A History of Palestine

A History of Palestine

FROM THE OTTOMAN CONQUEST
TO THE FOUNDING
OF THE STATE OF ISRAEL

Gudrun Krämer

Translated by Graham Harman and Gudrun Krämer

PRINCETON UNIVERSITY PRESS

PRINCETON AND OXFORD

First published in Germany under the title *Geschichte Palästinas: Von der osmanischen Eroberung bis zur Gründung des Staates Israel*
© Verlag C.H. Beck oHG, München 2002

English translation © 2008 by Princeton University Press

Published by Princeton University Press, 41 William Street, Princeton, New Jersey 08540

In the United Kingdom: Princeton University Press, 3 Market Place, Woodstock, Oxfordshire OX20 1SY

ISBN-13:978-0-691-11897-0

The translation of this work was supported by a grant from the Goethe-Institut that is funded by the Ministry of Foreign Affairs

This book has been composed in Sabon

Printed in the United States of America

A Book Club Edition

CONTENTS

ILLUSTRATIONS

FIGURES

MAPS

NOTE ON ILLUSTRATIONS

Figures 1–12 and 14 come from the collection of historical photographs of Palestine held at the Faculty of Theology of Humboldt-Universität zu Berlin. The holdings include around 2,000 glass-plate slides that were collected by Hugo Greβmann, who taught at Humboldt Unversität from 1907 to 1927, and who traveled to Palestine in 1906. While he took some of the photographs himself, others were made by Gustav Dalman and participants in his classes. (Dalman served as the first director of the German Protestant Institute for the Study of Antiquity in the Holy Land in Jerusalem from 1902 to 1916.) Other collections such as that of the American Colony were later added to the existing one. It was only in 1994 that the glass-plate slides, which until then had been housed in various places and many of which were in a precarious state due to war damages, could be assembled in a central location. For this reason, the precise origin of many slides remains unclear. For the same reason, it is impossible to reconstruct exactly when and by whom the slides reproduced in the present book were taken. They are reproduced with the kind permission of the Faculty of Theology of Humboldt-Universität zu Berlin.

TABLES

PREFACE

To WRITE A HISTORY OF PALESTINE that is not strictly focused on politics is no easy task, as the conflict between Arabs and Jews casts its shadow well beyond current affairs. To a large extent it molds our perceptions of the past, and not just the most recent one, which is often seen as a mere prelude to the present. In this book I have tried to write a history of modern Palestine that does not take its point of departure from the arrival of the first Zionist immigrants in 1882, the transformation of the Jewish community in Palestine, and the foundation of the State of Israel in 1948. Under both Ottoman and British rule, Palestine was predominantly Arab. For this reason, the book focuses on the Arab majority of the population. I will of course discuss the evolution of the Jewish Yishuv, the coexistence of Jews, Christians, and Muslims, and their relations to the various state authorities. But doing so involves more than politics narrowly defined. To give adequate expression to their entangled histories, and to write a "relational history" worthy of the name, remains a challenge, given the tendency of both contemporary and later observers to focus on either the Jews *or* the Arabs. It is not for nothing that we speak of a "tunnel vision." The social, economic, and cultural encounters between Arabs and Jews, formal as well as informal, still require closer attention. It is to be hoped that the present study will serve to stimulate others to go further in this direction.

This book is the revised and updated version of my *History of Palestine*, which first appeared in German in 2002. Working on both the German and English versions, I benefited greatly from my readings and discussions with others. Students in classes, participants in conferences, and readers of the German original kindly shared some of their impressions and criticisms. I am no longer able to offer credit for every insight and idea received over a period of several years. But I would like to give special thanks to Thomas Berchtold, Mark Cohen, Susanne Enderwitz, Thomas Philipp, Sabine Schmidtke, Philipp Speiser, and Stefan Wild, who at different stages were kind enough to read portions of the manuscript and to help me with their knowledge of the field. Their suggestions have been assimilated into the book (or at least I hope so). Any errors that remain are my own. I would like to thank Angela Ballaschk at the Institute of Islamic Studies at Freie Universität Berlin and the editors at Princeton University Press, Jill Harris and Marsha Kunin, who assisted me in preparing the manuscript, index, and proofs. Anyone who has ever tried to bring a book to press within a reasonable period of time knows what this entails. "Reasonable" is of course a relative term: Brigitta van Rheinberg, who oversaw the book for Princeton University Press, had to show great patience with the various foreseeable and unforeseeable events that delayed completion of the manuscript. So did my husband, who was probably the most patient of all. Without their support this book would not lie before the reader today.

Finally, special thanks are due to the Faculty of Theology of Humboldt-Universität zu Berlin, and to Peter Welten, who until 2001 held the Chair for the Study of the Old Testament, Biblical Archaeology, and Iconography, who allowed us to use samples from their rich "Collection of Historical Photographs of Palestine" and to publish them here. It would be wonderful if this helped the collection find even more admirers.

Berlin
July 2007
Gudrun Krämer

ABBREVIATIONS

A.D.	Anno Domini
AEC	Arab Executive Committee
AHC	Arab Higher Committee
ALA	Arab Liberation Army
AWA	Arab Women's Association
B.C.	Before Christ
GDP	Gross Domestic Product
IPC	Iraq Petroleum Company
IZL	Etzel
JCA	Jewish Colonization Association
JNF	Jewish National Fund
MCA	Muslim-Christian Association(s)
OETA	Occupied Enemy Territory Administration
PAWS	Palestine Arab Workers' Society
PICA	Palestine Jewish Colonization Agency
PLL	Palestine Labor League
SMC	Supreme Muslim Council
UN	United Nations
UNSCOP	United Nations Special Committee on Palestine
WZO	World Zionist Organization
YMCA	Young Men's Christian Association
YMMA	Young Men's Muslim Association

A History of Palestine

Chapter One

NAMES AND BORDERS

THERE ARE NO INNOCENT TERMS, especially in geography. For centuries Palestine, as known under the British Mandate in the twentieth century, formed no independent geographical and political unit. Its names and borders changed, and so did its population.[1] As a part of the Fertile Crescent extending from the Mediterranean to the Persian Gulf, and from the Taurus and Zagros Mountains in the north to the Arabian desert in the south, Palestine was always a land of passage. For this reason it was also a site of cultural encounter and exchange. As part and parcel of "greater" Syria, Palestine has few natural landmarks, and aside from the Mediterranean it has no "natural borders." The Jordan Valley provides one geographical marker and the Sinai Peninsula another. But neither of them offered any "natural" protection to the inhabitants of the area against hostile incursions. Its borders were largely man-made and hence variable, often determined less by the local population than by powerful neighbors. Still, over time an entity emerged that stretched from the Mediterranean to the Jordan Valley and sometimes beyond, depending on the state of settlement of the Syrian desert. In the north, it included parts of present-day Lebanon as far as the Litani River; in the south, it contained portions of the Negev, but not the Sinai. In political terms, Palestine in part or in whole was usually a province within a great empire; only rarely, and even then only for short periods, did it form an independent political unit.

In the context of the Jewish-Arab conflict over Palestine, places and place-names have acquired great significance to all efforts to legitimize particular historical rights to the land. To be able to establish the *names of things* serves as one of the most telling indicators of political and cultural power.[2] For this reason the various terms used to designate the

---

[1] Place-names will be given according to contemporary usage (Lebanon, Syria, etc.).

[2] Benvenisti (2000), esp. ch. 1; Enderwitz (2002), ch. 4. R. Khalidi (1997), ch. 2, highlights different usages not just between Jews and Arabs, but also between Muslim and Christian Arabs; with a different approach, see also Lewis (1980); Biger (1990), pp. 2–4; Biger (2004), ch. 1. For the role of archaeology in this competition over historical rights and political claims, see also Neil Asher Silverstein, *Between Past and Present. Archeology, Ideology, and Nationalism in the Modern Middle East* (New York 1989), and Nadia Abu El-Haj, *Facts on the Ground: Archeological Practice and Territorial Self-Fashioning in Israeli Society* (Chicago 2002).

land of "Palestine" are instructive, reflecting as they did the dominant perspective and by the same token prevailing power relations. As is well known, the terms "Near" and "Middle East" make sense only when viewed from Europe, but were nonetheless adopted into the political vocabulary of these regions themselves. Regarding Palestine, the dominant perspective has clearly been informed by biblical associations, on the basis of which even the borders of the British Mandate were drawn after World War I. This perspective, however, is distorted and distorting, affecting presentations of the land and its people as well as their history. It places the Jews at the center, pushing all other population groups (even if and when they formed a majority) into the background, if it considers them at all. This holds for ancient ("biblical") as much as for modern times. Remarkably, it also holds for Arab Christians, about whom we know far less than about the Jewish inhabitants of the area, at least for the modern period. Both Muslim and Christian Palestinians have complained about their marginalization in public perception and historical research. Still, the "biblical" approach is the prevalent one, and the most powerful historically. In the following it will be impossible to escape it entirely. The Jewish claim to Palestine as the "Land of Israel" (*Eretz Yisrael*) bases itself on biblical narratives and asserts the unbroken presence of the Jewish people in this land and their bond to it. The Arab claim, meanwhile, calls into question the uninterrupted presence of Jews, and points to Arab roots dating back over a millennium. Some will refer to the Canaanites, who settled in the land before the Israelites, as their own ancestors.

Both sides, then, claim priority in terms of chronology (the right of the firstborn, so to speak), both make use of archaeology, both draw maps, and both argue by means of place-names. Scarcely any spot on the map—whether it be Jerusalem (Urshalimum/Yerushalayim/al-Quds), the northern plain leading from the Mediterranean to the Jordan Valley (Esdra(e)lon and Jezreel/Marj Ibn Amir), or the hilly inland terrain (Judaea and Samaria in Hebrew)—is exempt from this contest. Palestine, or Eretz Israel, offers a textbook case of the "territorialization of history," in which political claims are anchored in historical geography. Biblical scholars have spoken of a veritable "geotheology."[3] For this reason we need to clarify not only designations such as "Canaan" or "Palestine" itself, but also "Eretz Israel," "Promised Land," and "Holy Land"—designations that were first used following Israelite settlement in a land previously controlled by the Egyptians, Hittites, or Assyrians, and inhabited by various ethnic groups.

[3] Thoma (1970), pp. 37–38.

"Canaan" and "Palestine"

Settlement can be traced back to earliest times. Already in the middle and late periods of the Old Stone Age (70,000–14,000 B.C.), characteristic differences appear between the coastal plain with its river valleys extending inland, and the central hills and mountains, differences that remained important up to the modern era.[4] In the Bronze Age (ca. 3,200–1,200 B.C.) an urban culture emerged among a population that took its name from the land of "Canaan" and became known under the generic name of "Canaanites." Little is known about Canaan and the Canaanites. The etymology of "Canaan" is unclear, and the precise location and extent of the territory so designated appear to have varied considerably over time. Contemporary testimony suggests that in the second millennium B.C., the term served primarily to designate individual population groups centered in and around a number of "city-states" rather than a well-defined territory. Only in the Hellenistic period was Canaan identified more or less consistently with Phoenicia, that is, with the Levantine littoral. The sources do not divulge the identity or origin of its inhabitants; we do know, however, that (like the Israelites) they spoke a western Semitic language or dialect, and we have some information about their material culture, religious life, and art, all of which showed Mesopotamian influence. In the Bible they are described with negative stereotypes, as barbaric idol-worshippers contrasting with the monotheistic Israelites, and portrayed with as much revulsion as the Egyptians and their cult of animals and idols.[5] While this tells us something about the self-image and perceptions of the biblical narrators, we should not take it as a reliable ethnographic description.

The regional powers ruling the area exercised control in varying fashion, and for the most part in a loose manner only. Under Egyptian domi-

[4] Redford (1992), ch. 10; Lemche (1991), pp. 152ff., and Lemche (1994). The maps found in Rasmussen (2000), pp. 90–103, and Aharoni et al. (2002), maps 17, 38, 46, and 68, rest on conventional assumptions (i.e., biblical accounts). The name "Canaan," first found in an inscription of Idrimi, king of the northern Syrian state of Alalah, from the fifteenth century B.C., is possibly derived from the Hurrian *kinnahu*, purple or crimson, a product that originated from Canaan and formed its most important trade commodity. This interpretation is also supported by the Greek designation "Phoinike" for the Levantine coast, which is said to be based on the Phoenician word for purple or crimson. However, the name could also be derived from the Semitic root *k-n-ʿ*, "low," signifying "low countries" (this would refer to the coastal plain and the valleys leading into the hinterland). Yet it is also possible that Canaan is simply an ancient place-name, of which we can say with some certainty that it is of Semitic origin, but not what it signifies.

[5] On the "Mosaic distinction" between monotheistic "purity" and polytheist "impurity," see Jan Assmann, *Moses, der Ägypter. Entzifferung einer Gedächtnisspur* (Munich, Vienna 1998).

nation, lasting from the middle of the sixteenth century (when it was at most intermittent and by and large confined to the lowlands) to the twelfth century B.C., "Canaan" appears to have denoted an Egyptian "province" (the term is to be used with caution and not to be conceived along the Roman model) whose area roughly coincided with later Palestine.[6] This at least would seem to follow from the Amarna Letters dating from the mid-fourteenth century B.C., when Pharaoh Akhenaten moved his residence to what is now Tell el-Amarna. Toward the end of the thirteenth century, we find the first mention of "Hebrews," who may have been identical with, or affiliated to, the bands of nomads, bandits, and brigands called "Apiru" or "Habiru" in Egyptian texts (the issue is much debated). The name "Israel" itself is first found on a stele of Pharaoh Merenptah, which according to the so-called middle chronology is dated c. 1210 B.C., and in which "Israel" designates a group of people, or to be more precise, a foreign people, not a given territory. "Israel" as depicted on this stele may well have been part of the population of seminomadic pastoralists described in contemporary Egyptian sources as "Shasu," living in the hilly terrain east and west of the Jordan, and sporadically raiding the lowlands, moving as far as Gaza.

The twelfth century was marked by the arrival of the Philistines, members of the so-called Sea Peoples, an Indo-European group from the Aegean region who, both peacefully and by force, entered the region later known as Palestine. The Philistines settled mostly on the coastal plain from the later Gaza to Mount Karmel, while the Israelites lived in the inland hills and mountains. The "Canaanites" and Philistines contributed greatly to the cultural and economic history of the Ancient Near East. The consonantal script developed by the Phoenicians of present-day Lebanon, which was to spread throughout the Middle East and Europe, is a case in point. Yet it was the Israelites (Hebrews, Jews) who profoundly shaped the subsequent history of Palestine, and with one major exception, also coined the place-names used to designate this land. The only designation recalling the Philistines is the one most widely used today, at least outside of Israel: "Palestine" itself. From the Assyrian "palastu" to the Greek "Palaistine," via the Latin "Palaestina," the term was ultimately adopted not only by the European languages, but also by Arabic, where it appears as "Filastin."[7]

---

[6] Redford (1992), pp. 170–71, 179, 195, and ch. 10; Weinfeld (1993), pp. 113–20, and ch. 5; Lemche (1991), pp. 13ff., 28ff., 39–40, 48, and 67–69; Miller/Hanson/McBride (1987); Weinstein (1981). On the so-called Israel stele of Pharaoh Merenptah (also Meremptah or Merneptah), see also Bimson (1991). Members of the Sea Peoples had already settled in Egypt around 1650 B.C.; cf. Dothan/Dothan (1992).

[7] In the Hebrew Bible (*gelilot*) *peleshet* (related to the old Egyptian *purusati* and the Assyrian *palastu*) originally refers to the southern coastal strip from Gaza to Mount Karmel. The term "Palestine" was used neither in the New Testament nor in the rabbinical

THE "LAND OF ISRAEL": PROMISED AND TAKEN

It may be bold, if not presumptuous, to attempt a brief sketch of the Jewish tradition concerning such central concepts as the "Promised Land," or the "land of the patriarchs." The Bible, on which this tradition is primarily based, does not provide us with a straightforward narrative stretching from Moses, Joshua, and the Judges to the minor prophets, beginning with the creation and ending with the expulsion of the people of Israel from the land of Israel, and their yearning for a return and redemption in this land. Instead, it offers a complex narrative fabric reflecting rival traditions. Their redaction and exegesis were of political relevance, especially with regard to the issue of land. Given the controversies over the nature of the divine promise, over God-given rights and their political consequences, it is worth considering more closely the biblical evidence cited in modern times. Here it is clearly not a question of exploring the intricacies of literary form, historical embeddedness, and shifting interpretation of individual terms, concepts, and textual passages, all of them subject to heated dispute in biblical scholarship. The aim can only be to briefly present the repertory to which later generations have had recourse, often without sufficient consideration for either text or context.

In the first instance we must distinguish between (1) Canaan or the "promised land," as described in the biblical stories of Abraham and Moses; (2) the area actually settled by the Israelites; and finally (3) the land of Israel as defined by Jewish law, the Halakha. All three (and this contributes considerably to the confusion) can be rendered in Hebrew as "Eretz Israel," or the land of Israel. The land that according to Jewish tradition Abra(ha)m and his children were promised through a covenant with God, that was later renewed with Moses and is known in the Jewish tradition as "the borders of the patriarchs" and in the Christian tradition as *terra promissionis*, appears in the Hebrew Bible (the Old Testament) in various forms, some of them quite vague, if not outright contradictory.[8] As much as they differ in detail, they include not just the territory of later Palestine, but also Lebanon as well as most of Syria. What the exegetes differ about is whether the Transjordanian lands south of Lake Tiberias ("Gilead," "Moab," and "Edom") should be viewed as part and parcel of the Promised Land or Eretz Israel. This is not the case in those parts of the Bible attributed to the so-called Priestly writer, and the rabbinical commentaries based upon them. They exclude

---

tradition. In the Talmud, it appears solely as a technical designation for one of the Roman provinces; Lewis (1980), pp. 1 and 6; Biger (1990), p. 9.

[8] Weinfeld (1993), pp. 52–75, and Weinfeld (1983), p. 27; Biger (1990), pp. 7–8. For the name change from Abram to Abraham after the Covenant, cf. Genesis 17:5.

the Transjordanian region from Eretz Israel, in both its promised ("ideal") and settled ("real") borders. The boundaries of Canaan as sketched in Numbers 34:1–12, describing the inheritance promised to the descendants of Moses, seem to reflect the borders of the Egyptian province of the same name, as established by Ramses II around 1270 B.C. after the battle of Kadesh, in his peace treaty with the Hittites. Its eastern border is formed by the Jordan River, whose crossing by the Israelites under Joshua is so vividly described in the Bible; the Euphrates is not even mentioned.

The broader conception of the "ideal borders" of Eretz Israel, in which the land east of the Jordan is included as part of the promise, appears to have arisen later, but was eventually to gain wide acceptance.[9] We find it in Genesis 15:18–21, where the borders reach far beyond the land of the Canaanites:

> On that day the LORD made a covenant with Abram, saying, "To your descendants I give this land, from the river of Egypt to the great river, the river Euphrates, the land of the Kenites, the Kenizzites, the Kadmonites, the Hittites, the Perizzites, the Rephaim, the Amorites, the Canaanites, the Girgashites and the Jebusites."

Here we already find the famous "from the river of Egypt to the river Euphrates," or even more succinctly, "from the Nile to the Euphrates," which plays such a prominent role in modern disputes over the aims of the Zionists and their alleged expansionist intentions. Modern scholars as well as rabbinical sources have identified the "river of Egypt" (*nahal mitzrayim* in Hebrew) not with the Nile or one of its branches in the eastern delta, but rather with the Wadi al-Arish in the Sinai Peninsula, which enters the Mediterranean about forty-five kilometers southwest of Rafah.[10] Still, there remains the daring presumption concerning the Euphrates—even if the "Euphratic hubris" (in Lothar Perlitt's phrase) was to remain wishful thinking.[11] Canaan, where God led Abraham's father Terah according to Genesis 11:31, formed only one part of the Promised Land as described in Genesis 15:18–21 quoted above. Two things are significant here: First, the land promised to Abraham was neither settled nor occupied by him or his kin, not even in part. Second, even if God's "eternal covenant" was made only with Isaac and his sons

---

[9] Weinfeld (1993), pp. 64–75, ascribes them to the deuteronomic source, school, or movement, and more specifically to the phase of renewed expansion of the kingdoms of Judah and Israel under kings Hiskia and Josiah in the seventh century B.C. All citations are from The Holy Bible, Revised Standard Version.

[10] Only in 1 Chronicles 13:5 can we identify the Nahal Mitzrayim with the easternmost tributary of the Nile (Shihor in Hebrew; on the latter, see also Josh. 13:10); cf. Biger (1990), p. 6; Weinfeld (1993), pp. 53–54, 57; Lewis (1980), p. 3.

[11] Perlitt (1983), pp. 51–53. According to the Bible, only Solomon controlled a territory that reached as far as the Euphrates (but not the Nile). More on this below.

(Gen. 17:19 and 21; Deut. 1:7–8), the descendants of Abraham that Genesis 15:18–21 refers to also included the sons of Ishmael, whom the Bible names as the ancestor of the "Ishmaelites" (commonly identified as an Arab tribal confederacy), and whom the Muslims recognize as one of their prophets.

Searching for precise geographical data, we find just as little help in those biblical passages that describe God's covenant with Moses and the land promised to his descendants (in the Jewish tradition "the land of those who came out of Egypt"). Here, too, we discover far-reaching descriptions in which individual geographical points are hard to identify, and which in later times were often identified differently. There is also no clear-cut definition of the rights accruing to the people of Israel on the basis of the promise, or the rights of those who do not belong to this people (a point that for obvious reasons attained new significance in modern times). Exodus 23:31–33 addresses this matter quite radically:

> And I will set your bounds from the Red Sea[12] to the sea of the Philistines, and from the wilderness to the Euphrates; for I will deliver the inhabitants of the land into your hand, and you shall drive them out before you. You shall make no covenant with them or with their gods. They shall not dwell in your land, lest they make you sin against me; for if you serve their gods, it will surely be a snare to you.

Much the same can be found in Deuteronomy 1:7–8 and 11:24 ("Every place on which the sole of your foot treads shall be yours; your territory shall be from the wilderness and Lebanon and from the River, the river Euphrates, to the western sea"). Joshua 1:1–4 reads as follows:

> After the death of Moses the servant of the LORD, the LORD said to Joshua the son of Nun, Moses' minister, "Moses my servant is dead; now therefore arise, go over this Jordan, you and all this people, into the land which I am giving to them, to the people of Israel. Every place that the sole of your foot will tread upon I have given to you, as I promised to Moses. From the wilderness and this Lebanon as far as the great river, the river Euphrates, all the land of the Hittites to the Great Sea toward the going down of the sun shall be your territory."

It is extremely difficult to discover the historical facts behind the biblical account, and to precisely define the land that was gradually settled or occupied by the Israelites. For obvious reasons, this is mined territory, and it would be pointless to tackle this issue here. Yet we cannot entirely avoid the controversy over the Jewish presence in Eretz Israel or Pales-

---

[12] The "Red Sea" or "Sea of Reeds" is generally identified with the Gulf of Aqaba; Weinfeld (1993), p. 67; Boehmer (1909), pp. 135–36; Biger (1990), map 8.

tine, because of its significance for Jewish identity and for the Arab-Jewish dispute over their right to "the land." Interestingly, both Jews and Arabs rely in essence on the biblical narrative, even in cases when they try to refute claims contained in this narrative. Historians and archaeologists of the Ancient Middle East, including leading Egyptologists, have a very different story to tell. Unfortunately, they do not tell the same story.[13] Again, controversy is due as much to religious and political conviction as to the nature of the evidence and its legitimate interpretation. Extra-biblical evidence, whether material, epigraphic, or literary (from buildings and pottery to coins, seals, steles, and statues, to documents and letters) is uneven in quality and quantity, and highly contested. While excavations have been carried out in many parts of Palestine since the mid-nineteenth century, they have not been possible in all places, and they are of course politically sensitive.

Still, we are not without clues. Archaeological and epigraphic evidence documents the presence of seminomadic pastoralists in the hilly inland terrain well before the twelfth century B.C., when we first learn of a group called "Israel." Several scholars hold the revisionist thesis that the Israelites did not move to the area as a distinct and foreign ethnic group at all, bringing with them their god Yahwe and forcibly evicting the indigenous population, but that they gradually evolved out of an amalgam of several ethnic groups, and that the Israelite cult developed on "Palestinian" soil amid the indigenous population. This would make the Israelites "Palestinians" not just in geographical and political terms (under the British Mandate, both Jews and Arabs living in the country were defined as Palestinians), but in ethnic and broader cultural terms as well. While this does not conform to the conventional view, or to the self-understanding of most Jews (and Arabs, for that matter), it is not easy to either prove or disprove. For although the Bible speaks at length about how the Israelites "took" the land, it is not a history book to draw reliable maps from. There is nothing in the extra-biblical sources, including the extensive Egyptian materials, to document the sojourn in Egypt or the exodus so vividly described in the Bible (and commonly dated to the thirteenth century). Biblical scholar Moshe Weinfeld sees the biblical account of the exodus, and of Moses and Joshua as founding heroes of the "national narration," as a later rendering of a lived experience that was subsequently either "forgotten" or consciously repressed—a textbook case of the "invented tradition" so familiar to modern students of ethnicity and nationalism.

To judge from the contemporary archaeological and later literary evi-

---

[13] Weinfeld (1993), chs. 5 and 6, esp. pp. 112–20; also I. Finkelstein (1988); Whitelam (1996).

dence, the land actually settled by the Israelites formed only part of the land "promised" to them under the covenant. Its borders were politically determined, and for this reason they varied considerably. A large portion lay on the eastern bank of the Jordan River. As a name for the land settled by the Israelites, "Eretz Israel" is repeatedly mentioned in the Bible. But it took hold slowly, and it is only in the Mishna ("repetition," "learning"), the oral exegetic tradition that was written down between A.D. 150 and 200 and incorporated in the Talmud, that it was regularly employed.[14] Of earlier use was the designation "from Dan until Beersheba," which apparently arose at the time of the undivided kingdom of David and Solomon (c. 1000–928 B.C.), whose boundaries are repeatedly specified in the Bible.[15] In 1 Kings 4:21, we read: "Solomon ruled over all the kingdoms from the Euphrates to the land of the Philistines and to the border of Egypt; they brought tribute and served Solomon all the days of his life." And in 1 Kings 4:24–25, we find: "For he had dominion over all the region west of the Euphrates. . . . and he had peace on all sides round about him. And Judah and Israel dwelt in safety, from Dan even to Beer-sheba, every man under his vine and under his fig tree, all the days of Solomon." According to these accounts, Solomon's realm stretched far beyond present-day Palestine all the way to the Euphrates and to the borders of Egypt, although it did not reach as far as the Nile. "From Dan to Beersheba" designated only a part of this area, a kind of core nucleus of Israelite land.[16] Interestingly, it describes the extension from north to south rather than the more usual east to west. Also, it does not refer to the actual borders of the kingdom but rather to two important cultic sites. The formula stamped itself so indelibly upon readers of the Bible that the British had recourse to it when planning the future of their conquests in 1917.

FROM THE "BABYLONIAN CAPTIVITY" TO THE DESTRUCTION OF THE TEMPLE

The undivided kingdom of David and Solomon proved to be fragile, lasting only about seventy years. If we follow the Bible, it split into the

[14] See especially 1 Samuel 13:19 and 1 Chronicles 13:2. Joshua 11:22 speaks of the "land of the children of Israel." Chapters 13–19 of Joshua offer more detail (see notably 13:2–5); see also Biger (1990), p. 9.

[15] Weinfeld (1993), pp. 52–53; Boehmer (1909), pp. 137–38; Biger (1990), maps 10 and 11. For critical remarks, see, e.g., Lemche (1991), pp. 80–81, and Whitelam (1996), pp. 129ff., 138, 150, 161, and 255.

[16] Further evidence is found in Judges 20:1 and 2 Samuel 24:2. Aharoni et al. (2002), pp. 80–89 (esp. map 105) transform the biblical text into cartographic material ("territori-

Map 1. Palestine, from Dan to Beersheva

---

alization of history"). The same holds true for Biger (1990), pp. 9–10 and, with a different chronology, Rasmussen (2000), pp. 116–23.

kingdoms of Israel and Judah around 928 B.C., who warred against each other ceaselessly.[17] The northern kingdom of Israel with its capital at Samaria, founded by the sixth king, Omri, was home to ten of the twelve tribes of Israel. Initially, it controlled much of Transjordan and Syria, but only part of the Mediterranean coast. Culturally, it gradually came under Phoenician influence. Between 732 and 721 B.C., Israel was conquered by the Assyrians under Tiglath-pileser III and Sargon II, who followed long-established practice by deporting part of the population to other regions of the empire. Assyrian rule already seems to have had an important impact upon the Israelites, giving rise to new religious ideas and practices. In place of the deported Israelites, other ethnic groups were brought to their country. According to the Bible, these groups mixed with the local population and formed the Samaritan community (who as a group situated between Jews and non-Jews were to capture the special interest of Western scholars and travelers in modern times).

The southern kingdom of Judah, comprising the region between Jerusalem, Hebron, and the Mediterranean coast, avoided conquest by submitting to the Assyrians in 721 B.C. However, the Assyrian Empire soon entered a phase of internal unrest. In 612 B.C. its capital Nineveh fell to the emerging New Babylonian Empire. The subsequent Babylonian conquest of Judah was to prove of far-reaching cultural and religious significance: In what appear to have been two separate campaigns, Nebuchadnezzar II had Jerusalem with its palace and temple destroyed, and its population deported to Babylonia: In 598–97 B.C., a great part of the Israelite elite and craftsmen were taken away, and when those left in the city rebelled under their king, Nebuchadnezzar destroyed the city in 586 and deported most of the remaining population. Nebuchadnezzar then annexed the conquered territory to the province of Syria, the "land beyond the river" (*eber-nahari*, with the river being the Euphrates), within which the former kingdom of Judah formed the subdistrict of "Yehud." It must be emphasized that not all Israelites were deported to Babylonia, especially in the countryside. But for those that were, the "Babylonian captivity" profoundly affected their self-image, culture, and religious ideas. For one thing, the name "Israelites" gradually gave way to the term "Jews." Upon their return, the resulting changes spread to those that had remained behind.

After the fall of the Babylonian Empire in 539 B.C., Palestine came under the control of the Persian Achaemenids, who allowed the Israelites

---

[17] Rasmussen (2000), pp. 124–39; Biger (1990), pp. 11ff.; Aharoni et al. (2002), pp. 90–109. For critical assessment, see Weinfeld (1993), pp. 186ff.; Asali (ed.) (1997), ch. 2.

(Jews) to return from Babylonia and to rebuild the Temple.[18] In the so-called Second Temple period, the Jews still appear to have formed a majority in the former kingdom of Judah (even there, their total number may have been as low as 11,000–17,000 between the sixth and the fourth centuries B.C.), but not in other parts of what they considered Eretz Israel. Already under Persian domination, the area began to be gradually Hellenized, accompanied by Greek colonization, especially along the Mediterranean coast. Both Hellenization and Greek colonization intensified after the conquest of Palestine by Alexander the Great in 332 B.C., even if the majority of the population continued to speak Aramaic rather than Greek. Despite internecine wars and extended struggles between the Ptolemies (who ruled Palestine from Alexandria during the years 286–200 B.C.) and the Seleucids (who controlled it from Syria during the years 200–167 B.C.), Palestine experienced a certain measure of economic prosperity.

The policy of forced Hellenization under the Seleucid Antiochos IV Epiphanes provoked a Jewish revolt in 167–66 B.C. Significantly, it was sparked by a threat to a sacred site, an issue that was to acquire new salience in the modern period: Antiochos had the Jewish temple in Jerusalem converted into a temple of Olympian Zeus where ("impure") sacrifices were made. Under the leadership of the Maccabees (also known as Hasmoneans), the Jewish rebels regained political autonomy, even if under Seleucid suzerainty, and were able once again to extend Jewish control beyond the Jordan River and into Lebanon. Their realm actually reached "from Dan to Beersheba" and further still to the "river of Egypt" (the Wadi al-Arish), albeit not to the Euphrates or, for that matter, to the Nile. As short-lived as the Hasmonean kingdom was, it informed later notions of the extent of Eretz Israel (in the Jewish tradition, "the borders of those who returned from Babylon"), as well as the boundaries of Eretz Israel as defined by Jewish law, the Halakha.[19] In the twentieth century, the combative spirit of the Maccabees also inspired Jewish nationalists in their struggle against the British mandate.

Pompey's conquest of Palestine in 63 B.C. proved another turning point, ushering in the era of Roman and Byzantine rule, which was to last for seven hundred years until the Muslim conquest in A.D. 636–38. Yet even as a Roman and Byzantine province, interrupted from A.D. 614–29/30 by a brief spell of Persian control, Palestine enjoyed a large

---

[18] Critical discussion in Eskenazi/Richards (eds.) (1994), esp. Charles E. Carter, "The Province of Yehud in the Post-Exilic Period: Soundings in Site Distribution and Demography," ibid., pp. 106–45 (with the population estimates on pp. 108 and 136–39); see also Whitelam (1996), p. 173; maps in Rasmussen (2000), pp. 140–52.

[19] Rasmussen (2000), pp. 153–59; Aharoni et al. (2002), pp. 140–58, esp. map 213; Biger (1990), p. 12 and map 13. For a different account, see Weinfeld (1993), pp. 52, 75.

measure of self-rule. Under Herod the Great (who overthrew the Hasmonean dynasty and ruled from 37 to 4 B.C.) and his successors, the province of Judaea was largely autonomous, whereas the Hellenized cities along the coast were governed by Roman officials. Still, relations between the Jewish minority and the Roman authorities remained tense, and in A.D. 66–70 and A.D. 132–35, two great Jewish revolts erupted with grave consequences for the local Jewish population.[20] The so-called Zealot Rebellion of 66–70, poorly prepared, badly coordinated, and weakened by internal strife, ended in failure. The Roman army under general Titus Flavius Vespasianus destroyed Jerusalem, along with Jaffa, Lydda, and other cities. In August A.D. 70 (reportedly on the ninth day of the month of Av, *tish'a be-av*, of the Jewish year), the Temple of Jerusalem, expanded and largely rebuilt by Herod, went up in flames. With it, the center of Jewish worship and pilgrimage and the prime symbol of Eretz Israel was finally destroyed. All that remained was part of its platform and a remnant of its western enclosure, later to assume new significance as the "Wailing Wall." In A.D. 73, a last group of rebels are said to have committed suicide in the fortress of Masada—a collective act of defiant despair, which, whether it actually happened or not, was later turned into a symbol of Jewish national history. After the foundation of the State of Israel, Masada was transformed into a national site, with the oaths sworn by military recruits invoking the heroic spirit of Jewish freedom fighters in the face of an overwhelming enemy ("Masada will never fall again!").

After A.D. 70, the troublesome region was elevated to the rank of a Praetorian province, opened up by systematic road construction and occupied by stronger military units. Nonetheless, another Jewish rebellion broke out around A.D. 132 under the leadership of Shimon Bar Kosiba, who was widely greeted as the Prince of Israel (*nasi*) and Messiah, and became known by the name Bar Kokhba (son of the star). The revolt appears to be have been sparked by among other things Roman plans to establish a military colony on the ruins of Jerusalem, and (once again) to transform the Temple area into a site of ("heathen") Roman worship.[21] The Bar Kokhba revolt as it became known was more carefully prepared than the previous one, although it largely remained limited to

---

[20] On both rebellions, see Aharoni et al. (2002), pp. 187–97; Rasmussen (2000), pp. 160–79. For the "Zealot Rebellion," see Berlin/Overmann (eds.) (2002), esp. ch. 15 (Neil A. Silberman). For a critique of the Masada myth, see further Sh. Cohen (1982); Shapira (1992), pp. 310–19, and Zerubavel (1995).

[21] Von Naredi-Rainer (1994), p. 43; Biger (1990), p. 14. The precise location of the Roman temple and statues is disputed; cf. Stemberger (1987), pp. 52–55. For rigorous source criticism, see Peter Schäfer, *Der Bar Kokhba-Aufstand. Studien zum zweiten jüdischen Krieg gegen Rom* (Tübingen 1981).

Judaea proper and even there did not involve all Jews; the Jews of Galilee barely participated, and the Judeo-Christians kept a distance, since for obvious reasons they could not recognize Bar Kokhba as the Messiah. After severe fighting the Romans were able to suppress the uprising—with disastrous consequences for the local Jewish population. Just as they had feared, Jerusalem was rebuilt as a Roman colony, named Aelia Capitolina after the Emperor Publius Aelius Hadrianus. Roman temples were dedicated and statues of Roman gods and emperors erected at the Temple Mount, the tomb of Christ, and the site of the crucifixion at Golgotha. Hence, the Jews were not the only ones to have their sites of worship and commemoration occupied and invested with "heathen" significance. But the Jews suffered more than the Christians: Circumcision was prohibited, and circumcised men were no longer allowed to enter the city, under penalty of death; they were replaced by large numbers of non-Jews, whom the Romans settled in and around Jerusalem. It may be doubted whether this ban was ever fully implemented. Emperor Constantine (ruled A.D. 306–37) is said to have allowed Jews to visit the remnant of the wall of Herod's Temple, which had survived the catastrophe of A.D. 70, and to mourn its destruction (hence the term "Wailing Wall").

As another element of retaliation, the Romans renamed the province of Judaea "Syria Palaestina" to erase any linguistic connection with the rebellious Jews. As mentioned earlier, the name "Palestine" in itself was not new, having already served in Assyrian and Egyptian sources to designate the coastal plain of the southern Levant. As a designation for a wider area including the interior along with the coast, it can be traced back to Herodotus (484–25 B.C.). Even after the defeat of the Bar Kokhba revolt, Syria Palaestina remained part of the Roman province of Syria. It was first enlarged through the annexation of neighboring territories and administrative units, and subsequently again subdivided. In the mid-fourth century, the province of Arabia (the former kingdom of Nabataea)—which comprised the Negev, the southern area east of the Jordan River, and parts of the Sinai—was made into Palaestina Salutaris, with its capital in Petra. Around 400, the rest of the province was divided into Palaestina Prima, with its capital in Caesarea in the south, and Palaestina Secunda, with its capital in Scythopolis (Hebrew Bet Shean, Arabic Baisan), in the north, which also included the Golan Heights. Palaestina Salutaris was renamed Palaestina Tertia.[22] The majority of the population were of Greek, Egyptian, Phoenician, or Arab origin and spoke Greek, Aramaic, or Arabic, and followed various Greco-Roman cults, which, however, were slowly losing ground to

[22] Lewis (1980), pp. 3–6; Biger (1990), pp. 15–17.

Christianity. By A.D. 300, Jews made up a mere quarter of the total population of the province of Syria Palaestina. Only in Galilee did they live in compact settlements. Two Samaritan revolts in 484 and 529, respectively, were crushed by the Romans, ending Samaritan attempts to establish independence in those parts of Galilee known as Samaria, with Mount Garizim as their holy site. By the fifth century, Jerusalem and Palestine as a whole had a Christian majority. At the same time, the Arab share of the population was growing steadily.

Palestine under Muslim Rule

Following their conquest of Syria and Palestine in A.D. 636–38, the Muslims largely retained the existing administrative order just as they did elsewhere. Within the Syrian province (*al-sham* in Arabic), the southern districts east and west of the Jordan River (formerly Palaestina Prima) were transformed into the military district (*jund*) of Filastin, with its capital first at Lydda and later at newly founded Ramla. To the north, Palaestina Secunda became Jund al-Urdunn (the military district of Jordan), with its capital at Tiberias. Further to the southeast, Palaestina Tertia, the former Nabataean kingdom with its capital at Petra, lost its status as a separate province, though it was only loosely controlled by the Muslim rulers. It was the Crusaders who once again created independent political units in Palestine, Lebanon, and Syria after 1099, including the Latin Kingdom of Jerusalem, the principality of Antioch, and the counties of Edessa and Tripoli. Saladin's (Salah al-Din al-Ayyubi) victory at the battle of Hittin in 1187 ended Christian rule over Jerusalem and Galilee; only the coast and some strongholds in the interior remained under Latin control with Acre as the capital. To prevent the Crusaders from recapturing Jerusalem and from there controlling Syria, an Ayyubid prince decided in 1218–19 to raze its walls and fortifications, leaving the city defenseless. Frankish rule was briefly restored not through conquest but through diplomacy, when in 1229 the Ayyubid sultan al-Malik al-Kamil granted Emperor Frederick II control of Jerusalem (excluding the Temple Mount) and certain towns in Galilee for a period of ten years. Local Muslim princes, however, prevented Latin authority from fully exerting itself. In 1244 Jerusalem was briefly occupied by Khwarezmian troops, originating from the region south of Lake Aral in Central Asia (now Uzbekistan), who had been called in by the Ayyubid sultan. Both soon faced a new danger: the Mongol armies under Genghis Khan and his successors, who within a few decades conquered vast portions of Asia from northern China to eastern Iran. In 1258, Baghdad fell to a Mongol army under Hülägü. The Mongols advanced on Syria and Palestine but were defeated in 1260 at Ain Jalut near Nazareth by the Mamluks, who had in turn overthrown their Ayyubid masters and "founded" the Mamluk dynasty. The fall of Acre in 1291 marked the end of Crusader rule in the Holy Land, removing the last challenge to Muslim rule over the area. Until the early sixteenth century, Palestine was controlled by the Mamluks residing in Cairo or their local representatives, who frequently acted quite independently of the sultan. Administratively, the horizontal partition into Jund Filastin and Jund al-Urdunn (terms not any longer officially used) was replaced by the vertical partition into Jerusalem (al-Quds) and the coast, which were further subdivided into various districts defined by their urban centers.

Under Ottoman rule, which began in 1516 and lasted for almost exactly four centuries, present-day Palestine was repeatedly subdivided and fused with neighboring administrative units. Official terminology changed over time, too. Ottoman documents occasionally referred to the "holy land" (*arazi-i muqaddese*). By contrast, the term "Palestine" fell out of administrative use, though it still figured in court documents, where evoking the Palaestina of Greek and Roman times, it apparently referred to the coastal strip, not the larger Jund Filastin of the Umayyad and Abbasid eras. "Al-Urdunn" was now limited to the Jordan River. And yet, the widespread view that the term "Palestine" was only revived at the time of the European Renaissance with its conscious reference to Greek and Roman antiquity, that it was never used by Jews, that it had been entirely forgotten by local Arabs, and that it was brought back to them by Arab Christians in touch with Europe, can no longer be upheld. We do, however, need historical studies that can document precisely when, how, and in what context the name was preserved in "collective memory," how it was utilized, and by whom.[23] What we do know is that the British seized upon the term and, for the first time in centuries, employed it to denote a distinct political unit. The boundaries of the mandate territory set up after World War I reflected biblical associa-

[23] Cf. Gerber (1998) as opposed to the standard version of Lewis (1980), p. 6, or Biger (1990), pp. 18–19; also R. Khalidi (1997), pp. 28–34. Rood (2004), pp. 44–46, suggests that in eighteenth-century Ottoman court records, *ard filastin* (the land of Palestine) referred to the coastal area comprising the towns of Gaza, Jaffa, Ramla, and Lydda, which did not belong to the districts of Jerusalem, Acre, and Nablus. This usage would seem to correspond to the ancient Greek Palaistine (cf. note 7 above). However, according to Biger (2004), pp. 15–16, the opposite was true in the 1890s, when in official Ottoman usage Filastin appeared to refer to the district of Jerusalem. Note that "Palestine" is to be distinguished from Ottoman concepts of a holy land (*arazi-i muqadesse*); see below, chapter 2, note 32. Porath (1974), pp. 7–9, stresses the importance of Christian notions of the Holy Land, which were also reflected in church institutions, for preserving a sense of a "Palestinian" entity within Syria, or *bilad al-sham*.

tions, since it was to stretch "from Dan to Beersheba." Already in the nineteenth century, this formula served to define the sphere of activity of the Palestine Exploration Fund.[24] It also served as an inspiration to David Lloyd George, British prime minister from 1916 to 1922. The year 1917, in which southern Palestine was conquered by the British army based in Egypt, he noted:

> saw a complete change in the attitude of the nations towards this historic land. It was no longer the end of a pipe-line here, the terminus of a railway there, a huddled collection of shrines over which Christian and Moslem sects wrangled under the protection of three great powers in every quarter. It was an historic and a sacred land, throbbing from Dan to Beersheba with immortal traditions.[25]

[24] Stoyanovski (1928), p. 205 (but see also below, chapter 7, note 8); Benvenisti (2000), p. 28.

[25] Cited from Frischwasser-Ra'anan (1976), p. 82. See also ibid., pp. 97, 100, 129.

Chapter Two

THE HOLINESS OF THE "HOLY LAND"

THE COMPLEX RELATIONS between the symbolic and the "real" are seldom more evident than when dealing with the holiness of the biblical lands. The fact that the "Holy Land" of Jews, Christians, and Muslims does not entirely coincide with the territory of modern Palestine renders things even more complicated. Holiness is commonly associated with the notion of continuity, if not eternity. Yet specific conceptions of the holiness of the Holy Land can be historically placed, or embedded, highlighting their changeability as much as their resilience. In different contexts, different images, ideas, and visions have been attached to the concept of holiness, and endowed it with ever-changing meaning. To contextualize these images, ideas, and visions in no way negates their power, and it may well be doubted that any "deconstruction" can erase their impact.

If we proceed by considering Jews, Christians, and Muslims in ostensibly chronological order, we quickly discover mutual influences and dependencies between their notions of holiness as translated into liturgy and ritual, image and language, music and poetry, space and architecture. In some instances, these representations unfolded in sequence, in others they did so simultaneously and under similar conditions. Hence the importance of mutual relations and mirror images, but also of the reversal of images as a means of deliberate demarcation. Exclusive claims, and the exclusion of others that these claims entail ("what is holy to us must be ours alone"), are of special relevance here. The accumulation of religious prestige or "symbolic capital" (in Pierre Bourdieu's phrase) in a land "holy" to all involved makes this topic so fascinating, so sensitive, and so potentially explosive.

JEWISH TRADITION

The significance of Palestine or Eretz Israel to Jewish tradition is beyond all doubt. And yet, its actual relevance to Jewish life and thought, and the practical consequences flowing from it, have always been subject to historical change. To begin with, the foundational myth of Israel is the exodus from Egypt, not the conquest of Canaan. According to the Bible, the twelve tribes of Israel had already been constituted *before* the land was taken. We need not discuss how this foundational myth was created in order to lend a form and sense to a much more diffuse process. Nor need we discuss that we are dealing with "representations" and "memories," not "(real) history."[1] In ancient Middle Eastern cultures, it was by no means uncommon to appeal to the gods to legitimize claims to land. What *was* unusual was the Jewish insistence that the Israelites were not indigenous to the land, but had come from outside, and that they had forcibly dispossessed and evicted others: This needed justification, and was justified with the divine promise. In the ancient Middle East, it was also common to think of the divine presence and power as manifest within a specific territory—not for nothing do we speak of "local gods." But again according to the Bible, the God of Israel revealed himself to Abraham, Moses, and Joshua outside of the land of Israel, even if he later "took up residence" there. Moses received the law in the Sinai, beyond the borders of Eretz Israel—even if some of its stipulations (that were elaborated much later) were fully valid only within these borders. Hence the importance of establishing the scope and extent of Eretz Israel according to Jewish law.

"Eretz Israel" can be considered a "geotheological" term[2] in which reference to actual space is bound up with the expectation of redemption. But what, according to Jewish tradition, is "holy" about Eretz Israel? Strictly speaking, it should not be "Holy Land," but rather "land (city, mountain) of the Holy"—holy because God is its owner and is present there; holy because in it his law is fully valid; holy because of its ritual purity. These aspects are obviously connected, but they do not altogether coincide. God as the "owner" (*ba'al*) of a territory (usually a city) is a familiar notion in the ancient Middle East. In the Hebrew Bible, it appears in many variations. Biblical scholars have analyzed the pertinent evidence, pointing to the important shift from the "land (of Israel)" as a whole to Zion-Jerusalem, and more specifically to the Temple in Jerusalem, following the return of the Jews from the Babylonian exile in 539 B.C. As already mentioned, the biblical evidence is abundant: At its heart are passages declaring that God "dwells" in "his land," in "his city," or on "his holy mountain."[3] The term "Holy Land" can be found in Zechariah 2:12 ("And the LORD will inherit Judah as his portion in the holy land, and will again choose Jerusalem."). Psalms 46:4 and 48:1–3 are of special relevance here, the latter reading: "Great is the LORD and greatly to be praised in the city of our God! His holy

---

[1] Anderson (1991); Hobsbawm/Ranger (eds.) (1983).
[2] Thoma (1970), pp. 37–38.
[3] Weinfeld (1983), esp. p. 108.

mountain, beautiful in elevation, is the joy of all the earth, Mount Zion, in the far north, the city of the great King. Within her citadels God has shown himself a sure defense."

We have already considered the dimensions of the "Promised Land," whose demarcations proved to be both vague and shifting. Yet for the purposes of worship and for the payment of taxes incumbent on Jews within Eretz Israel, it was always important to determine its bounds with precision; both worship and taxation were linked to the purity and impurity of man and space.[4] The legal and fiscal dimension is unique to Jewish conceptions of the holiness of the Holy Land; nothing in the Christian or Islamic traditions corresponds to it. But even according to Jewish law, the boundaries of Eretz Israel were not permanently fixed, for they depended on whether the site in question actually contained Jews who followed the law. Hence it was not so much a matter of political control over a given territory, but rather of individual and collective religious observance of its Jewish residents that determined its halakhic status. For the same reason, the halakhic borders had to be periodically revised. While the law itself refers to Eretz Israel in the borders of "those who returned from Babylon" (after 539 B.C.), the boundary lists at our disposal, especially the so-called Tannaitic boundary index, actually reflect the situation in the Hasmonean era, that is, in the second century B.C. While in Palestine west of the Jordan River, it excluded several of the predominantly Greek coastal cities from the territory regarded as ritually pure, it included settlements and areas in Transjordan as well as in present-day Lebanon and Syria as far as Damascus.

The special status of Eretz Israel—and here it is often difficult to distinguish between the "ideal borders" of divine promise and the "real borders" of Jewish settlement—had further legal consequences, which took on new importance in modern times. As the land was granted by God to the people of Israel as an "everlasting possession" (Gen. 17:8), it was in principle unalienable and could neither be sold nor rented to non-Jews. Leviticus 25:23 explicitly states: "The land shall not be sold in perpetuity, for the land is mine; for you are strangers and sojourners with me."[5] This statement obviously did not fully reflect existing condi-

[4] The impurity of both was determined, above all, by two factors: contact with corpses and the practice of pagan rituals. Yet the situation was complicated: A place could thus be exempted from taxation and nonetheless declared "pure." In contemporary Lebanon and Syria there were "mixed zones." Cf. Safrai (1983), pp. 204–10; Klein (1928), pp. 204ff., 227, 234ff., 240ff.; also W. D. Davies, *The Territorial Dimensions of Judaism* (Berkeley 1982) and D. Mendels, *The Land of Israel as a Political Concept in Hasmonean Literature* (Tübingen 1987).

[5] This is similar to Isaiah 60:21: "Thy people also shall be all righteous: they shall inherit the land for ever, the branch of my planting, the work of my hands, that I may be glori-

tions. Thus it can be shown that after the Second Temple was destroyed and the Jews banished from Jerusalem and its environs in A.D. 70, the rabbis proclaimed a duty for all Jews to remain in Eretz Israel or to acquire land there, and that they encouraged the immigration of Jews and threatened to punish any sale or rent of land to non-Jews, or any act of emigration. They would not have felt obliged to do so had these practices not existed. In the twentieth century, the Zionists, later followed by Islamic activists and Arab nationalists, took up this idea of Palestine as a divine gift or trust, unalienable and nonnegotiable.

In the same context, Jewish scholars invoked the obligation that the Bible imposed on the Israelites to "ban" all non-Jews from the conquered land, a ban (*herem*) that could range from their expulsion to the killing of their children, the elderly, and even their animals. Irrespective of how the ban was understood and to what extent it was ever implemented, two points are clear: It denied the claims of others to "the" land and banned all social contact with those who remained, or were permitted to remain, against God's law and command. Deuteronomy 7: 1–6 explicates the reason for such draconian strictness: The heathens must not be allowed to lead the Israelites to unbelief. Other biblical passages refer to the impurity of non-Jews.[6] Little can be said about actual practice, except that biblical accounts indicate a lack of success in driving all heathens out of the "Promised Land," or of eradicating them altogether. We also learn that Jerusalem first became Israelite under David and Solomon, and that the Hasmonean era saw renewed attempts (based on Deut. 12:2–3) to destroy pagan places of worship and convert non-Jews to Judaism. Those who resisted were apparently not killed but permitted to emigrate (a practice amounting to actual expulsion). What we can establish, then, is a scale of options ranging from

---

fied." Yet according to Safrai (1983), pp. 210–12, land transfers to non-Jews (whether through sale, lease, or rent) are well attested.

[6] Deuteronomy 7:1–4 reads as follows:

When the LORD thy God shall bring thee into the land whither thou goest to possess it, and hath cast out many nations before thee . . . [which were] greater and mightier than thou. And when the LORD thy God shall deliver them before thee; thou shalt smite them, and utterly destroy them; thou shalt make no covenant with them, nor shew mercy unto them. Neither shalt thou make marriages with them; thy daughter thou shalt not give unto his son, nor his daughter shalt thou take unto thy son. For they will turn away thy son from following me, that they may serve other gods: so will the anger of the LORD be kindled against you, and destroy thee suddenly.

See Weinfeld (1993), pp. 86–98, and chs. 4, 5, 8; further W. Horbury, "Extirpation and Excommunication," in *Vetus Testamentum* 35 (1985), pp. 19–38. On the impurity of non-Jews, see Numbers 35:34, Isaiah 52:1, and Joel 3:17. On the treatment of foreigners, see also Leviticus 19:33–34; cf. Talmon (1970), pp. 147–48.

the integration of non-Jews from a position of Jewish strength, to ethnic segregation in the name of Jewish self-preservation, to the actual expulsion of non-Jews.

Jerusalem has held special rank within Eretz Israel since at least the period of the Second Temple, as evident from hundreds of references in the Hebrew Bible that served as a source of inspiration for later generations.[7] Perhaps founded as "Urshalim(um)" or "Urusalim," the city is thought to have been first mentioned outside the Bible in Egyptian "execration texts" dating from the nineteenth century B.C., in which specific enemies of the Egyptians were named and cursed. In the Bible, it appears for the first time—as enemy territory not ruled by the Israelites—in Joshua 15:63 ("But the Jebusites, the inhabitants of Jerusalem, the people of Judah could not drive out; so the Jebusites dwell with the people of Judah at Jerusalem to this day") and Judges 1:21 ("But the people of Benjamin did not drive out the Jebusites who dwelt in Jerusalem; so the Jebusites have dwelt with the people of Benjamin in Jerusalem to this day"). David's conquest of Jerusalem, following his unification of the Israelite tribes, is generally dated at about 1000 B.C. Folk etymology later equated (Jeru)Salem with "peace" (Hebrew *shalom*, Arabic *salam*), so that Jerusalem became the "city of peace"—which historically speaking is precisely what it hardly ever was.[8] "Zion," which was later frequently used as a synonym for Jerusalem as well as the land and people of Israel, changed its geographic reference and significance for sacred history more than once. Originally it seems to have designated a fortress on a hill south of the later Temple Mount (known in the west as Ophel Hill), on which the Canaanite (Jebusite) settlement was located that for a long time bore the name of Jerusalem.

Under David, Jerusalem was elevated to a royal city and religious center of the Israelites. David renamed the fortress of Zion the "city of David" (2 Sam. 5:7–9 and 1 Chron. 11:5–7) and built a palace there. The transfer to Jerusalem of the Ark of the Covenant from Shiloh, which had previously served as a religious center, and the construction of the Temple under David's son Solomon lent an aura of holiness to the city

[7] It is important to remember the historical context of the biblical passages. In the entire Pentateuch we find only two possible mentions of Jerusalem, and about a dozen in Joshua and Judges, which were written at a time when the city had not yet attained its later importance. By contrast, Jerusalem plays a great role in the historiographies of court and temple (Samuel, Kings, Ezra-Nehemiah, and Chronicles) as well as in the Psalms, which were at least in part composed at the behest of the king to be used in temple services; cf. Talmon (1970), pp. 136–39; also Asali (ed.) (1997), ch. 1 (al-Hiyari).

[8] For references to Salem, see, for instance, Genesis 14:18–19 or Psalm 76:2: "In Salem also is his tabernacle, and his dwelling place in Zion." Cf. Fohrer (1969), p. 217; Baltzer (1990), pp. 5–6, 10–12. On Jerusalem as the city of peace, see, e.g., Psalm 122 and Hebrews 7:1–2; cf. Talmon (1970), pp. 140–41, and Weinfeld (1983), pp. 102–103.

as well as to the royal house.[9] The founding of the state by David and Solomon marked a major turning point in the history of Israel: the transition from a tribal to a dynastic order, and from mobile shrines to solid temple. Such novelty required religious justification, and was expressed in a new covenant with David analogous to God's covenant with Abraham and Moses. The founding of the dynasty and the construction of the palace and Temple—the two were closely linked architecturally—may thus be interpreted as signs of a "normalization of Israel," with parallels in ancient Middle Eastern concepts of court and empire. Still, the Temple did not replace other sacred sites that continued to exist especially in northern Palestine. In Jerusalem itself, other population groups and religious cults remained, although biblical passages from that period refer to a future "purification" of the city.

Jerusalem emerged as the sole religious center only after the Babylonian exile, when in 539 B.C. the Persian king Cyrus II granted the Israelites (Jews) the right to return to their city and rebuild the Temple, which was allegedly constructed with the aid of the Persian state treasury. The exile—religiously interpreted as a sign of divine punishment—led to far-reaching reinterpretations of Jewish life and thought. One consequence was a reorientation away from the *land* of Israel, inhabited in the meantime by growing numbers of non-Jews, while at the same time a Jewish diaspora had formed beyond its borders (not all Israelites or Jews who had been deported to Babylonia decided to return to Palestine). The focus now shifted to the *people* of Israel, and to the city of Jerusalem and its Temple, which seemed better suited to provide the dispersed people with a focal point of reference.[10]

Even after the Temple, palace, and kingdom were destroyed in A.D. 70, there remained the importance of Zion/Jerusalem as a symbol of the Jewish people, which could be endowed with a wide range of meanings. The motif of the sacred site threatened by others ("heathens") repeatedly provoked armed Jewish uprisings. Their failure gave added strength to another, spiritual expression of the yearning for Zion that focused on a "heavenly Jerusalem" at a time when the earthly one—at least in Jewish

---

[9] The motif of the temple city (often also "the city on the mount") as the center and navel of the world was perhaps first developed in Nippur in Mesopotamia, and was later taken up not only in Ugarit, Babylon, and Assyria, but also in Greece (Delphi). See Weinfeld (1983), pp. 75, 85ff., 111–14; Weinfeld (1993), pp. 89ff., 104–14; Talmon (1970), pp. 143–45; also F. E. Peters (1987). On the pagan cults practiced locally, see Miller/Hanson/McBride (eds.) (1987). No traces remain of the First and Second Temples, and only parts of Herod's reconstruction and expansion of the Second Temple, begun around 19 B.C.; cf. Theodor A. Busink, *Der Tempel von Jerusalem von Salomo bis Herodes*, vol. 1 (Leiden 1970); Bieberstein/Bloedhorn (1994); Kaplony (2002). For Zion and the city or citadel of David, see also Asali (ed.) (1997), ch. 1 (al-Hiyari) and ch. 2 (Little).

[10] Weinfeld (1993), pp. 202, 206–207; Baltzer (1990), p. 10; Talmon (1970), p. 141.

eyes—gave so little cause for idealization. First indications of this "spiritual" understanding, pointing to a "heavenly Jerusalem," can be traced back to the eighth century B.C. It grew stronger in the Hellenistic period, especially in circles living in the expectation of the end of times, but never replaced the yearning for the earthly Zion.[11]

Reality was indeed grim: From the defeat of the Bar Kokhba revolt in A.D. 135 until the Muslim conquest in 636–38, that is, for half a millennium, Jews were banished from Jerusalem and its vicinity (though it is doubtful whether the ban was always enforced). Only on the ninth day of the month of Av, the day of the destruction of the Second Temple rebuilt by Herod, were they allowed to lament their loss at the "Wailing Wall." The center of gravity slowly shifted to Galilee. Local Jewish scholars were no longer able to play a leading role for the Jews of Palestine and the diaspora.[12] The seat of the Sanhedrin, the highest religious and judicial authority of the Jewish community, presided over by the patriarchs from the House of Hillel, was eventually moved to Tiberias, a city founded by Herodes Antipas in A.D. 18 in honor of Emperor Tiberius, where it remained until the Muslim conquest. With the death of Gamliel VI in around A.D. 425, the line of the Palestinian patriarchs came to an end. That Jews were readmitted to Jerusalem after the Muslim conquest therefore marked an important moment.[13] Another positive sign was the purification of the Temple Mount, which according to both Muslim and Jewish sources, had degenerated under Byzantine rule into a heap of rubble and refuse. By the seventh century, the center of Jewish prayer and pilgrimage had shifted from the Temple Mount and the Wailing Wall (close to which the Jews may have maintained a small synagogue during the Umayyad and Abbasid periods) to the Mount of Olives, which also served as a gathering place for the community. In the

[11] Isaiah 65:17ff. speaks of a new creation, if not a "new" or "heavenly" Jerusalem: "For, behold, I create new heavens and a new earth: and the former shall not be remembered, nor come into mind." Cf. Weinfeld (1993), pp. 217ff.; Talmon (1970), pp. 148–50; Thoma (1970), pp. 41 and 48–50. Jeremiah 31:38–40 paints a rather realistic vision of the rebuilt Jerusalem as the navel and capital of the world.

[12] In the tenth century, the Sanhedrin was transferred to Jerusalem, only to return to Tiberias at the end of the eleventh century. From the end of the sixth century to the middle of the eleventh, the heads (ge'onim) of the rabbinical academies of Sura and Pumbedita in Babylon (Iraq) were regarded as the highest religious and judicial authorities for all Jews. In the twelfth and thirteenth centuries, the gaon of Cairo had jurisdiction over the Jews in Ayyubid and Mamluk domains. But there were also Babylonian communities in Palestine, so that there existed no clear division of power and influence between the Jewish authorities in Cairo and Iraq; Gil (1997), pp. 110–14, 470.

[13] See Gil (1997), esp. pp. 65ff., 71ff., 86, 626ff., 636ff., 648; F. E. Peters (1987), pp. 126–31; Lazarus-Yafeh (1981), p. 60. The prophet Ezekiel saw the shehina (God's presence or "inhabitation") leave Jerusalem from the Mount of Olives after the destruction of the city by Nebuchadnezzar; Thoma (1970), p. 50.

sixteenth century, Bedouin incursions caused the sites of worship and gathering to be moved to the interior of the city, whose walls were rebuilt by Suleiman the Magnificent in the 1530s. He also allowed the Jews to open a prayer room at the Wailing Wall. Given that according to contemporary records, the Wailing Wall itself first had to be cleansed of a mound of filth and debris, it appears to have played no prominent role in Jewish religious life until then. The notion of the Wailing Wall as a focal point of holiness was only popularized in literary and pictorial form in the nineteenth and twentieth centuries. The idea that there are "four holy cities" in Eretz Israel—Jerusalem, Hebron, Safed, and Tiberias—developed in connection with fund-raising for the Jews in Eretz Israel, the Halukka, which seems to have been carried out more systematically after the Ottoman conquest in the sixteenth century.

It is true that after the destruction of the Temple and the Jewish kingdom as a whole, the vast majority of Jews did not live in Eretz Israel. But they lived "turning to the land":[14] All synagogues were oriented toward Jerusalem (just like mosques toward Mecca), and the seven-armed candelabrum, the Menorah, symbolized the Temple. The yearning for Zion was expressed in liturgy and ritual, in visual art and poetry. The most familiar passage is certainly Psalm 137:1–6:

> By the waters of Babylon, there we sat down and wept, when we remembered Zion. On the willows there we hung up our lyres. For there our captors required of us songs, and our tormentors, mirth, saying, "Sing us one of the songs of Zion!" How shall we sing the Lord's song in a foreign land? If I forget you, O Jerusalem, let my right hand wither! Let my tongue cleave to the roof of my mouth, if I do not remember you, if I do not set Jerusalem above my highest joy!

In ritual prayer, Zion or Jerusalem stood for Eretz Israel as a whole. Among the best-known references is surely the saying "next year in Jerusalem," spoken at the close of the Passover seder, the liturgy commemorating the exodus from Egypt. Especially important is the fourteenth of the nineteen blessings of the daily Amidah prayer, which is modified on the Sabbath and on holidays: "To Jerusalem Thy city, return with compassion, and dwell within it as Thou promised; rebuild it soon in our days—an everlasting structure; and speedily establish in its midst the throne of David. Blessed art Thou, O Lord, builder of Jerusalem." Daily table prayer as a central component of household liturgy consists of four blessings. In the third, the so-called *boneh yerushalayim* ("Build Jerusalem"), a prayer is made for Zion/Jerusalem and for the restoration

---

[14] Thoma (1970), p. 51; also Safrai (1983), p. 212; Budde/Nachama (eds.) (1996); Kaplony (2002); Ben-Arieh/Davis (1997).

of the Davidic dynasty and the Temple. Jerusalem also plays an important role in the *piyyutim* (liturgical poetry), where depending on the
context, it is praised or lamented. The land of Israel as a land "flowing
with milk and honey" (Exod. 3:17) was idealized in the non-normative
rabbinical tradition (Aggada) and in folk tradition, embellished with miraculous tales and legends. Like religion in general, the form and function of liturgy changed over time. In the age of emancipation, Reform
congregations, whose goal it was to integrate diaspora Jews into their
non-Jewish society, went so far as to strike from the prayer books those
passages that spoke of a return to Zion/Jerusalem. Such passages were
deterritorialized and spiritualized. The Holocaust was to change this as
it changed so many other things.

Concerning the practical implications of the yearning for Zion, we
have little information for the period up to the late nineteenth century.
Jewish pilgrimage, which must have been of major importance in the
period of the Second Temple, came to a halt with its destruction. The
attempt of Emperor Julian the Apostate (ruled A.D. 361–63) to rebuild
the Temple was ended by his early death.[15] Yet pilgrimage to the Holy
Land at large continued as did immigration of Jews, for which we have
evidence across the centuries. Already in the third century A.D., we hear
of the burial or transfer of the dead to Palestine (and not only to Jerusalem), although it cannot be quantified. Against the initial resistance of
the rabbis, who after the destruction of the Temple would rather see the
living in Eretz Israel than the dead, there developed the notion that
burial in the Holy Land was especially commendable, both as an expiation of sins, and to join the ranks of those whom the Lord would
awaken first on the Day of Resurrection.

CHRISTIAN TRADITION

In Christian tradition, we find perhaps an even greater variety of images
and ideas concerning Zion/Jerusalem and the biblical land at large than
in Jewish tradition. On the one hand, we witness a tendency toward
abstraction from concrete space ("deterritorialization"), reflecting a conscious attempt at differentiation from, if not reversal of, Jewish notions
of the Holy Land. But we also witness the exact opposite, emphasizing
the Christian bond with the Holy Land, and requiring political control
of this particular space. Especially significant for Western cultural history, both then and now, is the transfer of the biblical motifs of the

---

[15] Stemberger (1987), pp. 151–74. On Jewish pilgrimage and travel reports, see Kaiser
(1992), pp. 41ff. On Jewish burials, see Gafni (1981).

"chosen people" and "promised land" to a variety of Christian groups and communities—from the early Christians, who regarded the "old covenant" of the Jews as replaced by the "new covenant" of Christianity, to the Russian Orthodox Church and the English Puritans of the seventeenth century to American preachers and politicians of our own day. These concepts, based on different notions of the significance of the land for religious practice and communal identity, occasionally reflected very specific interests. For all the similarities of Jewish and Christian "land theologies," there are also basic differences: Whereas the Jewish land theology is based on the divine promise and covenant, its Christian counterparts are more focused on persons, transferring the holiness of individuals —not only Jesus, the apostles, and Christian martyrs, but also the biblical patriarchs, kings, and prophets—to the territory in which they were active.

The idea of Palestine as the "Holy Land" (*terra sancta*) spread in the Roman Empire from the end of the fourth century, following the adoption of Christianity as the official religion of the empire.[16] But it was only during the Crusades that it became a permanent part of European consciousness and linguistic usage. Prior to that, an indifferent attitude toward the biblical land had prevailed, which must be understood as a conscious differentiation from Judaism. The apostles were not united in their appreciation of Jerusalem and the Holy Land: In the Gospels, Jerusalem is, above all, the place of the passion and death of Christ and for that reason is viewed rather negatively. The Gospel of John is an exception—and yet it is here that we find the clearest dissociation of space and redemption. The "heavenly Jerusalem" that John speaks of (especially in John 4:19–24) designates neither a space nor some parallel world to the earthly sphere, but rather an inner state of mind. The abstract, or spiritual interpretation is above all reflected in chapter 21 of the Book of Revelation, which speaks so powerfully of a "New Jerusalem," and in the letters of the apostles, particularly Hebrews 11:16 ("But as it is, they desire a better country, that is, a heavenly one") and Galatians 4:26 ("But the Jerusalem above is free, and she is our mother"). Here, Christian authors were able to refer to the Hebrew Bible, especially the prophets Daniel, Isaiah, and Ezekiel. The motif of a heavenly Jerusalem was interpreted in various ways: For Origen (185–254) and Ambrose (340–97), heavenly Jerusalem was the faithful soul, while for Paul and Augustine (354–430), it was the community of believers. The Middle Ages created new spaces, institutions, and communities as sites

---

[16] For what follows, esp. representations of "heavenly Jerusalem," cf. Konrad (1965); Kühnel (1987); Budde/Nachama (eds.) (1996); von Naredi-Rainer (1994), pp. 46ff.; Stemberger (1987), pp. 184–236.

and presentations of a Christian order, among them the monastery and
the cathedral, where the glory of heavenly Jerusalem was reflected in the
Gothic stained-glass windows.

In parallel with this tendency toward abstraction, we observe a gradual appropriation of the Jewish concept of the promised land by Christian authors and authorities. In the early fourth century, Emperor Constantine made a conscious effort to transform Jerusalem into a holy city
of Christianity. Like others before and after him, he embarked on a
construction program, directed toward the (presumed) sites where Jesus
had been active.[17] In 325, the emperor ordered Bishop Makarios of Jerusalem to tear down a temple of Venus. On the very spot, the tomb of
Jesus was "discovered" only two years later. Eusebius (c. 260–339),
religious advisor and biographer of the emperor, who as bishop of his
native Caesarea had previously followed the religious upgrading of Jerusalem with considerable reserve, interpreted the discovery as a sign of
Christian triumph and impending victory over the Jews and heathens.
During the construction of the Church of the Holy Sepulcher, dedicated
in 335 with great ceremony, the cross of Christ was "found," a discovery that was later ascribed to Constantine's mother, Helena. The Church
of the Holy Sepulcher itself was invested with high symbolic meaning:
The basilica (*martyrion*) was dedicated to the passion of Christ; the rotunda (*anastasis*) with the tomb of Christ was held to be the site of the
resurrection; the rock of Golgotha was also thought to be the grave of
Adam as well as the site of the sacrifice of Isaac. In the fourth century,
numerous churches and monasteries were built in Jerusalem, Bethlehem,
and the "Holy Land" at large, funded by Byzantine dignitaries and
wealthy patrons from Christian Europe, among them many monks who
had visited the Holy Land as pilgrims. At the same time, ever new "discoveries" of tombs and relics of biblical prophets and Christian martyrs
were made, complete with more easily obtainable and multipliable
goods such as soil, oil, pieces of the cross, and Jordan River water,
which greatly helped to render "sacred memory" concrete and tangible.
Christian liturgy incorporated references to the holy sites. In later times,
the stations of the cross made it possible for believers to visualize, if not

---

[17] Stemberger (1987), pp. 49–51, 99–102, 154. On the Church of the Holy Sepulcher,
cf. Krüger (2000). With the Persian conquest in 614, the church went up in flames. It was
rebuilt on a smaller scale and again destroyed in 1009 by the Fatimid caliph al-Hakim bi-
amri 'llah. The Byzantine emperor Constantine IX Monomachos had the rotunda of the
Sepulcher rebuilt in 1048. It was renovated by the Crusaders in Romanesque style, who
also erected a monumental new building in place of the basilica. Both were reconstructed
in the nineteenth century following a fire and earthquake, and periodically renovated in
the twentieth century (such as following the earthquakes of 1927 and 1937). On relics
and replicas, see Wharton (2006).

experience, the sites of Christ's passion in the most distant places. Image, sound, and word made the biblical sites appear familiar in a manner unmatched by any place outside people's immediate environment.

The earliest remaining depiction of Christian Jerusalem, presented in idealized oval form on the mosaic floor in Madaba in present-day Jordan, dates back to the sixth century. Interestingly enough, European maps did not for a long time reflect the new (Christian) vision of the world, with Jerusalem as its center and navel.[18] Only from the close of the twelfth century, in the time of the Crusades, do we have a map that places Jerusalem in the center of the (Christian) world. Its significance for Christianity should not be overrated, for at the very time that Jerusalem (the site of the passion of Christ) attained new status, it was Rome (the site of the persecution of the apostles and the "Babylon" of the early Christians) that became the true center of the Christian universe. By the fifteenth century, cartographers returned to models based not on sacred geography, but on the latest scientific discoveries.

Renewed interest in the holy sites was also reflected in pilgrimages, for which there is evidence soon after the discovery of the tomb of Christ.[19] A few pilgrims had undertaken the journey even earlier. It became somewhat less dangerous when in 311, Emperor Galerius halted the persecution of Christians in the western Empire (in the east they only ended in 324). Beginning in the fourth century, we have the reports of the anonymous pilgrim of Bordeaux who traveled to the Holy Land in 333, of the Roman ladies Paula and Eustochium (385–86), the nun Egeria or Aetheria (393–96), and the Gallic bishop Arculf, who was among the first European pilgrims to visit Palestine in 670 or 680, a few decades after the Muslim conquest. In the course of the Middle Ages and the early modern period, the motives of the pilgrims became increasingly diverse: While the spiritual dimension must always have been strong, there were also the indulgences granted by the Church, as well as the search for prestige, and the love of adventure. In the nineteenth century, the pilgrimage was often part of an educational journey, or one of the "grand tours" of good society (or their male portion, at least). Still, the great majority of pilgrims did not come from Latin Christianity, but from the east, whether from Byzantium or from regions controlled by

---

[18] Nebenzahl (1986); Rubin (1999); von Naredi-Rainer (1994), pp. 46, 88–89.

[19] For western Europe, see Röhricht (1890); Stemberger (1987), pp. 84–92; Kaiser (1992), pp. 44ff.; also Herbert Donner, *Pilgerfahrt ins Heilige Land* (Stuttgart 1979). Around 1500, the "travel description" written around 1356 by John Mandeville (who never visited the Holy Land) was one of the most popular pieces of European travel literature, which was then receiving a new impetus from the printing press; von Naredi-Rainer (1994), pp. 61ff. For Orthodox pilgrims from eastern Europe, see Stavrou/Weisensel (1986).

the Muslims. Even in the nineteenth century, Russian and Middle Eastern visitors made up the majority of Christian pilgrims and travelers in the Holy Land.

For Christians just as for Jews, notions of sacred space and holy sites were closely linked with the exclusion of others—even though Christian conceptions were not based on similar concepts of ritual purity and impurity, and were largely confined to Jerusalem.[20] In the Crusader period, the policy of exclusion was mainly directed against Muslims. After the conquest of Jerusalem in 1099, the Dome of the Rock was transformed with little architectural modification into a Christian church (the "Temple of the Lord," *templum domini*), and al-Aqsa Mosque into "Solomon's Temple," *templum Salomonis*. The Order of Templars, founded in 1118–19, established their headquarters there. This clearly showed a spirit of competition and the attempt to outdo the Muslims just as the latter had done four centuries earlier by constructing the Dome of the Rock. Representations of Solomon's temple and the New Jerusalem were to have a deep impact on European art and culture. Witness the various attempts at reconstructing the Temple as a prototype of ideal architecture, from the Hagia Sophia to the Sistine Chapel to the Escorial. In each case, the ideal form was defined differently, whether in circular shape or as strict axial symmetry.[21] In the eighteenth century, the Freemasons referred to the Temple as a metaphor for virtuous society. In the fifteenth and sixteenth centuries, Venice, Kiev, and Moscow all portrayed themselves as the New Jerusalem. The Anabaptists in Munster and Cromwell's Puritans viewed themselves as renewers of the Old Testament covenant. Similar attempts were made in America: The first European emigrants became known as the "Pilgrim Fathers." Later, the "opening" of the west was identified with the exodus, as reflected in nineteenth-century landscape painting. As early as 1685, Samuel Wakeman, a New England preacher based in Hartford, put it so well: "Jerusalem was, New England is, they were, you are God's own, God's covenant people."[22]

MUSLIM TRADITION

The historicity of all notions regarding the holiness of the biblical lands, or at least part of these lands, can also be traced through the Muslim

---

[20] Kaplony (2002); Asali (ed.) (1997), ch. 5 (al-Hiyari) and ch. 6 (Little). See also Sylvia Schein, "Between Moriah and the Holy Sepulchre: The Changing Traditions of the Temple Mount in the Central Middle Ages," in *Tradition*, 40 (1984), pp. 175–95; Helen Rosenau, *Vision of the Temple: The Image of the Temple of Jerusalem in Judaism and Christianity* (London 1979).

[21] Von Naredi-Rainer (1994); Wharton (2006).

[22] Cited from Davis (1996), p. 14; see also Merkley (1998), pp. 54–55.

tradition. Like its Christian counterpart, it was from the beginning marked by competing visions. The very richness of the Qur'an and the Prophetic Tradition (Sunna) made it possible for diverse conceptions to be legitimated in Islamic terms. Not surprisingly, it was mostly local scholars and mystics who advocated the special status of Jerusalem and its vicinity; others like the famous theologian Taqi al-Din Ahmad Ibn Taimiyya (d. 1328), himself a native of Syria and a favorite of modern Islamists, adopted a critical stance.[23] In Islam we find a new chain of arguments characteristic of the subtle pattern of inclusion and exclusion that Muslims displayed toward the other revealed religions: While they inserted themselves into the grand monotheistic tradition, they marked their distance toward its previous adherents. Just as in the Christian view, the "new covenant" corrected and superseded the old, so did the revelation sent down to Muhammad renew and supersede the earlier ones, which were thereby devalued without being utterly deprived of value. The Qur'anic reference to Abraham as the spiritual ancestor of Muslims, Jews, and Christians served to lend to the new community and its prophet the prestige and recognition that were denied to them by actual representatives of the monotheistic tradition, the Jews and Christians inside and outside of the Arabian Peninsula. According to the Qur'an itself, it contained the divine message pure and uncorrupted, which the Jews and Christians had received too, but deviated from, or even falsified outright. The most visible token of this complex relation was the change of the direction of prayer (qibla) from Jerusalem to Mecca (Sura 2:142–50), which according to Muslim tradition occurred soon after the hijra in 622, possibly as a result of the violent conflict between Muhammad and the Jewish tribes in Medina, who he had hoped to win over to his mission.[24]

Muslim conceptions of the holiness of the Holy Land clearly built on themes from the Jewish and Christian tradition, but they also endowed them with new meaning. To begin with, the significance of sacred space in Islam is not easy to determine.[25] The case of Mecca and the pilgrimage (hajj) there suggests that strictly speaking, holiness applies to a combination of space, time, and a state of consecration. The latter presupposes ritual purity, which entails (at least potentially) the exclusion of the "impure" and the unbeliever. For this reason, mosques were at various times

---

[23] See Matthews (1936) and Muhammad Umar Memon, *Ibn Taimiya's Struggle against Popular Religion* (The Hague, Paris 1976). Also Elad (1995); Asali (ed.) (1997), ch. 4 (Duri).

[24] Neuwirth (1993) and (1996), pp. 24ff. Muhammad's mosque in Medina was also called the "mosque of two prayer directions (*masjid al-qiblatain*)." Jerusalem is still known today as the "first of the two prayer directions (*ula al-qiblatain*)."

[25] See F. E. Peters (1986).

declared to be sacred spaces (*haram*), taboo for unbelievers. Until the mid-nineteenth century, this held for the "noble district" (*al-haram al-sharif*) on the Temple Mount, including the Dome of the Rock and al-Aqsa Mosque, as well as for specific places like the Tomb of the Patriarchs in Hebron (*mahpela* in Hebrew).

For Muslims, too, Jerusalem enjoyed high religious status, as traced to the Qur'an and the Sunna. According to Muslim tradition, it was the original direction of prayer (*qibla*) and the site of the so-called night journey of Muhammad (*isra', mi'raj*), a narrative, whose individual elements were woven together over a lengthy period of time. The Umayyad caliphs lent new prestige and a specifically Islamic character to the city when they built the Dome of the Rock and the Aqsa Mosque, a construction program that should be viewed in light of competition with the Christians. In the aftermath of the Crusades, the Ayyubids and Mamluks carried out construction work with similar intent, later followed by the Ottomans. The literature on the merits of Jerusalem (*fada'il al-quds*), too, was disseminated above all during the time of the Crusades, though it had been created much earlier. By contrast, the notion of Palestine as a religious endowment (*waqf*), a divine and unalienable trust of the Muslims, who in the seventh century conquered the land for Islam, appears to be modern. In addition to the normative tradition, there is, of course, the large stock of stories and legends connected with Jerusalem, many of which were shared by Jews, Christians, and Muslims alike.

When the Muslims conquered Jerusalem in 638, it was a purely Christian city. It is difficult to determine what it meant to them at the time: The caliph Umar b. al-Khattab (ruled 634–44) seems to have briefly visited Jerusalem and to have arranged for the purification of the Temple Mount. But it is unclear, whether he was persuaded to do so by Jews or by local Christians.[26] To emphasize the direction of prayer toward Mecca, Umar had a simple wooden structure erected to the south of the rock (which in some way was already connected with Abraham). The building served the Muslims as a place of gathering and prayer, and was described by the Gallic bishop Arculf in 670, or perhaps 680. Apart from this, the "holy city" does not appear to have attracted special notice. In Arabic, it was still called "Iliya" (Aelia). Only much later were *al-quds* ("the holy") or *bait al-maqdis* ("house of the holy") used to designate Jerusalem.

The Umayyad caliphs, who ruled the Islamic lands from 661 to 750, attached high value to Jerusalem, or at least to the Temple area, as can be deduced from their extensive construction program. Their chief motive seems to have been competition with the Christians, who since the

---

[26] See Lazarus-Yafeh (1981), pp. 60, 66; Enderwitz (1996), p. 34; Gil (1997), pp. 65ff., 90ff., 96, 636ff.; also Stemberger (1987), pp. 56–57, 94, 97.

time of Constantine had erected a series of buildings in Jerusalem that were truly magnificent, at least by local standards. In fact, it was primarily *buildings* that marked the "noble district" (*al-haram al-sharif*) as an Islamic site. The Dome of the Rock (*qubbat al-sakhra*), which the Umayyad caliph Abd al-Malik b. Marwan had built in 691–92, only two generations after the death of Muhammad, was situated in the place where according to Muslim tradition, Umar had prayed during his short visit to Jerusalem.[27] The thesis of the eminent Islamic scholar Ignaz Goldziher, based on a minority tradition within Muslim historiography, that the Dome of the Rock reflected competition with the "anti-caliph" Abdallah b. al-Zubair, who had seized control of Mecca and Medina, has been widely discarded. According to Goldziher, the Dome of the Rock was to divert the Muslim pilgrimage from Mecca and establish a pilgrimage center in Jerusalem under Umayyad control. What the Umayyads aimed at was not so much their Muslim rivals, but the Christians, and to a certain extent also the Jews. Abd al-Malik, incidentally, seems to have identified the rock on the Temple Mount as the site of Abraham's sacrifice, not of Muhammad's heavenly journey (a legendary story that may not even have been known to him yet in full detail). Here too, then, it was initially a question of occupying an "Abrahamic site."

The Dome of the Rock was never a mosque, but rather a place of Muslim assembly, pilgrimage, and individual prayer, designed as a visible sign of Islam's triumph over the Christians, Jews, and all other rivals and opponents. The inscriptions and pictorial program show as much. We are less well informed about the history of al-Aqsa Mosque—in religious terms the most important building in the "noble district," and from early on a special subject of Muslim anxieties. We learn from Egyptian papyrus scrolls that the Aqsa Mosque was probably completed between 706 and 717, only a few years after the Dome of the Rock, under Abd al-Malik's son and successor al-Walid. Little seems to have remained of the original structure following numerous renovations, reconstructions, and expansions, and after the fire of 1969 it was thoroughly restored.

Along with the construction program, various genres of literature evolved that established the status of the Dome of the Rock, al-Aqsa Mosque, and the city of Jerusalem as a whole as holy sites of Islam. In

---

[27] The literature on the Haram in general and the Dome of the Rock in particular is extensive. Cf. especially Kaplony (2002); Raby/Johns (eds.) (1992); Elad (1995); also Priscilla Soucek, "The Temple of Solomon in Islamic Legend and Art," in Joseph Gutman (ed.), *The Temple of Solomon* (Missoula MT, 1976), pp. 73–123. Amikam Elad is one of the few specialists to support Ignaz Goldziher's thesis (*Muhammedanische Studien*. Reprint, Hildesheim, New York 1971, Part II: 35–36); see his "Why did 'Abd al-Malik build the Dome of the Rock? A re-examination of the Muslim Sources," in Raby/Johns (eds.) (1992): 33–58.

Figure 1. Al-Aqsa Mosque on the Temple Mount, or "noble district" (*al-haram al-sharif*). Anonymous photograph, c. 1900.

the Umayyad period, first efforts were made to systematically relate passages of the Qur'an to al-Haram al-Sharif, Jerusalem, and Palestine or the Syrian land (*bilad al-sham*), which did not necessarily suggest such a relation.[28] Sura 5:21, for instance, does mention the "holy land" (*al-ard al-muqaddasa*)—but here it is Moses speaking to the Israelites, telling them of God's promise. Sura 30:3 speaks of a Byzantine defeat in the "nearest" or the "neighboring land" (*adna al-ard*), which was understood as a reference to Syria and Palestine. Only later was this reference taken as related to al-Aqsa Mosque, even though *al-aqsa* literally means the "furthest" place of prayer. Where to place the "furthest place

[28] Busse (1968) and (1991); Neuwirth (1993) and (1996).

of prayer" (*al-masjid al-asqa*) mentioned in Sura 17:1, "the area around which we have blessed," was and still is a matter of dispute: on the Arabian Peninsula in the vicinity of Mecca, on the Temple Mount in Jerusalem, or indeed—clearly resonating with the notion of "heavenly Jerusalem"—in heaven itself? The prevalent identification of this "furthest site of prayer" with al-Aqsa Mosque places it among the three mosques to which Muslims, according to scholarly opinion, can and should make pilgrimages. But Mecca and Medina always retained higher status: The pilgrimage to Jerusalem was a *ziyara*, a religiously meritorious "visit," not a religious duty (and indeed a pillar of Islam) comparable to the *hajj* to Mecca.

The story of Muhammad's night journey to heaven presents a complex narrative fabric linking two distinct elements: the Qur'anic report of his night journey (Sura 17:1; Sura 17 is called *surat al-isra'* in Arabic), in which God took his servant from the "sacred place of prayer" (*al-masjid al-haram*) to the "furthest place of prayer" (*al-masjid al-aqsa*), and Qur'anic allusions to Muhammad's ascent to heaven (*isra'*), and even unto the presence of God (Suras 53:1–18 and 81:19–25).[29] The stories are told with more detail in the Prophetic Tradition (Sunna) and in extra-Qur'anic tradition more generally, which later had an effect on Qur'anic interpretation and appear to have been influenced by Jewish eschatological notions. In the most elaborate versions of the story, in which the night and heavenly journeys are combined, Muhammad travels by night on the miraculous mount Buraq to the "furthest place of prayer" on the Temple Mount in Jerusalem. From the rock (where the imprint of his foot was later identified), Muhammad ascended to heaven, where he prayed with the prophets Abraham, Moses, and Jesus, and where the correct form of obligatory prayer was revealed to him. The night and heavenly journeys later came to be further embellished and interpreted in ever new ways: mystically, allegorically, psychologically. In Islamic art and literature, Buraq achieved special status, a magic creature familiar from other religions. It is Buraq after whom the Wailing Wall is named in Arabic, because it is here that Muhammad is said to have tethered his mount before ascending to heaven.

Like the literature of praise, the story of Muhammad's nightly ascent to heaven seems originally to have been produced locally, and was clearly inspired by non-Muslim sources, whether Jewish or Christian. Already by the time of Muhammad, stories about the patriarchs, first and foremost Abraham, had been dissociated from their specifically Jewish and Christian context and integrated into popular imagination. The notion that prayers said in Jerusalem carry special weight betrays the

[29] Busse (1991).

influence of oriental Christendom. The idea that the resurrection will take place in Jerusalem would suggest Jewish influences; it contributed to the fact that more and more Muslims sought to be buried there, too, or at least to have their dead taken and interred there. In a similar way, biblical sites were integrated into Islamic tradition; Hebron, for instance, was said not only to contain the tombs of Abraham (Ibrahim al-Khalil, hence "al-Khalil" as the Arabic name for Hebron), Sarah, Adam, Joseph, and other Old Testament figures, but also to have served as a way station on Muhammad's night journey. The Hebron mosque with the so-called tombs of the patriarchs (*mahpela*) remains to the present day one of the most important, and contested, religious sites in Palestine.[30]

The literature on the merits of Jerusalem (*fada'il al-quds*) formed a heterogeneous genre whose origins reach back to the Umayyad era; *fada'il* literature incidentally was by no means limited to Jerusalem, but was a popular part of praise literature in general.[31] Most of the *fada'il* literature in praise of Palestine, and Jerusalem more particularly, was disseminated in the early eleventh century, that is to say relatively late, though predating the First Crusade. It does not provide us with precise descriptions of the nature and geographic scope of the "Holy Land" according to Muslim views: Jerusalem is not clearly distinguished from the surrounding area, or from Syria at large; many authors refer to *bilad al-sham* as a whole. Later reports display a similar lack of precision: When in the sixteenth century, the highest Muslim authority in the Ottoman Empire, *sheih ül-islam* Ebussu'ud Effendi, was asked about the location and scope of the "Holy Land" (*arazi-i muqaddese*), he mentioned Palestine (*filastin*) and Syria.[32]

Thus, over the centuries Palestine was not so much the actual center of Jewish, Christian, or Muslim life, but rather a symbol and reference point of highly charged emotions, to which believers could connect in ever changing ways.

---

[30] Canaan (1927); Gil (1997), pp. 42, 99, 633–34; also Benvenisti (2000), pp. 286–87; Wagner (2002).

[31] Sivan (1995), pp. 67–106. See further Kamil al-'Asali, *Makhtutat fada'il bait al-maqdis* (Amman 1984).

[32] See Mehmet Ertuğrul Düzdağ, *Seyhülislam Ebussuud Efendi Fetvaları. Isiginda 16. Asır Türk Hayatı* (Istanbul 1972) and Colin Imber, *Ebu's-su'ud, The Islamic Legal Tradition* (Edinburgh 1997), pp. 135–36. Imber makes it clear that in this context Ebussu'ud is largely concerned with taxation. See also R. Khalidi (1997), esp. pp. 28–32.

Chapter Three

CONTRASTS: PALESTINE, 1750–1840

SO FAR WE HAVE SPOKEN MOSTLY OF IMAGES, images of Palestine as the Holy Land formed by Jews, Christians, and Muslims at various times. The power of images is undisputed, and returns in force in the nineteenth and twentieth centuries. But what do they tell us about economics, culture, and society in Palestine in the Ottoman period? One is tempted to say: little or nothing. The notions of pilgrims, travelers, and diplomats from east and west who visited the country in the eighteenth and nineteenth centuries were as a rule exalted, their expectations high, and their disappointment over conditions on the ground often all the greater. Not surprisingly, Jerusalem was the place where these feelings were most vividly expressed. A well-known biblical scholar and archaeologist thus wrote in 1838:

> The glory of Jerusalem has indeed departed. From her ancient estate as the splendid metropolis of the Jewish commonwealth and of the whole Christian world, the beloved of nations and the "joy of the whole earth," she has sunk into the neglected capital of a petty Turkish province; and where of old many hundreds of thousands thronged her streets and temple, we now find a population of scarcely as many single thousands dwelling sparcely within her walls. The cup of wrath and desolation from the Almighty has been poured out upon her to the dregs; and she sits sad and solitary in darkness and dust.[1]

The vision of ancient splendor expressed here (and characteristically translated into a demographic argument) is striking but by no means unique. Western notions of "Oriental despotism," corrupt, ineffectual, and incapable of anything but the oppression of its own people was of some relevance in this context. European travel literature transmitted these clichés, but it was not alone in doing so, as the following passage will illustrate:

> At the beginning of the 19th century Palestine was but a derelict province of the decaying Ottoman Empire. The Sublime Porte [the Ottoman authorities in Istanbul] only showed interest in it because of the holy places and

[1] Edward Robinson, *Biblical Researches*, vol. II (London 1838), p. 81, cited from Ben-Arieh (1984), p. 53. Yet Robinson's impressions were not all negative, as the lines preced-

the meagre revenue extorted from the wretched habitants. The country was badly governed, having no political importance of its own, its economy was primitive, the sparse, ethnically mixed population subsisted on a dismally low standard; the few towns were small and miserable; the roads few and neglected. In short, Palestine was but a sad backwater of a crumbling empire—a far cry from the fertile, thriving land it had been in ancient times.[2]

The author is Yehoshua Ben-Arieh—not some Bible enthusiast traveling through the Holy Land, but rather a respected historian of the nineteenth century whose works on Jerusalem are widely read. These few sentences contain almost everything that can be found in contemporary and later writings, whether from European observers or Jewish settlers, Arab nationalists or Islamic activists: The past appears distant and glorious, the present dismal and desolate, the land poor and neglected, the people downtrodden and wretched, the administration inept and despotic. Ruins, nothing but ruins, is what the German traveler Ewald Banse saw in the entire "Orient" as late as the 1930s:

> Wherever one goes in the Orient, everywhere one encounters decay, dust, and mildew. And worst of all, the feeling always prevails that it used to be much better and more beautiful than it is now. Here it is not only ancient ruins that lie in rubble. Even the living present is now only the rubble of what has passed away.[3]

Not everyone saw things so negatively. Yet the leitmotif is one of decay, which Ben-Arieh like many others traced back to the poor administration of the "Turks." The clichés assembled here found their ultimate expression in the idea that at the end of the nineteenth century the Jewish settlers found a country not only devoid of people, but utterly deserted, a "land of ruins," squalid and desolate: Palestine, a "still life."[4] The image would seem quite apt, since it was disseminated through paintings, engravings, and photographs that were in turn guided and inspired by Holy Scripture. Hence the well-known phrase that the Jewish pioneers "made the desert bloom." Here the desert is not only to be

---

ing this quote prove; for a fuller citation, see Rood (2004), pp. 28–29, and chapter 4 below.

[2] Ben-Arieh (1979), p. 11; Ben-Arieh (1984), Part I, chs. 2–5, and Part II, chs. 4 and 5, paint a similar picture. Cf. also A. Cohen (1973), pp. 1–4. For critiques of the "Orientalist view," see Whitelam (1996), pp. 40ff.; Doumani (1995), pp. 6–7, 216; R. Khalidi (1997), pp. 178–79.

[3] Banse (1934), p. 67.

[4] Divine (1994), p. 13. In sarcastic vein, see also Benvenisti (2000), ch. 2. On the relation between scripture and image, see, e.g., Davis (1996); see also Wharton (2006).

taken literally, for it also designates a cultural, intellectual, and even spiritual desolation. New life and vitality, so the argument ran, retrieving greatness lost (but remembered by others, at least!) was only possible through the intervention of external powers; the entry into civilization required a clean break with local customs and habits.

Stereotypes are notoriously persistent and can survive strong attacks, no matter how well these attacks are grounded in facts. It is a long way from scholarly research to public awareness—especially in cases when politics intervene at every level. Historians have been working for some time to revise our image of the Ottomans, attempting a reevaluation or even rehabilitation of Ottoman politics, culture, and society, including the alleged period of decadence and decay when the Ottomans (or rather, the Turks) were perceived in Europe as "the sick man of Europe."[5] Arab historians, who under nationalist auspices had long viewed the era of Ottoman rule as negatively as their European and American colleagues, have joined in the revisionist effort. Arab memoirs and autobiographies largely retain the negative image. By contrast, scholars now increasingly emphasize the strengths of Ottoman rule, first and foremost its flexibility and adaptability to local conditions, which permitted it to control large parts of the Arab world for just over four centuries. In the process, they do not always escape the danger of a romanticism that depicts the Ottoman Empire, in sharp contrast to Western modernity, as a space of free movement and free negotiation of social relations. This tendency is especially marked in studies on women, family life, and Islamic law.[6]

Historians have also turned their attention to local actors: not just members of the elite, but also "the common people," urban as well as rural, both settled and nomadic, who in earlier works were often discussed all too briefly. They no longer present them merely as victims of foreign domination and exploitation. Rather, they ask about perceptions, identifications, and the demarcation of boundaries; they sketch spaces of action, refer to complex interrelations, to the inherent openness of every historical situation and the contingency of all historical

---

[5] Czar Nicolas seems to have been the first to speak of the "sick man" in regard to the Ottoman Empire (or Turkey, as it was usually called at the time), when in a meeting with George Hamilton Seymour in 1853 (held in connection with the Crimean War) he said: "We have on our hands a sick man—a very sick man." Cited from Burton Stevenson (ed.), *Stevenson's Book of Quotations*, fourth edition (London 1943), p. 2061. I owe this reference to Stefan Wild.

[6] On the paradigm of decline, see Christoph Herzog, *Geschichte und Ideologie: Mehmed Murad und Celal Nuri über die historischen Ursachen des osmanischen Niedergangs* (Berlin 1996); also Faroqhi et al. (1994), pp. 467ff., 552ff. For Palestine, see Reinkowski (1995); Doumani (1992) and (1995). A moderate version of the romanticizing approach can be found, for instance, in Tucker (1998), pp. 179–86.

events. Their aim is to make the inhabitants of Palestine visible again as agents of their own history, and to overcome the "tunnel vision" that has left them out of consideration for too long. It is a promising research program, though by no means accomplished. Men still figure much more prominently in the sources than do women, which has an obvious influence on how history is written and stories are told.

The sharper focus on local conditions and "subaltern" subjects, along with the revisionist view of the Ottoman Empire as a whole, has had a definite effect on historical periodization in the modern era. Critical historians no longer look primarily for external actors, whether the French army under Napoleon Bonaparte or the troops of the Egyptian governor Muhammad Ali, whether the European consuls and missionaries, the Württemberg Templars, or Jewish settlers. They pay greater attention to local or regional actors, processes and developments, recognizing that these, too, did not act or occur in isolation and for that reason cannot be dissociated or disentangled from external influences. As a result, the temporal horizon is broadened, and the boundaries of political change and economic revival are shifted. In certain regions of Palestine this revival can be dated to the end of the eighteenth century, in others to the last third of the nineteenth. The year 1882—the beginning of Zionist immigration—loses its status as the date of Palestine's entry into modernity.

State and Society in the Late Ottoman Period

From 1516 to 1918, and hence for almost exactly four hundred years, Palestine (defined here as always by the boundaries of the later Mandate) was ruled by the Ottomans. Throughout this period it was not perceived as a distinct political, administrative, or economic unit within *bilad al-sham*. The coastal strip, the valleys leading to the interior, and the mountainous interior itself formed "geohistoric" units that, conditioned equally by natural and political factors, each followed their own path of development. These "geohistoric" units did not coincide with the administrative units created by the Ottomans, who frequently altered and adapted their boundaries in response to changing political goals and demands. Here we have a textbook case of Ottoman pragmatism as highlighted by revisionist historians, though the frequent alterations and inconsistent use of terminology make it difficult for the modern scholar to obtain a clear picture of the situation at a specific point in time.[7] As

[7] For what follows, cf. Schölch (1986), pp. 17–24; Birken (1976), pp. 242ff.; Gerber

a permanent factor we have a number of cities—above all Damascus, Sidon, and Beirut—acting as the political, economic, and cultural centers of their surrounding districts (*sanjak*, Arabic *liwa'*, both meaning "flag") and provinces (*eyalet* or *vilayet*, Arabic *wilaya*). For the local population, administrative districts were of only slight significance. Family, cultural, and economic ties were as little determined by them as were feelings of ethnic and religious solidarity.

It was of paramount interest to the Ottoman central government to secure the pilgrimage route from Damascus to Mecca and Medina, a route that led through Transjordanian territory. This also helps explain why the districts of Jerusalem and Nablus were assigned to the province of Damascus, an arrangement that held until the 1870s. Only during the 1830s, when the Sublime Porte attempted to counter the expansionist policies of its Egyptian governor, Muhammad Ali, was there a brief experiment with a unification of most of the "Palestinian" districts. From the late nineteenth century until 1918, the northern part of the country was oriented northward: the districts of Acre and Nablus (renamed Balqa) were part of the province of Sidon, and beginning in 1888 of the newly formed province of Beirut, while the districts east of the Jordan River belonged to the province of Damascus. From 1872, the southern areas including Jerusalem, which after 1840 had been first assigned to Sidon, and then to Damascus, formed an "independent" district (*mutasarrifiyya*) divided into the subdistricts (*kaza*, Arabic *qada*) of Jerusalem (Jabal al-Quds), Hebron, Jaffa, Gaza, and (in 1909) Beersheva.

One point is of primary importance here: The Ottoman administrative units were mostly relevant for the purposes of tax collection. At the district borders, tariffs could also be levied on certain goods. But the situation was complicated, if not to say confusing: administrative and juridical units did not always coincide. For example, the jurisdiction of the Islamic judge (*kadi*) of Jerusalem reached all the way to Nablus and Gaza, even though his actual power always remained dependent on the status and personality of the incumbent officeholder. The church hierarchy—and this was later to become important for the formation of Palestinian identity and national sentiment—transcended Ottoman administrative borders and encompassed large parts of Palestine. The authority of the Orthodox patriarch of Jerusalem extended across the three ancient Roman provinces both east and west of the Jordan; the Protes-

---

(1985), pp. 93–96; Rood (2004), pp. 44–48, 96–97; also Himadeh (ed.) (1938), pp. 4–6. On the *kadi*, see Singer (1994), pp. 28–29; Manna' (1992), p. 76, and below, note 26. On the pilgrimage route, see below, n. 8.

tant diocese of Jerusalem (founded in 1841) and the Catholic Latin Patriarchate (reestablished in 1847) did not coincide with the Ottoman
administrative units, either.

Local and interregional ties created a complex web of interrelations.
Palestine was of course connected to regional trade, caravan, and pil-

Map 2. Commercial and Pilgrimage Routes of the Eighteenth Century

grimage routes, yet these routes either followed the central mountain ridge before turning at the height of Jenin toward the coast, or else led through Transjordanian territory. In their majority, they ran in a north-south direction. East-west connections, which still existed in the seventeenth century, had largely disappeared by 1800.[8] The *via maris*, which had run along the coast since ancient times and was used above all for military purposes, was not reinforced; this made travel by ship and boat between the Mediterranean ports all the more important. In the interior, only a few roads connected the various towns and villages, and of these only a small number were paved. Overland movement occurred by foot, or by horse, donkey, mule, and camel, with the animals also carrying loads. Horse carts and carriages, which required well-founded roads, first came into use in the last quarter of the nineteenth century. Until the development of a suitable network of roads and trails, internal commerce was predictably slow and burdensome. There was no infrastructure to sustain an integrated "Palestinian" economy and society. Yet in the eyes of the local population, there were good reasons not to develop a sound infrastructure: Roads not only facilitated the traffic of goods and persons to the benefit of the local community, or at least some of its members; they also gave the authorities better access to the local population and their possessions. To evade the regular imposition of taxes, possible recruitment, or confiscation of livestock, local communities sometimes decided against connections with the outside world when the choice was given to them.

The issue of autonomy counts among the most interesting aspects of societal action and organization, and not just of the Ottoman Empire and Palestine: Most village and urban communities appeared to their members and to outsiders as autonomous, and the defense of this autonomy greatly mattered to them. Yet autonomy should not be confused with isolation, splendid or otherwise, let alone with autarchy. Just as in other parts of the Middle East, local communities in Palestine were horizontally and vertically connected through family, clan, and genealogical ties, through trade and industry, credit and patronage, and not least through religious ties provided by Sufi brotherhoods, holy sites, rites and celebrations that even created common links between Muslims, Christians, and Jews. In the late Ottoman period, Muslim pilgrimage to the Haram in Jerusalem was less important than the pilgrimage to the shrine of the prophet Moses (Nabi Musa) near Jericho, which in the first half of the twentieth century would attain such political significance.

---

[8] Philipp (1998) and Schölch (1986), the latter including maps. On the seventeenth century, see Ze'evi (1996), pp. 11, 205.

Town and Countryside

Around 1800, after having suffered significant losses in the last third
of the eighteenth century through war and general insecurity, Palestine
numbered between 250,000 and 300,000 inhabitants.[9] For the same period, the population of the Ottoman Empire as a whole was estimated
at between 25 and 32 million people, divided roughly equally between
Anatolia and Rumelia, that is, between the Empire's Asian and European territories. Istanbul had between 300,000 and 350,000 residents
within its city walls (*intra muros*), and 600,000 in the wider metropolitan area. (Istanbul alone was thus more populous than the whole of
Palestine, and its metropolitan population twice as large.) Cairo had
around 210,000 inhabitants in 1800; Edirne, Damascus, Aleppo, and
Tunis each about 100,000; Baghdad, Sofia, and Saloniki around 70,000;
Mosul and Bursa some 65,000. Even if some of these figures can be
disputed, they still give a rough indication of the relative size of these
cities. Palestine, at least outside of the inland hills and mountains, was
indeed sparsely populated, and its demographic weight within the Ottoman Empire was small.

The vast majority of the population lived as peasants. The number of
Bedouins was estimated at the beginning of the nineteenth century at
about 16,000. Though the urban share of the population was less than
in Syria proper, it reached 20 to 25 percent. Compared with large parts
of Europe, that constituted a significant rate of urbanization.[10] Villages
ranged in size from a few dozen inhabitants to several hundred. Patrili-
nial families and clans (*hamula*) served as the basic unit of solidarity, of
physical and social security, mediation and arbitration. While the houses
in the plains were built mostly of perishable clay brick, in the mountains
they were made mostly of stone, which of course made them more dura-
ble and offered better protection to their residents from all kinds of
danger. If we count towns of 8,000 to 10,000 inhabitants as "large"
and those with 1,000 to 3,000 as "small," then only Jerusalem, Acre,
Gaza, and Nablus could be classified as large: Around 1800, Jerusalem
registered between 8,000 and 10,000 inhabitants, Gaza 8,000, and
Nablus 7,500. Safed and Hebron numbered from 5,000 to 6,000; Tiberias, Ramla, and Jaffa 2,000 to 3,000; Bethlehem, Nazareth, and Haifa

---

[9] Divine (1994), p. 17, and Faroqhi et al. (1994), pp. 646–55. More on this below,
chapter 7.

[10] On the rate of urbanization, see Abdel-Nour (1982), pp. 35–41, 72–74. For the
Negev in 1830, Bailey (1980), p. 75, gives a population of 16,000. For 1850, Gerber
(1979), pp. 317–18, estimates the total number of Bedouins at 18,590, compared with
140,385 city dwellers and 333,700 villagers. On the villages, see also Völger et al. (eds.)
(1987), pp. 92–98. For Acre, see Philipp (2001).

each had 1,000 to 2,000. How great the decline in population was in the late eighteenth century, and how strongly the numbers could fluctuate, can be seen from the example of Acre, whose population sank from around 20,000 to about 8,000 to 12,000 from 1780 to 1810, that is, within a single generation. For security reasons, most large settlements were surrounded by a wall, behind which fruit and vegetable gardens as well as vineyards were planted.

Only about a third of the land could be cultivated with the methods available at the time. Nonetheless, agriculture formed the basis of the local economy and society, and like everywhere else in the Mediterranean region, grain, vines, and olives were the most important crops. In some areas almonds, figs, watermelons, pomegranates, dates, and other fruits were grown, as well as sesame, tobacco, and cotton. Olive farming offered wide-ranging possibilities, from food to heating to the production of soap and souvenirs. It is no coincidence that the olive tree was eventually chosen as a national symbol of Palestine, analogous to the Lebanese cedar and the German oak.[11] The cultivation of cereal grains and various winter and summer crops was extensive, since especially in the interior it was based almost exclusively on rain-fed fields (dry farming); as a result, it was very labor intensive. Until well into the nineteenth century, traditional farming methods prevailed, which did without the newly developed seed, modified crop rotation, modern machines and appliances, or artificial irrigation. Yet agriculture was not confined to subsistence farming. In the seventeenth and eighteenth centuries, local rulers promoted cotton growing in Galilee, Jabal Nablus, and the northern coast with the explicit aim of exporting the produce and thereby entering the regional market. At the same time, Palestine imported various foods for luxury consumption, from coffee and sugar to spices and rice—none of them produced locally.

As for commercial goods produced locally, these were mostly simple cotton fabrics and soap, along with glassware (Hebron) and souvenirs (Bethlehem, Nazareth, Jerusalem), which were sold to Christian, Jewish, and Muslim pilgrims to the Holy Land, who in the nineteenth century were joined by tourists.[12] Around 1800 soap, cotton, and tobacco formed the most important export goods to Egypt, Lebanon, Syria, and Europe, most of them shipped from the Mediterranean port of Acre.

---

[11] Everything about olive farming can be found in vol. 4 of Dalman's monumental study of the manners and customs of Palestinian peasants; Dalman (1935), pp. 153–290. See also Schölch (1986), p. 85, and Doumani (1995), pp. 33, 178–79. On landscape and memory, see Shama (1995) and Benvenisti (2000). Along with the olive tree, wild thyme (za'tar) or oranges also served as symbols of the homeland.

[12] On crafts and industry, see Schölch (1986) and A. Cohen (2001); on the pilgrimage, see Ben-Arieh (1984) and Abu Jabir (2004).

Figure 2. Steep paths and heavy burdens: a glimpse of transport and communication. Anonymous photograph, c. 1900.

Gaza had lost its former importance toward the end of the seventeenth century. In the first instance, however, local handicraft and industry—textiles and construction, food, soap, and woodwork production—served internal demand.

Only a portion of the total area was cultivated, whether seasonally or year-round. Like everywhere in the Ottoman Empire, land ownership was of less importance than claims to income from agrarian production as well as water and pasturage rights.[13] Arrangements for the use of

---

[13] For what follows, see Gerber (1987), pp. 11–15, 22–24, 30, 50ff., 69–70, 84ff., and Gerber (1985), p. 217. See further Rood (2004), pp. 30–44; *Survey of Palestine* (1946), pp. 232–33, 256; Owen (ed.) (2000).

land, which rested on various combinations of local custom (*'urf*), Sharia law, and sultanic statutes (*qanun*), served a twofold purpose: to regulate the rights to and control over a given piece of land, and to determine tax-paying and other duties attached to it. In this connection, the Ottoman government, in contrast with classical Islamic law, disregarded the religious affiliation of those concerned, and thus ascribed the same rights and duties to Muslims and non-Muslims. Roughly stated, three types of land can be distinguished with differing claims to revenue over it: state land (*miri*), private property (*mulk*), and land held by religious endowments (*waqf*, pl. *awqaf*). In reality, things were a good deal more complicated.

The greater part of the cultivable area was regarded as state land (*miri*) that, if it was regularly cultivated, could be farmed, mortgaged, and leased either individually or communally. From a legal point, however, it could be transformed into neither private property nor religious endowment. All that could be transmitted and inherited was the claim to revenue over the land and the right to usufructuary possession, or usufruct for short (*tasarruf*). Only the sultan and his closest family members were entitled to establish religious endowments on *miri* land (so-called sultanic *awqaf*). To preserve sustainable economic units and avoid an extreme fragmentation of land-holdings, succession was as a rule limited (in clear contradiction to Islamic inheritance law) to sons and daughters to the exclusion of other legal heirs as defined by the Sharia. Often enough, daughters too were either excluded or only allowed to enter into the inheritance by payment of a special fee. In accordance with Islamic law, all movable property as well as all buildings found on the land would be divided among the legal heirs. *Miri* land that was not cultivated for a specified period—generally three years—could revert to the state as option land (*mahlul* or "idle"), while land that had been cultivated at least once in the course of three years could not be confiscated by the state. Unclaimed land lying at a distance from areas of cultivation (*mawat*), including hilly, scrub, or woodlands, swamps and grazing grounds, which in Palestine as in other regions of the Empire made up a large part of the total area, could be taken into possession and cultivated by whoever wished to do so upon payment of the requisite fees and taxes. Private property in freehold (*milk*, in Syria and Palestine pronounced as *mulk*) existed only for land inside of villages and towns, as well as for orchards and vineyards in their immediate vicinity.

Like almost everyplace else in the Islamic world, religious endowments (*waqf*, pl. *awqaf*) were of great importance to the Palestinian economy and society, and made up a significant share of urban real

estate and its buildings and facilities as well as of agricultural income.[14]
With the establishment of a religious endowment, the founder intervened into the normal course of business and inheritance (the literal
meaning of *waqafa* is "to stand" or "to stop"). The property was transferred to God "for eternity" and therefore, at least in theory, could neither be substantially altered, nor sold, mortgaged, or inherited; it could
also not be confiscated by the state. In addition, it was subject to lower
taxes. The revenue from the endowment—whether derived from dues
and taxes paid by a village, the profits realized by a market stand, an
artisan's shop, or a bathhouse, or the rent of a building or apartment—
went either to a charitable cause (termed *waqf khairi,* and including
religious facilities such as mosques, Qur'anic schools, and madrasas located either in the same place or in Mecca, Medina, and Jerusalem, and
public facilities such as wells, hospitals, orphanages, and soup kitchens),
or to the family of the founder of the endowment (termed *waqf ahli* or
waqf dhurri—how "family" was defined in each case is of major significance for social history). Family endowments, although of doubtful
status from the point of view of Islamic law, made up the vast majority
of *awqaf* in late Ottoman Syria and Palestine. In many cases, both purposes were combined and revenue was accordingly shared among family
members (or other designated individuals) and charitable institutions.
The goal was primarily to protect the property in question from the
grasp of the authorities, to reduce the tax burden, and to circumvent the
stipulations of Islamic inheritance law, which tended toward the fragmentation of estates. The institution of the *waqf* also reflected the relation of city and countryside: while the income was often produced in
the countryside, the benefits accrued largely to urban dwellers. Village
mosques and their personnel constituted a notable exception, to the extent that they were maintained by religious endowments. At the same
time, it was as a rule urban scholars ('*ulama*') and urban descendants of
the Prophet (*ashraf*) who were entrusted with the profitable administration of the *awqaf*.

Hence, in Palestine as in most parts of the Empire (Egypt was a special
case) private property in agricultural land was not legally recognized.
Nonetheless, individual and communal rights of tenure and usufruct
were recognized and defined by both local custom and state law. Special
mention must be made of the so-called *musha'* system, which was practiced in large parts of Palestine, though scholars still disagree as to its

---

[14] Cf. art. "wakf," in: *Encyclopaedia of Islam*, vol. 11 (Leiden 2002), pp. 59–92; for
waqf and family, cf. Doumani (1998). For *waqf* in Palestine, cf. Dumper (1994), pp. 7–15;
Kupferschmidt (1987), ch. 5; Gerber (1985), pp. 178ff., 183, 192; Rood (2004), pp. 33–
38; Reiter (1996), pp. 13ff. It should be emphasized that Christians and Jews also maintained religious endowments in Palestine and elsewhere.

exact scope and impact.[15] In contrast to common assumptions, *musha'* entailed not so much collective property, but rather joint farming of a given plot of land, combining communal and individual rights and duties. The plot in question was periodically redivided into equal shares according to customary quotas and/or the capacity of those entitled to a share, and then cultivated for a specified period of time by these individuals or their families. In theory, *musha'* only pertained to cultivated areas, mostly devoted to field crops, not to orchards, olive groves, or vineyards; in actual fact there were many exceptions to this rule. Finally, pasture rights were of prime importance for the rural economy and society, both settled and nomadic. Woodlands, rivers, and pasture land lying in the vicinity of a village or a group of villages (*matruka*) were common land, defended against any kind of encroachment, and defended as well in the state courts.

PEASANTS AND BEDOUINS

Relations between sedentary farmers and Bedouin nomads were not always as conflictual or antagonistic as it would appear from the reports of Ottoman officials and outside observers. From ancient times, there always existed mixed and transitional forms between the economies of peasants and nomads. In part mediated by traders, farming and livestock breeding were components of an integrated economic system.[16] Yet the anti-Bedouin bias shared by Ottoman officials and European observers alike also goes back to antiquity. At its core lies the notion of Bedouin banditry and lawlessness that depicts them as the chief danger to public security and a settled lifestyle, or civilization, similar to the barbarians of ancient times. A quote from a study of eighteenth-century Palestine, teeming as it is with violent terms, serves to illustrate this point. The Bedouins, we read, were

> the chief cause of the destruction of the countryside and the subsequent ruin of agriculture and commerce. These powerful nomads infested the Syrian provinces, pillaged caravans and travellers along the roads, ravaged

[15] Nadan (2003) and (2006), ch. 6; El-Eini (2006), pp. 289–302; for the Hawran, see Schaebler (2000). According to Firestone (1990), *musha'* prevailed in the mountainous and hilly areas; according to Gerber (1985), pp. 206–15, and Gerber (1987), pp. 31–33, 61–62, 77–78, 147–48, it was in the plains.

[16] See Anatoly M. Khazanov, *Nomads and the Outside World.* Second edition (Madison, Wisconsin, 1983); Lewis (1987), ch. 1, and Dowes (2000), ch. 1; for the Ancient Orient, see also Whitelam (1996), pp. 78–79, 98ff. For Palestine, cf. Ze'evi (1996), pp. 87–114; Doumani (1995), pp. 201ff.

large pieces of cultivated land, and even dared to raid villages that were situated on the outskirts of big towns.[17]

By contrast, recent studies tend to highlight the fact that from very early on, peasants and pastoralists were part of an integrated economic system creating not just interdependencies between both modes of life and economic activity, or even certain forms of hybridity, but also a variety of shifts and transitions between sedentary and nomadic life that could be either short-term or long-term, voluntary or enforced. Neither excluded conflict, of course. Not only was nomadic livestock breeding sometimes combined with small-scale farming. Even in the absence of political pressure, it could make economic sense for individual communities to withdraw into the steppe during periods of drought, and to concentrate on farming in periods of sufficient rainfall. In times of emergency, sedentary farmers could literally seek refuge in pastoralism. Incidentally, this did not necessarily entail instant changes in their cultural outlook. With regard to Palestine, transitional forms are most relevant to the northern and central plains, and less so for the interior hills and mountains or the Negev where complementarity rather than hybridity was the rule.[18] Bedouins were thus indispensable to the production of soap in Nablus and Jerusalem or the glass industry in Hebron, to which they supplied important raw materials such as alcalic soda (*qilw*). We also notice important processes of sedentarization. Historically speaking, it was of course not new; nor did it always occur against the will of the former nomads. Otherwise, the founding of the Islamic Empire and of numerous cities during the Muslim conquests would have been unthinkable and impossible. In Palestine itself, the process is well documented for the sixteenth, seventeenth, and eighteenth centuries. A number of well-known families of the mountainous and hilly regions were of Bedouin stock, and in the nineteenth century were quite conscious of their tribal origins. But it is only from the close of the nineteenth century that the trend toward sedentarization, now strongly encouraged (if not enforced) by the Ottoman authorities, can be considered irreversible.

In spite of persistent conflict, and indeed very much as a result of their "nuisance" potential, Bedouins could also become partners with the Ottoman government and its local representatives, acting among other things as guardians and protectors of individual stretches of road, especially along the pilgrimage route from Damascus to Mecca. Up into the

[17] Ma'oz (1968), p. 9; also Gerber (1985), pp. 14, 20–27.
[18] For Syria at large, see Lewis (1987), ch. 1; Douwes (2000), ch. 1; for Palestine, see Spyridon (1938); A. Cohen (1973); Hoexter (1973), pp. 272–73; Steppat (1974); Schölch (1986), pp. 167, 171ff., 185–95; Ze'evi (1996); Asali (ed.) (1997). For Gaza, see Bailey (1980), pp. 75–80.

Figure 3. Rural idyll near Jerusalem: olive grove in the Josaphat Valley. Anonymous photograph, c. 1900.

mid-nineteenth century, the Ottoman authorities pursued a policy favorable to the Bedouins by which they hoped to attract Bedouin immigration to certain areas where their presence was deemed desirable. For this purpose, land was placed at their disposal through which they would have unlimited freedom of movement. Whenever possible they were taxed, but given their mobility and the limited means of enforcement available to tax collectors, taxation was rare and inconsistent. Even in the second half of the nineteenth century the Bedouins were not drafted for military service. Up until the end of the nineteenth century, possibilities to exercise effective control over them were quite limited. Jerusalem and its environs remained especially susceptible to Bedouin attack, since the area was easily accessible on all sides and surrounded by uncultivated land. Still, economic complementarity and mutual dependence, which occasionally even led to alliances of peasants, urbanites, and Bedouins against both the Ottoman authorities and external foes, could not entirely efface existing conflicts. The extortion of protection money (the term *khuwwa* suggested ties of brotherhood), for instance, did little to endear the Bedouins to merchants and travelers. On the whole, then, mutual perceptions were negative, and quite devoid of romance, with each side feeling superior to the other.

GOVERNANCE, LAW, AND ADMINISTRATION

In regional terms, the demographic weight of Palestine remained small into the nineteenth century, and its economic potential insignificant. Its importance for the Ottomans was less economic than strategic, with the strategic dimension largely determined by religion. Ottoman interest manifested itself in the renovation, new construction, and financial contribution to the religious sites in Palestine, more specifically in Jerusalem, so assiduously patronized by the Fatimids, Ayyubids, and Mamluks. Without neglecting the large endowments in favor of al-Aqsa Mosque and the Dome of the Rock, or in favor of the poor, the Ottomans were much concerned with the security and supply of the city itself. In the 1520s and 1530s, Sultan Suleiman the Magnificent had the Jerusalem city walls, which had been largely destroyed during the Crusades, rebuilt; the precarious water supply improved; several public wells constructed; and the Dome of the Rock renovated by restoring the cupola and covering the outer wall with ceramic tiles. Playing on his name, inscriptions referred to him as the "second Solomon."[19] The religious significance attached to Jerusalem can be gathered from the fact that the *kadi* sent there from Istanbul held a higher rank within the Ottoman scholarly hierarchy (*ilmiyye*) than did his administrative and military counterparts in the city.[20]

But more important than the holy sites of Palestine themselves was the protection of the Islamic pilgrimage route to Mecca and Medina, which was crucial to the legitimacy of the Ottoman dynasty and the local rulers.[21] To protect the route, the Ottomans constructed roads, ports, and fortifications, stationed troops at critical points, and main-

---

[19] Auld/Hillenbrand (eds.) (2000); Rood (2004), pp. 26–28; Ze'evi (1996), p. 4; for the inscriptions, see Tütüncü (2006), esp. pp. 20, 35. On Mamluk Jerusalem, cf. Burgoyne (1987).

[20] Singer (1994), pp. 28–29; Birken (1976), p. 14; Doumani (1995), pp. 249–50.

[21] On the Hajj route in the eighteenth century, cf. Philipp (1998), p. 13. On taxes, see Schölch (1986), p. 166, and Faroqhi (1990).

tained facilities such as rest areas, wells, food and water. This in turn required circumspect dealings with the Bedouins, who were at one and the same time the greatest threat to the security of trade and pilgrimage routes and indispensable as guides and escorts for the pilgrim caravans. For this reason, a great part of the taxes levied in the area flowed into the coffers of the official responsible for the pilgrimage (amir al-hajj). Beginning in the early eighteenth century, this was the governor of Damascus. As in other parts of the Empire outside the capital of Istanbul, which was subject to stricter control, Ottoman government in Palestine concentrated on a limited range of functions, which can be summarized as the guarantee of security, law, and order as understood by the Ottomans. This involved political and military control of the territory, defense of its borders, protection of its subjects from domestic and foreign dangers, administration of justice, as well as collection of revenue. How these functions were carried out in detail varied greatly according to the period and local conditions. Systematic interventions in the local economy, social structure, customs, and practices were neither envisaged nor even possible up until the mid-nineteenth century. All the more significant, then, were the changes brought by the Tanzimat reforms. Up to that point, central control was exerted over certain groups of people and areas for certain periods, always adapted to local conditions and therefore quite variable. By and large, Ottoman authority may have been recognized by the local population as legitimate; at least there are scant indications pointing to the opposite other than the defense of local autonomy or "traditional rights." But the sultan was far away, and his representatives had little presence outside the urban centers.

In the Arab provinces in general, and Palestine in particular, Ottoman state power was represented by a few persons and institutions whose actual capacity to impose their will varied strongly according to the situation and personality of the officeholder.[22] They included the provincial, district, and subdistrict governors with their staffs of scribes, guards, and other personnel; the regular and irregular troops with their commanders, who also fulfilled police functions; the judge (kadi) of Jerusalem with his deputies in the various district centers; and finally tax farmers and tax officials. While some were sent from Istanbul, others were recruited from among the local population. Given this limited personnel and their equally limited means of coercion, effective control of the population was only possible with the active cooperation of key figures

---

[22] Faroqhi et al. (1994), pp. 658–79; Findley (1980) and (1988); Kunt (1983). According to Scheben (1991), p. 18, the entire Ottoman bureaucracy comprised only 1,500 officials in 1800. For sixteenth-century Palestine, see Ze'evi (1996), pp. 41ff. Both Hoexter (1975), pp. 251ff., and Schölch (1986), pp. 164–77, describe the complex power relations prevailing in Jabal Nablus. For Acre, see Philipp (2001).

among the local elite—urban notables, Muslim as well as non-Muslim, village sheikhs, clan leaders, and tribal chiefs. Hence, Ottoman rule was based on intermediaries just like British "indirect rule" was later to be. It was also constantly changing. From the eighteenth century onward, governors and their deputies were increasingly recruited from the civilian hierarchy, no longer solely from the military as had been the rule in the fifteenth and sixteenth centuries. The provincial governor (Arabic *wali*, or often simply *pasha*) was sent from Istanbul for a fixed period, often no more than one or two years. He named deputies in the districts and subdistricts under his control (Arabic *mutasarrif* and *mutasallim*—in the later nineteenth century, the latter were known as *kaimakam*, from Arabic *qa'im maqam*). The formal ranking of all officials in an empire-wide hierarchy should not mislead us as to the actual freedom of action enjoyed by the local representatives of state power such as the governors of districts and subdistricts. Like the deputies of the *kadi* and the tax farmers, the subgovernors generally came from leading local families, who tended to regard specific functions and offices as quasi hereditary.

The regular troops stationed in the provinces were as a rule subordinate to the governor, but paid from the central treasury. The idea behind this practice was of course that the governor must not be able to control their loyalties through financial means. This did not prevent energetic *walis*, especially in the seventeenth and eighteenth centuries, from creating an independent power base in their provinces by recruiting Mamluks (manumitted white military slaves), mercenaries, and other retinue through their own funds, so as to create what were de facto private troops. The number of Ottoman forces stationed in Palestine in the eighteenth and nineteenth centuries was small. In addition to regular cavalry, artillery, and infantry units, paramilitary militias were recruited from the Arab population.[23] The defense of Jerusalem was given highest priority, reflecting the city's religious prestige rather than military needs strictly speaking. More in accordance with military concerns, the port city of Acre was strongly fortified up into the early nineteenth century. Cannons positioned on the city walls and fortifications were of special importance in this context, as was the field artillery used in military campaigns. Otherwise, the possibilities of military intervention were limited. The life of most soldiers was miserable, the pay low, and its payment irregular. Hence the temptation to take part in local economic life, which in theory was inconsistent with military status. Occasionally, individual contingents of troops would even unite with peasants and city

[23] A. Cohen (1973), pp. 270–92; Philipp (ed.) (1992), p. 5, and map 3; Divine (1994), pp. 19–20, 51; Doumani (1995), pp. 34ff., 53.

dwellers against the Ottoman pasha. The governors reacted in turn by recruiting Mamluks, mercenaries, and other forces that might include Bedouins and even peasants to use them against their enemies.

Contrary to common assumptions, the peasants were by no means defenseless against Ottoman officials, Bedouin raiders, and foreign attackers. Despite a government ban on firearms, the inhabitants of the hill and mountain country possessed a great number of them, including rifles (baruda), though only rarely did they own pistols. While these weapons might have been outdated in comparison with the arsenals of European armies, the Ottoman troops stationed in the region around 1800 were hardly better equipped (if we except the few cannons and pieces of field artillery just mentioned). Even in the middle of the nineteenth century, local feuds and conflicts were carried out with the aid of swords, daggers, lances, clubs, and sticks. In his chronicle covering the period from 1821 to 1841, the Greek monk Neophytos records numerous uprisings by locals against the authorities: When the opportunity arose, villagers did not hesitate to expel the soldiers who had come to collect dues and taxes, or to prevent their entry in the first place.[24] Contemporary records are replete with local feuds that pitted the Qais against the Yaman, two groups claiming descent from northern and southern Arabs respectively, evoking the tribal conflicts of Umayyad times when these groups, "imagined communities" par excellence, first emerged.[25]

Like the governor, the Sunni kadi of Jerusalem was as a rule sent from Istanbul and usually stayed for only one to two years.[26] The kadi of Jerusalem always represented the Hanafite school of law that predominated within the Ottoman Empire, whereas a large part of the population of Palestine belonged to the Shafiʿi school, which at least in Jerusalem had judges and legal experts (muftis) of their own. The deputies of the kadi and the scribes were usually appointed from prominent local families and merely confirmed in office by the kadi. Their wide-ranging tasks were not confined to judicial matters in the modern sense, whether

[24] Spyridon (1938), pp. 73ff; also Schölch (1986), pp. 192, 197. For the sixteenth century, see Singer (1994), pp. 89–118. For the Jerusalem garrison, see Ben-Arieh (1984), pp. 135–36. For arms and armor more generally, see Parry/Yapp (eds.) (1975).

[25] Hoexter (1973); Macalister/Masterman (1906), pp. 43–44; also Benvenisti (2000), pp. 86–87; Enderwitz (2002), pp. 136–38. For the Umayyad period, see Eva Orthmann, *Stamm und Macht. Die arabischen Stämme im 2. und 3. Jahrhundert der Hiğra* (Wiesbaden 2002), and Patricia Crone, "Were the Qays and Yemen of the Umayyad Period Political Parties?" in *Der Islam*, 71 (1994): 1–57.

[26] See notes 7 and 14 above, as well as Rood (2004), pp. 50–61, 87–88; Ze'evi (1996), pp. 25–27; Tucker (1998). In the nineteenth and early twentieth centuries, local elite families held influential positions at the court of Jerusalem and served as kadis of other cities such as Nablus, Acre, or Gaza; see the entries in Manna' (1998), and below, chapter 10.

Figure 4. Armed Bedouin. Anonymous photograph, c. 1900.

inside or outside of the Islamic Sharia court or *mahkama* (before which
non-Muslims sought justice as well). Their tasks also included registration and notary functions, ranging from commercial contracts, loans,
and real estate transactions to questions of marriage, divorce, and the
division of inheritances. They were charged with the supervision of urban buildings, markets, and most importantly, of religious endowments,
which were of tremendous importance for urban life. The *kadi* as the

representative of Ottoman central power, tied in to an empire-wide hierarchy (*ilmiyye*), was at one and the same time judge, arbitrator, notary, and registrar, and for this reason—even if he was an outsider, and often unskilled in spoken Arabic—he was a central figure in local (urban) society. But he had no independent means of power or coercion that would have enabled him to challenge the governor, or the local troop commanders, let alone the sultan himself.

While it was the main function of the *kadi* to adjudicate conflicts, muftis issued legal opinions (fatwa, pl. *fatawa*) on the basis of the normative sources (i.e., the Qur'an and prophetic Sunna) and the authoritative legal tradition. In the Ottoman Empire, some muftis were integrated into the official hierarchy of the *ilmiyye*, whereas in most other Muslim societies, they acted in a private capacity only. Unlike the *kadi*, muftis that had joined the official hierarchy could be in office for decades, and were mostly of local origin.[27] Unlike in the Rumelian and Anatolian provinces, but also unlike in Damascus, the muftis in Palestine (at least in the seventeenth and eighteenth centuries) seem not to have been integrated into the *ilmiyye*, and to have been less closely tied to the state courts than was the case in Istanbul, Bursa, or Edirne. To attain influence, they therefore needed local recognition, which was for obvious reasons most easily gained by someone belonging to a respected family, who added learning, achievement, and possibly charisma to his inherited rank and status. In the nineteenth century the trend toward greater bureaucratization also reached Palestine, so that here too the function of the mufti was increasingly formalized and defined more strictly in terms of the imperial hierarchy.

Having said this, we have to admit that our knowledge is largely restricted to what happened in the cities. We know much less about the countryside. In the villages, the scribe and preacher (*khatib*) seems usually to have also worked as notary, prayer leader (*imam*), and Qur'anic schoolteacher, in charge of circumcisions, marriages, and burials and also responsible for announcing official communications. There were frequent complaints about their poor level of education, low performance, and venality, but at the same time they had to live off rather modest commissions and remunerations. There is much to indicate that, here as elsewhere, conflicts were settled whenever possible outside of the court system and in accordance with local custom, which was influenced by the Sharia but not identical with it, and which apparently was followed not only by Muslims but also by Christians.[28] Religious and social

[27] Birken (1976), p. 13; Tucker (1998), pp. 1–36, esp. 20–21; Kupferschmidt (1987).
[28] On customary law, see Hoexter (1973), pp. 302–303; Baldensperger (1893), pp. 314–36; al-ʿArif (1944); Tibawi (1956), p. 75; Steppat (1974), p. 239. In the region of Hebron, customary law was known as "the law of Abraham" (*shariʿat al-Khalil*, after the Arabic

life in the villages was focused primarily on the shrines of saints (*ma-qam*) and the veneration of saints in general, who could be Muslim, Christian, or Jewish; mosques and churches were found mostly in the cities.[29]

There remains the issue of taxation.[30] As in other parts of the Ottoman Empire, several forms of tax collection existed that could be practiced either simultaneously or consecutively: They included direct taxation that required salaried officials, and two indirect forms of taxation that employed middlemen to collect the taxes. These middlemen were either recipients of stipends, most of them land grants (*timar, zeʿamet, and hass* in order of increasing size), which provided hereditary and nonhereditary income in exchange for military service, or they were tax farmers (*multazim*). Tax farms were usually acquired for a period of up to three years via sale, loan, or auction, but from about 1700 could also be acquired for life (*malikane*). Tax farming (*iltizam*) could easily be combined with other functions: Thus a governor could also act as a tax farmer in his own province, or a mufti could purchase the farm of specific dues, tariffs, or taxes. Tax farming offered one of the most important routes of social advancement to members of local society. While the *timar* system had disappeared in large parts of the Ottoman Empire around 1800, it could still be found in certain parts of Palestine until the mid-nineteenth century. Despite all efforts, even the reformers of the Tanzimat period were unable to abolish tax farming. The greatest part of the tax burden always fell on the peasant population, who beyond the tithe (*ʿushr*), which in fact usually amounted to more than 10 percent of the assessed harvest and was usually paid in kind, also had to pay a variety of regular and irregular taxes and dues (*awariz*). Urban craftsmen, merchants, and shop owners were also regularly taxed. A significant share of tax revenue came from the poll tax (*jizya*) imposed upon non-Muslims, which was levied in cash, and which whenever possible was collected by state officials rather than tax farmers to ensure that it went directly to the state treasury.

From the seventeenth century onward, taxes (with the important exception of the tithe) were increasingly levied in cash rather than in

---

epithet for Abraham, Ibrahim al-Khalil); Finn (1878), vol. 1, p. 216; but see also Rood (2004), p. 53. On the *khatib*, see also Kupferschmidt (1987), pp. 76, 133–34.

[29] Canaan (1927); also Baldensperger (1893), pp. 315–20; Macalister/Masterman (1904–1906); de Jong (1983).

[30] For the Ottoman Empire at large, see Shaw (1975); Faroqhi et al. (1994), pp. 55–142, 436–38, 531–75, 661, 710–23; Gerber (1987), pp. 12–13, 20–22, 50–56. For Palestine, see A. Cohen (1973), pp. 247ff.; K. Stein (1984), pp. 16–20; Gerber (1985), pp. 160–77, 226–36, and 323, note 30. On the *timar* system, see Schölch (1986), pp. 164–69; Zeʾevi (1996), p. 37; Rood (2004), pp. 38–44.

kind—further evidence that the local economy did not rest solely on subsistence farming. From this followed a close connection between tax collection on the one hand and the credit and lending business on the other. The peasants in particular became dependent on credit if they were required to pay their taxes prior to sale of the harvest. In Syria and Palestine this happened during the yearly "round" (*dawra*) that the governor conducted in the company of a strong military escort, in order to gather the taxes and make state power locally seen and felt.[31] As brutal as this exercise in state power may often have been, its limited nature still made it easier for the subjects than in later times to evade their tax obligations. As a rule, taxes were paid only under duress, and when this was lacking they went unpaid as often as not. Only a small portion of the taxes and dues collected locally, whether regular or irregular, legal or illegal (which were still levied by local strongmen despite repeated government interdictions) ever reached the treasury. A considerable portion flowed to various intermediate agents and agencies, from the village sheikh to the tax farmer to the governor, who with the funds collected had to fulfill a variety of tasks. A good part of the revenue flowed back directly into the local economy.

THE PURSUIT OF AUTONOMY: ZAHIR AL-UMAR AND AHMAD AL-JAZZAR

Contemporary observers and modern historians have identified signs of Ottoman decline, as evident in the worsening quality of the administration and the military, as early as the mid-sixteenth century. In the seventeenth and eighteenth centuries, powerful local figures made determined efforts toward autonomy in various parts of the Empire. Unlike the "warlords" who emerged at the same time in Rumelia and Anatolia (where they were known as *ayan* or *derebeys*, "valley princes"), local strongmen in the Arab provinces came mostly from the Ottoman state apparatus itself. True, many of them had entered it as it were from the outside, not having been educated at the Istanbul court schools, which from a legal point of view, would have made them "slaves" (*kul*) of the sultan. In the eighteenth century, they included the Jalili dynasty in the Iraqi city of Mosul, the Shihab al-Dins in Mount Lebanon, the Azms in Damascus, and the Mamluk beys Ali al-Kabir and Muhammad Abu l-Dhahab in Egypt.[32]

---

[31] On the *dawra*, see Doumani (1995), p. 266, note 5. Spyridon (1938), pp. 74ff. provides a vivid description for the year 1825.

[32] Ze'evi (1996), pp. 35–62; Gerber (1985), pp. 103–104, 232; Schölch (1986), pp. 164–77, 185–95; Rood (2004), pp. 48–50, 61–64; Doumani (1995), pp. 40ff. For Syria, cf. Abu-Husayn (1985); for the Ottoman Empire at large, cf. Inalcik (1977); Faroqhi et al. (1994), pp. 467ff., 552, 658–79. See also chapter 4 below.

These local rulers, who unlike the nationalists of the nineteenth and early twentieth centuries did not intend to break away from Ottoman rule, displayed a number of common traits. All made use of a special form of patrimonial rule in which their "household" was not clearly separated from public administration, and in which their personal retinue, some of them slaves, served as "public" officials and functionaries. All tried to centralize politics and administration at the district and provincial levels, in some cases with the explicit permission of the sultan, in other cases against his declared will. All established de facto monopolies over key agricultural products and increased trade with Europe; some even entered into political and military alliances with European powers. Finally, as a result of these measures, all facilitated (often unintentionally) a stronger control of the urban elite over rural resources, not only at the expense of the rural population, but also of the central government in Istanbul. A military buildup based on modern equipment and the enlistment of mercenaries; a monopoly over power and resources; the promotion of trade and agriculture; and intensified contacts with Europe served the cause of political autonomy. The consolidation of local power, and even more so its determined expansion, may appear exclusively as an expression of centrifugal tendencies. But it is not to be equated with decline or decay. Seen from a local perspective, it could offer new and improved opportunities to various sectors of the population, since local rulers invested in the development of agriculture and urban infrastructure, founded charitable institutions, and in some instances even promoted culture and science. Seen from the same perspective, it also had its disadvantages, since these rulers exploited their subjects more systematically than the central power, which was able to intervene only sporadically and intermittently. "Decline" is obviously a concept reflecting imperial interests, and the historian need not adopt it as his or her own.

Throughout the eighteenth century, the Levantine coast from Beirut to Jaffa gained importance, as did its hinterland. This was largely a result of increased trade with Europe, especially France, and the port city of Marseilles in particular.[33] It is therefore no coincidence that two local rulers could become established in this region, Zahir al-Umar and Ahmad al-Jazzar, who conformed closely to the pattern outlined above. Yet they followed two rather different paths.

Zahir al-Umar al-Zaidani (c. 1690–1775), originally a trader and tax farmer of Bedouin origin, managed to create an autonomous power base in his home region of Galilee.[34] Galilee belonged to the province of Si-

---

[33] A. Cohen (1973), pp. 312–13, 317–19; Philipp (2001).

[34] Safi (2004), pp. 15–20; Philipp (2001) and (1992); also Joudah (1987); Doumani (1995), pp. 40ff.

don, which at the time comprised large parts of what is today southern Lebanon and northern Israel and Palestine. Under Zahir, Acre, a strategically positioned former Crusader fortress and the most important port on the Syrian coast, began to prosper. Zahir's great innovation, at least in a local context, was his (successful) attempt not only to promote the export of cotton, grain, olive oil, and tobacco, but to monopolize it. The revenue from this trade allowed him to build an independent military power base in competition with the Ottoman governor of Damascus. In the face of constant conflict with the Ottoman central authorities on the one hand and the resistance of local rural clans on the other, Zahir was able to extend his power beyond Galilee and the northern coastal region well into the northern hinterland. This included the fertile if sparsely populated plain of Marj Ibn Amir with the market city of Nazareth. By contrast, he was never able to conquer Nablus, whose hinterland was developing into the most important cotton-growing region in Palestine. Jerusalem, as well as the south, remained beyond his grasp. Within Zahir's domain, the cultivation and trade of cotton reached high levels, contradicting the widespread image of progressive economic decay toward the close of the eighteenth century.[35] Economic prosperity inevitably attracted migration toward Acre, a trend that continued under his successors. Having previously sought confirmation of his position by the sultan and his local representatives, Zahir felt strong enough to develop his own "foreign policy," aligning himself with Ali bey al-Kabir, one of the powerful Mamluk beys in Egypt. Together, they occupied Damascus in 1770 and, to strengthen their position vis-à-vis the Porte, entered into an agreement with Russia—always the nemesis of the Ottoman Empire. After the Russo-Ottoman War of 1768–74, the sultan turned against the rebel: In August 1775, an Ottoman fleet took Acre, and Zahir himself was killed shortly after.

Of a different caliber altogether was the Bosnian Mamluk Ahmad al-Jazzar (the "butcher") who established himself as a regional power for almost three decades, from 1776 to 1804. As an outsider without previous connection to the land, he managed to rise as high as governor of Sidon and Damascus, to which large parts of Lebanon and Palestine then belonged, retaining a lifelong tax farm (*malikane*) for this area.[36] His power base, like that of Zahir al-Umar before him, was centered in Acre. But unlike Zahir, Ahmad Pasha al-Jazzar was himself the representative of the Ottoman state apparatus, and carefully saw to it that all dues and taxes were collected promptly, while at the same time pursuing his own ambitions. His prestige was greatly bolstered when in early

[35] On cotton production, cf. Doumani (1995), pp. 95–130; Schölch (1986), pp. 81ff; Gerber (1985), p. 6; for Jabal Nablus, see also Hoexter (1973), p. 251.

[36] Philipp (2001); Safi (2004), pp. 20–26.

1799 his troops successfully defended Acre against the French army under Napoleon Bonaparte, an operation that ended for the French in resounding defeat, and in their retreat from Syria and Palestine with heavy losses. Ahmad al-Jazzar was well aware that political and military power required a sound economic basis. He managed to obtain a monopoly on trade in cotton and grain, finally eliminating the French traders who had invested in cotton cultivation in the Jaffa region since the 1720s. The development of agriculture and trade gave rise to prosperity in his domain. This was accompanied by efforts to suppress the Bedouins, who in the 1740s had moved into northern Palestine in great numbers from the Syrian district of Raqqa, and to attract settlers including even Christians and Jews. Intensive construction work contributed to the continued rise of Acre. Income from taxes, tolls, commerce, and sheer extortion permitted Jazzar to recruit a motley army of Kurds, Albanians, Maghrebinians, and Afghans, who secured and widened his power base. Through the elimination of autonomous actors like the Bedouins, he undoubtedly improved security in his domain; in this sense he stood for order, though certainly not for law and order. At the same time, a ruthless taxation policy increased the burden on the population and thus spurred emigration to neighboring zones and regions. Deliberate settlement and de facto expulsion worked at cross purposes. In Palestine as in the Ottoman Empire more generally, centralization thus did not necessarily improve the lives of the rural and urban population.

For all their differences in origin, status, and strategy, Zahir al-Umar and Ahmad al-Jazzar displayed a number of similarities. First, they shared insight into the nexus between political-military strength and economic performance. While not especially original in the Ottoman context, they translated this insight into a policy of monopolization. Both made use of European trade, especially in cotton, grain, and olive oil, to obtain weapons, Mamluks, and mercenaries. While actively encouraging immigration and offering better protection against the Bedouins, both exploited their subjects ruthlessly. In this way, pockets of prosperity formed along the northern coast and in Galilee, though they remained susceptible to political reversals and economic crises. Whatever the energy of their actions, neither Zahir al-Umar nor Ahmad al-Jazzar developed new ideas and institutions, and neither set into motion any irreversible dynamism of economic and social development. Also, neither of them thought in terms of national categories: Their frame of reference was not "Palestine," but rather a regional zone of power and influence encompassing Galilee, the Levantine coast, and southern Syria, sometimes reaching as far as Damascus. Jazzar ruled the province of Damascus from Acre, which in 1777 had become the seat of the pasha of Sidon. The pursuit of autonomy was continued by Jazzar's less brutal successor in the office of pasha of Sidon, Sulaiman Pasha al-Adil ("The Just"), who belonged to Jazzar's household and was in power from 1805 to 1819. In his fight against rural clans, his own successor, Abdallah Pasha (who ruled from 1819 to 1832) placed himself once again at the service of the sultan (Mahmud II), helping him to enforce the policies of fiscal and military reform in those parts of Syria and Palestine under his control. Not surprisingly, conscription led to widespread dissatisfaction, resistance, and open rebellion among the populace.[37]

The experiment of local rule in Galilee and southern Syria ultimately failed not so much because of imperial pressure, but because of another expansionist project, which lent a new flavor to the autonomizing tendencies within the Ottoman Empire. The Ottoman governor of Egypt, Muhammad Ali (who ruled from 1805 to 1848 and assumed for himself the princely title of *khedive*) systematically extended his influence to other Ottoman provinces, including Syria and Palestine. By the 1820s the expanding Egyptian cotton trade had already eclipsed the cotton trade in the Acre region. In 1831 Egyptian troops marched into Palestine and Syria and in 1832, they destroyed Acre, and with it the power base of its local rulers.

EGYPTIAN OCCUPATION, 1831–40

The Egyptian occupation, which lasted scarcely ten years, has come to be seen as a turning point in the modern history of Syria and Palestine, if not as the beginning of their modernization. For this reason, it deserves special attention. Egyptian expansion, aimed primarily against the Ottoman central authority and therefore ultimately against the sultan himself, which was at the time actively seeking to impose fiscal and military reforms, seems to have been viewed quite positively in Palestine in the second half of the 1820s, that is before *khedival* troops had actually invaded the area.[38] For Muhammad Ali, Syria was of strategic relevance and economic importance as a source of certain raw materials (wood, among others) and a potential market for Egyptian exports. Religion does not appear to have inspired Muhammad Ali: No special interest in

[37] Rood (2004), pp. 73ff.; Safi (2004), pp. 22–26.

[38] Rood (2004), chs. 3 and 4. She prefers to speak about "*khedival*" rather than "Egyptian" rule to make it clear that the principal agent was Muhammad Ali, who had assumed the Persian title of *khedive*, and that there was not yet such a thing as an Egyptian state or nation able to act on the regional stage (pp. 6–7). See also Safi (2004), ch. 1, and pp. 174–78; Divine (1994), pp. 53–72. On Muhammad Ali, cf. art. "Muhammad ʿAli Pasha" (Ehud R. Toledano), in *Encyclopaedia of Islam*, vol. 7 (Leiden 1993), pp. 423–31; Marsot (1984) and Fahmy (1998).

Jerusalem or the "Holy Land" as a whole can be discerned among *khedival* policies. When the Egyptians invaded Palestine in November 1831 under the command of Ibrahim Pasha, the stepson of Muhammad Ali, they did so with a sizeable fleet and the largest army the country had seen since the Ottoman conquest in 1516. After a prolonged siege, they took Acre in May 1832, which under Ahmad al-Jazzar three decades earlier had withstood the French troops and now was utterly destroyed. The Egyptian triumph made a deep impression locally. According to the Greek monk Neophytos, the conquest of Acre was greeted with tremendous joy by the inhabitants of Jerusalem, which by then had been occupied by the Egyptians too (though according to him the Muslims had certain forebodings):

> The conquest of Ptolemais [Acre] was celebrated in Jerusalem with illuminations, dancing, and music, in every street and place of the city. For five days the people of Jerusalem, Moslems, Greeks, Franks, Armenians, and even Jews, made merry. All were happy and delighted at the thought that Egyptian entry meant freedom (as it really did.) The Moslems alone could not hide their sorrow and sullenness (although they danced with the rest), because they had a presentiment that Egypt would use its power against them. They felt that they could not continue to act as they wished, and that hereafter Jerusalem and all Palestine would be reformed. They heard and saw things which they hated to hear and see, namely regular soldiers wearing tight trousers and carrying terrible fire-arms and musical instruments, and marching in formation after the European fashion.[39]

The description of the celebrations with lights, music, and dance "in every street and place" is noteworthy, especially since it emphasizes the fact that Muslims, Christians, Jews, Arabs, Greeks, and Armenians were all united in their joy. Equally noteworthy is the reported distaste of the local population for the Egyptian troops who appeared uniformed in the European style and playing (European-sounding) military music. In this they were not alone: Already in 1807, Sultan Selim III (who ruled from 1789 to 1807) had been toppled over his attempt to force the Ottoman auxiliary troops to wear "Frankish" uniforms. His successor Mahmud II (ruled 1808 to 1839) made a renewed attempt, and in 1826 ordered the army to wear European-cut uniforms, boots, and the fez or tarbush, which shortly thereafter was made mandatory for all members of the bureaucracy with the exception of the '*ulama*', who were allowed to continue wearing the turban. The dislike of Ottoman troops of tight-fitting pants is widely attested. They also seem to have resented the bay-

---

[39] Spyridon (1938), pp. 84–85.

onet, which for them allegedly looked similar to a cross, and was therefore interpreted as "Christian."[40]

Yet the entry of the Egyptians was not immediately viewed as a new beginning. For one thing, the locals remembered earlier incursions from Egypt: The Mamluk beys had marched in only fifty years earlier, and the French too had invaded Palestine and Syria without having left any lasting imprint. At first, Ibrahim Pasha did not alter the formal status of the districts, and even sent the customary tribute to Istanbul; the Sultan in his turn continued to appoint religious and other dignitaries there. In the first few years, Ibrahim Pasha spent his time too far away in other parts of Syria or in Anatolia for his orders to be obeyed in Palestine (where he was represented by Husain Abd al-Hadi, from the Jenin area). Ibrahim Pasha issued his orders, and they were blithely ignored. In its initial phase, the Egyptian presence thus seemed to bolster local autonomy rather than weaken it.

The year 1833 brought important changes, however. Egyptian measures taken to remedy the lack of funds, soldiers, and equipment, and resulting more from necessity than the will to reform, caused deep offense. Increased controls were placed on the local population, and the rural elite was threatened with a reduction of its power and influence.[41] Dissatisfaction mounted with the introduction in 1834 of new regular and irregular taxes, especially a head tax (*ferde*, in Arabic *firda*) for all male Muslims aged fourteen or older, excluding only '*ulama*' and foreigners. To the Muslims (and not only to them), it looked as if the *jizya* levied on non-Muslims were now to be imposed on them too. The fact that these taxes were not at first collected regularly did not appreciably lessen the disaffection. Other measures were understood as attempts to improve the lot of the Christians and Jews, as announced to European consuls before and during the invasion in order to gain their sympathy and support, or at least their acquiescence. These measures did indeed attract great attention in Europe. (It is no coincidence that in Protestant circles the idea of a "restoration of the Jews" to Palestine, which would be a sign of the coming of the Messiah, began to circulate during these

---

[40] Abir (1975), pp. 299–301 (esp. note 75), 303, 308; Rood (2004), pp. 73–74; Elliot (2004), pp. 110–111, 117. On the complex issues of dress, fashion, status, and order, cf. Faroqhi/Neumann (eds.) (2004); also Norton (1997); Quataert (1997); Kreiser (2005). See also note 42 below.

[41] Rood (2004), chs. 4 and 5; for non-Muslims, see esp. pp. 89–92, 183–93; for the *firda*, pp. 115–19; for advisory councils, pp. 98–109. Safi (2004), ch. 2, provides detailed information; for non-Muslims, see pp. 146–64, 181–82; for the *firda*, pp. 122–24; for education and health, pp. 165–73. See also Spyridon (1938), pp. 99, 123–26. On the policy toward Christians and Jews, see further Yazbak (1998), pp. 18–22; Abu Jabir (2004), ch. 2. On the fear of Crusaders in the seventeenth century, see below, note 43. On the idea of a return, or restoration, of the Jews, see chapter 7 below.

years.) Among other things, Ibrahim allowed local Christians and Jews to renovate their churches, monasteries, and synagogues, which according to classical Islamic law, as documented in the so-called Pact of Umar, was permitted only under limited circumstances if at all. This touched upon a sensitive aspect of Muslim and non-Muslim relations—especially in Palestine, where as late as the seventeenth century the fear of a return of the Crusaders remained alive. At the same time, Christians and Jews were represented in the urban advisory councils (*majlis al-shura*), now invested with new, or partly new powers. This gave them their first experience of public participation in local government.

In accordance with these policies, Ibrahim Pasha presented himself in the time-honored manner of rulers as the fatherly protector of the weak, first and foremost the non-Muslims. Christians and Jews were indeed able to conduct themselves more freely under Egyptian rule than before. The German traveler Heinrich Petermann reported from Nablus, a city regarded as especially fanatical:

> In general, Nablus is a place feared by Jews and Christians. Before the occupation of Ibrahim Pasha, scarcely a single European dared to set foot in this city, at least not in European dress. The few Greek Christians who were here lived under harsh oppression, and had to wear dark brown turbans to distinguish them from the Muhammadans and, throwing their cloaks over their heads, had to sneak through the alleys, always being careful not to come too close to the clothing of a Muslim, or to pass one on the right-hand side. And even if they dutifully followed all of this, they still had to listen patiently to insults and abuse against their religion. This ceased once and for all when Ibrahim Pasha took possession of Syria. The Christians once again breathed freely, and even Franks (Europeans) travelled unchallenged in their normal dress through this city. But once the power of the Egyptians was broken, and when following their expulsion the Turkish government once again displayed its former weakness, fanaticism began to display itself again in every way. One began to abuse the Christians once more, and especially to insult the Franks.[42]

That the Egyptians permitted the British a few years later, in 1838, to open the first diplomatic missions in Damascus and Jerusalem, and at the same time granted to Christian missionaries greater freedom of ac-

---

[42] Petermann (1976), p. 261. He describes some of the discriminating regulations contained in the so-called Umar Pact (dress codes, signs of respect in public, etc.) that held in parts of Palestine up to the close of the nineteenth century. The dress code gradually fell out of use without being officially abolished. Changes began with Sultan Mahmud II's decree imposing the fez on Ottoman courtiers and officials, which at least in the cities gradually superseded most of the existing types of headwear indicating status and religious affiliation; see note 40 above. For a broader picture, see Elliot (2004); for Jerusalem, cf. Ben-Arieh (1984), pp. 190–201, 284–85.

tion, reinforced the suspicion that "Christian interests" were given pref-
erence at the expense of Muslims.[43] All of this disturbed the established
rules of Muslim-Christian relations, without Ibrahim Pasha ever changing the legal status of non-Muslims as "protected people" (dhimmis),
which required them to pay the poll tax. At the same time, many Muslims were alarmed at the establishment of Egyptian-style state schools
and civilian courts. The 'ulama' regarded these not just as incursions
into their domain, but also as attacks on Islam as such. Though he occasionally resorted to religious language, Ibrahim himself had the reputation of not following Islamic prescriptions too closely. His (bad) reputation was confirmed by the confiscation of large religious endowments
such as the Khasseki Sultan Waqf in Jerusalem, whose kitchens served
the local poor. Even more provocatively, he quartered troops in mosques
and madrasas.[44]

Yet these were not the decisive steps that led to the revolt that erupted
in April 1834, before the British consulates in Damascus and Jerusalem
were even opened. Rather, it was the announcement that troops would
be recruited for the Egyptian army from the local Muslim population,
to be carried out by local notables, and accompanied by a disarmament
of the population (Christians and Jews continued to be exempted). The
revolt was led by Ahmad al-Qasim from Jabal Nablus, who in 1832–33
had briefly served Ibrahim Pasha as deputy governor of Jerusalem. It
was followed by uprisings in southern Syrian Hawran and Mount Lebanon.[45] In the Nablus region alone, tens of thousands are said to have
fought against the Egyptian occupation, though many Christians stayed
out of the fighting, arguing that under Islamic law they could not take
up arms against Muslims. While it is true that many Muslims were indeed opposed to arming Christians, the latter still took part in the feuds

[43] Safi (2004), pp. 146–56; Ben-Arieh (1984), pp. 178–89. After the Ottoman reconquest, a Prussian consulate opened in Jerusalem in 1842, soon followed by other diplomatic missions: France and Sardinia in 1843 (the latter was replaced in 1849 by an Austrian consulate), the United States in 1844, Spain in 1854, and Russia in 1858 (Ben-Arieh
(1984), p. 148). In the early 1620s, the first French consul in Jerusalem was driven away
by the local population after a few months, having been regarded as a kind of modern
Crusader; Ze'evi (1996), pp. 21–22; Asali (ed.) (1997), p. 209. R. Khalidi (1997), pp.
29–32, dates a strikingly similar event to the year 1701. In the eighteenth century, a
French vice consul resided in Ramla, which was of commercial interest due to the regional
cotton and textile industries; Tucker (1998), p. 28.

[44] Kupferschmidt (1987), p. 111; Divine (1994), pp. 65ff.; Safi (2004), p. 182.

[45] On conscription, disarmament, and the revolt, cf. Safi (2004), pp. 92–104, and ch. 3;
Rood (2004), pp. 119–21, and ch. 5. On the Qasim family, see also Hoexter (1973), pp.
266ff. For earlier attempts at conscription under Abdallah Pasha, acting on behalf of Sul-
tan Mahmud II, see Safi (2004), pp. 20–26. On military policies in Egypt and the Ottoman
Empire at large, cf. Khaled Fahmy, All the Pasha's Men. Mehmed Ali, His Army and the
Making of Modern Egypt (Cambridge 1997), and Zürcher (ed.) (1999), esp. ch. 4.

and fights of the eighteenth and nineteenth centuries. They also participated in the revolt of 1834.[46]

In his chronicle, Neophytos illustrates the conflict between Egyptian
policies and local perceptions. At a meeting in Jerusalem in April 1834,
the people assembled argued that they had learned to fight from their
fathers and needed no special military training. To this Ibrahim Pasha
retorted: "War is not the place for a herd of useless men: technique and
skill are required." At this, they decided on revolt: "It is far better to die
with our arms in our hands than to give our beloved children to everlasting slavery, without the hope of ever seeing them again!"[47] Some of the
captured rebels were later brought to Egypt, in order "to learn the art
of war in a royal manner and not after the fellah fashion." Equally
instructive was Ibrahim's behavior toward the Bedouins who, after the
destruction of the city of Karak in Transjordan, came to him in order
to gain his favor:

> He replied to them that if they were his subjects, they should bring their
> arms to him and stop wandering from place to place with their tents, and
> settle down and build houses like other Arabs, and plant vines and olives
> and become civilized. They laughed and replied that they would surely die
> if they were to remain in one place for two months.[48]

The uprising failed, like others before and since, largely because of
the lack of coordination and unity among the rebels, who did not shy
away from plundering friend and foe alike—beginning with the weakest
members of society, Jews and Christians. According to Neophytos they
pillaged "immense wealth" from the Jews of Safed and Tiberias—a
statement difficult to reconcile with many others insisting on the great
poverty of the Jews in the Holy Land.[49] Jerusalem was also looted when
the peasants briefly occupied the city in May 1834. The conflicts between rural and urban society manifested here (as well as one hundred
years later in the uprising of 1936–39) call for further study, yet
sources that could present the peasant point of view are scarce. The
revolt was weakened by the divergent interests of peasants and Bedouins on the one side, and urban and rural notables on the other. Following a familiar pattern, the notables made efforts to mediate between
their supporters and the authorities in order to maintain their tradi-

---

[46] Spyridon (1938), p. 102. On pp. 67ff., covering the year 1821, Neophytos mentions
the disarming of the Christians in Jerusalem in connection with the Greek rebellion. On
the participation of Christians in local conflicts, see also Hoexter (1973), pp. 289–91.

[47] Spyridon (1938), p. 90; cf. also Safi (2004), pp. 188–91.

[48] The citations are taken from Spyridon (1938), pp. 109, 117.

[49] Ibid., pp. 95–96, 104, 126–32; also Parfitt (1987), pp. 11–12, 69–70, 80ff.; but see
Safi (2004), p. 195.

tional position (or under Egyptian rule, their newly attained position).[50] The superior equipment of the Egyptian army, reinforced in 1834 by troops under Muhammad Ali's personal command, succeeded after a few months in suppressing the revolt, without being able to entirely break the resistance.

Egyptian rule in Syria and Palestine was ultimately ended not by local resistance, but rather by the European powers, who at this point would not tolerate an internal threat to the Ottoman Empire.[51] Like the French invasion of Egypt and Syria about thirty years earlier, Egypt's own invasion of Syria and Anatolia posed the "Oriental question": How could the Ottoman Empire, with its vast territories, be included in the European concert of powers without disturbing the balance of power in Europe and provoking uncontrollable regional conflict? In 1839 Great Britain, Russia, Prussia, and Austria resolved to intervene and expel the Egyptian army from Syria and Anatolia. A British naval blockade of the Levantine coast, the bombardment of Beirut, and the entry of Ottoman troops into the theater, combined with local uprisings, finally forced an Egyptian withdrawal with terrible losses in the winter of 1839–40.

How decisive was the impact of the Egyptian occupation on local economics, society, culture, and politics? This raises once again the issue of rupture and continuity, and of the criteria with which to measure them. In the decade from 1831 to 1840, commercial and diplomatic relations with Europe were systematically promoted. For the first time, the Ottoman districts in *bilad al-sham* were brought under one roof, with its center in Damascus. Palestine was not perceived and treated as a distinct entity by the Egyptians. What is more, Palestine did not serve as a frame of reference for the rebels, either; nor did their revolt reflect patriotic aspirations, to say nothing of Syrian and/or Palestinian nationalism. The integration of urban elites into local government through the introduction of urban advisory councils proved to be of lasting effect. So did the disarming of the rural population. Investments in agriculture gave rise to increased yields and hence increased revenue, but just as in Egypt itself, this entailed greater burdens on the peasant population, including forced labor. The settling of peasants, including Egyptian fellahin, in the Jaffa region and other parts of the coastal plain as well as on Bedouin land in the Sinai and the Negev contributed to agrarian change. Largely independent of European influence, cultivation and settlement

---

[50] See especially Divine (1994), pp. 59–60. Examples are found in Spyridon (1938), pp. 105ff. On the occupation of Jerusalem, see Rood (2004), pp. 127–30; Safi (2004), pp. 191–95, 205–206. For the different roots and functions of the urban and rural elites, see Rood (2004), pp. 54–64. On the "politics of notables," see below.

[51] Safi (2004), chs. 4 and 5; Rood (2004), ch. 7; also Fahmy (1998), pp. 165–78.

gradually extended to the south.[52] At the same time, repeated attacks of locust swarms, a cholera epidemic in Jaffa, an outbreak of plague, and an earthquake in Jerusalem, followed in 1837 by an even more serious earthquake in northern and central Palestine, took their toll.[53] The combined effects of economic, fiscal, and political measures worked differently for each of the subregions of Palestine. By and large, they had positive effects on the coastal plain and the valleys leading inland: Jaffa for instance experienced an economic upturn in the first decades of the nineteenth century. Acre, by contrast, never entirely recovered from its destruction by the Egyptian army, and was soon overshadowed by a rapidly expanding Beirut. The interior hills and mountains were negatively influenced by the Egyptian intermezzo. Not for nothing were they the center of revolt against the Egyptian occupation.

[52] Safi (2004), pp. 125–46, 259–85; also Divine (1994), pp. 63ff., 70ff., 102ff.; Doumani (1995), pp. 44ff.; for Jerusalem, see Rood (2004), pp. 142–52. Egyptian fellahin continued to move into Palestine up to the end of World War I; Ben-David (1990), pp. 186–87.

[53] Spyridon (1938), pp. 91ff. Also Divine (1994), p. 64; LeVine (2005), pp. 28–33.

Chapter Four

THE AGE OF REFORM, 1840–1914

THE SIGNIFICANCE OF THE REFORMS that became known as "Tanzimat" (literally "regulations," or "reorganization") can scarcely be exaggerated. Central to these reforms, which culminated in the imperial decrees of 1839 (the *hatt-ı sherif* of Gülhane) and 1856 (the *hatt-ı hümayun*), were the concepts of security, order, and efficiency. The instruments employed to this end included a census, compulsory military service, direct tax collection, and the formation of new political institutions for the integration of local elites. The "reorganization" originally aimed at a strengthening of the state apparatus, not at a liberalization of state and society. Only in the mid-nineteenth century did constitutional and in some cases even liberal ideas enter into the reform program. In 1876 the movement of reform led to a constitution followed by elections to a national assembly, which met in the same year in Istanbul. Two years later in 1878, Sultan Abdülhamid II suspended the constitution as well as the parliament, and from that point ruled autocratically. This however did not signify the end of reforms, which were pursued, even if in authoritarian form, until the Young Turk Revolution in 1908 and beyond. The reform program itself was certainly broad and multilayered. It was rendered even more complex because it coincided (and not accidentally) with the integration of the Mediterranean region into the world market dominated by Europe. The intricate interplay of intended and unintended effects and side effects, of internal and external factors, makes the Tanzimat era fascinating to the modern observer. For those living at the time, the changes it brought could be quite disorienting.

Today the importance of the reforms for the Empire at large is undisputed. Less clear is the impact they had on local society, and the ways local elites dealt with the "stimuli," both positive and negative, sent out from Istanbul. The view from above, which is commonly adopted when discussing the Tanzimat reforms, is as conventional as it is justified, for the reform measures were conceived and introduced in the capital with a view to challenges that essentially emanated from Europe, and were therefore external. Local actors were of course neither silent nor passive with respect to the new "regulations." But their actions were essentially a reaction to impulses from outside, and from above, and they moved within a framework that they themselves had not established. Naturally,

the reforms devised in Istanbul were received and implemented differently in different parts of the Empire. It happened more rapidly and with
broader effect in areas that were either close to the capital, or easily
accessible, or of strategic importance, and more slowly and with slighter
effect in distant, or strategically less important regions, or those that
were less accessible due to their terrain or sociopolitical conditions. Palestine, and its mountainous and hilly parts in particular, counted among
the second group. The growing European presence in Jerusalem and the
"Holy Land" at large, however, steadily raised its importance for the
Sublime Porte.

LAW AND ORDER

In the two decades following the end of the Egyptian occupation, the
Sublime Porte succeeded in gradually imposing its centralizing reforms,
against considerable resistance, on Syria and Palestine as well. By 1860
the Palestinian interior was essentially "pacified." The fact that Ottoman
policies could build on previous Egyptian efforts certainly helped: Central control was perhaps not altogether popular with the local population, but not unfamiliar either. The resistance of local groups in defense
of their autonomy was suppressed with the help of the modernized
army.[1] From the start, "progress," whose banner the Ottoman reformers
began to carry ever more openly, was therefore linked with violence.
And yet, the "modernization" of state and society cannot be reduced to
the use of force, or the threat thereof. Ottoman attempts to create a
standing army trained and organized according to modern methods
alongside (and later *instead of*) the existing cavalry, artillery, and infantry units from the *sipahis* to the Janissaries, reached back to the late
eighteenth century. They entered a new stage when in 1826 Sultan Mahmud II had the Janissaries stationed in Istanbul massacred (the act, in
which thousands of Janissaries perished, became officially known as the
"auspicious event," *vaq'a-i hairiyye*). Having destroyed the Janissaries,
the sultan raised new troops, not to supplement existing units, but rather
to replace them.[2] In 1838 compulsory military service was introduced
for Muslims, and in 1839 new regular troops (*nizamiyye*) were raised
alongside irregular units (*redif*) of varying quality and composition. The
goal was to strengthen the Empire by means of a standing army, profes-

[1] Ma'oz (1968); Hoexter (1973), pp. 308–9; Schölch (1986), pp. 184ff.; Doumani
(1995), pp. 49ff.
[2] Zürcher (1999); Shaw (1978), pp. 327–28. For Palestine, see Hoexter (1973), p. 262;
Abir (1975), p. 299; Gerber (1985), pp. 14–27; Divine (1994), pp. 83ff. According to
Schölch (1986), p. 211, the last *sipahi* units were dissolved in Jabal Nablus in 1859.

sionally trained and recruited from the subject population on the basis of selective conscription, and to eliminate autonomous armed groups of every kind, whether they were Bedouins, local dynasties, warlords, or rural leaders as found in the Palestinian mountain range, the Negev and Sinai. Success was not immediate, though: Muhammad Ali, whose army was built according to the same principles as the sultan's, defeated his sovereign's forces in the battles of Konya (1832) and Nezib (1839). Only with European support was the sultan able to counter the threat emanating from his own governor.

In view of Ibrahim Pasha's difficulties with military conscription, Palestine remained exempted from compulsory service until 1862. In Syria the last remnants of the *timar* holding *sipahi* cavalry were dissolved in 1845, and from the end of the 1850s, the locally stationed Ottoman troops were converted into gendarmerie units. In the second half of the nineteenth century, the number of regular troops stationed in Palestine was remarkably small, amounting to a total one thousand men in 1858–60 and a mere eight hundred in 1877. Their ranks thinned even further during the Russo-Turkish War of 1877–78, leaving only poorly trained and equipped irregular units to suppress any local unrest that might develop. There can be no doubt that the modernization of the military was of the greatest importance to the Ottoman Empire as a whole, but in Palestine itself it played no great role once the hilly uplands had been "pacified" in the 1850s.

The same is not true with regard to the modernization of the bureaucracy. It entailed centralization and expansion no less than professionalization, including the separation of military and civilian powers and hierarchies, and the integration of local nonmilitary elites into political advisory and decision-making bodies. During the Tanzimat, the reorganized and vastly expanded bureaucracy reached the ordinary subject or citizen for the first time, even in provincial towns and settlements. The provincial administration itself was thoroughly revised through the Vilayet Law of 1864 and the Electoral Law of 1876.[3] Two assemblies were of special importance here: the district and provincial councils (*majlis al-idara*), whose members, drawn mostly from local families of notables, were appointed by the governor and were granted broader powers in the 1840s, and the municipal councils (*majlis baladi*), newly established in the 1860s, whose members were elected from and by the propertied classes of the local (urban) population. As in most parts of Europe, the active and passive right to vote was premised on property and the ability to meet certain tax obligations. From the 1870s, general councils (*majlis 'umumi*) made up of elected deputies were established at provincial level

---

[3] Avci/Lemire (2005); also Gerber (1985), pp. 93–142; Scheben (1991).

Figure 5. Arrayed in row and column: Ottoman soldiers in the citadel of Jerusalem. Anonymous photograph, c. 1900.

and represented those members of the local population considered to hold some authority and therefore able to carry out the decisions taken by the council. Mediated though their elites, local populations gained their first direct access to political and administrative decision-making, from city planning and land assignments to the allocation of tax farms so important socially and economically. Here lay the beginnings of the "politics of notables" that was to attain such importance in the twentieth century. Like the British after them, the Ottomans pursued what was essentially a conservative policy of support for, and co-optation of, existing social elites, provided they were not capable of independent armed action.

The Tanzimat reforms introduced the state to new domains, involving higher claims on both the state and its subjects, who as citizens were made subject to new and more extensive dues and services. The state intervened more forcefully in the fields of economics, law, and infrastructure, in which it had already been active, albeit with varying intensity. But it also became engaged in public education and health, in which until then it had not taken any part. Here the new provincial, district, and city councils played a major role, now considering functions and activities that were previously left to private initiative, if indeed they were considered at all, as "public tasks": They saw to it that the streets were clean and well lit, they established parks and green spaces, and they improved the sewage systems as well as health conditions and education in general. The clock towers erected in various cities served as the new symbols of time in more than one sense.[4] So did the new government buildings—from city hall to train station, and from post and telegraph offices to schools, hospitals, and jails—that were built for the purposes of new tasks and familiar tasks redefined. In Palestine state intervention remained limited at first, and largely overshadowed by European initiatives, which also stimulated representatives of local society to stronger involvement.

As for the education system, the newly opened Ottoman state schools initially remained of limited significance.[5] Theoretically, school attendance was compulsory and public instruction was free; in practical terms, comprehensive schooling for the entire population could not be financed. The new state schools were modern and also secular to the extent that their curricula offered not only the traditional subjects of Islamic education, but also subjects ranging from European languages to mathematics to history, which seemed indispensable in view of current changes. Equally new were the teaching methods and the entire layout of the schools: The students who had formerly gathered around the teacher on mats on the floor now sat on chairs and benches, usually clad in school uniforms. The teachers were provided with textbooks, some of them even illustrated (which occasionally created problems in view of Islamic reservations concerning the representation of living beings). Yet

[4] On the wider meaning and function of these clock towers, i.e., to manifest state power at the local and provincial levels, see Deringil (1998), pp. 29–30. In Haifa, the great clock was attached to the Friday Mosque; Seikaly (1998), p. 16. In Jerusalem, a modern clock tower was first erected in 1901–1902 to celebrate the silver jubilee of Sultan Abdülhamid II, followed by a larger one dedicated in 1907 (and blown up by the British in 1922); Ben-Arieh (1984), pp. 34, 36, Part I, ch. 1, and Part II, ch. 4, for urban infrastructure more generally; also Tütüncü (2006), p. 136, and figures 131–34a.

[5] For the Empire at large, see Deringil (1998), ch. 4; Somel (2001). For Palestine and Jerusalem, see Tibawi (1956), pp. 19–23, 58–59; Ben-Arieh (1984), pp. 136–39; also Safi (2004), pp. 165–68.

for this "modern" instruction there were at first barely any "modern" teachers with a secular education available, so that the 'ulama' did not immediately lose their status and influence in the early phase of the Tanzimat reforms.

At the outbreak of World War I, Palestine had 95 state primary schools and 3 secondary schools with a total of 8,250 students, as well as 379 private Islamic institutions, which were predominantly Qur'anic schools of the traditional type (*kuttab*) with some 8,700 students, and a considerable number of foreign private schools concentrated in the Jerusalem area. The private Rawdat al-Ma'arif School opened in 1908 in the Haram al-Sharif following the Young Turk Revolution quickly earned a good reputation. Its students and graduates were later to play an important role in Palestinian political life. While 1,300 girls were registered in the state schools, a mere 130 attended Muslim private schools. Higher education, whether of a religious or nonreligious kind, could be obtained only outside of Palestine. For religious education, al-Azhar University in Cairo played the most important role, while for secular education it was the corresponding institutions in Istanbul and Beirut. The rural population, aside from village Qur'anic schools that imparted only rudimentary reading and writing skills, remained neglected. All in all, the level of education was low; in 1914 the rate of illiteracy still stood around 80 to 90 percent.

By contrast, the health system showed some interesting developments.[6] In Palestine as elsewhere, diseases and epidemics such as cholera, typhus, yellow fever, smallpox, and malaria, accounted for a high mortality rate, especially among infants and children. They were caused by the familiar factors of malnutrition combined with the effects of insufficient ventilation, hygiene, litter and sewage removal that were all too well known to major European cities such as London or Paris. All were especially pressing in Jerusalem, as best documented for the Jewish Quarter. But in the "Orient," they were customarily explained by the moral and political deficiencies of its inhabitants, Oriental inertness combined with Oriental despotism. Filth, squalor, and neglect are topoi of Western travel literature (which does not mean that they did not exist, though perhaps not to the extraordinary degree the authors make us

---

[6] See Ben-Arieh (1984), Part I, chs. 4 and 5, for health, sanitation, and water supply in the Old City of Jerusalem (for leprosy, ibid., pp. 98–101). Wulf (2005), chs. 2–6, focuses on malaria. See also Gerber (1985), pp. 46–47, 70–75; for the Jewish population of Jerusalem, cf. Schmelz (1975) and Ben-Arieh (1984), Part IV, esp. ch. 4, and Part V. For conditions in the seventeenth and eighteenth centuries, see A. Cohen (2001), pp. 70–74; Safi (2004), pp. 168–72. For the plague more generally, see Daniel Panzac, *La Peste dans l'Empire ottoman* (Louvain 1985) and LaVerne Kuhnke, *Public Health in Nineteenth Century Egypt* (Cairo 1992), esp. chs. 3 and 4. See also the statistical survey below, chapter 8.

believe). In 1864 the British doctor Thomas Chaplin gave the following report from Jerusalem:

It cannot be said that sanitary measures are entirely neglected in the Holy City. Many European residents and the principals of the larger convents are aware of their importance, and put them in practice so far as their own dwellings and the streets in which they are situated are concerned. Recent Pashas also have, both by example and authority, done a good deal in promoting cleanliness and decency, and the city has consequently become much cleaner than formerly. Nevertheless, if judged by European standards, it is shamefully and abominably dirty. Some ancient drains are still in existence; but they are imperfect, and not one house in fifty has its cesspools connected with them. This would not matter so much if the cesspools were emptied at proper times and into proper places; but a citizen of Jerusalem, after his privy has been running over for some weeks, when he begins at last to bestir himself, too often digs a hole *in the street*, puts the contents of the latrine into it, fills in the earth, and congratulates himself upon his energetic attention to health and cleanliness. Occasionally he shows more foresight, and establishes an opening between the place of convenience and the street, thus saving himself the expense and trouble of emptying his cesspool by never allowing it to become full. All kinds of animals and vegetable matter are allowed to lie and rot in the streets. If a dog or a cat dies, it putrefies in the roadway, or is eaten by one of its companions. In a walk through the city during the cold weather, a dozen of these animals may be seen lying dead. The remains of horses, donkeys, and camels are usually dragged outside the city, and left just under the walls to be devoured by dogs and jackals. There is no end to the melon-rinds, stalks of grapes, dung, feathers, bones, and refuse of all sorts which find their way into the street. The Oriental's notion of a street would appear to be a *receptacle for whatever is useless*; and as there are no scavengers, and it is only by lodging a complaint at the Seraille that a person can be compelled to remove a nuisance, the public ways are almost always disgracefully dirty. More disgusting than all to a European is the shameless indecency with which the thoroughfares are turned into places of convenience. For seven months of the year there is no rain, and the air during this long dry season becomes filled with the loathsome dust and odour which result from so much impurity.[7]

Some diseases such as cholera spread even more rapidly than before along the new communication lines, with their increased traffic in people and goods. In 1865–66 a cholera epidemic led to thousands of deaths

[7] Cited from Schmelz (1975), pp. 123–24. Ben-Arieh (1984), pp. 90–91, has another quote from Chaplin. For a different impression, see the noted biblical scholar and archae-

in northern Palestine, and in 1902 hundreds more perished. Even in the 1920s, a small leper colony existed outside the gates of Jerusalem. One of the most widespread diseases, malaria, was caused primarily by stagnant water that was found not only in low-lying swampy areas fed by winter rains, but also in the cisterns used to store rainwater in Jerusalem and many other places. Malaria remained endemic even in the second half of the nineteenth century. Traditional means of fighting the disease such as planting eucalyptus trees, which served to drain swampy grounds, proved of limited effectiveness. Only after 1898, when the anopheles mosquito was finally identified as the carrier of malaria, could effective countermeasures be taken. It was different with the plague, which had periodically decimated the population, but which by 1830 was largely eradicated, recurring at most in the port cities (as for example, in Jaffa in 1834 and 1838). The reasons for this are not entirely clear. They may have to do with the disappearance of infected rats, which occurred quite independently of scientific discoveries. Yet it seems likely that improved precautionary and sanitary measures such as quarantine, which Ibrahim Pasha had introduced in the 1830s, also played a role. However, even in the second half of the nineteenth century, many quarantine stations operated under the most difficult conditions. In the mid-nineteenth century, European and American missionaries opened the first hospitals furnished with modern equipment in urban areas. European, or European-trained doctors, came to be in greater demand. Around 1900 modern pharmacies were established in many places. To what extent these establishments also served the rural population remains unclear.

Not all observers were impressed with the progress made. In 1881 the Jewish physician Dr. Schwarz described local conditions in words as harsh as they were melancholic. Referring to contemporary conditions in the Western capitals of London, Vienna, and Paris, he wrote with regard to Palestine:

> Not so in the Orient. Here, hygiene is altogether unknown. Any tourist who has travelled through the Orient is familiar with the lack of interest of oriental authorities in the cleanliness of the streets, where refuse and animal corpses fill entire neighborhoods with their stench. The Turk, with his ruinous finances, offers travelling princes royal hospitality at the expense of the districts in question, but has not a cent left over for the improvement of his cities. What for? Allah Kerim! The gods themselves fight in vain against fatalism.
>
> Yet the consequences are terrible.

---

ologist Edward Robinson, writing in 1838, as cited in Rood (2004), pp. 28–29. See also the Masterson quote below.

What has become of this realm once divinely blessed? What has become of these wonderful landscapes! Where are the many peoples of whom ancient lore tells us and whose glory is handed down by world history! Gone! All gone! Rubble and debris cover the former glories and magnificent ruins. In their shadows, wretched descendants vegetate in wretched huts, to bear witness to long-vanished splendor.

Entire regions are deforested, the high plateaus are stripped of their fertile soil. In vain does the weary eye seek for anything green. Only where small brooks wend their way, nourished by half-dry springs, is there some sign of life, some trace of vegetation—and where the hands of foreign colonists are there to show what human industry can achieve.[8]

The report of a British medical doctor working in Jerusalem, Ernest Masterson, published in 1913–14, still describes some of the basic problems identified by Chaplin fifty years earlier. But he also highlights one aspect of the problem that is often overlooked: While it is true that European and American institutions contributed significantly to the improvement of public health and hygiene in the country, and in Jerusalem more particularly, they also created a major obstacle to the implementation of Ottoman reform measures. Under the provisions of the Capitulation treaties, foreign subjects and institutions were exempted from Ottoman jurisdiction in important ways, and to all practical effects were beyond the reach of the Ottoman authorities. New laws and stipulations required the consent of all Capitulary powers concerned, as represented by their local consuls:

There is no proper public water supply, no sewers worth the name, vaccination is not enforced even when small-pox is epidemic and there is no attempt to isolate those suffering from infectious diseases. This state of things is undoubtedly largely due to remissness and ignorance on the part of the Turkish Government, but the situation is made very complicated and difficult on account of the "Capitulations" by which all foreign subjects are practically independent of the Local Authority and accept no orders except through their own Consuls. It is easy to see that any government in the world would find it exceedingly difficult to enforce measures of public health—which are often in our own lands obstructed as far as possible by lay persons—under circumstances like these. The inhabitants of a single Jewish tenement-house may be representatives of perhaps half a dozen nations and not one step can be taken by the Local Authorities to get rid of

---

[8] Cited from Luncz (1882), pp. 116–17. Chaplin at least had praised the efforts of the Ottoman governor to improve the situation; but see Avci/Lemire (2005) for the role of the local municipal authorities in urban modernization.

any public nuisance until the assent of the Consuls of all six "powers" concerned is obtained. To those who have had experience of human nature, it will not be surprising to learn that unanimity in such a case has so far been almost impossible to obtain.[9]

Modern scholars tend to support this critique, and to disagree with Schwarz and others. In fact, it was not only "the hands of foreign colonists" that stirred in Palestine in the late nineteenth century, as other visitors well noticed. For the first time, the Ottoman authorities began to show interest in the economic potential of Palestine, which was certainly modest by Ottoman standards, but not quite as minimal as later descriptions would have us believe. State interventions into the local economy were closely connected with the incorporation of the region into the expanding world market. The elements of this process of integration are essentially known, though their specific import may be disputed: the commercialization of agriculture and the development of an indigenous class of great landowners; increased commerce with Europe, which contributed to the shift of trade routes and the growth of Mediterranean ports; the replacement of local products, especially textiles, by goods manufactured industrially in Europe and the United States; and the social rise of a merchant and banking class, including both local and foreign non-Muslims.

For Palestine, the development of infrastructure and the expansion of agriculture that resulted, not so much from the introduction of new crops and new farming techniques, but from the altered political and judicial framework, were of great importance. While we cannot speak of an Ottoman economic policy in the narrow sense, the political changes introduced by the Porte were crucial for socioeconomic change.[10] The establishment of law and order, guaranteeing the security of individuals and their property in the immediate physical as well as in the legal sense, provided the requisite condition for economic growth in large parts of Palestine. Even the British, who generally viewed Ottoman rule with contempt, praised the orderly state of affairs that prevailed before World War I. Thus the Peel Report noted in 1937:

> It is right to recognize also that the rule of the Turk before the War was, in the matter of law and order, extremely effective. The *Vali* in Beirut retained in his own hands the portfolio of internal security. The Courts may have been corrupt; dishonesty may have pervaded public finance; the meth-

---

[9] Cited from Wulf (2005), pp. 24–25; see also Avci/Lemire (2005), esp. pp. 77–79, 102–105, for consular interference and pp. 114–16 for municipal health and hygiene regulations.

[10] Schölch (1986), pp. 155–56.

ods employed for the prevention and detection of crime may have been antiquated and, like Turkish penology, repugnant to modern ideas; but the evildoer did not prosper. Sedition, banditry or robbery were put down with a firm hand. The Turkish policeman was feared—and respected. Except in a few outlying places the ordinary citizen could go about his lawful occasions unmolested.[11]

LAND REFORM

Agriculture received a vital impetus through the Land Code of 1858, whose purpose it was to regulate and formalize the acquisition, tenure, and transfer of state land in order to create clearly defined individual legal titles.[12] This was done not only with a view to creating a more efficient tax system. For the authorities it was also a matter of using land with a more long-term perspective, and by the same token more productively than had previously been the case. The new element was not codification as such: Ever since the fifteenth century, written land laws had been issued in the form of *kanunnames*. Nor was the differentiation and multiplication of various categories of landholding and ownership new. The distinction between state, private, and *waqf* land remained unaltered after 1858, at least for fiscal purposes, and the category of *miri* land with its attendant rights and duties was not replaced by unqualified private property (*mulk*). The novelty resided in another element, which attained considerable importance for Palestine, but also led to profound social change in Syria and Iraq: For the first time, it became possible to procure legal titles to uncultivated land (wasteland, *mawat*, which in Palestine mostly amounted to desert, shrub, and swamp land), without providing proof of actual cultivation. Technically speaking, uncultivated *mawat* land was no longer returned to the state as *mahlul*. Land could now be acquired solely on paper, without the new owner being present on the land itself. To achieve greater transparency in the actual state of land use and tenure, the lawmakers also sought to break up joint forms of ownership and cultivation like the *musha'* system, and to replace them with individual legal titles to clearly demarcated plots of land, ideally to be recorded in registers.

[11] *Peel Report* (1937), pp. 152–53.

[12] Owen (ed.) (2000) and Gerber (1987) correct a number of misunderstandings concerning the purpose, form, and effects of land reform that permeate the relevant literature; Gerber (1987), pp. 61, 71–72, 77–78, 84–85, 147–48. See also K. Stein (1984), pp. 7, 10ff., 20ff.; Metzer (1998), pp. 94–95; LeVine (2005), p. 346, note 6. On the *waqf* reforms, see Kupferschmidt (1987), pp. 114–17, 123ff.; Reiter (1996), ch. 1, esp. pp. 11ff., 29, 36. English text of the land law in Young (1906), Part II, vol. 6, pp. 38–83.

In 1867 foreigners were granted the opportunity to acquire land in their own name, in exchange for the corresponding tax obligations. In 1913 the state proceeded to put large endowments like the *awqaf* of Khasseki Sultan, Abu Madyan, and Nabi Musa under the control of the Waqf Ministry that had been newly created in the course of the reforms, and to direct their income toward public education, health, and welfare.

The commercialization of agriculture did much to stimulate the local economy. But it also created problems. One difficulty lay in the unequal and irregular enforcement of the new laws and regulations, which compromised the very principles of transparency and predictability of both process and outcome that they were designed to produce. Some problems were perhaps unexpected: Many peasants and Bedouins were reluctant to register the land that they farmed or otherwise used under their own names in the land registry, as required by the Land Code. Village notables and tribal sheikhs signed on their behalf, and in this way acquired large estates with one stroke of the pen. The peasants and Bedouins allowed this to happen not only because they feared taxation and possible military conscription, though they were justified in suspecting a connection between these measures and the new land titles. Some were simply not aware that registering the land under a different name would change existing practices in any way. Also, a fee was charged for registering the land titles. As a result, the actual state of land use and ownership could not be accurately documented. As late as 1925, several decades after the introduction of land registration, three quarters of the total surface of Palestine was still left unsurveyed and did not figure in the land registry. Existing entries did show the location, quality, and composition of individual plots, but only in the rarest cases did they contain maps to establish their exact position and boundaries (a problem that gained in importance in connection with Jewish land purchases). Combined with the complicated system of landholding and taxation, this made for a situation in which the land and real estate markets were severely lacking in transparency.

However, there is no evidence of large-scale expropriation and consequent pauperization of peasants, small-holders, and tenant farmers in favor of rural chieftains, urban notables, and external financiers, which is referred to in some of the scholarly literature, at least not for the densely populated hill and mountain range.[13] In a few cases the authorities did seek to enforce comprehensive land registration, but they were apparently faced with resistance on the part of the peasants concerned.

[13] Gerber (1987), pp. 67–90, esp. 72ff.; Stein (1984), pp. 17, 20–22; Schölch (1986), pp. 103ff.

Acre is a case in point. There, a survey was conducted in 1871 to determine the exact state of land ownership, and peasants were directed to register their land and to pay the relevant taxes, under penalty of unregistered land being put up for auction. But this is hardly the same thing as expropriating them in favor of local and foreign elites.

Another result of agrarian reform can be documented: the acquisition of large, previously uncultivated tracts along the coast, in the plains of northern and central Palestine, and in the Negev, which for the first time created large estates in these regions, and produced new social and political realities in Palestine. Three points are relevant in this context: First, these were not just *large* plots of land, but plots joined contiguously; by contrast, in the remaining parts of Palestine land was mostly parceled out in small plots. This was partly a result of Islamic inheritance law, which made division unavoidable (even if customary law as well as the authorities made efforts to restrict it), and partly due to a deliberate policy, which had used the allocation of small allotments (*timar*) to prevent the rise of a local landowning class. Second, the great size of the new estates allowed for their profitable use along capitalist lines with the introduction of new crops, techniques, and technologies (citrus plantations are the best example here). Third, large estates could be acquired by outsiders not resident in any of the Palestinian districts (who could be Ottoman subjects residing in other provinces of the Empire rather than foreigners). In this way, land reform favored not only the rise of a class of "absentee landowners," but also the purchase of land by foreign Jews, which could not have occurred on this scale prior to 1858.

To sum it up, agrarian reform led to important sociopolitical consequences beyond the emergence of great estates in certain parts of Palestine just mentioned. In many instances, pasture land of previously communal use was now privatized in a manner reminiscent of British enclosures, encroaching on traditional pasture and water rights that had been vigorously defended by the individuals, families, and communities concerned. Agrarian development heightened competition between local notable families over land and water, even in the more densely populated zones of the interior mountain range. Among the winners of agrarian reform, along with these notable families of urban and rural origin, was a number of wealthy banking and trading houses from Syria and Lebanon (especially Beirut), who invested in the expanding Palestinian agricultural sector. The best-known example is the Beirut entrepreneur Alfred Sursuq, or Sursock in Western sources, who in the 1870s purchased around 200,000 acres of land in the plain of Marj Ibn Amir. His investments allowed for the cultivation of previously fallow lands and the settlement of peasants and tenant farmers there. In 1882 even the

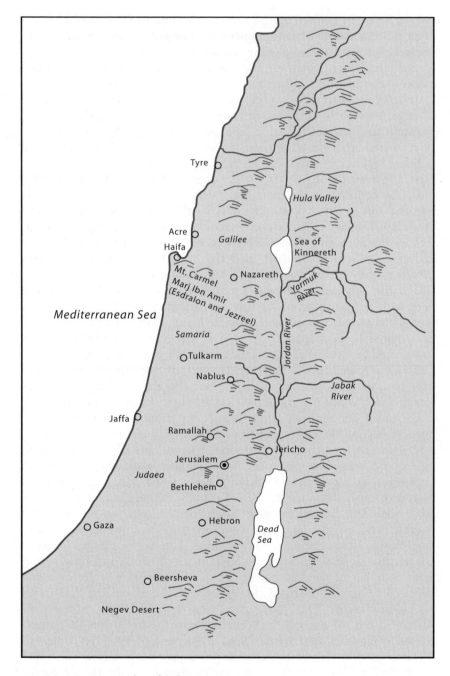

Map 3. Geography of Palestine

sultan himself acquired extensive estates in the western part of the plain.[14] An oft-cited description of the plain of Marj Ibn Amir, written by Sir Laurence Oliphant, a known sympathizer with the idea of a restoration of the Jews, after a visit in the year 1883, provides a vivid picture of the economic and social changes brought about by the Tanzimat:

> Readers will be surprised to learn that almost every acre of the plain of Esdraelon [Marj Ibn Amir] is at this moment in the highest state of cultivation; that it is perfectly safe to ride across it unarmed in any direction, as I can testify; that, so far from plundering and despoiling villages, the few Bedouins, whose "black tabernacles" are now confined to the southern margin of the plain, have in their turn become the plundered and despoiled, for they are all reduced to the position of being subject to inexorable landlords, who charge them exorbitantly for the land which they occupy, and for which they pay in hard cash, under penalty of instant ejection, which is ruthlessly enforced, so that the inhabitants of the villages, with which the plain is now dotted, live in perfect security.[15]

For the peasantry, the imposition of law and order in general, and agrarian reform in particular, produced contradictory results.[16] The Ottoman law-and-order policy did improve their personal security, as described by Oliphant. But it also made it easier for tax collectors as well as urban businessmen, creditors, usurers, and bankers to collect all kinds of taxes, debts, goods, and services. Simply put, from the 1860s onward capital could assert itself even without arms. It was no longer dependent on the support of local strongmen. But it also tended to be less embedded in personal ties and loyalties, and this could work to the disadvantage of the weaker elements of society. Contrary to widespread belief (transmitted not least by the nationalists of the twentieth century), the peasants, tenants, and agricultural laborers were indeed the weaker party, but they were not simply the passive victims of social change. They too benefited from rising land prices and mounting demand of both the urban population and Europe for their agricultural produce. Their greatest problem may have been insufficient access to cash, which was needed not only to purchase important goods, such as seed, livestock, and tools, but also to pay the taxes. Mortgages could be taken

[14] Schölch (1986), pp. 103ff., 144, 165–66, 194; Gerber (1987), pp. 80, 89.

[15] Laurence Oliphant, *Haifa or Life in Modern Palestine* (Edinburgh and London, 1887), p. 59, cited from Gerber (1987), p. 79; on Oliphant, see Shimoni (1995), pp. 63–64. However, parts of the plain were still marshland in the 1920s, so that not all of it had been drained or cultivated in the late Ottoman period; see, for instance, the photograph in Naor (1998), p. 17.

[16] Shafir (1989); Doumani (1995); Swedenburg (1988). On landlessness prior to the nineteenth century, see Gerber (1987), pp. 27ff.

out only on land that was officially entered in the registry, irrespective of who actually owned and worked it. If they could produce no legal title, their only sources of credit were private moneylenders, who as a rule charged interest rates as high as 30 percent. Given the unfavorable combination of uncertain income (conditioned by rain, drought, earthquake, swarms of locusts, and mice) and fixed expenditures, cultivators almost invariably ended in debt. By the end of the nineteenth century, a destructive path had evolved that showed its full force in the 1930s: vital expenses and tax obligations (levied at least partly in cash) leading to debt, forced land sales, flight from the countryside, and eventual proletarization. The process is hard to quantify, but can nonetheless be sensed in contemporary reports and documents.

The Bedouins were affected by the changes as well, especially by those elements of agrarian reform that concerned wasteland and fallow fields. During the 1880s Bedouins were already showing growing interest in becoming permanently settled, and not just at the fringes of existing zones of settlement and cultivation.[17] The mounting value of cultivable land also explains the increase of tribal conflicts in the border regions toward the end of the nineteenth century, in which stronger tribes or tribal factions ousted the weaker ones. At least in the Negev, the outcome of fighting in the years 1887–90 established the borders between tribal areas that lasted until 1948. Soon after Beersheva was founded as an administrative center of the Negev in 1900, it attracted, among other people, merchants from Gaza and Hebron into this developing zone. A growing number of tenant farmers from Egypt, the Sinai, and weaker tribes were enlisted as a labor force; at the same time, ever more Bedouins began to work the fields, marking an economic and cultural turning point for them. The Ottoman government played a much more active role in this process than had been the case before.

The changed legal framework, combined with better protection against Bedouin incursions and an expanded foreign trade, made investments in agriculture increasingly attractive. At the same time, population growth ameliorated the previous labor shortage. Higher investment and sufficient labor created the preconditions for expanded agricultural production. By the close of the nineteenth century, Palestinian agriculture was producing surpluses until population growth in the first decades of the twentieth century reversed the situation.[18] Not all outside observers were blind to the changes in agriculture and the landscape, or saw the Arab peasant as silent observer of changes introduced by others. Even

---

[17] Ben-David (1990), pp. 187ff. There is evidence of land conflicts as early as 1875; Bailey (1990), p. 35; Schölch (1986), pp. 154, 194.

[18] Schölch (1986), p. 76; Shafir (1989), pp. 28–29.

critical literature has its stereotypes, and the critique of the "Orientalist gaze" that perceives the Arab peasant only as a "biblical icon" (Doumani), silent, lazy, and immobile, is a good example.[19] Writing in the mid-1870s, the pious Dr. Thomson waxed quite enthusiastic about the beauty of the rural scenery:

> Lydd is a flourishing village of some two thousand inhabitants, embosomed in noble orchards of olive, fig, pomegranate, mulberry, sycamore, and other trees, surrounded every way by a very fertile neighbourhood. The inhabitants are evidently industrious and thriving, and the whole country between this and Ramleh is fast being filled up with their flourishing orchards. Rarely have I beheld a rural scene more delightful than this presented in early harvest, when I rode from Ramleh hither through the fields on the east of the common path. A thousand reapers, gleaners, and carriers were abroad and busy when the morning sun shot his first rays down through the olive-trees upon the animated groups. The wheat and barley grew among the olive-trees, which half hid, half revealed the merry harvesters—men, women, and children—the first reaping, the second gleaning and guiding the loaded camels, and the children at play, or watching the flocks and herds, which were allowed to follow the gleaners. But no description can reproduce such a tableau. It must be seen, heard, and enjoyed to be appreciated.[20]

One cannot help wondering at just how differently individual visitors experienced the land, veteran observers among them—what they noticed or did not notice, what they cared to transmit, and what they chose to ignore or suppress. It is hard to imagine a greater contrast than that between the nostalgic Dr. Schwarz and the lyrical Dr. Thomson. In any case, the travel literature is by no means as uniform as some of the critics of Orientalism describe it. While it is not difficult to find authors ranging from Ewald Banse to Ermete Pierotti that one cannot even cite today without being suspected of racism, others, including missionaries like Gustav Dalman or W. M. Thomson himself, who all spent long years in the country, are indispensable sources of social and cultural history.

PALESTINE TRANSFORMED?

Local trade, handicraft, and industry were stimulated by the growing influx of pilgrims and tourists, who benefited in turn from the improved

---

[19] In addition to Doumani (1992) and (1995), see the photographs in Elmendorf (1912); Landau (1979); Graham-Brown (1980); Gidal (1982); W. Khalidi (1984); Howe (1987), and Osman (1999). For an analysis of the photographic tradition, see Osman (1999), pp. 153–58, and Nir (1985).

[20] Thomson (1985 [1877]), p. 525.

Figure 6. The Orientalist gaze: Bedouin at the Jordan River. Anonymous photograph, c. 1900.

security situation, as well as the easier conditions for travel.[21] Regular steamboat connections between Europe and the Syrian Mediterranean ports of Beirut, Acre, Haifa, Jaffa, and Gaza that were opened in the late 1850s contributed greatly to this improvement. Still, the ports along the Palestinian section of the coast remained so inadequate that ships could be unloaded only at open sea, from which passengers and cargo were loaded onto boats and finally carried onto the shore. The 1860s marked the beginning of organized pilgrimages from Western Europe,

[21] Schölch (1986), pp. 57, 74, 134–36, 150–51. On commerce and handicraft, see A. Cohen (2001); Gerber (1985), pp. 62–73; Gerber (1987), pp. 48–50.

first from Marseilles, and then from Trieste. Shortly thereafter, the first
travel bureaus such as Cook & Sons took up their trade, taking both
pilgrims and tourists to the Holy Land. In the 1870s, thousands of pilgrims visited Jerusalem every year, most of them Russian, who did not
contribute to the tourism business only. In 1906 water from the Jordan
River was first exported to the United States. At the same time, the
infrastructure connecting the coast to the interior was improved, largely
owing to foreign and domestic private initiatives supported energetically
by the Ottoman state from the 1880s onward.[22] In 1868 the first paved
road was built between Jaffa and Jerusalem. In 1892 the first rail line
was established along the same route, shortening travel time from a
whole day to seven hours by horse-drawn coach or three and a half
hours by train. At the same time, Palestine was connected to the expanding rail network that led via the Orient Express as far as Vienna and
Paris. In 1905 the Hijaz Railway, designed to transport Muslim pilgrims
from Damascus to Medina, was completed, and established its headquarters in Haifa. A spur line from Haifa to Der'a in Transjordan, the
so-called Valley Line, built by a German engineer (Heinrich Meissner
Pasha), led through the plain of Marj Ibn Amir and contributed to enhancing land prices there. The railway lines from Haifa to Acre and
from Afula to Nablus were completed by 1914, linking Nablus to the
expanding regional infrastructure and by the same token facilitating its
control. Jerusalem was served by competing mail delivery services, beginning with the Austrian postal service in 1859, followed by the Ottoman in 1867, German and French services in 1900, a Russian service in
1901, and an Italian one in 1908.

Integration into the world economy, which would have been impossible without improved infrastructure, also brought about a gradual shift
of the export trade from Lebanon and Egypt (its most important trading
partners till then) toward Europe. The strongest growth in European
trade occurred between 1825 and 1875. The establishment of regular
steamship lines dramatically reduced transportation costs, though European trade did not benefit from this until moles were built in Jaffa and
Haifa that finally allowed the ships to dock. By 1914 Jaffa and Haifa
had developed into the most important ports (Jaffa in particular for agricultural shipments), while Gaza and Acre played a more modest role.

[22] Philipp/Schaebler (eds.) (1998); Kark (1990); travel times from Jaffa to Jerusalem,
Kark (1990), p. 75; also Schölch (1986), pp. 124ff., and maps 5–8; Frischwasser-Ra'anan
(1976), pp. 45ff. For the effects on Jaffa, see also LeVine (2005), chs. 2 and 3, esp. pp.
33–40. For postal communication established under Egyptian rule, see Safi (2004), pp.
172–73. For Christian pilgrimage, see Ben-Arieh (1984), pp. 198–201. On the Jordan
water, see Naor (1998), p. 35.

Figure 7. At the Jerusalem railway station. As can be seen, girls and women around 1900 wore headscarves (*mandil*) rather than veils. Anonymous photograph, c. 1900.

The most modern and most important port on the Syrian coast was Beirut.[23] Up to the 1870s, the "Palestinian" balance of trade was in the black: High exports to Europe were matched with low imports. Other than soap for the Egyptian and Syro-Lebanese markets, the exports consisted almost entirely of agricultural products. Foremost among them was grain, especially wheat for Italian pasta and French noodles as well as barley for the British beer and whiskey production. At the same, cash crops such as sesame, olive oil, tobacco, and also cotton (international markets permitting) were exported in growing quantities. Perhaps the

[23] LeVine (2005), ch. 2; Schölch (1986), pp. 76–157; Kark (1990), pp. 67–70.

most important innovation in Palestinian agriculture was the rapid
expansion of citrus cultivation after the Crimean War of 1853–56, first
and foremost of the Jaffa orange (*shamuti*), which was especially suitable for export due to its tough skin. However, the cultivation of oranges and other citrus fruits required higher capital investments, since
the trees yielded no profit for the first several years, and also had to be
irrigated during the dry season. Hence, the citrus plantations were
mostly owned by urban merchants and notables, not by small farmers.
But next to expanding European trade, we should not overlook local
and regional commerce in which soap continued to play a leading role.
The soap trade was controlled by merchants and traders of the provincial cities, who due to their intimate knowledge of markets, middlemen,
and credit conditions remained indispensable partners for the central
government as well as for Syro-Lebanese and European trading houses.

To sum it up, then, the local economy experienced considerable
growth between 1856 and 1880, accompanied by a marked population
increase matching parallel increases in Syria, Anatolia, and Iran.[24] The
economic upsurge was due primarily to the expansion of extensive agricultural cultivation, involving larger areas and an increased number of
fieldworkers. Apart from citrus farming, local agricultural production
underwent no structural transformation, such as the introduction of new
and more productive techniques and technologies, or new crops. There
were certainly innovations, but these were brought in by European immigrants. For example, the Templars of Württemberg, who settled near
Jaffa and Haifa from 1869, used fertilizer and machines on their farms
and, with the potato, even introduced a new crop to the region. It appears that they were imitated by some Jewish settlers, but not by the
local Arab peasantry.[25] While in certain regions the beginnings of modern economic activities could be detected even before the Land Code of
1858, and indeed before the Egyptian occupation in 1831, traditional
patterns of living and production persisted elsewhere until well into the
twentieth century. And yet, economic growth would not have been possible unless agriculture had been at least partially commercialized, that
is without the introduction of the cash economy and complicated forms
of credit, the integration of peasants into the local and regional economy, and the willingness of domestic and foreign investors to inject substantial capital into the local economy. True, the main impulse for
growth came from outside, or rather from above. But the reactions of
local peasants, traders, and merchants must be seen as an active engage-

---

[24] Shafir (1989), p. 28.
[25] On the Württemberg Templars, see Carmel (2000); Schölch (1986), pp. 71–73, 140–
42; Shafir (1989), pp. 28–30.

Figure 8. Street scene in Jerusalem. Anonymous photograph, c. 1900.

ment, not simply as a passive acceptance of change induced by others, and elsewhere. In Palestine, too, modernization had contradictory effects and consequences. But it was not a zero-sum game.

The Rise of the Notables

As mentioned above, the political, legal, and economic changes introduced by the Ottoman state worked to the advantage of civilian elites, who relied less on force, or the threat of its use, than on tax farming, credit, landed property, and membership in the local and provincial administration. Gradually, political power shifted from the countryside to the cities, reinforcing the control of urban elites over the surrounding countryside, whose residents became increasingly dependent on urban patrons. This ultimately resulted in new political alliances between the inhabitants of city and countryside.

The ideal type (to use a term introduced by Max Weber) of the notable, as it emerged in the second half of the nineteenth century, was defined above all by his political function of mediation.[26] A notable (the term usually occurs in Arabic only in the plural, a'yan, and they were apparently all male) held and exerted authority on the basis of family affiliation, wealth, personal conduct, performance, and connections. Power was exerted most effectively when it took account of local custom and expectations: hence the central importance of face-to-face relations, integrity, and honor. Status and honor resulted from, in Pierre Bourdieu's terms, a combination of "economic" and "cultural capital." As a rule, a notable belonged to a family that was already affluent and influential; many were merchants involved in long-distance trade, or scholars learned in religion and law. The link between family affiliation and notable status was strong, but not compelling. It was possible for an individual to be acknowledged as a notable on the strength of his individual achievements. Religious knowledge and a reputation of piety were of special use here, and could be reinforced by marriage into a scholarly family, charity, the founding and administration of a waqf, membership in a Sufi order, or religious office.

The notable mediated between his clientele (which was not necessarily fixed or stable, but could broaden or narrow according to changing circumstance) and the authorities, whether it be the local representatives of central government (the governor, city commander, kadi, etc.) or the central government in Istanbul, reaching up to the sultan himself. It was the combination of social status, locally recognized, and access to the authorities that made an individual a notable. The patron-client relationship on which rested the status of the notable as mediator can be viewed as an exchange of services and obligations that had to be continually renegotiated. Services and obligations were not limited to the economic realm, and patron-client relations cannot be trivialized as an exploitative relationship in which a narrow-minded, conservative, if not outright reactionary elite oppressed an ignorant and superstitious peasantry (more on this caricature below). The social ideals of solidarity, reciprocity, fair and just exchange, founded on a shared interest in the protection of local autonomy and expressed in the language of kinship, were not merely a mask of economic or political interest. And yet, the

---

[26] Hourani (1968); Muslih (1988), ch. 1; Abu-Manneh (1990); Doumani (1995), pp. 55–56, 67, 151; Yazbak (1998), pp. 42–46, and ch. 4. For Syria, cf. Khoury (1983); Gelvin (1998); Thompson (2000).

mediator was not just the unselfish honest broker either: mediation ultimately served to secure the position and self-interest of the notables
themselves. Mediation entailed the twofold task of passing demands and
complaints "from below to above," but also to ensure that such demands and complaints not disturb the existing order. Hence, mediation
usually involved the effort to hold tensions in check, and to have a
"moderating" effect on potentially rebellious groups. It is all the more
interesting, therefore, to study the instruments and mechanisms of leverage employed by the notables to secure and protect their status against
threats from both above or below. From the mid-nineteenth century, at
least in Palestine, they used military force only exceptionally. Concerning possible threats "from below," the classical institution of patronage
retained its importance in all spheres of life.

Quite a few of the notable families of Palestine can be traced back to
the seventeenth century; some had immigrated from neighboring Arab
territories, many were originally members of the Ottoman military and
administrative elite.[27] With the pacification of the provinces, and the
ensuing elimination of armed local elites, many rural clan leaders lost
their independent power base. The Tanzimat reforms strengthened the
position of the urban elites, although they also resulted in growing competition over land, as well as for positions in the administration and the
newly formed advisory councils. While the notables owed their position
primarily to their strong ties to specific groups and individuals within
well-defined geographical areas, the Tanzimat reforms served to widen
their contacts and to provide them with new institutions and new channels of communication reaching up to the highest level of political delib-
eration and decision-making: The Ottoman parliament, first convened
in 1876, included six representatives from the later Mandate area of
Palestine.

All of the notables previously referred to were Muslims. It is harder
to assess the role and status of local Christian and Jewish elites. Here we
must distinguish between the position of specific individuals and families
within their own communities and their status in the local (urban and
rural) hierarchy at large. Obviously, local Christian and Jewish communities and congregations were internally stratified. Just as obviously, they
had official and unofficial spokesmen and deputies who represented
them to the authorities and the external world in general. As among
Muslims, this role was traditionally filled either by educated, wealthy,
and influential individuals (merchants, doctors, financiers in the widest
sense) or else by those learned in religion and law (Christian clergy,

---

[27] Manna' (1992) and (1998); Abu-Manneh (1986) and (1990); for the 1830s and
1840s, see also Rood (2004), pp. 54–64.

Jewish rabbis). In the course of the nineteenth century, the so-called *millet* system granting recognition and specified rights to a number of non-Muslim communities including the Rabbanite Jews, Orthodox Christians, Armenians, Catholics, Georgian Orthodox, and Protestants was formalized and homogenized within the Ottoman Empire.[28] At the Sublime Porte, the various communities (*millets*) were represented by their highest-ranking clergy or the chief rabbi of Istanbul. At the provincial and district levels, representation was more varied and the role of laymen more prominent. Internally, the recognized *millets* enjoyed a large measure of autonomy in all questions defined as religious, from the exercise of their cult, to personal status matters, to education.

But a distinction needs to be drawn between representing a community to the outside world, and to the government in particular, and the role played by non-Muslims in a local social hierarchy dominated, at least in Palestine and Syria, by Sunni Muslims—whether in a city, village, or tribe. Representation of non-Muslims in provincial and municipal councils tells only part of the story, for during the Tanzimat era they were granted fixed quotas that in some instances went so far as to secure them a more favorable rate than the Sunni Muslim majority. When the amended Vilayet Law of 1913 repealed these quotas, the Christians decried the resulting abolition of privilege as a sign of discrimination.[29] It would be interesting to examine the extent to which the notables formed, beyond all confessional boundaries, a distinct social milieu or even class. A study on nineteenth-century Haifa suggests that in this port city, at least, this was not the case: Though an emerging class of Christian merchants, entrepreneurs, bankers, doctors, pharmacists, and so on, succeeded in attaining education and wealth, rising economically, and establishing themselves in society, they were not recognized as social equals by the local Muslim elite. Until the dissolution of the Ottoman Empire, the Haifa elite consisted only of Muslims.[30]

NABLUS

The social, economic, and political changes outlined above can be illustrated by looking at an area outside of Jerusalem: the district of Nablus. Thanks to a number of excellent studies, Nablus offers insight into provincial life of a kind rarely attained for nineteenth-century Palestine.[31]

---

[28] Braude/Lewis (eds.) (1982); Levy (ed.) (1994), pp. 42–71, 105–109. For Palestine, see also Steppat (1974), pp. 242–43.

[29] Porath (1974), p. 294.

[30] Yazbak (1998), ch. 4, esp. pp. 158–62, and ch. 6.

[31] Al-Nimr (1961–75); Doumani (1995); also Graham-Brown (1982). On the infrastruc-

Over much of this period, the city of Nablus was the most important center of trade and industry in the region, and indeed the center of a "geohistoric" unit with its own social and political character: Jabal Nablus (often called *jabal al-nar*, or "fire mountain"), which also included the city of Jenin. Jabal Nablus, which in the nineteenth century counted about three hundred villages, included some of the most fertile lands and several of the oldest settlements in Palestine. In administrative terms, the district was for the longest time part of the province of Damascus. In 1859–60 it was annexed to the province of Sidon (whose governor resided, as we have seen, in Acre after 1777), and finally, from 1887–88 to 1918, it belonged to the province of Beirut. Hence it was always oriented toward the north. When seen from an Ottoman or Syrian perspective, Jabal Nablus was the "periphery of the periphery" (Doumani): No international trade route led through the city and its environs, though it did host connecting roads that facilitated domestic and regional trade as far as Cairo and Damascus. The annual pilgrim caravan from Damascus to Mecca also brought some business. The most important export product was soap, whose main markets were in Egypt, Lebanon, and Syria. Until well into the nineteenth century, the main port for Nablus was Jaffa, though it was gradually superseded by Beirut, following the general economic trend. As no religious significance was ascribed to the city, it attracted few foreign visitors and travelers. One could indeed have written the history of Nablus and its hinterland without ever having heard of the "Holy Land."

Nablus itself, the ancient Flavia Neapolis, was widely identified with the biblical Shehem, and may actually go back to an earlier Canaanite settlement. Located in a picturesque setting, and surrounded by gardens and olive groves, Nablus was fortunate to have a number of springs. Thus, unlike many towns in Syria and Palestine (above all Jerusalem), it benefited from a secure water supply. The available data suggests that the population of Nablus had grown continuously throughout the eighteenth and nineteenth centuries: In the mid-sixteenth century the Ottoman census registered 5,000 to 7,000 residents, in 1800 over 7,000, and in 1850 more than 20,000.[32] From the mid-seventeenth century, there are reports of the influx of Bedouin families and members of the Ottoman military. Like Hebron and other settlements in the mountains,

---

ture, cf. Doumani (1995), pp. 23–25, 68–78, 94; Schölch (1986), pp. 146–49, 171–74, 195–212.

[32] Doumani (1994) and (1995), pp. 25–26, 34ff. Heinrich Petermann, who spent two months in Nablus in the early 1850s and was one of the very few foreigners to do so, left a vivid description; Petermann 1976 (1865), pp. 264–92. Thomson, who visited in the 1870s, was enchanted by the scent of blossoms and the song of the nightingales in the gardens of Nablus; Thomson (1985 [1877]), pp. 470–77.

Figure 9. View of Nablus. Anonymous photograph, c. 1900.

Nablus too was economically, politically, and culturally not sharply distinguished from the surrounding countryside, although the city was built of solid stone and the city gates were closed at night. In social and religious terms, the population was fairly homogeneous. Alongside the Sunni Muslims who dominated urban culture and society, there were around 800 Greek Orthodox and a small number of Protestant Christians, some 200 Jews, and around 150 Samaritans (who called themselves *shomrim*, guardians of the law, and sparked the special interest of Western travelers). In the first half of the century, the Samaritans were still heavily represented in the bookkeeping and administration of the city— classic functions of a minority in many Muslim societies.

The case of Nablus illustrates rather well the intricate links between local autonomy, imperial "decline," reform, and modernization. Beshara

Doumani points to a close connection between the loss of imperial control, relative prosperity, and economic growth in the remote district that was reflected in the population growth of the eighteenth and nineteenth centuries just mentioned.[33] To be removed from central control had its distinct advantages and was not coterminous with chaos or anarchy. A certain level of insecurity still allowed for a measure of prosperity, especially since profits were not systematically skimmed by a central fiscal administration, and the population was burdened with few duties and tax obligations. Unlike the greater part of *bilad al-sham*, Jabal Nablus was not ruled or controlled by the city itself until the middle of the nineteenth century. The peasantry was relatively autonomous, even armed, and well-protected in their sturdy stone houses. Ottoman punitive expeditions were designed to periodically restore and ensure the good behavior of the local population, whose leadership was gradually integrated into a local hierarchy. Until the 1850s, power in Jabal Nablus was shared by a few families with a power base in the hinterland. The Nimrs, Tuqans, Jarrars, Jayyusis, Abd al-Hadis, and others were in a position to mobilize peasant militias in their area, and their influence consisted to a large extent in their ability to make use of military force, or at least the threat of it. For the first half of the nineteenth century, enduring struggles have been documented between competing families and clans, which is not to imply that such struggles did not occur even earlier. The fortified family strongholds (*kursi*) in the equally fortified villages of the district testify to the state of insecurity and the importance of military force it entailed.

The Egyptian occupation permanently disrupted the local balance of forces, bolstering the position of the Abd al-Hadi family at the expense of their rivals. After the Egyptian withdrawal, the Ottomans campaigned vigorously in the 1840s and 1850s and ultimately broke the military power of the rural sheikhs. As urban influence on the hinterland gradually solidified, the district underwent increasing economic and political unification. The chief means of unification were nor longer military, but economic. The main beneficiaries of this process were urban businessmen who were able to build for themselves a stable network of contacts in the hinterland based on personal ties and an exchange of services. Beginning in the 1840s they also gained access to political decision-making via the newly established advisory bodies. Economic and political changes also led to a growing differentiation of the peasantry. European interests and influence helped to shift the regional center of gravity to Jerusalem, which gradually emerged as the political and administrative center of Palestine. At the same time, the center of economic activity

[33] Doumani (1995), ch. 1; Hoexter (1973); Abir (1975); Rood (2004), pp. 61–64.

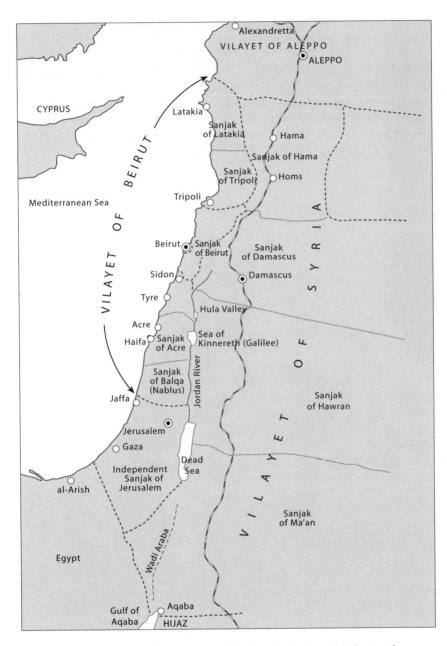

Map 4. Ottoman Administrative Districts in Syria and Palestine before World War I

shifted toward the coastal area, leading to the rapid development of Jaffa and Haifa in many ways similar to Beirut and Alexandria, albeit on a smaller scale. Under these circumstances, the Nablus merchants looked increasingly toward Transjordan, a development also reflected in the newly drawn boundaries of the district in the 1880s, which was now officially known as Balqa. Although increasingly deprived of military power and political autonomy, the district and its residents still preserved an independent character that would make itself known in the political struggles of the twentieth century.

Chapter Five

EVOLVING NATIONALISMS:
ZIONISM AND ARABISM, 1880–1914

TOO OFTEN, the history of late Ottoman Palestine is seen (and told) as a mere prelude to Arab-Jewish conflict in the twentieth century. As a result, the onset of large-scale Jewish immigration, and more particularly of Zionist immigration, in 1882 appears as a turning point in the modern history of Palestine, if not the region at large. The years 1881 and 1882 do of course mark an important time in Middle Eastern history: In 1881 Tunisia was invaded by the French, and in 1882 Egypt was occupied by the British, events noted with considerable alarm by the Ottoman authorities. But for Palestine, 1882 can only be taken as a turning point if history is written from its outcome—the foundation of the State of Israel. It makes no sense if the aim is to write a history of the Palestinian economy and society at large. Jewish immigrants, Zionist as well as non-Zionist, remained a marginal element until World War I, causing no rupture in the local economy, society, and culture. Even politics was not influenced for some time to come. Jerusalem may be considered an exception: Though not yet a center of Zionist activity, it was important for Jewish life in general, and increasingly attracted European interest.[1]

JEWS IN THE HOLY LAND: THE "OLD" AND THE "NEW" YISHUV

The spread of Zionism and the establishment of the Jewish Yishuv (the term commonly used for the Jews living in Palestine in the modern period, derived from the Hebrew verb *yashav*, "to sit" or "to settle") are generally told and explained with reference to European history. At the same time, ideological if not idealistic commitment to Zionism is privileged over practical considerations such as economic interest or the exis-

---

[1] The literature on nineteenth-century Jerusalem is very rich; cf. above all Ben-Arieh (1984) (who focuses on Jewish and European institutions); Asali (ed.) (1997); Auld/Hillenbrand (eds.) (2000). Gilbert (1994) provides interesting maps and illustrations, but his text is highly tendentious.

tence of political alternatives available to Jews.[2] Idealism, ideology, and convictions born from the European experience obviously cannot to be ignored in this context. And yet the evolution and characteristic features of the Jewish Yishuv, and later of Israeli society, were strongly influenced by conditions in Palestine itself. Only by considering the local and regional context can we understand certain characteristics that at least in the twentieth century, most Israelis regarded as basic to their society: the close connection between pioneers, settlers, and soldiers; the dominance of Ashkenazi Jews and the concomitant marginalization of Oriental and Sephardic Jews; the centrality of Labor Zionism to Jewish society and Israeli politics; the cooperative forms of social and economic organization; and the coexistence of what has been called the "inner collectivism" of the Jewish economy and society with a market economy within Israel after 1948.

FORERUNNERS OF ZIONISM

I will not attempt here to recount or reappraise the origins and development of Zionism—others have done so successfully.[3] What interests me here are a number of elements relevant to the history of Palestine. Among them, certain problems of terminology cannot be ignored, since they touch on the difficult distinction between Jews and Zionists (which still haunts political debate today) and the somewhat less politically charged but equally important differentiation between Zionism and Jewish immigration into Palestine. It is well known that the Zionist movement hoped to solve the "Jewish question (*Judenfrage*)," and that it spoke for the Jewish people at large, and ultimately posed as representative of all Jews around the globe. Yet not all Jews viewed Zionism as the solution to the "Jewish question," assuming that they even saw this question as existing in the first place. Most Jews in the Middle East, for instance, who tend to be ignored in this context, were not concerned with the *Judenfrage*. To narrowly focus on European and American Jews when dealing with the fate of Jewry in the modern age is as unacceptable as any other form of tunnel vision. And yet, such limitations are hard to avoid, since Zionism first evolved in Europe rather than the Middle East, and in the years up to the foundation of Israel, it was mostly European and American Jews who shaped the fate of Jews in Palestine or Eretz Israel.

---

[2] Here I basically follow Shafir (1989), esp. pp. xi–xiii, 2ff., 19, 49; see also Lockman (1996).

[3] Out of a large body of literature, see Shimoni (1995); Shilony (1998), ch. 2; Brenner (2002).

As a specific form of Jewish collective identity, Zionism was much like other forms of nationalism: never the only possible, natural or compelling way of defining collective identity, but only *one* of several possibilities of collective self-understanding and organization. As a cultural and political aspiration Zionism could of course build on the religious tradition of longing for Zion, which had remained very much alive in the Jewish diaspora.[4] But this did not make Zionism a guaranteed success; its early days were arduous, and resistance was considerable. The idea of preserving, renewing, and indeed redeeming Judaism through an "ingathering" of the Jewish people, or at least a part of it, in Eretz Israel, the "Land of the Fathers," had occasionally been voiced from the 1830s onward by men such as Rabbis Yehuda Alkalai (1798–1878) and Zvi Hirsch Kalischer (1795–1874). As observant (Orthodox) Jews firmly rooted in the tradition of messianic expectation, they reacted to the progressive emancipation of the Jews in western and central Europe and in the Balkans, accompanied as it was by the emergence of Reform Judaism. Hence their chief concern was not the physical oppression and persecution of the Jews, but rather their estrangement from their Jewish faith and identity through assimilation. What they cared for was a spiritual redemption of the Jewish people, not a national one. Neither did Moses Hess (1812–75) write under the fear of physical threat, when in 1862 he published his booklet "Rome and Jerusalem: The Last National Question" to proclaim the idea of a national unity and revival of the Jewish people, modeled on the recent unification of Italy. Significantly, his call went unanswered. Still, it is important to note that the idea of a national revival of the Jews in Eretz Israel developed *before* the rise of modern anti-Semitism. However, to the extent to which anti-Semitism took hold in various European countries, from Rumania and Russia to Austria, Germany, and France, it lent broader support to the Zionist project.

EMIGRATION AND "PRACTICAL ZIONISM"

Faced with poverty, marginalization, and persecution, the Jews of eastern and central Europe had various options at their disposal, even if the full range of choices was not available to all of them. One option was simply to continue living in an Orthodox way without searching for a new orientation, another was to assimilate to local society. Many east-

[4] For an overview, see Shimoni (1995), chs. 1, 2, and 8; for Alkalai and Kalischer, see pp. 71–82; for Hess, pp. 55–60. On the "yearning for Zion," see chapter 2 above; also Ben-Arieh/Davis (1997); Budde/Nachama (eds.) (1996); Rosovsky (ed.) (1996).

ern European Jews opted for socialism, or for a specifically Jewish form of socialism; some chose anarchism, others adopted some kind of Jewish "cultural nationalism," which could be variously defined, from Orthodox, to reform, to liberal. The great majority chose none of these possibilities to escape from their difficulties or to alter them decisively, but simply left them behind and emigrated to the New World. Between 1882 and 1914, around 2.6 million Jews left Russia and its neighboring territories, most of them to begin a new life in America.[5] For the most part they did so without reflecting deeply on identity and political change, and without making a conscious choice between individual and collective improvement, or even redemption. In the 1880s and 1890s, the decision in favor of Zionism and its realization in the promised land of Eretz Israel, was neither self-evident nor widespread. Of all the Jews who after the persecutions (pogroms) of 1881–82 emigrated from the Pale of Settlement, the area within the Czarist Empire assigned to Jews by Catherine the Great in 1790–91, less than 5 percent went to Palestine.

It is well known that there were already Jews in Palestine in the nineteenth century who became known as the "Old Yishuv" in contrast with the newcomers of the 1880s and 1890s.[6] "Old" here does not necessarily suggest deep roots, or a long-standing presence in the land. In fact, many members of the so-called Old Yishuv were first-generation immigrants themselves, while others descended from immigrants of the eighteenth and nineteenth centuries, who for the most part had followed Orthodox religious leaders to Eretz Israel. Yet others could boast a long line of ancestors in Eretz Israel. "Old" was above all a qualitative term used by the members of the "new," Zionist Yishuv, who stood for a cultural and national renewal of the Jewish people, to mark their difference from those who in their eyes embodied all they detested—tradition, immobility, and reliance on others. It was a moral concept, just as the Hebrew term 'aliya was a moral term for immigration to Eretz Israel, defining it not as mere migration, but rather as an "ascent" ('aliya referred originally to the "ascent" to the Jerusalem Temple, standing "up on the mountain"). In many of the reports from Jewish visitors (if they themselves were not Orthodox or ultra-Orthodox, haredi), one senses a certain fascination with the alien ways of Oriental Jews and decided reserve vis-à-vis the poor and pious eastern European Jews.

[5] Data taken from Metzer (1998), pp. 60–67; Shafir (1989), pp. 7–8, 49; Carmel/ Schäfer/Ben-Artzi (eds.) (1990), pp. 17–18, 156. For the Pale of Settlement, which was abolished only in 1917, see also Mendes-Flohr/Reinharz (eds.) (1995), pp. 379–80; for emigration to the United States, pp. 472–73.

[6] Parfitt (1987); Halper (1991); Kark (1990); Carmel/Schäfer/Ben-Artzi (eds.) (1990). For Sephardic Jews in Palestine on the eve of World War I, cf. Campos (2005).

Jerusalem has been a Jewish city from eternity to eternity. Driven away, they returned once more; driven away, they returned once more. . . . Here there dwell, in rags, the Kurdish Jewesses whose husbands are porters or stone-cutters. Here reside the worthy Sephardim, wearing the fez, with their cleanly wives. Here in vaulted shops Polish Jews, pale, bespectacled, their faces overgrown with blond, brown, or red beards, little black kippas on their heads, sit studying, a book in front of them, while all around a small shop, filled with junk, slowly gets covered with dust. Here reside the oriental Jews who come from Baghdad, from southernmost Arabia, from Yemen. The Jews from Poland wear fantastic garments, fur coats like they were worn around 1300, bronze- and olive-colored velvet coats that belong in the paintings of Rembrandt.

Here live the pious old who intend to die in Jerusalem, and the recipients of alms from all over the world. They have devoted their lives to God, their fellow humans must take care of their bodies.[7]

These were the Jews known to the local Arab population, and with whom they had lived more or less peacefully for ages. In the framework of the *millet* system, the Ottoman authorities regarded the Sephardic chief rabbi of Jerusalem, who was in turn subordinate to the Sephardic chief rabbi of Istanbul, as the head of the Jews in Palestine. The Ashkenazi Jews had no official status. At the close of the nineteenth century, the differences between "old" and "new" Yishuv were not always easy to discern, for even the Zionist immigrants were not all socialist agnostics or "freethinkers" as they were frequently called. From an early date, a religious branch, known as Mizrachi (derived from *merkaz ruhani*, spiritual center), evolved within the Zionist movement. At the same time, a number of local Sephardic and Oriental Jews, who were generally considered religious and non-Zionist, if not openly anti-Zionist, became engaged in cultural and social reform in their community, thereby closing the gap to cultural Zionism. Some even acted as middlemen between Zionist immigrants and the local authorities. Distinctions were most obvious in those cases where long-established Orthodox Jewish families were contrasted with freshly arrived Zionist pioneers who were sometimes nonpracticing secularists if not altogether revolutionary minded. Quite likely, such prototypes hardly ever met. In the course of the twentieth century, the boundary between old and new Yishuv was blurred even further, especially when Nazi persecution weakened the ideological reservations of Orthodox Jewry against Zionism.

The idea of a "productivization" of the Jews through physical labor in combination with a "colonization" of Eretz Israel was part of the

[7] Tergit (1996), p. 32.

emancipatory project advocated by spokesmen of the Jewish Enlightenment (*haskala*), who had already made first attempts to put these goals
into effect.[8] In 1870 the (decidedly non-Zionist) Alliance Israélite Universelle opened an agricultural school near Jaffa (Mikveh Israel) in
which many new immigrants would be educated from the 1880s onward. In 1878 and 1882, Petah Tikva and Ge'oni (later Rosh Pinna)
were established as the first rural Jewish settlements in Palestine since
antiquity—and they too were founded not by Zionist immigrants, but
by members of the "old Yishuv" from Jerusalem and Safed. Both settlements were designed as "model colonies." Hence, there was Jewish immigration and colonization before the formulation of a Zionist program,
and for decades neither was necessarily associated with Zionism.

Jewish immigration is usually divided into a series of waves (*'aliya*,
pl. *'aliyot*), to which precise numbers are attributed.[9] This reflects later
attempts to systemize a diffuse migratory movement that most of those
involved did not perceive as the first, second, or third lap of a well-
defined and linear process. The immigrants of the so-called First Aliya
(from 1882 to 1903–1904) were by no means all Zionists or socialists.
Nor were they all Europeans: A considerable number came from Middle
Eastern countries, especially from Yemen, Kurdistan, and the Maghreb.
The majority immigrated for religious reasons and settled down in the
cities, not in the countryside. Out of 20,000 to 30,000 Jewish immigrants, some 5,500 moved to twenty-eight rural settlements on both
sides of the Jordan River. At the same time, the number of Jewish residents of Jerusalem rose from 16,000 in 1882 to 35,000 in 1905.

Among the new immigrants motivated by ideology, one group would
attain significance for Zionism quite beyond its small numbers: the Bilu'im, whose name derived from the opening words of Isaiah 2:5 (*beit
Ya'akov lehu we-nelha*: "O house of Jacob come ye and let us go"). The
Bilu'im were a group of young Russian Jews who first met in 1882 in
Kharkov in present-day Ukraine, who in contrast to most of their fellow
immigrants not only wanted to set up agricultural settlements, but also
to create a Jewish state.[10] Their hopes and realities differed widely,

---

[8] On the intellectual and practical roots, forerunners, and beginnings of this movement,
in particular German colonization in Prussia and French colonization in Algeria and Tunisia, cf. Shafir (1989), ch. 3; Shimoni (1995), chs. 1 and 2; Shilony (1998), chs. 1 and 2;
Schölch (1986), pp. 68–73.

[9] Metzer (1998), pp. 65–67; Brenner (2002). Shafir (1989), p. xvi, provides a map of
the settlements from 1878–1918; Yemenite immigrants are discussed ibid., pp. 91–122.
See also Muhammad 'Abd al-Karim 'Ukasha, *Yahud al-yaman wa-l-hijra ila filastin, 1881–
1950*. Third edition (Gaza 1998).

[10] Shimoni (1995), ch. 3, for Pinsker, see pp. 32–35, and Salmon (2002); for their manifesto, dated 1882, see Mendes-Flohr/Reinharz (eds.) (1995), pp. 532–33. Their headquar-
ter was later moved from Kharkov to Odessa.

though: In 1900 the settlement of Gedera, which they established in 1884, numbered sixty-nine inhabitants. It was to remain the only one. The Bilu'im were part of a loosely knit grouping of "Friends of Zion" (Hovevei Zion) that included both religious and secular Jews. Deeply affected by the anti-Jewish riots in Russia, Rumania, and the Ukraine, they propagated emigration to Palestine and Jewish national revival there. Leo (Yehuda Leib) Pinsker (1821–91), a medical doctor and prominent representative of the Jewish Enlightenment, the Haskala, provided them with an ideological platform when in 1882 he published "Auto-Emancipation! Exhortation from a Russian Jew to His Kinfolk," which, significantly, was written in German. The same year also witnessed the foundation of the first Zionist settlement in Palestine, Rishon le-Zion ("First in Zion"), followed by some thirty other settlements, among them Gedera in 1884, Rehovot and Hadera in 1890–91, and Metulla in 1896; two others had to be abandoned after a short time. In 1884 the Hovevei Zion held their first conference in Kattowitz (in Upper Silesia, then belonging to Prussia). Meanwhile, they met with great difficulties in Russia. Only in 1890 was their organization Hibbat Zion (Love of Zion) recognized by the Czarist government as a "Society for the Support of Jewish Farmers and Craftsmen in Syria and Palestine" (better known as the Odessa Committee). Due to great practical difficulties and to political opposition on the ground, that is, in Palestine itself, the advocates of "practical Zionism" in and around Hibbat Zion were in no position to realize large-scale colonization projects. During this early phase the majority of settlers were supported and maintained by Jewish philanthropists such as Baron Edmond de Rothschild or the Alliance Israélite Universelle. One of the few exceptions was Gedera, which sought to preserve its financial independence.

THEODOR HERZL AND "POLITICAL ZIONISM"

Theodor Herzl (1860–1904) is generally regarded as the founder of the Zionist movement, yet he did not invent Zionism.[11] The term "Zionism" itself was first publicly used in the early 1890s by the Jewish writer Nathan Birnbaum, to distinguish the political movement from the efforts of "practical" settlement as advocated by various Jewish "colonization associations." In 1896, Herzl published *The Jewish State*, which served as the manifesto of the young movement. In 1897 he created the World Zionist Organization (WZO) at the First Zionist Congress in Basel,

---

[11] The literature on Herzl is extensive; for judicious treatment, see Shimoni (1995), pp. 88–100; Brenner (2002).

which would represent the Zionist movement in the decades to come. Unlike Alkalai, Kalischer, or Hess, Herzl spoke openly and daringly of a political project to alleviate what he called *Judennot* (Jewish plight): the foundation of a Jewish state on a suitable piece of land. In his view, this need not necessarily be Palestine, or Eretz Israel; it could possibly also be a piece of land in Africa or South America.[12] But it would have to be systematically planned and well prepared, and it would require international support. "The Jewish question," wrote Herzl in his Introduction to *The Jewish State* (p. 20),

> exists wherever Jews live in perceptible numbers. Where it does not exist, it is carried by Jews in the course of their migration. We naturally move to those places where we are not persecuted, and there our presence produces persecution. . . . I think the Jewish question is no more a social than a religious one, though it sometimes takes these and other forms. It is a national question, and in order to solve it we must above all make it a political world-question to be settled by the civilized nations of the world in council.[13]

Here we find the decisive element that distinguishes Herzl from the "practical Zionists": Herzl wanted to internationalize the issue and to systematically involve the European powers—a strategy later pursued by the Arabs as well. The solution of the Jewish question, Herzl was convinced, would benefit everyone, (European) Jews and (European) non-Jews alike, and it could be achieved through diplomatic appeals for support from the European powers and the Ottoman sultan. Ideally, it would be firmly established in an internationally recognized "pledge" or "charter." In *The Jewish State*, Herzl put his idea in a few sentences that would later be repeated time and again (p. 39): "Let the sovereignty be granted us over a portion of the globe large enough to satisfy our rightful requirements as a nation; the rest we shall manage for ourselves." In the same context, he continued with the famous passage (p. 43):

> Palestine is our ever-memorable historic home. The very name of Palestine would attract our people with a force of marvellous potency. Supposing

---

[12] After the Kishinev pogrom of 1903, there was serious discussion of the so-called Uganda Plan, under which the Jews would have been settled in this African country in order to escape persecution in Europe. Herzl supported this option. A considerable number of settlers in Palestine were prepared to abandon Eretz Israel (at least temporarily) in favor of Uganda. Nevertheless, the majority of Zionists rejected the Uganda Plan at the Seventh Zionist Congress, held in Basel in 1905 shortly after Herzl's death. Cf. Shimoni (1995), pp. 98–99, 334–39, and Mendes-Flohr/Reinharz (eds.) (1995), pp. 548–52.

[13] Here as in all subsequent quotes, I have adapted the English translation (*The Jewish State*, New York 1947) on the basis of the original German (*Der Judenstaat*, Berlin 1936). Page numbers refer to the 1947 English translation.

His Majesty the Sultan were to give us Palestine, we could in return undertake to regulate the entire finances of Turkey. For Europe we should form there a portion of the rampart against Asia, we should serve as an outpost of civilization against barbarism. We should as a neutral state remain in contact with all Europe, which would have to guarantee our existence. The sanctuaries of Christendom could be safeguarded by assigning to them an extra-territorial status recognized under the law of nations. We should form a guard of honor about these sanctuaries, answering for the fulfillment of this duty with our existence. This guard of honor would be the great symbol of the solution of the Jewish Question after eighteen centuries that for us were filled with pain.

Herzl viewed the efforts of the "practical Zionists" with skepticism ("An infiltration is bound to end badly," p. 42). He found the use of Hebrew as an everyday language ridiculous ("We cannot converse with one another in Hebrew. Who amongst us knows enough Hebrew to ask for a railway ticket in that language!" p. 99). No, there would have to be a state, and indeed a "model state," which Herzl anticipated in bold detail right down to the layout of the houses and the introduction of the seven-hour workday (a point to which he was especially committed). Work would shape society and allow the state to develop its full potential, for "the Promised Land is the land of work" (p. 66). The state "will seek to bestow the moral salvation (*sittliche Beseligung*) of work on men of every age and of every class." "Beggars," he continued, "will not be endured. Whoever refuses to work as a free man will be sent to the workhouse" (p. 79). Even so, life would not be entirely without joy. Herzl was a member of the bourgeoisie, not a socialist (p. 59):[14]

> Yes, the rich Jews who are now obliged to carefully hide their valuables, and to hold their uncomfortable feasts behind lowered curtains, will be able to freely enjoy their possessions over there. If they cooperate in carrying out this emigration scheme, their capital will be rehabilitated there. It will have proved its use in an unprecedented undertaking. If the richest Jews begin to build their palaces over there which are viewed in Europe with such envious eyes, it will soon become fashionable to settle over there in splendid houses.

---

[14] On p. 54 he says

We are only collectivists where the dreadful difficulties of the task demand it. Otherwise we wish to tend and care for the individual with his rights. Private property, as the economic foundation of independent people, shall be allowed to develop freely, and will be respected by us.

On Zionist concepts of labor and emancipation, cf. Shilony (1998), ch. 2, esp. pp. 49ff.

Religion, too, would have its place, albeit a limited one (p. 100):

> Shall we end by having a theocracy? No, indeed. Faith unites us, science
> makes us free. We shall therefore prevent any theocratic tendencies among
> our clerics. We shall know how to keep them within the confines of their
> temples just as we shall keep our professional army within the confines of
> their barracks. The army and the clerics shall receive the honors their beau-
> tiful tasks demand and deserve. But they must not interfere in the adminis-
> tration of the State which confers distinction upon them, else they will
> conjure up difficulties without and within.

The same could be expressed in more sarcastic terms: "We shall let
every man find salvation over there in his own particular way. This
holds above all for our dear Freethinkers, our immortal army, who are
continually making new conquests for humanity (p. 86)."

As can be gathered from his book, Herzl was not primarily concerned
with eastern European Jews, but rather with the Jewish and non-Jewish
elites of western Europe ("the cultivated men," p. 15). Yet he found his
largest audience in eastern Europe. The majority of the approximately
250 participants attending the First Zionist Congress, which Herzl organized in Basel in 1897 to provide Zionism with a structure, visibility,
and respectability that it had previously lacked, came from eastern Europe. The "Basel Program" put Herzl's vision into concise words. Zionism's primary aim, it stated, was "to create for the Jewish people a home
in Palestine secured by public law."[15] For the time being, however, Zionism was unable to win over the majority of Jews in Europe, America, or
the Middle East, and even met with sharp opposition.

After his early death in 1904, Herzl was revered as the father of the
Zionist movement, having already in his lifetime been styled as a "new
Moses." Like Moses, Herzl did not live to see his dream come true. But
he recognized like few others that for an idea to be effective it needed
organization as much as symbols—and these he either created or at least
helped to popularize. By the turn of the century, the Zionist movement
had acquired the nucleus of a modern organization and its accompany-
ing offices and functions. These included an increasingly better organized donation system (including the famous Shekel, a term later
adopted for the currency of the State of Israel, and the equally famous
blue collection box of the Jewish National Fund), a flag, and an unofficial national anthem known as the "Hatikvah" (from Hebrew *ha-tikva*,
hope). They were employed and displayed at the Zionist Congresses,
communicating the goals of the movement to a wider audience and giving their leaders a popularity well beyond their immediate circle of fam-

---

[15] Cited from Mendes-Flohr/Reinharz (eds.) (1995), p. 540.

ily, friends, and followers. From an early date, Zionism was rendered visible in a manner comparable to the established national movements in Europe and America, contrasting starkly with the Arab national movement emerging at about the same time. In the following decades several processes ran in parallel: diplomatic efforts of the World Zionist Organization to win international support for the Zionist project; steady immigration into Palestine by Jews of various origins, as well as the establishment and expansion of Jewish and/or Zionist institutions in both urban and rural settings, carried out by Zionists and non-Zionists alike. Gradually, "political" and "practical" Zionism merged, or at least complemented one another, in what became known as synthetic Zionism.

THE FOUNDING ERA: THE SECOND AND THIRD ALIYAS

With the Second Aliya (from 1904–1905 to 1914) and Third Aliya (from 1918–19 to 1923), the generation of pioneers and founding fathers (and mothers) who arrived in Palestine made every effort to distinguish themselves from the immigrants of the First Aliya and thoroughly transformed the Zionist movement in the country.[16] The decade preceding World War I was crucial for determining the values and self-views of Zionism for years to come. Among them was the idea of "productivizing" the "Jewish masses," by transforming Jewish *Luftmenschen* into workers. Rooted in the Jewish Enlightenment of the eighteenth and nineteenth centuries, this notion responded to the anti-Semitic stereotype of the Jews as parasites living off their "host societies." As important was the aim to establish an egalitarian Jewish society that would be largely self-contained and self-sufficient. In accordance with the idea of "productivization," labor was to be "Jewish labor," or rather "Hebrew labor" (*'avoda 'ivrit*), and the difference between the two is significant. In this context, two objectives were formulated: "the redemption of the land" (*ge'ulat ha-adama*) and the "conquest of labor" (*kibbush ha-'avoda*).[17] The basic values of the Zionist immigrants of the Second and the Third Aliya were a pioneering spirit, modest lifestyle, high esteem for manual

[16] Shafir (1989), pp. 2ff., 46–50. The distinction between the idealistic pioneers and the ("ordinary") immigrants guided by material interests can be traced back to Martin Buber, who speaks of election and vocation, and of the correspondence between inner and outer transformation. On the idealization of peasant life in Jewish travel literature, see Kaiser (1992), pp. 476ff.

[17] For the intellectual tradition of Labor Zionism, see Shimoni (1995), ch. 5. On the concept of the "redemption of the land," which combines legal notions with the expectation of salvation, see also Kaiser (1992), pp. 498–99. On "Hebrew labor," see below.

labor (especially agricultural labor), self-defense, self-reliance, and a future-oriented outlook. The idea was to revive *Hebrew* culture as opposed to the *Jewish* culture of the diaspora—the very epitome of everything they despised. The biblical patriarchs, the conquerors, kings, and "Hebrew" resistance fighters from Joshua and David to Judas the Maccabean provided the Zionists with their role models. In a similar manner, Muslim reformers looked to the "pious predecessors" (*al-salaf al-salih*), the first generations of the companions and successors of the Prophet, as their ultimate role models.

Zionist claims, hopes, and aspirations could be expressed in a variety of ways, and could be justified in religious or in secular terms. But no matter how it was done, there remained a certain tone of vibrancy, a sense of the greatness of the task that the settlers and pioneers faced. Their sense of mission seldom rested on deep familiarity with the land and its people. As late as 1935, a Zionist visitor repeated the familiar stock images of a desolate land "redeemed" through Jewish pioneers, which to him also entailed the redemption of the Jewish people, if not humanity as a whole:

> Today, 1,900 and 1,800 years after the two great massacres with which Titus and Hadrian mortally wounded the Jewish people in Palestine, the land is once again almost as desolate and deserted as Joshua found it. From Dan to Beersheva, and far beyond this southern point in the waterless desert of the Negev, wherever you go you find traces of former settlement and cultivation, ruins of towns, of buildings, water-pipes, streets, decayed terraces, sealed-up springs and wells. Before this land was taken land by this particular people, it was barren, deserted, and miserable; since the expulsion of this particular people, it is barren, deserted, and miserable, and only at the hands of this particular people has it been fertile, densely settled, and prosperous. This land and this people are like body and soul. Robbed of its soul the body lies as a corpse, left to decay. The soul torn from the body in which it dwelled wanders aimlessly through space, a phantom of itself, a terror for others. The Jews were just such a phantom after losing their land. . . . The day on which body and soul unite once more, on which this people returns to this land, is a happy day not only for this people and this land, but rather a happy day for the entire family of nations, who will be freed from a phantom, from a nightmare.[18]

THE "REDEMPTION OF THE LAND" AND THE "CONQUEST OF LABOR"

In Palestine as elsewhere, settlement was dependent upon a variety of factors. It required not only actual physical presence in the land and

[18] Hugo Herrmann, *Palästina heute: Licht und Schatten* (Tel Aviv 1935), p. 231, quoted from Kaiser (1992), pp. 93–94.

ownership of it, but also sufficient manpower. While Palestine was sparsely populated toward the end of the nineteenth century, it was by no means empty. Unlike North America or Australia, it was subject to a recognized political authority (the Ottoman sultan). Foreigners, including Jews, were in no position to take the land by force. They could only obtain it through purchase, and then only in those places where it was made available to them by the authorities or the locals. At the turn of the century, most Arabs still lived in the mountainous interior region—Jewish "Judea and Samaria" and also Galilee—where the majority of Jews had lived in antiquity. In the second half of the nineteenth century the Arab population densified in the coastal region and the river valleys connecting the coast with the interior. The Jewish settlements were concentrated in the vicinity of Jaffa, Haifa, and Safed. With the exception of Upper Galilee, these were not the regions in which the ancient Israelites had originally lived. Unlike Jerusalem and the other "holy cities"—Hebron, Safed, and Tiberias—these regions also lacked special religious status. It was not until 1910–11 that Jews acquired more extensive property in the fertile plain of Marj Ibn Amir. In Afula they founded the first cooperative settlement (Merhavia) which was protected by the Shomer (watchman), and which quickly became the target of both Arab attacks and lively debates in the Ottoman Parliament.[19] At the same time, Jewish-owned farms and plantations as well as the newly established settlements attracted residents of nearby Arab villages searching for new opportunities of work and income.[20] There is therefore some truth to the argument that Jewish immigration drew Arab immigration in its wake, even though the latter cannot be quantified. Zionist observers who remained in the country for a longer time and made an effort to be well informed about local conditions, were fully aware of the distribution of land and population, as seen from a report by Leo Motzkin to the Second Zionist Congress:

> One has to admit that the density of population does not exactly put the visitor to Palestine in a joyful mood. In large stretches of land, one constantly comes across big Arab villages, and it is a well-established fact that the most fertile regions of our land are occupied by Arabs.[21]

[19] On land acquisition, cf. Shilony (1998), ch. 5 (for the Jezreel Valley, Afula, and Merhavia, pp. 193–208), and ch. 6 (for Merhavia, pp. 245–58). Merhavia, founded in 1911, was transformed after World War I into a communal settlement or *moshav*, as the cooperative was not economically profitable. Maps of the settlements in Shafir (1989), p. xvi, and Aaronsohn (1990), p. 149. Maps of land use around 1880 can be found in *Tübinger Atlas des Vorderen Orients (TAVO)*, A X 9 (Southern Levant—Land Use Around 1880) and B IX 21 (Syria and Palestine at the close of the nineteenth century).

[20] Shafir (1989), pp. 52–53.

[21] Cited from the stenographic protocol of the transactions of the Second Zionist Congress, held in Basel from August 28–31, 1898 (Vienna 1898, pp. 99–127).

As we will see, the Ottoman authorities were from the outset resisting Jewish attempts to acquire land in Palestine. For this reason, land purchase and settlement had to be organized, and if possible coordinated. The Zionist movement made every effort to do so. An important example comes from the Ruppin Memorandum of 1907, which marked an N-shaped region between Jaffa and Lake Tiberias as the area of Jewish land purchases—an area that until the Arab uprising of 1936–39 did in fact form the heart of Jewish settlement activity in Palestine.[22] Until the turn of the century, colonization was largely carried out by European "colonization associations" such as the Hovevei Zion. The rural settlements (*moshav* and *moshava*), which at first employed local, labor-intensive methods of cultivation, yielded low profits and did not allow for a "European standard of living," to say nothing of the social and cultural amenities that the Jewish settlers and workers expected. The yields did not improve much when the settlements supported by Baron Rothschild adapted their mode of operation to the French colonial agriculture in Algeria and Tunisia, and produced cash crops such as almonds, grapes, olives, and citrus fruit, earmarked exclusively for export. Despite high investments, Rothschild was unable to make these enterprises self-supporting or profitable, and in 1900 he handed them over to the Jewish Colonization Association (JCA), founded in 1891 by Baron Maurice de Hirsch. The JCA was a non-Zionist organization for the support of Jewish emigrants, headquartered in Paris, which maintained settlement colonies, especially in North and South America (Argentina). Abandoning all philanthropic concerns, the JCA employed strictly economic criteria of profitability, even if this entailed dismissing Jewish workers. Repeated strikes and labor struggles could not hold up this process.

Already before World War I, a consensus was forming in Zionist circles that Jewish colonization of Palestine would be possible only through a "bifurcation" of the economy, requiring the establishment of new, and exclusively Jewish structures and institutions. However this could not sever the connections with and even dependence upon the local Arab economy and society—uneducated Arab labor remained indispensable for the so-called Jewish sector well beyond 1948. From 1918 onward, two institutions served as the main pillars of Zionist strategy: the Jewish National Fund and the General Federation of Hebrew Workers in Eretz Israel, known as Histadrut, which worked together to "redeem" the land and "conquer" labor.[23] The Jewish National Fund (JNF, *keren kay-*

---

[22] Shafir (1989), p. 43; K. Stein (1984), pp. 38, 64; Shilony (1998); also note 19 above.

[23] Shilony (1998), chs. 3 and 4, and Epilogue; p. 87 contains a useful diagram of the various organs of the World Zionist Organization. The Palestine Office was officially established at the end of 1907, but only operated from April 1908, when Ruppin arrived in Jaffa (p. 83). For the forestation campaign and the Herzl Forest, created in 1908 with the

emet le-yisrael) was set up in 1901 at the Fifth Zionist Congress and registered in London in 1907, with the proclaimed task "to purchase land for the Jewish people with donations from the people." All land acquired by the JNF was considered the property of the Jewish people. It could not be sold, but only leased for a period of forty-nine years, and only to Jews. In theory, non-Jews were not admitted as hired laborers (though this policy was not consistently enforced). In a way, JNF lands could be viewed as a secular counterpart to the religious endowments of Jews and Muslims. (In the 1930s, Muslim Arab activists adopted this idea when they declared Palestine to be a "sacred trust" of the Muslim community that could not be transferred to non-Muslims.) In February 1902, the Anglo-Palestine Company was founded in London, which served the World Zionist Organization as a credit institution; soon afterward, it opened branches in Palestine, beginning with Jaffa, Jerusalem, and Hebron. In 1903 there followed the Palestine Commission, with its headquarters in Berlin, which sponsored a series of surveys to explore the possibilities of systematic land development and settlement on both sides of the Jordan River. In 1907–8, the World Zionist Organization opened its Palestine Office in Jaffa (not Jerusalem). The head of this office, Dr. Arthur Ruppin, a lawyer and economist recently immigrated from Germany, would soon play a crucial role in Zionist colonization.

In line with Herzl, the various Zionist institutions spoke out against any "practical settlement" or "infiltration" unless supported by international guarantees for its existence, though they did approve of the colonization of Palestine after the model of German *Ostkolonisation*, internal colonization as pursued especially in the region of Poznan under Prussian domination. Only in 1910, when the advocates of "practical" Zionism were gaining ground within the World Zionist Organization, did the JNF seriously begin to acquire land for Jewish settlements. At the same time, an experiment was started that would later be identified with the Zionist project as a whole. With the support of the Palestine Office (which for a long time had resisted cooperative experiments and preferred private capitalist initiative), Russian immigrants founded the first communal settlement (*kvutza*). Soon renamed Degania, it was the

---

assistance of the so-called Olive Tree Donation, which sparked violent conflict over the principle of "Jewish labor" (Jewish laborers tore out the seedlings that had been planted by Arab workers and planted new ones), see pp. 115–35. Shilony, pp. 386–401 contradicts the notion that the JNF played a decisive role in the "redemption of the land" prior to World War I (until 1914, land purchased by the JNF amounted to a mere 24,000 dunam). Shilony emphasizes the JNF's research and promotional activities, which took place predominantly in an urban environment. On this point, see also Shafir (1989) and Metzer (1998), pp. 128–29.

nucleus from which the kibbutz movement subsequently developed. By 1918, Degania had been followed by three more cooperatives.[24]

At the same time, another element of the "conquest of labor" took shape: the defense of Jewish settlements, which eventually led to the Hagana, and in May 1948 to the Israeli army.[25] In 1906 the first units of Jewish watchmen (*shomer*, pl. *shomrim*) formed in Lower Galilee to defend Jewish settlements, vineyards, and other property against Arab attack. They never fully replaced the Circassians and Arabs that had previously been employed in this function. In September 1907 a small group of new immigrants around Yitzhak Ben-Zvi founded the secret society Bar Giora, named after Shimon Bar Giora, one of the leaders of the Jewish revolt of A.D. 70. They took as their motto "In blood and fire Judea fell—in blood and fire Judea will arise," a line from the poem "The Canaanites" by Ya'akov Cahan. Authorized by the Ottoman authorities, the Jewish society Ha-Shomer ("The Watchman") was founded in 1909 and, in 1916, established its first settlement in Upper Galilee.

Up into the 1920s, a plantation-type economy predominated in the Jewish agricultural sector, operating mostly with Arab labor. What was true of European settlers in French-occupied Tunisia or Algeria was also true of Palestine: Few Jewish farmers and landowners were rich and patriotic enough to employ Jewish rather than Arab labor, which, for them, was more attractive in almost every sense. Not only were Arab laborers physically strong and familiar with local modes of production; they were also unorganized, undemanding, and cheap. One Zionist observer spoke openly about the "lack of development" of the Arabs:

> Arab [workers] are distinguished . . . by one virtue that is much appreciated by the Jewish farmers, and it is their lack of development, as a result of which they do not know what to demand from the employers. . . . the Arab consents to be working every day of the week, and even continuously for full months without resting for a single day, and he demands no raise for all that [effort] of his regular wage.[26]

---

[24] Shilony (1998), chs. 5 and 6, esp. pp. 137–56 and 241–45. Naor (1998), pp. 51–52, has interesting illustrations.

[25] Shapira (1992), ch. 2, esp. pp. 61 and 71–72, underlines the aggressive masculinity adopted by the guardsmen, building on their ideas of Bedouin and Cossack life and mores; also Shafir (1989); Zerubavel (1995). Shilony (1998), pp. 150–56, and Naor (1998), pp. 32, 37, 43–45, 62, provide uncritical accounts of Hashomer, which in 1916 founded a first settlement in Upper Galilee.

[26] Moshe Smilansky quoted from Shafir (1989), p. 57; cf. also pp. 76–77. Shilony (1998), pp. 292–302, emphasizes the sense of sacrifice of the Jewish pioneers and the threat posed by the Arabs. Metzer (1998), pp. 123–37, esp. 128–29, provides data on labor wages.

One attempt to confront the problem without betraying the principle of "Jewish labor" came through the employment of Yemenite Jews. For this purpose, a Zionist envoy disguised as a scholar (Shmuel Warshaw-sky, later Shmuel Yavnieli) was sent to Yemen in 1911 (his conservative garb served the purpose of "making them receptive to the idea of emigration," since the Jews of Yemen were known to be deeply religious). Yavnieli did indeed manage to persuade some 2,000 Yemenite Jews to make the *aliya* to Eretz Israel. Mordecai Naor, a chronicler of Eretz Israel in the twentieth century, described the episode in the following terms:

> The men and women of the Second Aliya view themselves as workers out of conviction, yet they quickly realize that compared with the Arab farm workers, idealists like themselves almost always lose out. There, "workers" are needed who can endure the heavy physical work and oppressive living conditions. In their search for such productive manpower the men and women of the Second Aliya discover the industrious Yemenite Jews, some of whom have already come to the country at the time of the first Aliya. They plan to bring laborers from Yemen to Palestine. . . .
>
> As a result of Yavnieli's mission, 2,000 new immigrants come to Palestine. They build new neighborhoods and work very hard and for little pay in the farmers' fields. The Yemenites are patient workers who seldom complain about the harsh living conditions. For they believe that one would only be worthy of living in Eretz Israel if one "earns it through tribulation."[27]

A remarkable text. Despite their highly useful attitude toward redemption, land, and labor, the Yemenites did not solve the fundamental problem. For Jewish farmworkers, who unlike the Arabs had no other source of income (but higher expectations), living conditions were difficult and harsh.[28] What they were offered was usually poorly paid seasonal labor, not enough to feed a family. The strategy of "conquest of

---

[27] Naor (1998), p. 56 (translated from the German edition). As a general rule, the Yemenites immigrated with their entire families. According to Shilony (1998), pp. 302–309, the Yemenite Jews were well-suited to "push out" the Arab laborers, since they were accustomed to the difficult climate and working conditions, and since they obeyed their overseers and could survive on as low a wage as the Arabs; moreover, they spoke Arabic and they were Ottoman subjects. The Palestine Office regarded them as "natural workers": "All they had to do was show up on the labor market, and Arab workers would be easily ousted from the colonies" (quoted from pp. 302–303). Yet experience showed that the Yemenite Jews could not endure the climate and living conditions in Eretz Israel; infants and small children died in large numbers. In 1913 the experiment was largely brought to a halt. For a critical account, see Shafir (1989), pp. 91–122.

[28] Shafir (1989), pp. 53–57, 72–76. According to him, around 1,600 Jewish workers resided in rural settlements in 1900. In 1904 they totaled around 5,500 residents.

labor" failed in the face of hard reality, even though at least on the plantations the labor market was split into two: All of the more highly qualified and better paid positions were reserved for Jews; whenever Jews took over tasks that had previously been undertaken by Arabs, they would be better paid for the same kind of work. And yet they never attained "civilized" working conditions that fulfilled their needs and expectations, since seasonal labor and the lack of social amenities partly neutralized the higher wages. This explains the much lamented phenomenon of "vagabondage" among Jewish laborers, who would often leave a position after a short time in hopes of finding a better one elsewhere—and not necessarily in agriculture. It also helps to explain the high rates of emigration by Jews out of Palestine. All in all, Jewish workers succeeded in "splitting" the labor market, but not in "conquering" it. That would have required a total exclusion of Arab labor, the maximum goal of the Zionist workers' movement—an objective that proved impossible to achieve.

POLITICS AND CULTURE

Even in the heroic years of the First and the Second Aliya, a large number of the Zionist immigrants did not move to the countryside, but rather to the cities.[29] There, the poorer among them found employment as workers, craftsmen, and day laborers, while the better off opened businesses or sought positions in administration or the private sector; the better educated worked as teachers, journalists, doctors, lawyers, engineers, or nurses. As mentioned before, the activities of the Zionist organizations, including the Anglo-Palestine Company, the Palestine Office, and the Jewish National Fund, were in no way restricted to colonization or agriculture more generally. In 1909 lots were drawn for the first plots of land for a new Jewish residential area north of Jaffa, Ahuzat Bayit, which in 1910 became the city of Tel Aviv (Spring Hill, named after the Hebrew title of Theodor Herzl's book *Altneuland*, published in 1902). The period between 1900 and 1914 witnessed the foundation of various socialist Zionist organizations, unions of workers, craftsmen, and artists, professional associations, clubs, and newspapers from left-wing Zionist to Orthodox, creating a new Jewish sector that for the most part was Labor Zionist alongside the institutions of the "old Yi-

[29] Shilony (1998), esp. chs. 8 and 9. For Tel Aviv, cf. Schlör (1999) and LeVine (2005). For Lilien, cf. Arbel (ed.) 1996, and Michael Stanislawski, "Vom Jugendstil zum 'Judenstil'? Universalismus und Nationalismus im Werk Ephraim Moses Liliens," in Michael Brenner/Yfaat Weiss (eds.), *Zionistische Utopie—israelische Realität. Religion und Nation in Israel* (Munich 1999): 68–101.

shuv." In 1905 the first political parties were formed with the socialist Young Worker (*ha-Po'el ha-Tza'ir*) and the Workers of Zion (*Po'alei Zion*), which shortly after began to publish their own newspapers. In 1909 a Hebrew district court was established to deal with intra-Jewish affairs, an interesting extension of the legal autonomy enjoyed by non-Muslims in the framework of the Ottoman *millet* system. In 1911–12, a workers' sick fund was created from which the (Jewish) Sick Fund (*kuppat holim*) arose. At the same time, the anti-Zionist association Agudat Israel was founded in 1912 in Kattowitz, which would soon play a role in Palestine as well.

Education, art, and entertainment should not be ignored either: In the summer of 1902, a Jewish Library opened its doors in Jerusalem that also kept foreign books and newspapers; it later developed into the Israeli State and University Library. In various towns and Jewish settlements, Jewish orchestras were formed.[30] In 1905 the first Jewish high school was founded in Jaffa (the later Herzliah Gymnasium), which in 1910 relocated to the newly founded city of Tel Aviv (at least until World War I, its graduate certificates were written in French, Hebrew, and Arabic). There followed several boys' and girls' schools as well as additional secondary schools. In 1906 the Bezalel Academy of Arts and Design opened in Jerusalem, directed by Boris Schatz and the artist Ephraim Lilien. In Jaffa, the first Jewish plays were staged by local theater groups. When the rabbis in Jerusalem protested against such frivolity, Ottoman soldiers actually forced a performance to cease. Nonetheless, the Olympia Cinema opened its doors in Jerusalem in October 1908, followed in 1914 by the Eden cinema in Tel Aviv. At the initiative of the Hilfsverein of German Jews in Haifa, the cornerstone was laid for a Jewish Technical Institute, the Technion, in 1912, which immediately became involved in the so-called language conflict: Should instruction be in Hebrew as the Zionists demanded, or in German as the Hilfsverein wished? It was not until December 1924 that the Technion was finally able to open. Still in 1912, the Jewish Maccabi sports clubs—named after the Maccabean (or Hasmonean) dynasty who in the second century B.C. had founded a Jewish kingdom of considerable size, albeit under foreign suzerainty—created its own umbrella organization.

However important the goals and achievements of the founding generation were, one must distinguish between the ideal and the reality. The Second Aliya, triggered by the Kishinev pogrom (in present-day Moldova, then Bessarabia) of April 1903 and the Russian Revolution of 1905, which were followed by a fresh wave of anti-Semitism, brought 35,000–40,000 Jewish immigrants to Palestine, among them many of

[30] Mendes-Flohr/Reinharz (eds.) (1995), pp. 567–68; Brenner (2002), pp. 59–64.

the future leaders of the Jewish Yishuv, from David Ben-Gurion, Yitzhak Ben-Zvi, and Levi Eshkol, to Berl Katznelson and Joseph Shprin-
tzak. Yet the Second Aliya also had the highest percentage of emigrants
leaving Palestine again after a brief stay (*yordim,* literally "descenders"),
a percentage that in some years reached a full third of the immigrants
(*'olim,* "ascenders").[31] In 1914 about 12,000 Jewish farmers and fieldworkers lived in approximately forty Jewish settlements—and to repeat
it once again, they were by no means all Zionists. The dominant languages were still Yiddish, Russian, Polish, Rumanian, Hungarian, or
German in the case of Ashkenazi immigrants from Europe, and Ladino
(or "Judeo-Spanish") and Arabic in the case of Sephardic and Oriental
Jews. Biblical Hebrew served as the sacred language, while modern Hebrew (Ivrit) remained for the time being the language of a politically
committed minority that had devoted itself to a revival of "Hebrew
culture."

OTTOMAN REACTIONS

Rising Jewish immigration after 1880 did not go unnoticed in Jerusalem
and Istanbul, and yet the reactions to it cannot be simply classified as
"resistance," as later nationalist historiography would have it. Once
again, it is important to distinguish between different actors and interests at specific points in time, notably between the Ottoman authorities,
local Arabs, and Arab observers in neighboring countries. At the same
time we must distinguish specific themes and motifs: Opposition to Jewish settlement was not necessarily based on, or accompanied by, a developed sense of Palestinian identity, and this in turn was not coterminous
with the rise of an Arab-Palestinian national consciousness.

Ottoman policies toward Palestine and the Zionist movement can be
sketched here in their rough outlines only.[32] The interests of the central
government in Istanbul and of its local representatives in Palestine were
not always identical, or even in harmony, and in view of international
pressures, the Ottoman government had only limited room for maneuver. Ottoman policies did not so much reflect prejudice toward Jews as
a religious community, or special regard for Palestine as a Holy Land

---

[31] Metzer (1998), table 3.2, and the figures given below on demography; for linguistic
statistics during the Mandate period, cf. Himadeh (ed.) (1938), p. 38 (based on the census
of 1931).

[32] Brief summary in Reinkowski (1995), pp. 25–28; for more detail, see Karpat (1974);
Mandel (1976), ch. 1; al-Nuʿaimi (1998); Kushner (1999); Campos (2005), pp. 471–77,
and chapters 3 and 4 above. For the confusion surrounding the geographical definition of
Palestine, see Biger (2004), pp. 13–21.

for Muslims, Jews, and Christians. Ottoman policy makers were concerned about the risk of further European penetration of an area that was steadily growing in strategic importance to the European powers. Already in 1872, Jerusalem was raised to the rank of an independent district (Arabic *mutasarrifiyya*), so as to take into account European interests in the Holy Land in general and Jerusalem in particular. In view of the independence struggles in the Balkans and other parts of the Empire, decision makers at the Sublime Porte surmised (and not without reason) that there was a link between organized Jewish immigration and colonization on the one hand and European protection and intervention on the other—supported above all by the legal institution of the so-called Capitulations, which gave their beneficiaries far-reaching rights and privileges.

Even before the first immigrants of the Bilu'im had set foot on "Palestinian" soil (which occurred in Jaffa on July 6, 1882), and even before the first signs of resistance began to stir among the Arab population, the Ottoman authorities had been warned by their consul in Odessa. In response to this warning, they took first measures to prohibit immigration and land acquisition by foreign Jews in Palestine, a ban later extended to include Ottoman Jews who were not allowed to offer land or property to Zionist uses. This had nothing to do with anti-Jewish or anti-Semitic sentiment, but with politics. The Ottoman authorities perceived the immigrants not primarily as Jews, but rather as Europeans, or more precisely, as Russians, and therefore as members of a hostile power against which the Empire had just fought a war. For them it was not a question of hindering Jewish settlement in their territories in general: In fact, the pogroms in Czarist Russia triggered a fresh wave of Jewish immigrants into the Ottoman Empire beginning in 1881–82. A considerable number of Jews settled in Istanbul and other major cities, and quite a few made efforts to obtain Ottoman citizenship. They were perfectly free to settle in the Empire but not in Palestine (but as we know this was not a very precise term at the time). To this end, permission to stay in Palestine was now limited for Jewish pilgrims and businessmen to a period of one month, and later three months—a violation of the Capitulations that was immediately protested by foreign consuls. Official policy at first prohibited sales of *miri* land to foreign Jews; Ottoman Jews were obligated not to sell *miri* land to foreign Jews, or to open it to colonization. Two meetings between Theodor Herzl and Sultan Abdülhamid in May 1901 and June 1902, in which Herzl offered comprehensive debt relief to the Ottoman Empire in exchange for land in "Acre and its surrounding areas," proved fruitless.[33]

[33] Shilony (1998), p. 194. On Ottoman debt relief, see also Herzl (*The Jewish State*, p.

In the meantime, Arabs in Palestine began to react to Jewish land purchases and colonization, though they did so for a variety of reasons, and not necessarily for political ones only.[34] Until the Balfour Declaration of 1917 (and beyond) economic motives and interests remained decisive, and they worked in different directions: While some locals benefited from the new opportunities of work and income, others suffered, having been driven away by the sale of their leased land, or deprived of the water and pasturage rights attached to it. Until the mandate era, Jewish buyers mostly purchased uncultivated or sparsely settled land. For this reason, Arab losses remained quite small. A petition of Jerusalem notables in June 1891 against Jewish immigration and colonization is worth noting in this connection, since it shows that even then protest was occasionally voiced. Yet the petition seems to have had no effect other than the creation of a commission by these notables in 1897 to keep a watch on land sales to Jews.

Despite growing Arab protests, the Young Turks, who seized power in the Ottoman Empire in 1908, initially had other concerns than Palestine and Jewish immigration. They did however pass new bans on Jewish immigration and colonization in order to prevent the emergence of a "Jewish question" that would not only invite European intervention, but would also risk provoking Arab opposition that might possibly alienate the Arabs from Ottoman rule.[35] Religious motives, or to be more precise, anti-Jewish or anti-Semitic prejudice, can be largely excluded here: Prior to 1908, the Young Turks had found some support among Ottoman Jews, above all in Saloniki. Moreover, the chief rabbi of Istanbul, Haim Nahum Effendi, was known to sympathize with the movement. What impelled the Young Turks to intervene was political motives. Even so, government directives were followed only hesitantly by local officials and only partially executed. Corruption and bribery played a role in this, as did the pressure of local actors, both Arabs and Jews. The governors and their staffs interpreted their interests in different ways: While the governor of Jerusalem complained in 1900 over continuing violations of the law by the Jews, the subgovernor of Tiberias permitted the Jews in his district to arm themselves in the wake of Arab attacks. In the meantime, Jewish immigration into Palestine continued, and repeated interven-

---

43), quoted above. On Herzl's hope of obtaining support from Kaiser Wilhelm II as the kaiser visited the Holy Land and Istanbul in 1898, cf. Merkley (1998), pp. 26–34; Carmel/ Eisler (1999).

[34] R. Khalidi (1997), chs. 4 and 5; Mandel (1976), ch. 2. On land purchases, see notes 19 and 23 above, as well as chapters 9–11 below.

[35] Mandel (1976), chs. 3–5. This is not the place to discuss the alleged Jewish character of the Young Turk movement (according to which they were Crypto-Jews, or so-called Dönme); cf., e.g., al-Nu'aimi (1998), ch. 4.

tions, bans, and threats of punishment could not prevent illegal land purchases from taking place. Only during World War I were the Ottoman authorities able to block Jewish immigration in any serious way.

LOCAL RESISTANCE AND ARAB IDENTITY

Like Jewish nationalism, Palestinian Arab nationalism developed in the full light of history, acquiring its specific traits in the course of its struggle against Zionist activity, Jewish immigration, and later British occupation. For this reason, it has often been described as a mere reaction to, if not mirror image of, Jewish nationalism. This is certainly an oversimplification. All nationalisms are specifically modern articulations of what Benedict Anderson called "imagined communities," and consciously "constructed" under specific conditions while at the same time very much real.[36] This is also true for Arab and Jewish nationalism. Arab nationalism in Syria, Iraq, Palestine, and the Hijaz did not evolve, as it were, naturally and with the joyful participation of the masses, as Arab nationalist historiography would have us believe. Interestingly, nationalist narratives as they later developed never focused on a founding figure, real or mythical, that claimed or was claimed like Moses, Joshua, William Tell, Kemal Atatürk, or Theodor Herzl as a founding hero of the nation. Rather, Arabism was centered in three motifs: the unifying role of the Arabic language, the myth of the Arab uprising, and the trauma of European betrayal. The latter two only evolved during World War I and the postwar period, and were not yet in place at the turn of the twentieth century. To insist that all nationalisms are constructed makes it all the more imperative to clarify who did the constructing, who was included in the concept of the nation, and on what grounds, against whom the nation defined itself, and what the mobilizing potential of nationalism was for specific parts of the population at specific points in time. To put it differently: How were the boundaries drawn, and by whom? In the Arab, as in most cases (the Jewish example is especially instructive), identifications and loyalties were by no means exclusive. They could shift over time and be combined in various ways. In other words, Arab affiliation could coexist with other ways of identification and solidarity, from family and clan to religious community. This is especially relevant with respect to greater units that could be defined ethnically, religiously, or geographically, and to the combination of reli-

---

[36] Anderson (1991); R. Khalidi (1997). Morris (1987), p. 8, sums up the situation very well: For Arab-Palestinian nationalism, Zionism was at one and the same time a model, a provocation, and a threat.

gious and nonreligious motifs. The modern reform movements are a case in point: Both the Arab cultural renewal (Nahda) of the late nineteenth century and Arab nationalism in the early twentieth century were influenced more strongly by Sunni Islam than is widely thought, since nationalism was long identified with secularism and hence was regarded as a counterweight to religious ties and loyalties. It would be entirely wrong to identify Arab nationalism with secularism and to understand Arab nationalists and Islamic activists as polar opposites rather than as competitors in the political arena.

The Arab national movement of the twentieth century had a number of "forerunners," among them the movement of cultural renewal (Nahda), as well as scattered instances of local resistance against Jewish colonization, physical as well as verbal. Arabism thus crystallized in several variants.[37] Demands ranged from autonomy within the Ottoman Empire to Arab separatism (though the proposed Arab boundaries were as yet ill defined). It would be worth exploring the parallels between Arab renewal and Islamic reform on the one hand and Jewish Enlightenment (Haskala) on the other: Both were primarily concerned with cultural renewal through the revival of language and literature; both were rooted in the religious tradition, which they sought to revive in the present; and both gradually gravitated toward nationalist ideas, whether Arabism or Zionism. Yet for a long time, the Arab movement did not acquire a profile and visibility comparable to what Zionism had achieved so early in its history.

Cultural and political renewal were made possible in large part due to the spread of new media, including the growing availability of newspapers and printed books.[38] In this process an important role was played not only by European immigrants, Christian missionaries, and indigenous monks and monasteries, but also by private Arab citizens, both Muslim and Christian. In 1908, when the Young Turk government briefly adopted liberal policies easing the harsh censorship laws of the Hamidian era, some thirty Arabic-speaking newspapers and periodicals appeared in the later Mandate region, of which six were based in Jerusalem. In regional terms this was not a great number (in Beirut during the same period twelve Arabic newspapers were printed, and in Baghdad a total of sixteen), but by local standards the figure was noteworthy. In 1909 the newspaper *al-Karmil* (Carmel) was founded in Haifa, dedicated to the struggle against Zionism. It was followed in 1911 by *Filas-*

---

[37] For Arab nationalism in general, see R. Khalidi et al. (eds.) (1991); Kayali (1997); Gershoni/Jankowski (eds.) (1997); Nafi (1998), ch. 1; for Palestine, see R. Khalidi (1997), esp. chs. 2 and 5, and Ayyad (1999).

[38] Ayalon (2004); Khalidi (1997), ch. 3.

tin, which was published in Jaffa and quickly developed into one of the most important newspapers in Palestine. *Filastin* (note the title, which predated British occupation) sought to make its readers aware of the danger of Zionism through various means, including the translation of Zionist writings. As in other parts of the Ottoman Empire, especially in Greater Syria itself, a new "public sphere" emerged in the urban centers: It was made up of a new class of men (and some women) with cultural and political interests, educated in Ottoman state schools or European and Arab private schools, both religious and secular, who kept themselves informed through periodicals, newspapers, and books, which owing to improved communications (post, telegraph, and steamship) were distributed more quickly and easily than before. They were able to read in newly established reading rooms and libraries where the collections were not limited to religious literature, as was the case in mosques, churches, synagogues, and the schools linked to them. They would meet in private homes and public cafés, clubs, and theaters. Horizons were expanded in every respect, movement became more free, knowledge more easily attainable, and exchange less burdensome—at least in the cities, and at least for the male part of the population.

The Islamic Salafiyya movement owed much to the reform ideas that so deeply influenced Arab society at the close of the nineteenth century. The Salafiyya took its name from the "pious predecessors" (*al-salaf al-salih*), the first generations of Muslims in Mecca and Medina.[39] Like the Nahda, the Salafiyya was essentially a group of individuals sharing a common cultural outlook, and not a well-defined sociopolitical movement with a clearly defined social base. It too made use of the new means of communication, especially the press, and quite successfully so. If at the time its influence was mainly confined to religious scholars, journalists, and other members of the educated urban elites, it later made an impact on the Islamic as well as parts of the nationalist movement, which referred in one way or another to the Salafiyya.

The situation was different with respect to various currents of Arabism, organized around the turn of the twentieth century into a series of clubs and secret societies that consisted not only of students, writers, and journalists, but also of Arab officers in the Ottoman army. For the most part these clubs could only operate abroad (in addition to Europe, "abroad" also included Egypt). The literary and cultural associations tolerated by the Ottoman authorities were not always clearly distinct from political organizations, which met mostly in secret. Until World War I, local Arab elites and the emerging Arab intelligentsia were staunch supporters of the Ottoman Empire, and the Young Turk Revo-

[39] For Greater Syria, cf. Commins (1990); Tauber (1993); Nafi (1998), ch. 1.

lution of 1908 was at first greeted with great enthusiasm in Palestine and other parts of Syria.[40] The Turkification policies of the Young Turks, however, who fostered the exclusive use of Turkish in state schools (or at least in secondary schools), law courts, and official business, caused grave offense. So did their authoritarian policies, which aimed at strengthening the central government at the expense of local elites, including Arab ones. Hence it will not come as a surprise that the attempted coup staged in April 1909 by conservative followers of Sultan Abdülhamid II found support in Nablus, a place generally regarded as very conservative. The steady loss of Ottoman territory in the Balkans and North Africa (notably present-day Libya) further damaged the reputation of the Young Turks and increased fears of a collapse of the Empire. Yet even after 1909, the Young Turks could still count on supporters in the Arab provinces. In the heavily manipulated elections for the Ottoman Parliament in 1912, most of the "Palestinian" districts went to the Young Turk Committee for Unity and Progress, while in the somewhat freer elections of April 1914 a number of their critics and opponents were victorious.

One of the options discussed in the secret clubs, especially after 1909, involved autonomy within a decentralized Empire; prior to its dissolution, only a tiny minority considered national independence and sovereignty. The group al-Fatat (al-jam'iyya al-'arabiyya al-fatat), founded in 1911 by a group of Arab students in Istanbul who later moved to Beirut, Damascus, and finally Paris, advocated greater autonomy and cultural self-determination within the Ottoman Empire. Among their founders was Awni Abd al-Hadi, from a well-known Nablus family, who in the interwar period would play an important role in regional politics.[41] By contrast, the group al-Ahd (The Covenant), founded in Tripoli in 1913 following the Ottoman-Italian War, appears to have had no members from Palestine. Composed almost exclusively of Arab army officers, al-Ahd proposed a fundamental reform of the Ottoman Empire that would protect its "Islamic values." The Ottoman Decentralization Party (hizb al-la-markaziyya al-idariyya al-'uthmaniyya), formed in December 1912 in Cairo and one of the few political organizations to be able to work openly, did enjoy support in Palestine, where it even had some Jewish members. The number of people organized in these groups remained

[40] Nafi (1998), pp. 66–67, 78; Ayyad (1999), pp. 44ff., 56–57. For the enthusiasm evoked by the Young Turk Revolution, see Mandel (1976), ch. 3; Campos (2005); see also Rashid Ismail Khalidi, "The 1912 Election Campaign in the Cities of Bilad al-Sham." In International Journal of Middle East Studies, 16 (1984): 461–74. For the use of Arabic and Turkish in Ottoman schools under Sultan Abdülhamid II, see Deringil (1998), ch. 4; Somel (2001); Tibawi (1956), pp. 19–20; Khalidi (1997), pp. 46–53.

[41] Nafi (1998), pp. 35–47, 60–61; Tauber (1993).

small. An Arab Congress held in Paris in June 1913 attracted only two dozen participants; in Palestine, it was heavily criticized for not paying sufficient attention to the "Palestinian cause." Cultural associations proved more popular and attractive: The Literary Forum (*al-muntada al-adabi*), founded by Arab students in Istanbul in 1909, appears to have maintained numerous branches in the Arab provinces including Palestine, with a total of up to one thousand members. Its activities were only halted when during World War I its chairman was executed. Still in Istanbul, Arab high school and university students joined to form a society known as the Green Flag (*al-alam al-akhdar*) in 1912.

With the outbreak of World War I, Arabs from the later Palestine Mandate area were thus involved in a number of political and cultural associations from al-Fatat to the Literary Forum. Just like the local Arab press, they criticized the prevailing lack of awareness of the Zionist threat, not only in the Ottoman government, but among the public in general. In Palestine itself, however, Arabism remained a minority position until the collapse of the Ottoman Empire, never spreading widely among the Arab populace.[42] Even declared anti-Zionist associations such as the Society to Combat Zionism (*jam'iyyat mukafahat al-sahyawniyya*), active in Nablus around 1913, could not elicit much support. Only rarely was opposition to Jewish settlement and immigration motivated by nationalist sentiment. In most cases it was based on specific interests. The press, however, already reflected the close connection between Arabist feelings and the critique of Zionist designs. The anti-Zionism manifested here was essentially founded in practical concerns related to politics and economics, with religious arguments playing only a secondary role.

[42] Muslih (1988), p. 67, 96–100. Other authors ascribe more significance to them, such as Nafi (1998), pp. 59ff.; Ayyad (1999), pp. 39ff., 57ff. For contemporary notions of "Palestine," see Porath (1974), pp. 4–9; for early manifestations of Arabism and anti-Zionism, pp. 20–30.

Chapter Six

"A LAND WITHOUT A PEOPLE

FOR A PEOPLE WITHOUT A LAND"?

POPULATION, SETTLEMENT,

AND CULTIVATION, 1800–1914

THE FAMOUS, OR RATHER INFAMOUS, phrase that Palestine was "a land without a people for a people without a land" was a political argument that many took to be a demographic statement (more on this later): Accordingly, Palestine was seen and presented as empty, wretched, and desolate. Now it is true that at the beginning of the twentieth century, Palestine was indeed sparsely populated outside of the interior hill and mountain range. Both written sources and aerial photographs from World War I show as much.[1] But Palestine was no wasteland.

Despite a staggering number of books on the subject, in various European languages, the demography and settlement of Palestine were still widely unknown as Ottoman rule approached its end. In 1883 the German orientalist Martin Hartmann complained about the "confusion which prevails concerning place-names in Palestine that has been visited by so many." He suspected that this resulted from the difficulties of determining the exact location of places and of rendering Arabic place names in foreign language sources, especially in Ottoman Turkish ones.[2] Modern scholars have dealt with the subject extensively and arrived at a much subtler picture. Modern interpretations (or at least the more sophisticated among them) rest on a distinction between the development of settlement and cultivation on the one hand and of population on the other: Although the two are of course linked, they must be considered separately, and not just for specific time periods, but also for specific regions.

---

[1] Dalman (1925) published some of the (beautiful) aerial photos of Bavarian Airborn Division 304 from 1917–18. He also notes the season and the time of day for each photo; see also Gavish (1990). Schölch (1986), p. 59, and Himadeh (ed.) 1938 offer calculations of population density; for Jerusalem, see also Ben-Arieh (1984).

[2] Hartmann (1883), p. 104. References to the literature in Kaiser (1992), pp. 41–69.

The lack of reliable demographic data on Palestine for antiquity and the Islamic era has been much lamented. Even for the Ottoman period there is a problem of sources, for not only are they scarce and inconsistent, but they are also frequently politically biased.[3] Not until 1846 were the first birth and death registers created in Egypt and (other) parts of the Ottoman Empire. Parish and community statistics, registering births, marriages, and deaths, seem to be either unavailable or destroyed, if they were ever compiled in the first place. Palestine confirms the general rule that population data is politically tinged, and that demography is to a large extent "political arithmetic" (Gerber). This holds for every type of sources, whether Ottoman census data or the reports of non-Muslim religious communities and Western observers. The quality and size of the lens, if you will, used for specific purposes is of crucial importance here. Until the end of the nineteenth century, Ottoman surveys included only those subjects of the sultan who were liable to taxation and conscription, and thus took little notice of the subjects and protégés of other nations (often referred to collectively as "Franks"). By contrast, Western travelers, missionaries, and diplomats concentrated on biblical sites and landscapes and non-Muslim urban groups, paying little attention to the predominantly Muslim rural population. Moreover, their reports were mostly limited in scope and, for that reason, tend to give us small samples rather than a comprehensive population estimate. Their methods were at times quite unconventional: Some estimates were based on interviews with local residents and communal leaders, others on the number of houses, or of burials, or of animals butchered in the Islamic Feast of the Sacrifice as counted by the observer. From the 1830s onward, consular reports began to be available, such as the Bowring Report on Syria from 1840 ("Report on the Commercial Statistics of Syria"), which was more systematic and comprehensive than the random samples of Western visitors and travelers, not least because it incorporated official Ottoman data. As far as non-Muslims were concerned, and this is true for Palestine as for the rest of the Middle East, we are better informed about Jews than about Christians, even though the latter were far more numerous.

OTTOMAN SURVEYS: FROM HOUSEHOLD TO INDIVIDUAL

Western authors tended to hold Ottoman officials and their statistics in low regard. As Martin Hartmann wrote in 1883:

---

[3] On demography, see McCarthy (1990); Schmelz (1990); Cuno/Reimer (1997), esp. pp.

The Oriental has no understanding of the value and nature of good statistical material. The Turk in particular may be a great friend of "statistics," but this only means: precisely drawn and (by his standards) good-looking statistical *tables*. What is included in these tables, and whether any of it is correct, is of little concern to him. Turkish officials prepare lists of place-names as ordered by their superiors. But these people possess two qualities in too great a degree for us to take their work seriously: laziness and ignorance, the latter bound up with a presumption of knowledge that makes matters even worse. Their laziness means that when they are assigned a task that they loathe, and for which they can see no use whatsoever, they attempt to get it over with as fast as possible. Their ignorance—no Turkish official, even if he has spent half a lifetime in the Arabic-speaking provinces, has a good grasp of Arabic—allows them to misinterpret Arabic names completely. And their presumption of knowledge entices them all too frequently to correct the misunderstandings on their own.[4]

These remarks, tendentious though they may be, can certainly be applied to other "statisticians" besides the Ottomans. The problems were political as much as technical, and the objective of the survey conditioned its scope and depth. Before the modern era, population surveys mostly served a narrowly defined purpose: Usually it was taxation and military service, less frequently the allocation of privileges, rights, and entitlements. Modern surveys are as a rule more broadly conceived. Until the early nineteenth century, Ottoman surveys, like their European counterparts, mostly served the purposes of taxation, and for that reason were directed toward the taxable segments of the population, first and foremost sedentary adult males. The nonsedentary population, mostly nomads, were for the time being scarcely affected. The techniques and methods employed had a direct impact on the results obtained. Until the requisite bureaucracy was formed, the data were as a rule provided by representatives of those groups that were to be counted, groups that were in many instances defined for tax purposes in the first place, serving as it were as "fiscal units." The leaders of villages, neighborhoods, guilds, or religious communities other than Sunni Muslims, whose room for maneuver varied considerably, were held responsible for the accuracy of the data. Upon the conquest of a new territory, the Ottoman authorities would usually undertake a detailed survey of its

---

148, 203; Courbage/Fargues (1992); Faroqhi et al. (1994), p. 433. For Nablus, cf. Doumani (1994); for Haifa, Yazbak (1998), ch. 3.

[4] Hartmann (1883), p. 103. Nevertheless, he bases his list of towns and villages on the official yearbook (*salname*) for Syria for the year 1871, when Jerusalem still belonged to the province of Damascus.

economic and military potential, both with regard to the land (land registry) and the population (census).

For most of the time, the basic unit of Ottoman surveys was the "household" or "home" (in the Syrian provinces the Ottoman term "*hane*" was commonly used). What they actually counted were the heads of households, who were mostly male, and bachelors. The definition of a household is of obvious interest not only in connection with demography and tax collection, but also for the understanding of family and economic units in general. The Ottoman authorities do not seem to have had a clear definition until the census of 1931 where the *hane* was defined as a "commensual family (i.e., people sharing their meals), including dependents living in the house such as widows and servants."[5] At the same time, official documents such as passports (*mürur tezkeresi*) were given to *individuals* on the basis of the census registry, with the individuals assigned to a household, and this in turn to a neighborhood, village, and/or a religious community. As long as streets were still without names and numbers, the household also served as an address. Thus, the household was an entity formed for the purposes of administration and taxation; it did not necessarily coincide with the biological family, nuclear or extended. In fact, case studies show great regional and social diversity, not only with regard to actual family sizes, but also to styles of living and housing. Household sizes varied widely even within relatively restricted geographic areas. How many people, then, lived in an Ottoman household, on average? Numbers mostly range from five to nine, with five being the multiplication factor most commonly used for Ottoman as well as for premodern European society.

On certain occasions, the Ottoman authorities made surveys of males rather than households. More exactly, they counted men of age fifteen or older capable of using weapons, whose share in the population of preindustrial societies has been estimated at about one third, irrespective of religion, culture, and social organization. The head tax (*firda*) levied by the Egyptians in 1834 provided an earlier example of such a survey counting the number of men capable of bearing arms. The trend toward counting individuals and not just households became stronger during the Tanzimat reforms, once again with the primary aim of recruiting fighting-age males for the army. Until well into the nineteenth century,

[5] Schmelz (1990), pp. 18, 45–54 (the census of 1905 employed the Arabic term *maskan* rather than *hane*); see also Hütteroth (1978), pp. 16, 20. On individuals, households, and families, cf. Doumani (1998) and Doumani (ed.) (2003); Schölch (1986), pp. 42ff.; Gerber (1979), pp. 59–62; Yazbak (1998), pp. 98–102. For broader comparison, see further Duben, Alan/Behar, Cem, *Istanbul Households: Marriage, Family, and Fertility, 1880–1940* (Cambridge 1991); Cuno/Reimer (1997), pp. 196–97; and Peter Burke, *Städtische Kultur in Italien zwischen Hochrenaissance und Barock* (Frankfurt 1996), pp. 39–54.

the urban population was generally exempted from conscription. Egypt under Muhammad Ali made an exception when he gradually expanded military service from the 1830s onward to include both the rural and the urban population.

The Ottoman Empire adopted similar policies. Here, too, recruitment from the subject population was closely linked to military modernization. Although military service was introduced for Muslims in 1838 and expanded in 1855 into compulsory military service for all, Christian and Jews remained de facto excluded from it (as mentioned above, Palestine was exempted from general recruitment until 1862).[6] In place of the recently abolished *jizya*, non-Muslims paid a military substitution tax (*bedel-i askeri*). For this reason, it was in the interest of all groups concerned, Muslims as well as non-Muslims, to provide as low a figure of fighting-age males as possible. Gradually, the purposes of the population surveys were detached from purely military aims to include other duties, such as the construction and maintenance of roads, canals, and bridges, to which every male of working age was liable several days per year. Hence, the link between census registration and obligations placed on the subjects/citizens vis-à-vis the state remained in force. The surveys were not made to define citizen rights vis-à-vis the state. Accordingly, the wish to evade the census remained as strong as ever.

The figures of the Ottoman census of 1831 are generally considered incomplete, unreliable, and low. The same holds for the extrapolated data for 1835, 1838, 1844, and 1857.[7] But from the 1870s onward, the system was thoroughly revised with the assistance of foreign experts, resulting in important procedural changes. The state relied increasingly on its own personnel who cooperated with local committees (highlighting the role played by city councilors and village headmen of whom these committee were composed). Together they drew up three registers: (1) the number of males and, listed separately, their dependents, arranged according to their place of residence (village or neighborhood); (2) the total number of villages and towns, whose residents—at least in the towns—were grouped by religious affiliation; (3) the number of births and deaths as well as changes in the military status of the males (their fitness, etc.). In the last quarter of the nineteenth century, the data were entered into yearbooks (*salname*) that no longer served only military and fiscal purposes, but rather provided general information to the state and the educated public concerning conditions in individual prov-

---

[6] The men were divided into four age groups with differing military duties; cf. Karpat (1978), p. 240; Shaw (1978), p. 328; Zürcher (1999); Schmelz (1990), pp. 15–17.

[7] Schmelz (1990), pp. 29–30; Shaw (1978), p. 327; Karpat (1978), pp. 248–49.

inces and the Empire at large. The report of the Ottoman Council of State (*shura-yi devlet*) on the census of 1881–82 reads as follows:

> Above all, it should be noted that a government's interest in systematic population statistics springs not only from military considerations. It is a great achievement in matters of order and regularity when a government, which cares for justice, the guarantee of property rights, financial stability, as well as urban order and security, knows the exact totals of its population.[8]

The census of 1881 was the first to also count girls and women, who, however, could be represented before the committee by male family members, without their information being systematically verified. According to the new rules, it was now the provincial or city council that was responsible for the accuracy of the data, which could for this purpose add a local non-Muslim representative to its numbers. In conjunction with the census, personal identity cards (*nüfus tezkerezi*) were issued to those registered, which they had to keep on their person under threat of punishment.[9] The lack of uniformity in data collection over time and space constituted its greatest weakness. In the various counts, districts, subdistricts, religious and occupational groups were variously defined. In Ottoman as in other premodern surveys, "craftsman" served as a catch-all category to include anyone who fit nowhere else.[10] Like elsewhere, the data from rural areas were of inferior quality compared to those from the cities. Finally, updating statistics proved to be much more difficult than the initial survey; often, data from different years were combined to produce aggregate data in the statistical totals. Yet for all its flaws, the Ottoman census still offers us the most important source on demographic development in the Empire, Palestine included.

CULTIVATION AND POPULATION

Complaints about unreliable data for the modern period are often paired with notions of a decline since biblical times, first and foremost the time of David and Solomon—for which incidentally we have no verifiable demographic data whatsoever. For the centuries following the Islamic conquest, we have nothing better than rough estimates concerning popu-

---

[8] Cited from Karpat (1978), p. 242. For similar statements made by Muhammad Ali, see Cuno/Reimer (1997), p. 200.

[9] Karpat (1978), p. 253.

[10] Schmelz (1990), pp. 19, 41–44.

lation growth and distribution, broken down primarily according to religion, but no exact numbers.[11] In the early seventh century, Aramaic-speaking ("Nabatean") Christians seem to have made up the majority of the population, especially in Jerusalem and the countryside, while Jews were strongly represented in the remaining cities. The variations recorded thereafter were closely connected with political developments in Palestine and the surrounding region. Wars, disease, and epidemics caused great population loss, although this was partially counteracted by immigration from abroad, especially from the Maghreb. Nonetheless, the population seems to have been in decline until the thirteenth century. The process of Islamization is difficult to trace: We have reports on forced conversions in the late tenth century under the erratic Fatimid caliph al-Hakim bi-amri'llah, who in 1009 also ordered the Church of the Holy Sepulcher in Jerusalem to be destroyed. Yet in the Fatimid period, Christians still made up a majority, especially in the countryside and in Jerusalem itself.

Demographic information improves significantly for the Ottoman period: The Ottoman census of 1596 provided data on population, settlement, and cultivation, which were analyzed by geographers Wolf-Dieter Hütteroth and Kamal Abdulfattah and compared with the maps of the British Palestine Exploration Fund from the years 1871–76. Their conclusions, which admittedly have not gone unchallenged, support the thesis of a decline of settlement and population since the close of the sixteenth century. According to them, Palestine in the sixteenth century was richer, more densely settled and more productive agriculturally than the Ottoman Empire as a whole. For the 1870s, they estimate the total population at 206,290.[12] The majority lived in a network of interlinked villages, with compact settlement zones in the mountains around Jerusalem and Nablus, in Galilee, and in the plains north of Gaza. By contrast, the remaining coastal strip was only thinly settled. There appear to have been no villages registered in the plain of Marj Ibn Amir, the northern coastal plain, and the area around Haifa. In addition, Hütteroth and Abdulfattah identified approximately 1,384 isolated fields (mazra'a) where wheat was the primary crop. The total number of nomads appears to have been small, at least until the immigration of Bedouin clans

---

[11] Gil (1997); Carmel/Schäfer/Ben-Artzi (1990) with the corresponding TAVO maps; also Courbage/Fargues (1992).

[12] Hütteroth/Abdulfattah (1977); Hütteroth (1978). Cohen/Lewis (1978) also start from the assumption of a "population explosion" in the sixteenth century. By contrast, Haim Gerber (1979), p. 77, sets the total number of residents in 1548–49 at 213,660. On the Bedouins who entered the area, see Schölch (1986), p. 166, 171ff. On the early nineteenth century, cf. chapter 3 above.

from the Hijaz, Syria, and Transjordan in the seventeenth and eighteenth centuries. The cities, too, were surprisingly small.

In light of this study, some caution is called for when considering the thesis of decline (advanced by Hütteroth and Abdulfattah themselves), which is based not only on a reduction of cultivated areas ("desertion" or even "desertification") but also of the population ("radical depopulation"), and which was the topic of countless travel reports of the nineteenth and twentieth centuries, some of them cited above. In 1800 the total population of Palestine within the later Mandate borders—an estimated 250,000 to 300,000—was clearly higher than in 1596. Limited immigration under Zahir al-Umar and Ahmad al-Jazzar into northern Palestine and southern Lebanon was partly balanced by losses due to war, excessive taxation, and emigration. In the 1830s, Ibrahim Pasha encouraged immigration from Egypt as well as the entry of individual Bedouin clans, who were for the most part settled in Jaffa and the surrounding villages, in the region of Acre, and in the Jordan and Hula Valleys. At the same time, war, rebellion, natural disasters, and epidemics caused significant population loss.[13] For 1850, McCarthy makes use of corrected Ottoman census data to arrive at a total population of 340,000 (this includes Ottoman subjects only) of which 88 percent (or 300,000) were Muslims and Druze, as opposed to 27,000 Christians and 13,000 Jews.[14] Population growth declined slightly between 1840 and 1857 from 0.6 percent to 0.3 percent, mostly for political reasons: The sources refer to feuds between hostile clans and families in the mountainous region around Nablus, Jerusalem, and Hebron, as well as to Bedouin incursions, which increased when state power was weakened following the withdrawal of Egyptian troops.

Along with the demographic curve, the development of settlement and cultivation merits our attention.[15] The data of the 1870s on which Hütteroth and Abdulfattah rely show a retreat of the settlement boundaries since the sixteenth century, lower population density in almost all regions, a higher share of nomads, but also a growth in the number and size of the cities. Compared to the sixteenth century, there were fewer villages, but these villages were larger in terms of their inhabitants, suggesting a process of *densification* rather than desertion and depopulation. This can be seen most clearly in the lowlands. Around Gaza, half of the villages seem to have disappeared after 1596. With some 20 per-

[13] Shafir (1989), pp. 38–39; Rood (2004), pp. 197ff.; Safi (2004), ch. 1; Lewis (1987), pp. 38–40, and ch. 6.

[14] McCarthy (1990), pp. 10, 12.

[15] Shafir (1989), pp. 37, 40; Gerber (1979), p. 78. On settlement and cultivation in the plain of Marj Ibn Amir, see the Oliphant quote above, chapter 4, p. 85.

cent, the decline was significantly lower in the higher-lying, mountainous regions around Jerusalem and Nablus, as well as in Galilee. In Galilee 275 villages were registered in 1555–67 and only 176 in 1886, but the smaller number of villages had a total of 101,820 residents, as against 30,000 in 1533–39. In the vicinity of Jerusalem, the number of villages may actually have increased.

However, a cautionary note is called for here: A missing entry in the Ottoman register does not necessarily signal that the land in question was not cultivated or used for agricultural purposes. Again, we should recall the shift from the sedentary existence of peasants into a nomadic or seminomadic life that permitted them to withdraw from the control of the state, local landowners, or Bedouin sheikhs. The meaning of the term "*khirba*," on which Hütteroth and Abdulfattah based their desertion thesis, is of crucial importance in this context. A *khirba* is not necessarily an abandoned village but rather land that is either uncultivated, or else unsuited to cultivation and hence of little value.[16] In modern Arabic usage, *khirba* mostly refers to a "secondary" or "satellite" village where the villagers stay only intermittently—a phenomenon especially widespread in the drought-stricken region near Hebron. In fact, a *khirba* can be almost anything, including a ruin. In any case, the large number of *khirbas* identified by Hütteroth and Abdulfattah are no proof of widespread desolation in late Ottoman times.

In the mid-nineteenth century, most villages lay in the hilly and mountainous area from Galilee to Hebron, even though the coastal plains and the plain of Marj Ibn Amir were more fertile. The reasons for this may have been political: A lack of security against Bedouin incursions and heavy taxation are among the best-known factors that impelled cultivators to abandon fertile land. There were only a few settlements on the coast south of Gaza and north of Jaffa. The Jordan and the Hula Valleys were almost completely uninhabited, but in parts cultivated—one more indication of how carefully we must distinguish between settlement, cultivation, and population. In the 1860s, two powerful trends took hold: strong population growth ranging among the highest in the Middle East, and renewed settlement of the plains and the river valleys leading into the interior. Both were related to the Tanzimat reforms, which intensified state control and improved security along the coast and in the hilly regions, pushing back the Bedouins and allowing for the draining of swamps. This in turn helped improve health conditions, at least in the

---

[16] Gerber (1979), pp. 78–80, and Gerber (1987), p. 79; Doumani (1995), pp. 32, 269; Benvenisti (2000), pp. 80–81. Hartmann's definition (1883, p. 111) of *mazra'a* as "hamlet" is misleading. Rather, the *khirba* resembled the *gastina* known from Crusader times.

urban areas. Up until 1875, annual growth rates rose to 1.5 percent (higher than the European average of 1 percent), followed by a slight decline.[17] After the Ottoman reconquest in the 1840s and more particularly after the Crimean War of 1856–58, the authorities settled various refugee groups in Syria and Palestine, including Chechens and Circassians from the Caucasus, and Muslim refugees from Algeria, most of whom moved to Galilee. The main objective of the authorities was to heighten security near the borders and in trouble spots, and to raise tax revenues through expanded cultivation. For 1877, McCarthy computed a total population of 440,850 (Ottoman subjects only), with an unchanged percentage of Muslims at around 88 percent. In the Russo-Turkish War of 1877–78, thousands of Muslim soldiers from Palestine lost their lives. In the same period, however, more Muslim and Christian refugees originating from the Caucasus were settled in northern Palestine, especially Galilee and the Golan Heights, though many of them later left the region. Through immigration, the share of Jews doubled between 1872 and 1880 from around 13,900 to 26,000 (this number includes both Ottoman and foreign citizens). For 1880, McCarthy arrives at a total of 457,000 Ottoman citizens, of whom 87 percent (400,000) were Muslims, 9.4 percent (43,000) were Christians, and a little under 4 percent (15,000) were Jews.[18]

The combined effects of pacification, agrarian expansion, and the end of an epidemic cycle of plague and cholera set off a gradual shift of settlement and population toward the coast, which involved four groups in particular: residents of mountain villages who had already lived in low-lying satellite villages for extended periods of time; nomads and seminomads, above all in the region of Gaza; urban great landowners, who settled farmers and seminomads on the land acquired since 1858, whether as tenant farmers, shepherds, or fieldworkers (the land of the Sursuq family in the plain of Marj Ibn Amir provides the best example here); and finally immigrants, among them German Templars, American Protestants, and European and Middle Eastern Jews. As a result, three regions between the coast and the edge of the hills and mountains were

[17] Schölch (1985), p. 494, and Schölch (1986), pp. 145–46. For the Chechens and Circassians, see Lewis (1987), ch. 6.

[18] McCarthy (1990), pp. 10–11, 13–14; Shafir (1989), p. 39. Using data from the 1880s, Gottheil (1979), pp. 315–16 and 318, arrived at a markedly higher population total for 1875 of 492,675 people. Of this total, he estimated that around a third (140,385) lived in the sixteen towns, and two thirds (333,700) in the 613 villages. According to him the number of Bedouins amounted to 18,590. For 1881–82, Schölch (1985), p. 501, estimated a total population of 460,000 to 470,000. See also Karpat (1978) and Schmelz (1990), esp. note 48.

already densely settled in the 1880s: the southern littoral between Gaza and the later Rehovot, the region around Lydda in the central coastal plain, and the hills west of Hebron.[19]

From the 1880s, the number of non-Muslim immigrants from Europe, especially Jews, increased dramatically.[20] In 1895 around 28,000 Jews lived in Jerusalem, where they now formed a majority. In 1905 their number had risen to 35,000 (14,000 Ottoman citizens and 21,000 foreigners), and by 1914 it had reached 45,000 to decline sharply during World War I. The number of Christians registered in the Ottoman statistics reflects two opposite trends: an influx of Europeans and their increased adoption of Ottoman citizenship countered by outward migration of local Christians. At the outbreak of World War I, approximately 60 percent were Greek Orthodox, 28 to 30 percent Catholic, and the remaining 10 percent belonged to other churches from the Armenian, Georgian, Coptic, and Ethiopian to a variety of Protestant congregations. The Ottoman census of 1914, extrapolated from the data of 1905 in which individuals were counted, and not just households, registers a total of 722,000 residents of Palestine in the borders of the later Mandate.[21] According to McCarthy, the number of Muslims had declined to 83 percent (602,000); the percentage of Christians lay at 11.2 percent (81,000), while the number of Jews with Ottoman citizenship stood at around 5 percent (39,000). If these figures are accurate, the Muslim population had doubled in the period from 1850 to 1914, while the Christian population, who mostly lived in urban areas, had tripled. The number of Jews remains a matter of dispute—a clear sign of just how politically explosive the issue was and still is. The figure of 80,000 to 85,000 often cited in Western accounts (including Jewish authors of the time and later Israeli historians) cannot be reconciled with the Ottoman data even if one takes into account the high ratio of foreign citizens among them. By the end of the war, the British military authorities estimated the number of Jews living in the country at 65,300, which fits more closely with Ottoman and European figures for the prewar period.[22]

[19] Shafir (1989), pp. 39–40; cf. also the Thomson quote above, p. 87.

[20] Schmelz (1990), pp. 23ff., 27–29; McCarthy (1990), pp. 14, 20, and chapter 5 above.

[21] For 1914 Arthur Ruppin arrived at a markedly lower figure of around 689,000 inhabitants; his figures were incorporated into the British census of 1922. By contrast, Schmelz pleaded for a correction upward, since foreigners and Bedouins were not considered in the Ottoman count, immigration and emigration were not sufficiently included, and even the sedentary rural population outside the district (*kaza*) of Jerusalem was perhaps underrated; cf. Schmelz (1990), pp. 17ff., 57–59; Schölch (1985), p. 490; Metzer (1998), chs. 2 and 3; and chapter 8 below.

[22] McCarthy (1990), pp. 17–24; for 1919, cf. pp. 25–28, and *Peel Report* (1937), pp. 156–57; for the Jewish population of Jerusalem, see also Ben-Arieh (1984), pp. 351–63.

Chapter Seven

WORLD WAR I AND THE BRITISH MANDATE

EUROPEAN POLICIES TOWARD PALESTINE and the Ottoman Empire as a whole must be considered in the broader framework of colonial history, rather than of the Islamic or the Arab world, as Middle Eastern historians are inclined to do. The European powers were certainly concerned with the Ottoman Empire and, to a lesser extent, with the Arab territories under its rule (including Palestine), but their first priority was to maintain the European balance of power. This holds for both the nineteenth and early twentieth centuries, contrasting with the view of Middle Eastern nationalists as well as certain Middle Eastern historians who, sadly overestimating their own importance, saw European policy as directed first and foremost against Islam or the Arab (Turkish, Iranian) nation. Regarding European policy toward the Ottoman Empire, three distinct phases can be distinguished: the era of free trade from 1838 to 1878, the partition of Africa (also known as the "scramble for Africa") of the 1880s, and finally the breakup of the Ottoman Empire in World War I. Short of military intervention, European influence and penetration manifested themselves in the domains of trade, finances, and diplomacy as well as in institutions such as the protection of non-Muslim Ottoman subjects and the so-called Capitulations in favor of foreign citizens and protégés, whose importance was strongly felt in Palestine.

BREAKING UP THE OTTOMAN EMPIRE

In what follows the focus will be very much on Great Britain, even though in the nineteenth century Britain was by no means the paramount power in Palestine or Syria at large. Rather, it found itself in competition with France and Russia, and within certain domains even with Prussia, the United States, or the Vatican, who all pursued their separate interests through various means and with various partners, local as well as foreign. Great Britain emerged as the hegemonic power in Palestine only during World War I. Unlike the French, the Russians, or the Vatican, the British had no strong historic ties with Palestine and its people to look back to and rely on.[1] The notion found among Crom-

---

[1] Wasserstein (1978); Laurens (1999), esp. pp. 45–89, Frischwasser-Ra'anan (1976);

well's Puritans in the seventeenth century that they were God's chosen people, and the permission for Jews (who had been expelled from England by King Edward I in 1290) to "return" to England, had no practical effect on policies toward Palestine. The idea of a "restoration of the Jews," advocated in the 1830s and 1840s by the Earl of Shaftesbury and his friends who wished to "restore" the Jewish nation to the land of its fathers, did not translate into practical politics. Not until the mid-nineteenth century did the British try to follow the French, the Russians, and the Vatican in offering legal protection to local non-Muslims to gain influence in the Holy Land. But there were no longer many non-Muslim communities as it were available for British protection: Ever since the seventeenth century, France had claimed the right to protect the Latin (Catholic) Christians within the Ottoman Empire; Russia did the same for the Orthodox Church. By contrast, the British excelled in other areas, whether as travelers, missionaries, scholars, or scientists. The Palestine Exploration Fund founded in 1865 became one of the leading scientific societies of its day. In some ways, it did for Palestine what the French had done after occupying Egypt in 1798 by producing the famous "Description de l'Egypte."

In the nineteenth century, British interests in Palestine were primarily strategic in character. British policies of free trade during the period of 1838 to 1878 rested on the twin pillars of naval control and industrial superiority. The Open-Door Policy was based on the (not entirely peaceful) penetration of existing, formally sovereign entities, and relied for the most part on treaties, many of them unequal. Among them was the free-trade agreement between London and the Sublime Porte concluded in 1838, whose extension to Egypt in 1840 signaled an end to the state monopolies established by Muhammad Ali in the previous decades. The main concern of British imperial policy was to secure the sea and land routes to India, which mostly led through Ottoman or Ottoman-controlled territory. For this reason, the British had a strong interest in upholding the territorial integrity of the Ottoman Empire, at least outside of Europe. In the Greek War of Independence in the 1820s, the British, French, and Russians intervened on the side of the Greek insurgents. The strategic interest in maintaining imperial lines of communication and in the buffer function of the Ottoman Empire between the British and Russian spheres of influence in Asia occasionally led London to side with the Sublime Porte. In 1798 the British intervened against Napoleon Bonaparte as he set out to conquer Egypt and Syria, and they did so again when Muhammad Ali took control of Syria and Palestine from

---

Hopwood (1969). On the restoration of the Jews, see Kobler (1956); Vereté (1992); Shimoni (1995), pp. 60–65; Merkley (1998).

1831 to 1840, threatening the Ottoman Empire from within. Only in Mount Lebanon did the European powers, Britain included, intervene in violent communal strife in an early precedent of the policy of "humanitarian intervention." In 1861 they instituted a new political order under their own supervision, without formally encroaching upon the sultan's sovereignty over this unruly part of his domains.

The basic features of British Middle Eastern policy—known in Britain itself as the Eastern Question, linked to the Great Game in Asia—had already changed in the last quarter of the nineteenth century and were finally abandoned during World War I.[2] From the mid-nineteenth century onward, colonial expansion into Arab territories of the Ottoman Empire intensified. In 1830 France had already occupied Algiers, and in 1839 Great Britain had taken Aden, both very much on the periphery of the Empire and only weakly controlled by Istanbul. Radiating outward from Algiers, the French extended their power into the Algerian interior despite fierce local resistance, while in the rest of North Africa, the Levant, and the Persian Gulf region, European influence remained primarily cultural and economic. In the 1880s, creeping penetration gave way to more forceful intervention and ultimately to military conquest. Following the Russo-Turkish War of 1877–78, the Berlin Congress lent diplomatic recognition to the secession or occupation of former Ottoman territories in the Balkans and the Caucasus. In the course of the "scramble for Africa," the British, French, Spanish, and Italians took possession of North Africa and portions of the eastern Mediterranean region: If Cyprus was "ceded" to Britain by the sultan in 1878, Tunisia and Egypt were taken by force in 1881 and 1882, respectively. In 1911 colonial latecomer Italy annexed Tripolitania and Cyrenaica, later known as Libya. In 1912 northern Morocco was made into a French protectorate, while the southern part (including large parts of present-day Mauritania) fell to Spain, which already controlled the northern enclaves of Ceuta and Melilla. Bilateral und multilateral treaties and conventions among the major European powers confirmed the "partition on the ground."

During World War I, decisions were still made primarily with a view toward the European balance of power, rather than toward local actors and interests. The belligerent powers were thinking "in a larger context," as the division of the spoils of war was later to show. This is not to say that they viewed the region in coherent fashion, or acted according to a preexisting plan. Quite the contrary.

By the end of the war, the Entente powers found themselves with a tangle of agreements, all but one of them secret, which had been made

[2] Brown (1984).

during the war with the aim to influence its further course. These agreements proved to be mutually irreconcilable.[3] They included the Constantinople Agreement of March 1915, which in case of an Entente victory granted Istanbul, the Straits, and their adjoining territories, coasts, and islands to Russia. It was followed in April 1915 by the Treaty of London, which recognized Italian claims to Libya and the Dodecanese Islands off the Turkish coast and also promised Italy parts of southern Anatolia in order to attain its entrance into the war. The Husain-McMahon Correspondence carried out simultaneously in 1915–16 was aimed at potential Arab partners. The Anglo-French Sykes-Picot Agreement of May 1916 was followed in November 1917 by the Balfour Declaration—to say nothing of the various bilateral and multilateral, official and unofficial commitments, pledges, and declarations made by various actors and agencies in the course of war. Promises of independence to local populations, and support of the principle of "government by consent," were given to win local partners and to gain American support against the German Empire and its Ottoman ally. Some resulted from private initiatives that were not even discussed with the respective governments. The urge to seek security in a situation of great insecurity led to dishonest behavior and double games on all sides, including the Arab side. But the partners involved in the game were highly unequal.

Ever since in 1907 oil was discovered in southwestern Iran, a new element was added to the British concern to secure the imperial lines of communication. Its importance for the British Empire rose sharply when in 1912 the British navy converted to oil as fuel, with Iran as the chief supplier.[4] German influence within the Ottoman Empire (manifested among other things in the construction of the Baghdad Railway) was perceived as a direct threat to this strategic resource. When war broke out, the Entente powers were unable to secure the neutrality of the Ottoman Empire, which according to the German-Ottoman alliance treaty of August 1914 was obligated to enter the war on the side of the German Reich. On September 9 Istanbul unilaterally abrogated the Capitulations; on November 2 and 5, the Entente powers declared war on the Ottoman Empire, followed immediately by a British attack on Iraq. Britain annexed Cyprus and transformed Egypt and Kuwait into British protectorates. As early as November 1914, British policy makers spoke openly of partitioning the Ottoman Empire ("The Turk must go!"), though they did not as yet come up with a new map. Despite the reli-

---

[3] Fromkin (1989); Smith (1996), pp. 40–41, 64–65; Laurens (1999), pp. 285–319.
[4] Smith (1996), p. 38; also Helmut Mejcher, *Die Politik und das Öl im Nahen Osten*, 2 vols. (Stuttgart, 1980 and 1990).

gious and ideological value attached to the Holy Land, Palestine attracted little notice in this early phase of the war.

THE HUSAIN-MCMAHON CORRESPONDENCE, 1915–16

The confidential arrangements between the belligerent powers themselves were complicated enough. They were made even more complicated through pledges and commitments to regional actors, and the expectations they raised. Two documents lie at the heart of all later disputes: the secret Husain-McMahon Correspondence of 1915–16, which was not officially published by the British until 1939, and the Balfour Declaration of November 1917. We are still not entirely clear as to the events and motives leading to the exchange of letters between the British high commissioner in Egypt, Sir Henry McMahon, and the sharif of Mecca, Husain b. Ali (1852/53–1931), a prominent member of the Hashemite family, which traced its origins back to the clan of the Prophet, the Banu Hashim. What appears certain is that in 1914, through his son Abdallah, the sharif had already made first contact with the British so as to ascertain their attitude in case of a conflict with his suzerain, the sultan.[5] The British responded in the negative, but following the outbreak of war, they changed course and encouraged the sharif to rebel against the sultan, who had proclaimed a jihad against the enemies of Islam (i.e., Britain and France) in the hope of fomenting unrest in the eastern Mediterranean and the Islamic world at large. In his new function as war secretary, Lord Kitchener, the former British agent and consul general in Egypt, issued instructions to the Oriental secretary in Cairo, Ronald Storrs, which talked among other things of British support for the "Arab nation" and an "Arab caliphate" that Kitchener conceived of as a kind of "Islamic papacy." The letter, though, that Storrs then wrote to Husain in December 1914 appears not to have been

[5] According to Wilson (1987), pp. 22–28, and Shlaim (1990), pp. 18ff., the sharif's second son, Abdallah, at his own initiative, approached Lord Kitchener, the British agent and consul general in Cairo, in February 1914, that is to say well before the outbreak of the war, to ascertain the possibility of British support in case the sultan were to dismiss his father and the Arab tribes were to rebel. Kitchener responded negatively. According to Nafi (1998), pp. 47ff., and 181, note 149, Husain was still not ready to yield to British pressure for an uprising even after the outbreak of war. His attitude changed only when in 1915 the Ottoman governor of Syria, Jamal (Cemal) Pasha, adopted a harsh policy of oppression to crush Arab nationalism; cf. also *Peel Report* (1937), pp. 16–22. Shlaim (1990), p. 19, provides a Hashemite family tree. For additional reading, see Randall Baker, *King Husain and the Kingdom of Hijaz* (Cambridge 1979); Wilson (1987), ch. 2, as well as the contributions of Wilson and Ochsenwald in Khalidi et al. (eds.) (1991).

GUARDIAN of MECCA & MEDINA SINCE 10th C. > TOlERANT
4 SONS: Ali, ABDUllAH, FEiSAl, ZEiD HUSAiN.   ISlAm

ABDUl AZIZ IBN SAUD, RIVAl of THE HUSAINS &   ⇕
WAHHABISM — AUSTERE FORM OF ISlAm,   FANATICISM OF
MARGINAl MiDiEVAliSTS.   NEjD.

cleared with London on all details. In this letter Storrs announced British assistance in attaining Arab independence in exchange for Arab rebellion against the sultan. This in turn led to the so-called Husain-McMahon Correspondence, which was to become the subject of bitter controversy in the interwar period.[6]

In a note written in mid-July 1915, the sharif laid claim to an independent Arab caliphate that would encompass the whole of the Levant, Mesopotamia, and the Arabian Peninsula, excepting only the British presence in Aden. In his reply of August 30, 1915, the British high commissioner sounded somewhat more accommodating than London would have wished: McMahon asserted that the British hoped to bring about "the independence of the Arab countries," and were prepared to recognize a caliphate under "a genuine Arab of the blessed tribe of the Prophet" (i.e., the Hashemites, a requirement that the Ottoman sultan-caliph did not meet). As for the question of borders, McMahon declared that it was still too early to discuss them. For Britain, a pro-British caliphate held its distinct attractions, given the millions of Muslim subjects in India and other parts of the Empire. Not so for France. In the meantime, Husain had sent his son Faisal (later king of Syria and still later of Iraq) to meet with Arab nationalists in Damascus. In his reply of September 9, Husain insisted on an agreement on the proposed boundaries. This put the British under some pressure. On October 24 and December 13, 1915, McMahon sent Husain two letters that have been frequently cited since. Their deliberately vague diction, including confusing remarks on "regions," "districts," and "portions," with a population either "purely Arab" or "not purely Arab," has given rise to conflicting interpretations. They also fueled Arab feelings that they had been deliberately duped, cheated, and betrayed by the British.

The exchange makes one thing clear, though: when referring to "Arab" and "Arabs," Husain was thinking in terms of language and descent, and regarded as "Arab" those regions whose inhabitants, regardless of religious affiliation, were linguistically and ethnically Arabs. By contrast, McMahon clearly equated "Arabs" with "Muslims," and for this reason declared all regions as "not purely Arab" that had a high proportion of (Arab) Christians or Druze. Since sharp controversy later arose over the intended boundaries of the caliphate, McMahon's note of October 24, 1915, deserves to be quoted extensively. Referring to Husain's letter of September 9, the high commissioner wrote:

> It is with great pleasure that I communicate to you on their behalf [the British Government] the following statement which, I am confident, you will receive with satisfaction:

[6] The correspondence was officially published in 1939 under Cmd. 5957. (Unofficial)

The districts of Mersina and Alexandretta and the portions of Syria lying *to the west of the districts of Damascus, Homs, Hama and Aleppo* cannot be said to be purely Arab, and should be excluded from the proposed limits and boundaries. With the above modification, and without prejudice to our existing treaties with Arab chiefs [in the Arabian Peninsula and the Persian Gulf region], we accept these limits and boundaries, and *in regard to those portions of the territories therein in which Great Britain is free to act without detriment to the interests of her ally, France,* I am empowered in the name of the Government of Great Britain to give the following assurances and make the following reply to your letter:

Subject to the above modifications, Great Britain is prepared to recognize and support the independence of the Arabs within the territories included in the limits and boundaries proposed by the Sherif of Mecca. Great Britain will guarantee the Holy Places against all external aggression and will recognize their inviolability.

When the situation admits, Great Britain will give to the Arabs her advice and will assist them to establish what may appear to be the most suitable forms of government in those various regions.

On the other hand, it is understood that the Arabs have decided to seek the advice and guidance of Great Britain only, and that such European Advisers and officials as may be required for the formation of a sound form of administration will be British. . . .

I am convinced that this declaration will assure you beyond all possible doubts of the sympathy of Great Britain towards the aspirations of her traditional friends, the Arabs, and will result in a firm and lasting alliance, the immediate results of which will be the expulsion of the Turks from the Arab countries and the freeing of the Arab peoples from the Turkish yoke which, for so many years, has pressed heavily upon them.[7]

This did nothing to clarify the status of Palestine, which formed no administrative unit within the Ottoman Empire and thus had no well-defined boundaries. When Prime Minister David Lloyd George spoke of Palestine as the land "from Dan to Beersheva," this reflected biblical reminiscences that provided no basis for clear-cut borders to be recognized under international law.[8] McMahon's attempt to exclude the regions "to the west of the districts of Damascus, Homs, Hama and

---

English translation in Antonius (1969), pp. 413–27; see also Kedourie (1976); Kramer (1986), pp. 62–67.

[7] Cited from *Peel Report* (1937), pp. 18–19. The Arabic translation did indeed render "disctrict" as "*wilaya*" (province); cf. Smith (1996), p. 46; but on this point, see Porath (1974), pp. 44–46.

[8] According to Frischwasser-Ra'anan (1976), p. 100, Lloyd George was still unable, in 1919, to locate "Dan" on a map. See also pp. 74–96, and chapter 1, p. 17, above.

Aleppo" from an independent Arab caliphate was in any case unacceptable to the sharif, for if "districts" were used as an equivalent to Ottoman districts (*sanjak*) or provinces (*vilayet*), then the excluded "portions of Syria" would have comprised the entire Syrian Mediterranean coast, including future Lebanon and Palestine. Arab nationalists protested against such an interpretation after the war. In 1922 the colonial secretary, Winston Churchill, stated just as firmly that Palestine had in fact been excluded from McMahon's pledge:

> That letter [McMahon's letter of October 24, 1915] is quoted as conveying the promise to the Sherif of Mecca to recognize and support the independence of the Arabs within the territories proposed by him. But this promise was given subject to a reservation made in the same letter, which excluded from its scope, among other territories, the portions of Syria lying to the west of the district of Damascus. This reservation has always been regarded by His Majesty's Government as covering the vilayet of Beirut and the independent Sanjak of Jerusalem. The whole of Palestine west of the Jordan was thus excluded from Sir H. McMahon's pledge.[9]

This was and remains a matter of dispute. In any case, McMahon as interpreted by Churchill and others suggested a distinction between the lands east and west of the Jordan. In relation to French claims, which Great Britain was obligated to safeguard due to a yet another agreement, these letters were deliberately unclear. What could "Arab independence" amount to if a postwar arrangement for the Near East was to guarantee both French and British interests? McMahon himself defined the aims pursued by the British government in 1915 as follows:

> I do not for one minute go to the length of imagining that the present negotiations will go far to shape the future form of Arabia or to either establish our rights or to bind our hands in that country. . . . What we have to arrive at now is to tempt the Arab people into the right path, detach them from the enemy and bring them on to our side. This on our part is at present largely a matter of words and to succeed we must use persuasive terms and abstain from haggling over conditions.[10]

The sharif, who was never officially informed of the passage just cited, protested in further notes against McMahon's suggestions concerning the territory of the future Arab state, and expressly asserted his claim to the "(purely) Arab" Syrian coastline. The two parties retained their conflicting views, waiting for matters to be settled on the ground—after

---

[9] Cited from *Peel Report* (1937), p. 20. In 1937 McMahon expressed himself along these lines in a letter to the London Times; Frischwasser-Ra'anan (1976), p. 65.

[10] Cited from Kedourie (1976), p. 120.

all, the territories in question were for the most part still unconquered. In June 1916 Husain declared an uprising in the name of Islam against the Ottoman sultan-caliph and the Young Turk government, which he denounced as infidel. This did not end the dispute over the content and objectives of the wartime agreements. In the 1920s and 1930s, Arab nationalists referred to the confidential Husain-McMahon correspondence as a legally binding treaty that rendered the Balfour Declaration null and void.[11] Few were prepared to follow them in this interpretation.

THE SYKES-PICOT AGREEMENT, MAY 1916

Britain's secret arrangements with other allies, especially France, were just as problematic. They included the much-discussed Sykes-Picot Agreement of May 1916, which stood at the end of a series of informal talks about British, French, and Russian interests in the Near East.[12] The British, represented by Sir Mark Sykes, sought to create a British zone of influence from the Mediterranean to the Iranian frontier, but hoped to do so without creating a common border with Russia should the Ottoman Empire, which had previously served as a territorial "buffer," finally crumble. This function was now to be fulfilled by a French zone of influence. For their part, the French initially had ambitions toward the whole of Syria, Lebanon, and Palestine, where they could claim important economic interests as well as long-standing religious and cultural ties. In the course of the negotiations, however, they considerably lowered their demands. The secret agreement with the British, with its complicated and vague distinction between areas of "direct and indirect control," "exclusive spheres of influence," and "independence" already harbored the seed of future conflicts. By the terms of the agreement, central and southern Iraq would fall to the British, while the Syrian coastline and portions of southern Anatolia (Cilicia) would go to the French. Meanwhile, the greater part of Palestine and its holy sites, up to the line running between Gaza and the Dead Sea, would be subject to international administration to be jointly determined by Britain, France, and Russia. Haifa Bay with the cities of Haifa and Acre would remain a British enclave with special legal status, and Haifa would be connected

---

[11] Porath (1974), pp. 44–48, 52. Husain later refused to recognize the mandate system in which his sons Abdallah and Faisal were so prominently engaged; Nafi (1998), p. 147.

[12] See Frischwasser-Ra'anan (1976), pp. 58–96; Smith (1996), pp. 47–55; Laurens (1999), pp. 285–319. Unofficial English translation in Antonius (1965), pp. 428–30. For the British view, see *Peel Report* (1937), pp. 20–21. The secret agreement was published by the new Russian government after the October Revolution. For Arab reactions, see also Nafi (1998), pp. 53–54.

to Baghdad via railway.[13] The latter provision underscored Palestine's strategic importance as the terminus of a future oil pipeline from Iraq, where British troops were swiftly advancing following initial setbacks.

The British were fully aware of the potential conflict between this agreement and their commitments to the sharif. Not only did they intend to keep the Syrian and southern Anatolian coastline under European control, but the ("independent") Arab state that they promised Husain was to accommodate two European spheres of influence, or interest: a French zone "A" (also known as the blue zone), comprising the area from the line of Aleppo, Hama, Homs, and Damascus (and including these cities) to the border of Iran, with Mosul as its center in northern Iraq, and a British zone "B" (also known as the red zone) that was to reach from the Sinai to the border of a British-dominated southern and central Iraq, centered in Kirkuk. Thus, only those parts of the Arabian Peninsula controlled neither by local chiefs and princes nor by the British were marked for independent status under Hashemite rule. While the British did recognize that their pledges to the Arabs were at odds with French claims, and vice versa, they hoped that the British military would ultimately decide the matter to their advantage. However, during World War I, the various commitments drifted even further apart, as the Entente powers made ever more generous promises to the Arabs while at the same time offering the Zionists the prospect of Palestine as a national home of the Jewish people.

THE BALFOUR DECLARATION, NOVEMBER 1917

British interest in Palestine grew more pronounced in 1917. In December 1916 the Conservative government of Herbert Asquith was overthrown and replaced by a cabinet under Prime Minister David Lloyd George, who had close connections with Chaim Weizmann, a prominent representative of the Zionist Organization. The change of cabinet also enhanced the status of Sir Mark Sykes, who was able to act quite independently even as he consulted with Lloyd George. A series of new developments made the British rethink their earlier plans. The appeal by U.S. President Woodrow Wilson for a "peace without victory" called into question the wartime arrangements of the Entente powers. The Russian ("February") Revolution of March 1917 threatened to weaken the anti-German front, while in the Middle Eastern theater Baghdad was conquered by the British in the same month. At a different level, there were disconcerting rumors of an imminent German declaration in sup-

---

[13] See Biger (2004), pp. 43–46; Stoyanovsky (1928), pp. 8ff. On the railway lines more generally, see Kark (1990) and Frischwasser-Ra'anan (1976), pp. 45–57.

port of Zionism. In Great Britain itself, Zionism could count on the sympathies of influential circles that saw Palestine as the land of the Bible and homeland of the Jews. While some still upheld the idea of a "restoration of the Jews," the majority thought in terms of a "national rebirth" of the Jewish people in Palestine. In the nineteenth century, well-known writers such as George Eliot had already expressed their support for Zionism. At the same time, the prospect of Jewish self-government in Palestine provided a useful screen for British control of the region—which according to the Sykes-Picot Agreement was to be for the most part placed under international administration without need of formal annexation. In June 1917 the French government signaled its acquiescence to Zionist aims. Interestingly, the main objections came from Lord Curzon, an influential member of the War Cabinet, and Sir Edwin Montagu, the incumbent minister of munitions and only Jewish cabinet member, who feared for the integration of the Jews in Europe and elsewhere if they were recognized as a people with national rights in Palestine (rather than Britain, France, or Italy). For the same reason, the Board of Deputies of British Jews, the official representative of British Jewry, openly declared itself against the Zionist aim to obtain a charter. Lengthy deliberations resulted in a declaration whose primary audience were the Jewish communities in the United States, Russia, and the German Reich if not world Jewry at large. It was hoped that they would pressure their own governments in the interests of the Entente.

The declaration was not published as an official government paper but as a letter from the British foreign minister, Lord Arthur Balfour, to the honorary president of the Zionist Federation of Great Britain and Ireland, Lionel Walter Rothschild, second Baron Rothschild. The text had previously been submitted to President Wilson who had voiced no objection. The Balfour Declaration of November 2, 1917, published in the British press on November 9, ran as follows:

Dear Lord Rothschild,

I have much pleasure in conveying to you, on behalf of His Majesty's Government, the following declaration of sympathy with Jewish Zionist aspirations which has been submitted to, and approved by, the Cabinet. "His Majesty's Government view with favour the establishment in Palestine of a national home for the Jewish people, and will use their best endeavours to facilitate the achievement of this object, it being clearly understood that nothing shall be done which may prejudice the civil and religious rights of existing non-Jewish communities in Palestine, or the rights and political status enjoyed by Jews in any other country."

I should be grateful if you would bring this declaration to the knowledge of the Zionist Federation.[14]

---

[14] Cited from *Peel Report* (1937), p. 22. For background information, see L. Stein

The letter was phrased ever so carefully. Note the rights explicitly stated and those not mentioned of the population groups concerned; the rights of the Jewish people "in" Palestine, not to the whole of Palestine; the adoption of the term "national home," first mentioned at the First Zionist Congress in 1897 and unknown in international law, which allowed for far-reaching interpretations without imposing any specific obligations on the British.[15] Most important, the letter speaks of a "Jewish people," but refers to the Arab Muslims, Christians, and Druze in Palestine as "non-Jewish communities," a mere residual group formed on the basis of this difference. The Declaration was motivated by the consideration of who would be most useful to British interests under the given circumstances. At the time, this seemed to be the Jews—and not just the Zionist Jews. For this reason, they were offered the chance to make their dream of a national home (or state?) come true, starting from modest beginnings until, it was thought, they would form a demographic majority in the country and gradually make it their own. In 1937 Lloyd George addressed the members of the Peel Commission along these lines:

> The idea was, and this was the interpretation put upon it at the time, that a Jewish State was not to be set up immediately by the Peace Treaty without reference to the wishes of the majority of the inhabitants. On the other hand, it was contemplated that when the time arrived for according representative institutions to Palestine, if the Jews had meanwhile responded to

---

(1961); Frischwasser-Ra'anan (1976), pp. 74–96; also Segev (2000), ch. 2. Mendes-Flohr/Reinharz (eds.) (1995), pp. 580–81, publish an anti-Zionist letter to the *London Times*, sent in May 1917 by the presidents of the Board of Deputies of British Jews and the Anglo-Jewish Association in an attempt to prevent official British support for political Zionism. In it, they stated that

> Emancipated Jews in this country regard themselves primarily as a religious community, and they have always based their claims to political equality with their fellow-citizens of other creeds on this assumption and on its corollary—that they have no separate national aspirations in a political sense.

On Wilson and the American philo-Semitic tradition, cf. Merkley (1998), chs. 7–10, esp. pp. 87–94.

[15] Stoyanovsky (1928), pp. 70–82. According to him (p. 80), the Jewish people has a legal claim *to* Palestine, whereas its Arab inhabitants merely enjoy (certain) rights *within* Palestine. This interpretation is problematic insofar as the Balfour Declaration (as well as the later Mandate treaty) speaks explicitly of a Jewish national home *in* Palestine, not of a Jewish right *to* (the whole of) Palestine. Yet it illustrates that from the very beginning, the Jewish people, that is to say Jews all over the world, were addressed, and not just the Jews living in Palestine at the time. The British, too, did not distinguish between Jews and Zionists. The concept of a "national home" was also brought up in the context of the so-called Armenian question during debates in the League of Nations in 1921. See also Segev (2000), ch. 2, esp. p. 46.

the opportunity afforded them by the idea of a national home and had become a definite majority of the inhabitants, then Palestine would thus become a Jewish Commonwealth.[16]

Sharif Husain, whose knowledge of the Balfour Declaration was as vague as it had been with respect to the Sykes-Picot Agreement, was appeased with incorrect information. Chaim Weizmann joined in this effort when in April 1918 he traveled to Palestine and Syria at the head of a Zionist Commission hoping to counter local fears over the intentions of the Entente and the Zionist movement. In Palestine itself, the Balfour Declaration was not officially published until 1920, though it had already been made known through excerpts in the Egyptian press.[17] The immediate gain was minimal. The Balfour Declaration was hailed by many Jews in Russia, but was eclipsed by news of the October Revolution. The new Bolshevik government quickly ended Russian participation in the war. And when the United States sent troops to Europe in greater numbers in January 1918, they did not do so because of Jewish pressure.

THE CONQUEST OF PALESTINE

When at the outbreak of World War I Sultan Mehmed V Reshad proclaimed a jihad against the Entente powers, he received pledges of loyalty from crowds in Nablus, Jerusalem, and a number of other towns. For the most part, the Jews living in Palestine also remained loyal. Many actually took Ottoman citizenship when the Sublime Porte abrogated the Capitulations and began to expel the citizens of enemy states, affecting above all Russian and American Jews. Thousands more left the country because of poverty and fear of harassment. The Arab population remained loyal to the sultan despite harsh repression under the new Ottoman military governor Cemal (Jamal) Pasha and the Arab revolt of 1916, which even in Syria received only limited support from Arab reformers and nationalists.[18] Strict press censorship prevented any form of public critique. Between August 1915 and May 1916, dozens of actual

[16] Cited from *Peel Report* (1937), p. 24.

[17] Khalidi et al. (eds.) (1991), pp. 179, and 319–20, note 31; Kedourie (1976), chs. 5 and 6; Smith (1996), pp. 56–57.

[18] Nafi (1998), pp. 47ff., 80–82; Muslih (1988), pp. 89ff., 97–98; Porath (1974), pp. 70ff.; Kramer (1986), ch. 5, esp. p. 55. Enderwitz (2002), pp. 99–102, points to lacking identification with Ottoman rule; Ayyad (1999), pp. 59–60, claims great enthusiasm for the Arab cause. For a pro-British espionage Jewish ring known as Nili, which was discovered by the Ottoman authorities in 1917, see the popular account by Anita Engle, *The Nili Spies* (London 1959).

and presumed Arab nationalists were arrested, tortured, and publicly
executed in Damascus and Beirut, many others were deported; in Jerusalem, twelve men were hanged. Nablus was apparently untouched by any
of this. A good number of young men enlisted at recruitment bureaus
set up by the British in 1917 for the army of the sharif. But the Arab
revolt also met with critique and opposition, which focused on the sharif's alliance with the British. Arab nationalism was still far from having
any mass base of support. And yet in the postwar era, it was to become
a broad movement that channeled a variety of aspirations and interests
into national resistance against the British, the French, and the Zionists.

The British conquest of Syria and Palestine had little to do with the
Balfour Declaration. Rather, it reflected strategic considerations that
made Syria and Palestine an important land bridge between Egypt, Mesopotamia, and Anatolia. As early as September 1914, the Ottomans had
sent significant troops to Palestine, commanded by Cemal Pasha, prominent member of the Young Turk movement and head of the Fourth
Army based in Damascus, and reinforced by German and Austrian units.
In 1917 the Anglo-Egyptian Expeditionary Force under General Ed-
mund Allenby conquered the Sinai, Negev, and southern Palestine up to
Gaza. Ottoman resistance was strong, and both sides suffered heavy
losses. The British took Jaffa on November 16, and Jerusalem on December 9.[19] Two days later, on December 11, 1917, Allenby entered the
Old City of Jerusalem on foot to proclaim an allied military government.
There were reasons for his modest behavior: Kaiser Wilhelm II, during
his visit to the Holy Land in 1898, rode on horseback through Jaffa
Gate, which had been widened for this purpose. (In all fairness, the kaiser had protested against this measure and later climbed down from his
horse in order to show his respect to the holy sites.) Allenby came as a
conqueror, but without imperial gestures.[20]

The Anglo-Egyptian Expeditionary Force was made up of troops from
the British Empire, including Indians, Australians, and New Zealanders,
as well as large numbers of Egyptians drafted into the British army,
and small French and Italian contingents. Local Arab forces played no
significant role in the conquest of Palestine west of the Jordan, but they
joined the troops of the Arab revolt when they took Aqaba and what
was later to become Transjordan. Unlike the later conquest of Damascus, Arab troops and symbols were consciously excluded when Allenby

[19] Laurens (1999), pp. 290–319; Muslih (1988), pp. 96–100; on the Anglo-Egyptian
Expeditionary Force, see also Segev (2000), pp. 24–27, 43, 74–76; for more detail, see A.
P. Wavell, *The Palestine Campaigns* (London 1928) and Anthony Bruce, *The Last Cru-
sade: The Palestine Campaign in the First World War* (London 2002).

[20] Carmel/Eisler (1999), p. 51. Yet he entered on horseback. See also Landau (1979),
pp. 42–43; Sherman (1997), pp. 35–36.

entered Jerusalem. The Jewish Battalions (also known as the Jewish Brigade or Legion), which had been mainly recruited in Britain and America by Vladimir (Ze'ev) Jabotinsky to assist the allied war effort, also tried to enlist local Jews. However, they were only employed in Palestine after Jerusalem had been taken and saw little military action. (In Hebrew, they are referred to as *Hebrew* rather than Jewish Battalions, not to be confused with the Zion Mule Corps, which had been dissolved in June 1916 following the Gallipoli campaign, and which is also often referred to as the Jewish Legion.) Northern Palestine, Lebanon, and Syria remained under Ottoman control until the fall of 1918. Haifa fell on September 23, Damascus on October 1, Beirut shortly after; Aleppo was occupied on October 25. On October 30, 1918, the Ottoman government signed the Armistice of Mudros, ending the war in the Levant. Conditions in Syria, Lebanon, and Palestine were bordering on the catastrophic, particularly for all those dependent on outside help.

In the meantime, General Allenby made new and extensive promises to the local population. In the so-called Declaration to the Seven (a group of seven Syrian nationalist leaders residing in Cairo who in April 1918 had responded to news of the Sykes-Picot Agreement with the declaration of Arab self-determination), issued in Cairo in June 1918, the British confirmed the principle of "government by consent." The Anglo-French declaration of November 7, 1918, addressed to the "peoples" and "populations" of Syria and Iraq after the Ottoman surrender, clearly contradicted the agreements they themselves had made. According to this document, France and Great Britain aimed at

> the complete and definite emancipation of the peoples so long oppressed by the Turks, and the establishment of National Governments and administrations deriving their authority from the initiative and free choice of the indigenous populations. In order to carry out these intentions France and Great Britain are at one in encouraging and assisting the establishment of indigenous Governments and administrations in Syria and Mesopotamia. . . . Far from wishing to impose on the populations of these regions particular institutions, they [France and Britain] are only concerned to secure by their support and by adequate assistance the regular working of Governments and administrations freely chosen by the populations themselves.[21]

Arab hopes of "complete liberation" and of freely elected government therefore did not rest on the elusive Husain-McMahon Correspondence alone. Even so, the future of Palestine was never unambiguously ad-

---

[21] Cited from *Peel Report* (1937), p. 25. Stoyanovsky (1928), p. 12, contains a slightly different wording. See also Porath (1974), pp. 42ff.; Smith (1996), p. 58; Gelvin (1998), pp. 68–69, 95, 154–55; Nafi (1998), p. 143.

dressed in the various British and French declarations. The same is true for President Wilson's famous "Fourteen Points," which in January 1918 proclaimed the principle of the right of self-determination. With regard to the "nationalities" under Ottoman rule (Arabs, Kurds, Armenians, Jews?), Wilson used guarded language, speaking somewhat vaguely of "security" and "autonomous development," not of sovereignty:

> The Turkish portions of the present Ottoman Empire should be assured a secure sovereignty, but the other nationalities which are now under Turkish rule should be assured an undoubted security of life and an absolutely unmolested opportunity of autonomous development.[22]

PALESTINE UNDER ALLIED MILITARY GOVERNMENT, 1918–20

Through a slow and meandering process, a new regional order began to take shape under the auspices of the mandate system, which was formally effected in 1923. No justice will be done to the historical situation if we forget how indeterminate the situation was by war's end. The British and French had no ready plans for further action, and no concrete ideas about how to implement their contradictory agreements. On the Arab side, there was scarcely anyone with well-defined conceptions, either. Only the Zionists had clearer ideas of their larger objective, yet even Zionist plans could not be carried out immediately.

For the Entente powers, their first priority was to establish firm control over the occupied areas in the face of international competition and local resistance. Wartime arrangements were soon revised: The military governments they formed in Syria, Lebanon, Palestine, and Iraq, did not fully coincide with the territorial entities sketched in the Sykes-Picot Agreement. The British and French competed over Palestine, and the Zionists too made far-reaching territorial claims. Even before the opening of the Paris Peace Conference in 1919, Chaim Weizmann delivered a memorandum to the British containing suggestions as to the boundaries of a future British mandate. According to this document, the mandate would stretch beyond Galilee and the northern mountain range ("Samaria") into Lebanon as far as the Litani River, and would also include the Syrian wheat-growing region of Hawran, the sources of the Jordan River ("Dan"), and its eastern bank ("Gilead") as far as the Hijaz Railway. In the south it would include the Sinai up to the line between Aqaba and al-Arish. The proposed boundaries took into ac-

---

[22] Cited from *Peel Report* (1937), p. 25.

count economic assets such as water supplies, vital to the success of an eventual Jewish national home. Yet they were utterly at variance with existing agreements among the British, the French, and the sharif.[23]

The delineation of the occupation zones was therefore not a given, but resulted from lengthy negotiations between London and Paris. By and large they went in favor of the British, who did in fact occupy the territories in question. Contrary to long-standing claims in Western and Zionist literature, the geographical concept of "Palestine" (*filastin*) had not been altogether forgotten among the local population. There are strong indications that at least in the seventeenth century, Palestine was locally known and employed. Eighteenth- and nineteenth-century Ottoman court records used the term "Palestine" to denote the coastal plains. One of the best-known Arab journals (*Filastin*), founded in 1911, bore its name.[24] But under British rule "geohistoric entities" with their distinct socioeconomic features and sociopolitical elites were joined to form the political unit of Palestine, which corresponded closely to the three Ottoman *sanjaks* of Jerusalem, Balqa (Nablus), and Acre. Previously linked only loosely, they were united by the British without the consent or even advance knowledge of the local population. And yet, like other colonial creations in the Middle East, this proved to be a lasting arrangement.

The personnel of the Occupied Enemy Territory Administration (OETA), South, was exclusively British and began work in late 1917. It was hastily thrown together and most of its members lacked administrative experience. In 1937 a witness recalled the situation as follows:

> It is important to remember how this Administration grew up in Palestine. It was started by complete amateurs, led by amateurs. There was practically nobody in the Administration who had ever worked in an administration. . . . It was the blind leading the blind, and that is what this country suffered from for years.[25]

The tasks of military government were not confined to security and administrative issues. It was more a matter of relief and rehabilitation measures designed to improve the living conditions of the population, who had suffered greatly during the war.[26] The recruitment of fighting-

---

[23] Biger (2004), pp. 58–79; Frischwasser-Ra'anan (1976), pp. 84–140. For Britain, see Wasserstein (1978), pp. 18ff.; Ingrams (1972), ch. 4; Storrs (1945).

[24] Porath (1974), pp. 4–9; Khalidi (1997), pp. 58–59; Gerber (1998), and chapters 1 and 3 above.

[25] Cited from *Peel Report* (1937), p. 160. See also pp. 172ff.; *Survey of Palestine* (1946), pp. 15–17; Wasserstein (1978), pp. 1–2, 15–20; Biger (2004), pp. 51–58.

[26] Divine (1994), pp. 169–90. For population figures, see *Peel Report* (1937), p. 156, and McCarthy (1990), pp. 19–24. For Jewish suffering, see Segev (2000), ch. 3; Pappé

age men, the confiscation of animals, food, fodder, tools, vehicles, fuel, and motors, the chopping down of olive and fruit trees for firewood (delivery of coal was cut off during the war), the cessation of the import trade including food and other donations for the highly dependent Jewish Yishuv, plunder, and other forms of destruction had all caused serious hardship. Although the Ottoman government announced a moratorium on debt, the needs of the military drove many peasants into indebtedness and financial ruin. In parts of Syria and Lebanon, the allied sea blockade, combined with severe supply problems (in part conditioned by politics), had led to famine, aggravated by disease. In Palestine politically suspicious individuals and their dependents—both Arabs and Jews—had either fled or been deported. The Jewish population of Tel Aviv had been expelled. In light of the British advance, Gaza had been evacuated. To make matters worse, the country was struck in 1915 and 1916 by devastating locust plagues. All told, about 6 percent of the inhabitants of the later Mandate area of Palestine are thought to have perished during the war years. At the end of March 1919, the military authorities gave a population estimate of 648,000 people, among them 551,000 Muslims, 65,300 Jews, 62,500 Christians, and 5,050 "Others" (Druze, Armenians, Baha'is, and others). It appears that the hardships of war, though somewhat alleviated by American aid, had significantly reduced the number of Jews. According to British reports, around 15 percent of the residents of Jerusalem depended on external assistance in 1918. But they were not the only ones to have suffered: The ruthlessness of the Ottoman military had aggravated the situation of the population as a whole, at least of its poorer segments, hitting women and children especially hard. Known as *safarbarlik* (wartime mobilization), it left negative memories of "the Turks" in the minds of the local populace. Orientalist stereotypes of "Ottoman decadence" and "Oriental despotism" later served to reinforce this negative image.

The retreating Ottoman troops had seized not only provisions and supplies, but also records, documents, and fiscal logs. Under these conditions, it was of vital concern to the British to restore peace and order, not least with the aim of reducing the costs of occupation: The territories of the Empire, if possible, were to be self-supporting.[27] The practical

---

(2004), p. 69. Arabic narrative sources may merit closer attention; cf. Enderwitz (2002), pp. 99–102, 235–37. For a lively account of a Swiss German medical doctor, see Gerda Sdun-Fallscheer (who spent 1915–17 in Nablus, Jerusalem, and Aleppo), *Jahre des Lebens* (Stuttgart 1989), pp. 470–545. For Syria and Lebanon, see Schatkowski Schilcher (1992); Thompson (2000), pp. 19–38; al-Qattan (2004). For wider comparison, see Farschid/ Kropp/Dähne (eds.) (2006).

[27] K. Stein (1984), pp. 31, 146. The Mandate administration even earned surpluses dur-

assistance provided by the military administration was much appreciated by the local population since the British distributed food and allocated credit to the peasants for the purchase of livestock, seed, and tools.[28] But this did not make them forget politics altogether. While the British understood their task primarily in administrative terms, they were soon confronted with adverse political developments and strong demands that focused on three issues: political participation and self-determination, Jewish immigration, and Jewish land purchases. On each of these issues, Zionists and Arabs took opposite stands. Further, British military administrators in Palestine and their superiors in London often differed in their assessment of local conditions and the policies to be adopted. Many local British officials saw the Balfour Declaration as the main obstacle to establishing law and order. In London, by contrast, it was seen by many as the very foundation of British presence in the country.

Faced with conflicting demands and expectations, the military administration quickly lost credibility. Many Jews viewed it as pro-Arab, and some even as anti-Semitic, or at any rate anti-Zionist. That genuine neutrality could hardly be preserved under these circumstances was echoed in the Peel Report of 1937, charged with determining the background of Arab-Jewish tensions:

> There was a constant tug-of-war and the Government was accused by both sides of being either pro-Arab or pro-Jew, and it has developed into the feeling that if one is pro-Arab one must necessarily be anti-Jew, and *vice versa*, which is not necessary at all.[29]

To secure law and order, the authorities at first did not allow the Zionists to engage in activities that might provoke Arab protests, such as singing the Zionist anthem "Hatikvah" or displaying national flags and symbols in public. Above all, the authorities initially halted Jewish immigration as well as any kind of land transaction, mostly because the relevant land records had disappeared, making it next to impossible to establish legal claims and titles. Jews were especially embittered by the decision not to allow the Jewish Brigade to protect Jewish institutions and interests, which some viewed as yet another sign of anti-Semitism among British officials. This fed into the sense of "betrayal," a betrayal

---

ing the interwar period, although in view of looming unrest they were quickly eaten up by military and security expenditures.

[28] K. Stein (1984), pp. 29, 40; also Munayyir (1997), pp. 11ff.

[29] Cited from *Peel Report* (1937), p. 163. For what follows, see pp. 153–72; also Wasserstein (1978), pp. 22ff., 34ff., 42, 67–68, and ch. 7; Porath (1974), pp. 124–26. On land transactions, see K. Stein (1984), pp. 23–24, 33, and 39ff.

of which the British were accused by all sides. Here it was the Zionists, with their expectations that Jewish self-rule would be installed immediately upon British entry into Palestine, who saw themselves deceived and betrayed.

As might be expected, the Jews were not the only ones to be critical of the British and dissatisfied with their performance. The Arabs, too, had placed some hopes in the new rulers. A memorandum sent by a newly formed Muslim-Christian Association from Jaffa in the autumn of 1918 reflects the prevalent mood immediately after the end of the war:

> Palestine is Arab, its language is Arabic, we want to see this formally recognized. It was Great Britain that rescued us from Turkish tyranny and we do not believe that it will deliver us into the claws of the Jews. We ask for fairness and justice. We ask that it protect our rights and not decide the future of Palestine without asking our opinion.[30]

They, too, were to be sorely disappointed. Like other groups among the Palestinian population, the Arab elite grew progressively disillusioned, leading to greater ambivalence and mistrust of Western powers, and of Britain in particular. And yet, the hope that outsiders might establish justice where one's own powers seemed unable to do so has been preserved in some form to the present day, although it has shifted, under changed political conditions, from the British to the Americans and to a more vaguely defined world opinion.

THE SYRIAN OPTION

After the fall of the Ottoman Empire, Arab nationalism was left as the only political option available to the Arabs in Palestine, even if an unattractive option for many. Following the conquest of Syria by the Anglo-Egyptian Expeditionary Force and troops of the Arab Revolt, an independent Arab government was proclaimed in Damascus on October 5, 1918, under Emir Faisal, third son of the sharif of Mecca, who in October 1916 had himself proclaimed king of the Arabs (a title subsequently toned down to king of the Hijaz). Faisal's government initially raised great hopes and some enthusiasm in Palestine, as Palestinian Arabs assumed various important posts in his government and administration. This gave a fresh impetus to the "Syrian solution," in which Palestine, or rather Southern Syria, would form an integral part of the greater Syrian land (*bilad al-sham*).[31] In June 1919 Palestinian delegates at-

---

[30] Citation taken from Ayyad (1999), p. 76; see also al-Hut (ed.) (1979), pp. 1–11.
[31] Porath (1974), ch. 2; Muslih (1988), pp. 119ff., 147–54, 200–202; al-Hut (1981),

tended a General Syrian Congress in Damascus that spoke out against Zionism in general and the Balfour Declaration in particular.

Yet sympathies with the creation of a Greater Syria were not as firmly rooted in Arab collective consciousness as Arab nationalists would have us believe, especially in later years. The notion that in World War I the Western powers had "dismembered" the Arab nation is mistaken, for there was as yet no such body to be dismembered; it only developed later. Even so, regions that previously had been only loosely connected were joined together and others were torn asunder. To the older generation of Arab notables, with their lives and outlook shaped by the Ottoman experience, a focus on Palestine or an even smaller area seemed more appealing, especially since it offered the prospect of evading Syrian dominance, or rather dominance of the Syrian urban notables. It was different for the younger generation, who were as a rule less attached to the Ottoman past.[32] To the extent that Arab nationalists opted in favor of the Syrian solution, they did so for political reasons and not because it came naturally to them. In Palestine as elsewhere, local loyalties and interests generally took precedence over a broader Arab identification, especially since Arab nationalism came up from the very beginning against British and French imperialism. The idea of Arab unity ultimately failed not only because of European machinations, but also because of the particular aims and interests of the Arabs themselves.

The Syrian option quickly lost its attractiveness, and not only through external pressure. In Syria itself, the Arab Government proved unable to remedy the catastrophic conditions created by the war and aggravated by local resistance to the new rulers, who although Arab had only weak roots in Syria itself.[33] Faisal, who spent months in Europe negotiating over the creation of an Arab state in the Arabian Peninsula and Greater Syria, was never able to attain full control over Syria and Lebanon. Wartime hunger and suffering were hardly overcome. The precarious state of supply was worsened through the steady influx of refugees from other parts of the former Ottoman Empire. Strikes, demonstrations, and protests revealed how brittle the legitimacy and authority of the new national leadership really were. Once again, the issue of military service turned out to be especially controversial; in vain did Faisal's government try to implement compulsory service, even for the eminently national goal of defending Syria's independence in the face of French aggression.

---

pp. 116–19. In Syria, the Palestinians were viewed as "outsiders" (*ghuraba'*), Muslih (1988), pp. 152–53; also Nafi (1998), pp. 140–41.

[32] Muslih (1988), pp. 103ff., 152–54, 174ff., 201ff., 214. Cf. also chapter 5 above.

[33] Muslih (1988), pp. 115ff.; Gelvin (1998), pp. 25ff., 36ff., 44ff., 141.

The Faisal-Weizmann Agreement

At the same time, Faisal came under attack in connection with Palestine. The so-called Faisal-Weizmann Agreement of January 3, 1919, produced violent reactions not only among the Palestinians living in Damascus, but also in Palestine itself. A protest note was sent from Nablus, reminding Faisal of the Arab view of the situation.[34] The agreement had been prepared in June 1918 during a meeting with Chaim Weizmann near Aqaba. Speaking in the name of the Arab Kingdom (or rather of his father Husain b. Ali, since he was hardly qualified to speak for the Arabs of Palestine), Faisal made wide-ranging promises to Chaim Weizmann as the representative of the Zionist Organization relating to the Arab state and independent Palestine, both still to be created. Among other things, he promised the closest possible collaboration, based on the most cordial goodwill and understanding, of the Arab state with Palestine, the implementation of the Balfour Declaration, and the promotion of large-scale Jewish immigration and settlement upon the land, with the holy sites of the Muslims remaining under their own control. To all appearances, Faisal was thus prepared not only to open Palestine to Jewish immigration, but to allow the establishment of a "Jewish national home." With this he seems to have hoped for Jewish capital and assistance against the French, whose designs on Syria he understood all too well. For its part, the Zionist Organization offered the Arab state its good services. Yet Faisal attached a handwritten note to the agreement, in Arabic, containing an all-important stipulation: the agreement to Arab independence by the powers gathered at the Paris Peace Conference. If this was refused, the Faisal-Weizmann agreement would be rendered void. Whether this was truly a missed opportunity for peaceful understanding between Arabs and Jews (one of the many "missed opportunities" often referred to) may safely be doubted. Faisal represented the interests of the Hashemite family rooted in the Hijaz. In no way was he authorized by the inhabitants of Palestine to speak on their behalf. Nor had he asked them how they imagined their own future.

From Military to Civil Administration

In this situation, the U.S. government insisted on dispatching an allied commission, which, following the principle of "government by con-

[34] Al-Hut (ed.) (1979), pp. 18–19; English text in Antonius (1965), pp. 437–39. Background information in Caplan (1983); Muslih (1988), pp. 121ff., 133, 150–51, 202–203. When the British refused to allow a Palestinian delegation to travel to the Paris Peace

sent," would try to ascertain the wishes of the local population. Since the British and French refused to participate, it was a purely American commission that went to Palestine, Lebanon, and Syria in June 1919, led by Dr. Henry King, president of Oberlin College, Ohio, and Charles Crane, a Chicago businessman. The Arab side met them in Jerusalem with "three demands": "complete independence" for Syria from the Taurus Mountains in the north to Rafah in the south; internal autonomy (*istiqlal dakhili*) for Palestine (Southern Syria) within this Syrian state; rejection of Zionist immigration and of a Jewish national home in Palestine, though with the recognition of those Jews who had long resided in Palestine as citizens with equal rights and duties (*wataniyyun lahum ma lana wa-'alaihim ma 'alaina*)—a formula derived from the Islamic legal tradition.[35] The report of the King-Crane Commission, which recommended an American or possibly a British mandate over Greater Syria (including Lebanon and Palestine), was not discussed by the delegates at the Paris Peace Conference and only published in 1922. In September 1919 Paris and London agreed on a British withdrawal from Syria, with French troops to enter the region as provided under the Sykes-Picot Agreement (zone "A"). For the time being, the fate of the Syrian interior controlled by the Arab Government, including the cities of Damascus, Hama, Homs, and Aleppo, remained open. But the district of Mosul, which equally was supposed to form part of the French zone "A," was to remain under British occupation. Unimpressed by both internal and external opposition, a General Syrian Congress, including delegates from Palestine, proclaimed Faisal b. al-Husain king of an independent Syrian-Arab state on March 8, 1920.[36] The proclamation found a lively echo in Palestine that was further enhanced by the simultaneous publication of the Balfour Declaration by the British military administration.

Despite all of its domestic problems, the Arab Government ultimately failed not as a result of local resistance, but of French military superior-

---

Conference, the Jerusalem Muslim-Christian Association in February 1919 did authorize Faisal to represent them at the conference, but only in order to demand Palestinian autonomy within Syria as an independent Arab state; Porath (1974), pp. 85–86. Again according to Porath, pp. 322–23, note 41, the English version was drafted by T. E. Lawrence ("Lawrence of Arabia"). See also Nafi (1998), p. 85, note 197; Ayyad (1999), pp. 73, 79ff.

[35] Al-Hut (1981), pp. 109–14, with the list of demands on p. 110. A delegation from Jaffa expressed itself along similar lines, apparently inspired by the famous slogan of the Egyptian Wafd—*al-din lillah wa-l-watan lil-jami' lahum ma lana wa-'alaihim ma 'alaina*: "religion is for God and the fatherland for all, same rights, same burdens." See also Porath (1974), pp. 60–62; Wasserstein (1978), pp. 39–40; Laurens (1999), pp. 292–96; and chapter 8 below.

[36] Muslih (1988), pp. 125–29; Porath (1974), pp. 95ff.; Gelvin (1998), pp. 47, 102ff., 246–52.

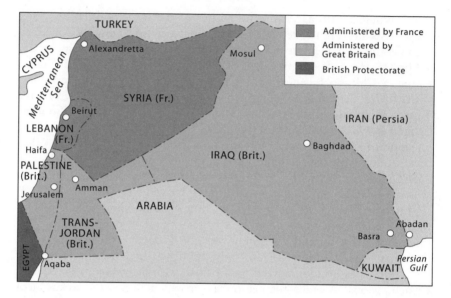

Map 5. The Near East following the San Remo Conference (1920)

ity. In April 1920 the Supreme Council of the Paris Peace Conference, convened at San Remo, reached an understanding over the division of the British and French mandate territories in the Middle East. In July of the same year, the League of Nations ratified the decision. In anticipation of the formal, internationally recognized transfer of the mandate, Great Britain established a civilian government in Jerusalem under the committed Zionist Sir Herbert Samuel on July 1, 1920. After the British had granted them a free hand, the French defeated the remainder of Faisal's army on July 24, 1920 in the battle of Maisalun, occupied Damascus, and transformed Syria into a French mandate. The fall of the Arab Kingdom in Syria also signified the end of hopes for a Greater Syrian Arab state. At a conference in Cairo held in March 1921 and chaired by Winston Churchill, the new regional order was put in place. Secretary of state for war in 1919, Churchill was now colonial secretary, and in the latter capacity acquired responsibility for the British mandates in the Middle East. To appease Faisal, he offered him the newly created throne of Iraq. Shortly after, his elder brother Abdallah was charged with taking care of Transjordan, which until July 1920 had been administered as part of the Arab Kingdom of Hijaz, and was now subject to the authority of the British high commissioner in Jerusalem. On July 24, 1922, the Supreme Council of the League of Nations approved the British mandate over Palestine. In September 1922 it made arrangements, couched in difficult language, to exclude Transjordan from the stipulations relating to the creation of a Jewish national home. Hence the Balfour Declaration was not to apply to the territories lying east of the Jordan River.[37] In the Treaty of Lausanne signed on July 24, 1923, Turkish independence was recognized. After further delays, the British mandate in Palestine officially went into effect on September 29, 1923, simultaneously with the French mandate in Syria.

[37] In a note to the general secretary of the League of Nations, the British government explicated the meaning of the stipulations; cf. Stoyanovsky (1928), pp. 84–85; *Peel Report* (1937), p. 37. On the eventual delimitation of boundaries, cf. Biger (2004), chs. 2–6; for Transjordan, see Wilson (1987), pp. 40–53.

Chapter Eight

DOUBLE STANDARD, OR DUAL OBLIGATION

Palestine is very small. It is the size of Sardinia or a German province. But it extends from the sea to snow-capped mountains, and includes plains, mountains, the lowest point on the earth's surface, and both desert and the greatest fertility. There is cold Jerusalem and blazing Jericho. In this tiny bit of land, there is six weeks' difference in the harvest time for grain between the Jordan plain and the mountains. There are northern fruit trees along with tropical bananas, acacias, and palms. The land lies stretched between the Mediterranean and the Jordan, which forms the boundary today from north to south—a narrow strip along the eastern Mediterranean. Across the way lies Greece. . . . The same sea is here as there. But here there is no relation between land and sea. The sea washes up against the land, that is all. . . . The sea is lifeless on the coast of Palestine. The face of the land is turned toward the desert.*

THE MANDATE TREATY

The mandates system was essentially colonial rule in a new guise, and was understood as such locally. The main concern for the European powers was to determine their overseas spheres of influence in agreement with the United States, which had not joined the League of Nations when it was formed in 1919. The tutelage implied in mandates was couched in a quasi-religious language of responsibility, which plainly alluded to the "white man's burden." Under the new regime of international law, the conquered territories were handed as a "sacred trust of civilization" to the guardianship or tutelage of experienced (Western) powers. In Article 22 of the Covenant of the League of Nations of June 1919, this was expressed as follows:

To those colonies and territories, which as a consequence of the late war have ceased to be under the sovereignty of the States which formerly gov-

---

Epigraph. Tergit (1996), p. 19. Gabriele Tergit (pen name of Elise Reifenberg, née Hirschmann, 1894–1982) lived in Palestine 1933–38; cf. Joachim Schlör, Nachwort, Tergit (1996), pp. 147–58.

erned them, and which are inhabited by peoples not yet able to stand by themselves under the strenuous conditions of the modern world, there should be applied the principle that the well-being and development of such peoples form a sacred trust of civilisation, and that securities for the performance of this trust should be embodied in this Covenant.

The best method of giving practical effect to this principle is that the tutelage of such peoples should be entrusted to advanced nations.[1]

The Arab inhabitants of the former Ottoman Empire qualified for the highest category of the so-called A mandate. According to Par. 4 of Article 22, they had attained a state of development that enabled them to seek independence under the guidance of a European power. In the precise words of the treaty,

Certain communities formerly belonging to the Turkish Empire have reached a state of development where their existence as independent nations can be provisionally recognised subject to the rendering of administrative advice and assistance by a Mandatory until such time as they are able to stand alone. The wishes of these communities must be a principal consideration in the selection of the Mandatory.[2]

Palestine was the exception here. Unlike Syria (including Lebanon) and Iraq it was in fact not treated as an A mandate, since according to British understanding it was subject to special regulations. Thus, Palestine from the outset was given a special status that derived from the "Jewish question," more specifically from Zionist claims to national self-realization (to avoid the more explicit concept of political "self-determination"). Arab rights and demands seemed to pale by comparison.

"A LAND WITHOUT A PEOPLE FOR A PEOPLE WITHOUT A LAND"

The fact that Palestine was treated differently from Syria and Iraq brought into sharp relief what the phrase "a land without a people for a people without a land" actually meant. Often wrongly attributed to Theodor Herzl or to early Zionists like Israel Zangwill (1864–1926), it actually goes back to the philo-Semitic Earl of Shaftesbury, who coined the memorable phrase as early as the 1840s.[3] What it meant was not that there were no people in Palestine (although in the early twentieth

---

[1] Cited from *Peel Report* (1937), p. 29. Like the other mandates, Palestine was subordinated to the Colonial Office.

[2] Cited from *Peel Report* (1937), p. 29. On the A mandates, itself a diverse category, see also Stoyanovsky (1928), pp. 40–48.

[3] Garfinkle (1991).

century there were still writers who thought that the Holy Land was
both backward and empty). Rather, it meant that the people living in
Palestine were not *a* people with a history, culture, and legitimate claim
to national self-determination of their own; to the extent that any of this
existed, it was regarded as inferior in value to the history, culture, and
claim of the Jewish people. Put differently, Palestine contained "people,"
but not "*a* people." There were people who (possibly) had their *homeland* there, but they lacked a national identity and thus had no claim to
national self-determination, let alone a state. The argument, then, was
about politics, not numbers, and it could not be defeated by citing demographic data. In Palestine more was at stake than the people currently
living there.

A lengthy citation from the Peel Report can perhaps illustrate British
views at the end of the war, which informed British attitudes toward Palestine and its people. In a thoroughly memorable opening paragraph, the
authors begin by declaring that with the defeat of the Jewish revolt in A.D.
135, "Palestine steadily sank into obscurity" (p. 4). The end of Jewish
power was therefore the end of Palestinian history, its further development scarcely worthy of mention, and the present miserable and wretched.
The reforms of the nineteenth century had apparently left no traces:

> In the twelve centuries and more that had passed since the Arab conquest
> Palestine had virtually dropped out of history. One chapter only is remem-
> bered—the not very noble romance of the Crusades. In economics as in
> politics Palestine lay outside the main stream of the world's life. In the
> realm of thought, in science or in letters, it made no contribution to mod-
> ern civilization. Its last state was worse than its first. In 1914 the condition
> of the country was an outstanding example of the lethargy and maladmin-
> istration of the pre-war Ottoman regime. The population, still overwhelm-
> ingly Arab in character, eked out a precarious existence mainly in the hills.
> On the plains, where life and property were less secure, such irrigation-
> works as had existed in ancient times had long disappeared. Oranges were
> grown round Jaffa, but most of the maritime belt was only sparsely popu-
> lated and only thinly cultivated. Esdraelon for the most part was marshy
> and malarious. Eastwards beyond Jordan nothing remained of the Greek
> cities of classical times save one or two groups of deserted ruins. South-
> wards in Beersheba, once the site of several prosperous towns, all trace of
> urban life had long lain buried under the encroaching sand.[4]

To this point, the text sounded familiar to readers of European travel
literature, even if divergent voices could be heard in that genre as well.
Yet unlike many observers before and since, the authors of the Peel Re-

---

[4] This citation and the following one are taken from *Peel Report* (1937), p. 6.

port did not conclude from the supposed backwardness of the country that its inhabitants were not rooted there. For they continued:

> But, poor and neglected though it was, to the Arabs who lived in it Palestine—or, more strictly speaking, Syria, of which Palestine had been a part since the days of Nebuchadnezzar—was still their country, their home, the land in which their people for centuries past had lived and left their graves.

The Arab inhabitants regarded Palestine as their home—that much had to be granted. But in the British view, this did not mean that they had legitimate political claims to Palestine comparable to those of the Jewish people with its unique tradition, a tradition basic to Western Christian culture. Lord Balfour stated this clearly enough when asked to clarify why the principle of self-determination should not apply to Palestine and its (Arab) inhabitants. In a letter to the British premier dated February 19, 1919, he wrote:

> The weak point of our position of course is that in the case of Palestine we deliberately and rightly decline to accept the principle of self-determination. If the present inhabitants were consulted they would unquestionably give an anti-Jewish verdict. Our justification for our policy is that we regard Palestine as being absolutely exceptional; that we consider the question of the Jews outside Palestine as one of world importance and that we conceive the Jews to have an historic claim to a home in their ancient land; provided that home can be given them without either dispossessing or oppressing the present inhabitants.

The latter point would be taken up again in the late 1930s. According to Balfour, "Palestine presented a unique situation," where, he argued, "We are dealing not with the wishes of an existing community but are consciously seeking to re-constitute a new community and definitely building for a numerical majority in the future."[5]

To "re-constitute" a "new community" has a strange sound to it. Also worth noting is the numerical argument that Balfour projected into the future. He used it not to describe Palestine as empty of people, wretched, and desolate, but rather to make room, both politically and physically, for a future Jewish majority. Lord Milner, who described himself as sympathetic to the Arab cause (and who like McMahon before him equated "Arab" with "Muslim"), spoke in the same vein before the British House of Lords in 1923:

[5] Cited from Ingrams (1972), pp. 61, 73. A British observer was later to characterize this line of thinking as "charity of heart coupled with woolly thinking"; Sherman (1997), p. 176.

Palestine can never be regarded as a country on the same footing as the other Arab countries. You cannot ignore all history and tradition in the matter. You cannot ignore the fact that this is the cradle of two of the great religions of the world. It is a sacred land to the Arabs, but it is also a sacred land to the Jew and the Christian; and the future of Palestine cannot possibly be left to be determined by the temporary impressions and feelings of the Arab majority in the country of the present day.[6]

Milner was demanding much of the Arab majority, whether Christian or Muslim, whose "temporary impressions and feelings" should count for nothing against the claims of the Jewish people and indeed of history writ large. Even Balfour realized as much. In July 1920 he addressed the expected difficulties of a postwar arrangement:

Among these difficulties I am not sure that I do not rate highest, or at all events first, the inevitable difficulty of dealing with the Arab question as it presents itself within the limits of Palestine. It will require tact, it will require judgment, it will require above all sympathetic good will on the part both of Jew and Arab. So far as the Arabs are concerned—a great, an interesting and an attractive race—I hope they will remember that . . . the Great Powers, and among all the Great Powers most especially Great Britain, has freed them, the Arab race, from the tyranny of their brutal conqueror, who had kept them under his heel for these many centuries. I hope they will remember that it is we who have established the independent Arab sovereignty of the Hedjaz. I hope they will remember that it is we who desire in Mesopotamia to prepare the way for the future of a self-governing, autonomous Arab State. And I hope that, remembering that all, they will not grudge that small notch—for it is no more geographically, whatever it may be historically—that small notch in what are now Arab territories being given to the people who for all these hundreds of years have been separated from it.[7]

A remarkable logic that already linked the territorial argument with the historical one, and interpreted both in favor of the claims of the Jewish people to the "land of the fathers." Here too we find the idea that the Arabs had so much land at their disposal that they could do without this "small notch" to the benefit of the Jewish people who had only *this one* land—and had it as of right, not on sufferance, as the Churchill Memorandum of 1922 tried to establish.

---

[6] Cited from *Peel Report* (1937), p. 27.
[7] Cited from ibid., p. 31.

POLITICAL REPRESENTATION

The right to self-government of the Arab population (the "existing non-Jewish communities" referred to in the Balfour Declaration) was defined in the Mandate Treaty for Palestine in even more restrained fashion than for Syria and Lebanon. In the latter territories, the Mandatory was obligated to work out an Organic Law in coordination with the local "authorities" within three years, and to prepare the population for independence. The Mandate Treaty for Palestine contained no such provisions.[8] The Mandatory retained full legislative and administrative powers, to be exercized by the high commissioner. He was assisted by an Executive Council (that was exclusively British) and an Advisory Council initially composed of ten British officials and ten appointed members (four Muslims, three Christian Arabs, three Jews), among whom the Muslim majority was clearly underrepresented (Muslim representation was augmented in the Palestine Order in Council enacted in August 1922). British officials also headed the central and provincial administrations, the police and the gendarmerie, as well as the justice system. The Mandatory's obligation was restricted to facilitating the creation of self-governing institutions of the local population. The Mandate Treaty already included a clause referring to a "Jewish agency" to look after Jewish interests. The Balfour Declaration was part of the Mandate Treaty, and therefore binding under international law. The Preamble made it the main task of the Mandatory to implement the Balfour Declaration. Article 2 included its wording, albeit with interesting modifications:

> The Mandatory shall be responsible for placing the country under such political, administrative and economic conditions as will secure the establishment of the Jewish national home, as laid down in the preamble, and the development of self-governing institutions, and also for safeguarding the civil and religious rights of all the inhabitants of Palestine, irrespective of race and religion.[9]

Article 3 obliged the Mandatory to "encourage local autonomy"— "so far as circumstances permit." Article 4 dealt with the recognition of a Jewish agency to advise the Mandatory in "such economic, social, and other matters as may affect the establishment of the Jewish national

---

[8] The Palestine Order in Council of August 10, 1922, supplemented by the Palestine (Amendment) Order in Council of 1923, served as a substitute for a basic law. Neither the Arabs nor the Jews were formally involved in preparing these documents; Stoyanovsky (1928), pp. 166ff., and 363–84.

[9] Cited from Stoyanovsky (1928), p. 356.

home and the interests of the Jewish population in Palestine" more generally. For the time being, these tasks were to be met by the Zionist Commission representing the Zionist Organization—a newly formed political agency based in London, with no prior presence in Palestine. Given strong opposition to Zionism within the Jewish communities of Europe, the United States, and the Middle East, the Zionist Organization might attempt to speak on behalf of the Jewish people, but could hardly claim to represent the Jewish people as a whole. There were no corresponding arrangements for representing the Arab population.[10] Article 6 established the obligation, "while ensuring that the rights and position of other sections of the population are not prejudiced," to "facilitate Jewish immigration under suitable conditions," and to encourage, in cooperation with the Jewish agency, "close settlement by Jews on the land, including State lands and waste lands not required for public purposes." Article 22 defined English, Arabic, and Hebrew as official languages of Palestine.

"DUAL OBLIGATION"

From the outset, the situation was characterized by a marked imbalance of power and rights. The British were well aware of their difficult position, since they themselves introduced the concept of "dual obligation" or "two-fold duty"—dual because the Mandate Treaty obliged them to develop self-governing institutions in Palestine, and the Balfour Declaration committed them to securing the establishment of a Jewish national home there.[11] This entailed unequal treatment of the two major population groups: the Jews (or rather, the Zionists) had to be assisted in their endeavors, and the Arabs to be held in check insofar as they opposed these endeavors. Arab wishes and aspirations were taken into account to the extent that they did not stand in the way of other interests and obligations. Politically speaking, the British did not actually pursue a status quo policy in Palestine, even if, with regard to the Arab population their interests lay in upholding the existing social and political order by not in infringing upon the position of local Arab elites.

The situation was complicated still further by the interplay of strategic interests, political goals, and broader sympathies (or the lack thereof) that could be directed toward Jews as well as toward Arabs and Muslims. British officials were by no means all pro-Zionist or sympathetic to the Jews; there was prejudice against Jews and Arabs alike. This came

---

[10] Ibid., pp. 87–100; *Peel Report* (1937), pp. 47–50.
[11] *Peel Report* (1937), pp. 41–42, 181–84; Y. Miller (1985); Wasserstein (1978).

out strongly with regard to the Arabs. The majority of Palestinian Arabs did not live in the desert, and thus had little in common with the Bedouins of the Arabian Peninsula, who many British writers and officials admired as noble and racially pure—true gentlemen as to descent and lifestyle. It is no coincidence that the Hashemites, descended from the clan of the Prophet and represented by the sharif of Mecca and his sons, were widely regarded in Europe as the "natural leaders" of the Arab nation. By contrast, Arab city dwellers were viewed as "Levantines" of doubtful origin and dubious character—superficial, pushy, and cunning. Worse yet, their elite spoke French, albeit with a heavy accent. Anti-Arab prejudice was by no means confined to the British as a survey of the relevant literature would readily show.[12]

Still, ambivalence and prejudice had deeper roots, deriving from the colonial situation as such. In official usage, all inhabitants of the Mandate territory were "Palestinians" (to avoid confusion I will not be using the term for Jews), who were all subjects of the British Crown, regardless of origin, race, language, and religion. Yet the Jewish Palestinians were mostly Europeans while the Arabs were natives of the Middle East ("Orientals" as writers of the time would have said). In relation to the Arabs, British perceptions were relatively well defined: Even wealthy and educated Arabs (especially the Muslims, but also the Christians, who were for the most part members of the Eastern churches) were *colonized* and for this reason could not be part of ruling society. The Arab elite tended to see things quite differently, viewing themselves as aristocrats in their own society. Their genealogy could easily match that of most British colonial officials. In some cases it could be traced back to the military elite of the Mamluks, in others to the family of the Prophet himself—scarcely any British family could boast such ancient origins. Unlike most of the British officials in Jerusalem, Arab elite families were wealthy, if not actually rich. They were educated and, unlike most of the British residents in Jerusalem, were fluent in four or five languages, even if English was often not one of them. They were widely traveled. In short, they were cosmopolitans, or saw themselves as such. Indeed, there was no reason why a Raghib al-Nashashibi, who combined all of these qualities in his own person, should look up admiringly upon a member of the Scottish gentry who felt superior to the natives for the simple reason that he was British.[13] Nonetheless, the Arab "effendi"

---

[12] For sarcastic comment, see Kedourie (1978), pp. 72–77; also Wasserstein (1978), pp. 12–14, and (in a very different vein) Banse (1934), pp. 109–12. For vivid description, and much pro-Arab sentiment, see Sherman (1997). For the idealization of the Bedouin by Zionist pioneers, see Benvenisti (2000), p. 59; also Shapira (1992), ch. 2.

[13] Nashashibi (1990), pp. 14–21, 64–66; for the notable families, Manna' (1998).

posed no social and cultural challenge for the British. This was all the more true for the Arab peasant and Bedouin.

It was different with the Jews who represented the "new" Yishuv and the Zionist movement more generally. In social terms they were highly diverse, with some coming from a very modest background in an Eastern European shtetl, others from the cultured and affluent milieus of the large Western European cities. For the most part, they were well educated, often fluent in English, thoroughly familiar with European customs (including the British variety), and entirely lacking in any feelings of inferiority. The Zionists among them were at one and the same time colonized and colonizers. As Europeans, they saw themselves as the bearers of civilization who had come to Palestine to establish by means of "model colonies" a modern society on Western lines. The civilizing mission that the British claimed for themselves as the Mandatory was also claimed by the Zionists. Not only did they not feel inferior to the British: They continually made demands, they prodded, they criticized, they urged, and they reprimanded; they were impatient, and they were presumptuous. In the 1920s an American journalist described the irritation resulting from the colonial situation:

> The English want to be just, and try to be just, in Palestine. But they feel at home with the Arabs as they do not, and probably never can, feel at home with the Jews. These Arabs are natives in the real sense of the word. They behave as the English have found natives behaving in other parts of the earth. They are indigenous to their own strange soil. Therefore the English know what to do with them and how to treat them. They can play their pipes as they have played them in a hundred lands.
>
> . . . the English, as the governing authorities of Palestine, do not like the Jews as a subject population. In fact, they do not know what to make of them, as in all their imperial experience they have never had to deal with people of just this kind before. As comprising a part, and a large part of the inhabitants of the country, the Jews must of course be classified as natives. But they do not seem like natives. They are acquainted with Western culture; they are themselves cultured, in the true English sense of the word; many of them speak the English language, and are familiar with English ways. What is more, these Jews do not act like natives. They are not submissive, and obedient, and grateful for benefits received. . . . The Jews are trouble-makers . . . and thus are regarded by the English . . . with the active dislike of a superior class for an inferior class which does not know and keep its place.[14]

---

[14] John Holmes cited from Shamir (2000), pp. 19–20. Shamir speaks of a *dual colonialism* in relation to Jews and Arabs (ibid., ch. 1).

A British official put similar feelings in simpler words when in 1939 he noted in a private letter:

> One cannot help having the greatest admiration for the Jews in their industry, their boundless enthusiasm, & their loyalty to each other: it is strange that so intelligent & gifted a race should as a whole be so completely devoid of tact which has made their relations with both British & Arabs increasingly difficult—it is simply incredible how they manage to rub you up the wrong way![15]

In a difficult situation, the British took courage from the belief in their own usefulness. They saw themselves in the role of "honest broker," acting as mediator and guarantor of security, well-being, and development, a belief that also served to legitimize the continuation of Mandatory rule. Even in the most difficult times, they persisted in the argument that Palestine would derive economic benefits from the Mandate in general and the Jewish national home in particular, as Jewish immigration, settlement, capital, and labor would benefit the country as a whole and help to improve the state of the Arab peasantry, whose distress was strongly felt. The Peel Report expressed these two notions concisely:

> It is clear, then, that the policy of the Balfour Declaration was subjected to the operation of the Mandate System in 1919 in the belief that the obligations thereby undertaken towards the Arabs and the Jews respectively would not conflict. And this belief was still held when the draft Mandate was confirmed by the Council of the League in 1922. Already by then the Arab leaders had displayed their hostility to the Mandate and all it involved; but it was thought that this hostility would presently weaken and die away. . . . It was assumed that the establishment of the National Home would mean a great increase of prosperity for all Palestine. It was an essential part of the Zionist mission to revivify the country, to repair by Jewish labour, skill and capital the damage it had suffered from centuries of neglect. Arabs would benefit therefrom as well as Jews. They would find the country they had known so long as poor and backward rapidly acquiring the material blessings of Western civilization. On that account it was assumed that Arab fears and prejudices would gradually be overcome.[16]

This argument was based on several assumptions. There was the notion that Palestine had previously been neglected (a stock image of travel

---

[15] Sherman (1997), p. 158. Another observer remarked in the 1940s that most British officials were "either pro-Arab or strictly impartial in detesting both sides. . . . Off the record, most of the officials here will tell you that the Jews are above themselves and want taking down a peg." Cited on pp. 27–28. For more comment in a similar vein, see pp. 26–30.

[16] *Peel Report* (1937), p. 41.

reports, white papers, and much of the scholarly literature). There was the belief, rooted in the liberal ideals of self-help and improvement that the situation in Palestine could quickly be ameliorated through Jewish labor and capital, or Jewish competence and efficiency (Herzl had sought to persuade the sultan with this very argument). There was the conviction that at its core the problem was not *political* but *economic* (as the Zionists argued), or that at any rate political conflicts could be overcome through economic prosperity (as the British thought until growing more skeptical in the mid-1930s). The Zionists did not invent the idea that the Jewish national home would contribute to the welfare of Palestine. It actually went back to the Earl of Shaftesbury. But they used it with remarkable consistency, and also linked it to two further arguments. First, they claimed that if the peasants or *fellahin*, uneducated and limited in outlook as they were, opposed Jewish immigration and colonization, they did so because they were misled by a corrupt and selfish Arab upper class (the "effendis") who said "nationalism" and meant "exploitation" (a classic case of "false consciousness" on the part of the masses). Second, they insisted that violence must not be rewarded.[17] As late as the 1930s, a Zionist observer wondered whether

> the "national liberation movement" of the Arabs corresponded to an actual inner need of the Arab people, or whether it was only to be seen as the machinations (*Mache*) of the effendis who wished to block the immigration of the Jews for their own purposes.

Another observer provided the answer:

> The Arab effendi [he wrote] who suddenly finds his large estate, worked by enslaved fellahin, lying next to socialist workers' colonies, speaks of Muhammad (whose creed is the sword), but what he means is agrarian rent (*Bodenrente*).[18]

In the Zionist view there was indeed an "Arab problem," but it could be solved rationally as long as one did not yield to the pseudonationalist agitation duping the ignorant peasants. Hence, the British should not seek an understanding with the effendis. Rather, they should put the Balfour Declaration into effect. No premium must be placed on violence. By contrast, British officials did not perceive of Arab protest as artificially created and stirred up solely by a corrupt upper class. They saw it as real—and as harmful to British interest. Accordingly, the Zionists were to restrain themselves, and not turn the Arabs and Muslims against

---

[17] Wasserstein (1978), pp. 26–28, 140; Stein (1984), p. 37. For Shaftesbury, cf. Merkley (1998), p. 40. For an interesting comparison with French attitudes in Syria, see Provence (2005), esp. pp. 47, 52.

[18] Both citations from Kaiser (1992), pp. 494–95.

themselves (and thus against the British Crown) with their offensive arrogance. Rather, they should seek an understanding with the Arab elite, preferably with the pro-British Hashemites.

This did nothing to alter the imbalance of forces that was reflected at every level, including access to financial resources and influential circles in Palestine, Europe, and the United States. Access to the European and U.S. public as well as to the highest decision makers in London was at least as important as a solid organization on the ground—and here, the Zionists were infinitely better positioned. It was in this context too that the distinction between Jews and Zionists was most difficult to make. As opposed to the Zionists, or the Jews involved more generally, Palestinian Arabs had scarcely any independent financial means at their disposal, especially abroad. That made for a high dependence on the Mandate government for carrying out social and political projects. This in turn reinforced the paternalistic attitude of the British toward Arabs and Muslims, and toward Arab peasants more particularly—who, as a British official put it, "obviously *couldn't* . . . manage their own affairs satisfactorily."[19] The result was an unstable triangle: With the help of a wider Jewish public, Zionists set out to build their national home and demanded that the British prevent Arab opposition to this objective. Arabs were opposed to the Mandate in general and the Balfour Declaration in particular. There was a conspicuous lack of interaction between Arabs and Zionists or Jews, based in large part on a lack of trust. Naturally, this left ample room for the spread of suspicion, fear, and rumors of every kind. In a number of instances, the British actually did become involved as honest brokers.

It soon proved impossible to create self-governing institutions within the framework of the Mandate that could bring together Jews and Arabs under British auspices. Instead, separate institutions gradually formed. Among the Jews, this process of self-organization proceeded more rapidly, and comprehensively, than among the Arabs, partly because it met with fewer obstacles. Even within the Mandate administration itself, in the police and the security forces, there was constant friction over how to distribute various posts and responsibilities.[20] This placed the British

[19] G. S. Symes cited from Wasserstein (1978), p. 13. See also pp. 14, 133. A similar account can be found, in a different context, in Laurens (1999), p. 290. The same "humanitarian-paternalistic" approach was common among the Zionist left; see Benvenisti (2000), p. 61.

[20] In June 1921, Arabs made up two thirds of Mandate employees (1,633 out of 2,490), yet they mostly filled the lower and middle ranks. In the upper ranks, they made up only 40 percent of the total (145 out of 360). See Wasserstein (1978), chs. 8 and 9, and table 246; Tibawi (1956), pp. 13–14. Stoyanovsky (1928), pp. 184–97, and *Peel Report* (1937), pp. 158–68, describe the complicated justice system, in which Arab officials, judges, state attorneys, and lawyers prevailed. In the security forces, both Jews and Arabs were repre-

in a dilemma. On the one hand, they had a low opinion of the administrative abilities of non-Europeans. On the other hand, Arab officials
were cheaper than British or Jewish ones. In order not to leave the administration entirely to the Arabs, the Zionists subsidized the salaries of
Jewish Mandate employees. In this context, it was not just the relationship between Muslims, Jews, and the British that mattered, but also that
between Muslims and (Arab) Christians, as the latter were traditionally
overrepresented in administrative positions compared with their share
in the total population. British efforts to redress the balance added fuel
to the conflicts within the Arab community.

"Tunnel Vision" and "Entangled History"

It has often been noted, and widely lamented, that contemporaries and
modern observers rarely take account of Palestinian reality in its entirety
and that a "tunnel vision" prevails in which one community takes center
stage (as a rule the writer's own). The tunnel vision is evident in the
works of eminent Israeli and Western scholars who fail to refer to the
works of equally eminent Arab historians and social scientists (the reverse is less common, highlighting once again the asymmetries that rule
academia as well as any other field). Up to the early twentieth century,
communities were generally distinguished on the basis of religion. The
British census still listed individuals as Muslims, Christians, Jews, and
"Other." The distinction between Jews and Arabs, whose internal differences were largely ignored, reflected political criteria. In recent years,
however, there has been growing emphasis on history as "relational,"
urging historians to consider individuals, groups, and societies not in
isolation, but in their manifold interactions. Colonial history in particular has been defined as "shared" or "entangled" history, to indicate that
not only were the colonized influenced by their European colonizers, but
that the reverse was also true. This is especially relevant to the history
of Palestine, which cannot but be written as "relational," "entangled,"
and indeed "shared." How the Jewish Yishuv was shaped and influenced
by its local environment, how Palestinian resistance to Zionism and Brit-

---

sented: The military units stationed in Palestine were reduced during the 1920s, from
25,000 men in 1920, to 7,000 in May 1921, to a mere 2,800 in December 1922. In
addition, there was a British and an Arab-Jewish Palestinian gendarmerie, each subject to
civilian control. In 1926 they were dissolved amid drastic austerity measures that reduced
British troops to a minimum. But in their stead, the police were strengthened and a new
military unit was created in the form of the Transjordan Frontier Force. Moreover, British
troops stationed in Malta and Egypt were also available in cases of crisis; Wasserstein
(1978) and Kolinsky (1993).

ish occupation transformed into an Arab-Palestinian national movement (without being totally absorbed by it), how Arab agriculture changed under the impact of Jewish immigration and Zionist settlement—all of this can only be understood by taking account of these webs of relations. None of these phenomena developed autonomously, nor can they be understood in this way.

And yet, the "mental separatism" that was noted and criticized by numerous contemporaries and later observers is not entirely unfounded. The communities were certainly part of a complex web of relations and interdependencies, and to a large extent developed in conflict with one another. But this does not imply that their individual members lived *with* the other (rather than *alongside* the other), or that they maintained personal relationships as good neighbors, or friends, or even mere acquaintances. Often enough, this was not the case. There were obviously personal encounters in the street, in the marketplace, and in business more generally. The British Mandate authorities employed Jews and Arabs, Muslims and Christians in the same offices. Arab laborers and employees worked on Jewish farms, settlements, and industrial enterprises. Jewish kibbutzim had Arab neighbors. They might visit the same doctors, hire the same craftsmen, or live in the same neighborhoods, the same streets, or even the same buildings. Yet both communities were primarily inward oriented, or self-centered, and preoccupied with their own problems, hopes, and aspirations. Their knowledge of the other was limited, not least due to the lack of a shared language. Anxiety and prejudice were deeply rooted, leaving much space for rumors and insinuations. In the tense atmosphere of the early 1930s, a Jewish observer wrote:

> Though relations between the two Semitic peoples are not exactly intimate, they remain more or less good neighbors. They grumble about each other, eliminate competition as much as possible, and separate work and business. But the Arabs ride in the Jewish buses and the Jews in Arab carriages, they make purchases in the market. Preferably however they try to ignore each other.[21]

Even those in the labor movement and among the communists who in the name of class solidarity were actively committed to fostering personal contacts between Jews and Arabs met with little success. The legal

---

[21] Grete Fischer, alias Joseph Amiel, *Palästina, das erlaubte Land* (Paris 1934), p. 69, cited from Kaiser (1992), p. 494. For a poignant description, see also Benvenisti (2000), ch. 2, aptly entitled "Through a Glass Wall." But see also Sakakini (1987), Vester (1988), Lockman (1996), Bernstein (2000), and a number of Arab authors (cf. Enderwitz 2002), who tell more nuanced stories of formal and informal relations and encounters, which still await systematic exploration.

Figure 10. Street in the so-called Jewish Quarter of Jerusalem. As can be seen from the clothing and headgear, it was frequented by Jews as well as non-Jews.

system, in accordance with both Islamic and Jewish law, upheld religious autonomy in personal status matters (pertaining to marriage, divorce, custody, wills, and inheritance). This served to maintain barriers in the private sphere, and by the same token preserved the influence of their religious authorities. Mixed marriages were rare. In science and in the arts, Jews and Arabs largely went their separate ways.

A Segmented Society

Education

The division of society manifested itself in the educational system, which under the Mandate developed into separate Jewish and Arab branches.

Within the Yishuv, education was further divided into an Orthodox "Jewish" and a national "Hebrew" branch, while on the Arab side important distinctions existed between Muslims and Christians.[22] On the eve of World War I, there were ninety-eight Ottoman state schools in Palestine with some eight thousand Arab and Jewish students, as well as about five hundred local and foreign private schools, including hundreds of Qur'anic schools, that were attended by twelve thousand students of both sexes. Nonetheless, the rate of illiteracy among the Arab population was high. During World War I, almost all of the foreign schools were closed (only German, American, and some Jewish schools were permitted to remain open). The British allowed most of them to reopen after the war and incorporated most Ottoman schools into the new system with the significant exception of the secondary school in Jerusalem. However, the British did not introduce compulsory schooling. Due to a lack of public funds, villagers were obliged to contribute to the construction of schools in their villages. As a result, education developed along highly differentiated lines. In addition to the reorganized Ottoman state schools and foreign private schools, there were now Arabic-speaking private institutes, both religious and nonreligious, that attracted virtually no Jewish students and teachers. Jewish private schools, whether religious or secular, in which instruction was given in Hebrew or in a European language, only attracted Jewish students and teachers. Under Article 15 of the Mandate Treaty, the schools were largely free to set their own syllabi and teaching methods.

For all practical purposes, the "Jewish educational sector" operated independently of the state schools, which were attended mostly by Arab students. From the outset, the Zionist immigrants placed great emphasis on creating their own school system, which unlike the traditional *Jewish* institutions (the *heder*, Talmud Torah school, and *yeshiva*) was to be both national and secular, expressing a new *Hebrew* spirit, inspired by ancient glories, and breaking with the traditions of diaspora Judaism. The institute of higher learning opened in 1925 was characteristically called the *Hebrew* University (not the *Jewish* University). The results of this educational drive were impressive in every respect: By 1931 only 6 percent of Jewish men and 26 percent of the women over fourteen years old were illiterate. Put differently, 93 percent of the men and 74 percent of the women were able to read and write (a notoriously vague definition). Seventy-three percent of Jewish children and youths from the ages of five to fifteen attended school in 1931, and 77 percent in 1944.

Among the Arab community, interest in improving the educational system was equally strong, especially in the countryside. For Arabs and

[22] Ayalon (2004), pp. 16–42; *Survey of Palestine* (1946), pp. 635–78, 715–18; Metzer

Jews alike, private schools made a significant contribution to the education and professional training of children and adults. During the Mandate period private institutes formed an estimated 40 to 50 percent of all schools teaching in Arabic. One could almost speak of a thirst for education that fed largely on the assumption that education could improve an individual's social status. Still, the rate of illiteracy remained very high by international standards. It seemed especially unfavorable when compared with the exceptionally well-educated Jewish community, though not when compared with other Middle Eastern societies such as Turkey. In 1931 the rate of illiteracy in the group over age fourteen still lay around 80 percent (70 percent of Arab men and 90 percent of Arab women; among Jews the average was about 14 percent). Nineteen percent of Arab children and youths from the ages of five to fifteen attended school in 1931, while in 1944 it was 25 percent. The average duration of school attendance among Jews was 7.3 years, as compared to 4.4 years among Arabs. However, there were great differences according to religion and sex: Among Arab Christians, 76 percent of boys and 44 percent of girls could read and write, but only 25 percent and 3 percent among the Muslims. In 1944–45, nearly 100 percent of all Jewish and Christian children from ages five to fifteen attended school for at least some time, but only around a third of all Muslim children of this age group. Despite a considerable expansion of the rural school system, cities on the one hand and boys on the other remained privileged. The modest level of education among the Muslim community was problematic in every respect, not least with a view to recruitment into the Mandate administration, where the overrepresentation of Christians was strongly resented by Muslims. For this reason, it would have made sense for the Mandatory to promote Arab education, and Muslim Arab education in particular. Insufficient budgets put a tight limit on this.

Village schools (and not just in Palestine) were designed to impart practical skills, not an academic education. In the words of a British colonial official, the goal was to "enlighten the peasant, make him a contented citizen and keep him on the land." Preventing a rural exodus and the resulting emergence of an urban proletariat that would threaten stability was always one of the top priorities of Mandate policy toward the peasantry. The moral "betterment" and material "welfare" to be derived from primary education was thought to be considerable:

(1998), pp. 52–55, and table B.1; Nadan (2006), pp. 151–59. Qualitative factors are also discussed in Tibawi (1956), pp. 20–72; Y. Miller (1985), pp. 62–70, 90ff., 100ff., 110–11; Fleischmann (2003), ch. 2, esp. pp. 34–48. For Arab Christians, see also Abu Jabir (2004), chs. 3 and 6, and Ben-Arieh (1984), Part III.

Improved cultivation will increase prosperity; malaria and eye disease will diminish; infant mortality will decrease; serious crime will wane; the burden of debt will vanish. In a single generation much can be achieved.[23]

Yet it proved impossible to keep the project of "betterment" within the narrow limits regarded as useful by British officials. In Palestine as in other colonial societies, education was closely connected to emerging nationalism. Education had been one of the core concerns of the earlier reformers, belonging to both the Nahda and the Salafiyya, who saw education as the key to progress, power, and development.[24] In some ways, British rule offered Arab reformers and nationalists better conditions than had the Ottomans. For one thing, Arabic was now the main language of instruction in the state schools, so that *this* battle was won for the Arab cause. At the same time, state schools were attended by both Muslims and Christians, allowing for a shared sense of destiny to develop, and personal friendships to evolve even beyond confessional boundaries. Arabs did complain, however, that Arabic language and history classes were neglected. Arab private schools paid more attention to them, and as a result developed into the most important site of nationalist thought and activity. From the 1920s onward, the Islamic educational and welfare institutions played a significant role, most of them supervised by the Supreme Muslim Council, which devoted a considerable share of its budget to education.

Even so, no institution of higher education was created for Arabic-speaking Palestinians, and no university. The British opened only one Teachers Training College, which was again "practically" oriented and open to women as well as men. Plans to found an Islamic university came to nothing. While educated Jewish youth could choose among a growing number of excellent schools and institutes of higher learning within the country (including the Technion in Haifa and the Hebrew University in Jerusalem, opened in 1924 and 1925), Arabic-speaking students still had to pursue their studies abroad. While this enlarged the horizons of those who were actually able to go to Beirut, Cairo, Baghdad or Paris, contributing to their cultural and political awareness, and generating personal ties and connections beyond the narrow confines of Mandate Palestine, it also restricted access to advanced education to the sons (and very few daughters) of the elite.

Demography

Social and cultural differences between Arabs and Jews, or more precisely between Muslims, Arab Christians, and Jews, retained their im-

---

[23] Both citations from Y. Miller (1985), p. 109; see also Fleischmann (2003), pp. 34–38.
[24] Tibawi (1956); Y. Miller (1985), pp. 69, 91, 99, 112, 184; Fleischmann (2003), ch.

portance under the British Mandate. A variety of demographic data testify to the structural differences between these communities. After a
lengthy period in which demographic data were extrapolated by the Ottoman authorities on the basis either of earlier counts or limited surveys,
the British conducted a new census in October 1922. Among other
things, this census was meant to provide the basis for an adequate political representation of Arabs and Jews.[25] The introduction of birth and
death registers (already begun by the Ottomans, though we know little
about their actual functioning) may have enhanced its accuracy. The
census of 1922 yielded a total population of 752,048, including 589,177
Muslims, 83,790 Jews, 71,464 Christians, and 7,617 "Others" (most of
them Druze, with about 350 Baha'is and 180 Samaritans), corresponding to 89 percent Arabs and 11 percent Jews. The census of November
1931 documented the changes of the 1920s: Out of a total population
of 1,035,821, the number of Muslims had risen to 759,712, that of Jews
to 174,610, of Christians to 91,398, and of "Others" to 10,101.

In political terms, the most important result was surely the increase in
the Jewish population, amounting to an average 8.4 percent per year, as
compared to 3 percent among Christians and 2.6 percent among Muslims. Jewish population growth resulted mostly from immigration,
which under British rule—unlike under the Ottomans—was not seriously curtailed until 1939 (more on immigration policy below). Among
Arabs, immigration remained on a more modest scale, and during the
entire Mandate period did not exceed a total of 40,000 to 42,000, most
of it from 1932 to 1935, and hence probably a result of a more favorable economic situation. Muslim and Christian population increase was
therefore due primarily to natural growth, not to immigration.[26] The
great majority (43 percent) of those who immigrated into Palestine from
1919 to 1936 (virtually all of them Jews) came from Poland, 10.5 percent from the Soviet Union, nearly 10 percent from the German Reich
(climbing from 4 percent in 1926–32 to over 17 percent in 1933–36),
5 percent from Rumania, and about 3 percent from Lithuania. European
Jews thus formed the great majority, while 3 percent of the Jewish immigrants came from Yemen and Aden, 2 percent from Turkey, and 1 percent from Iran. The number of Jews and Arabs who entered the land
illegally (whether as tourists, merchants, or smugglers) is of course diffi-

---

2; for Arab memoirs, see also Enderwitz (2002), ch. 7, esp. pp. 227–29. For British agricultural training, see also El-Eini (2006), chs. 2–4.

[25] Metzer (1998), ch. 2; McCarthy (1990); Lister G. Hopkins, "Population," in Himadeh (ed.) (1938), ch. 1, pp. 1–40. On the political context, see also Wasserstein (1978),
p. 120.

[26] Metzer (1998), pp. 30–32. For the hotly disputed issue of Arab or rather non-Jewish
immigration, see also Benvenisti (2000), pp. 82–83.

cult to ascertain, especially since beginning with the European persecution of the Jews in 1934, illegal immigration was systematically promoted by Jewish organizations.

The high level of Jewish immigration inevitably shifted the demographic weight of the individual religious communities, and was thus of great significance for the social, cultural, and political development of the Mandate area.

Taken together, the population of Palestine under the British Mandate grew by about 1.1 million people (from 816,000 registered in the first census in 1922 to 1.94 million in 1946). The number of Jews increased by more than a half million from 93,000 to 600,000, with the highest growth rate in 1932–35, when the number of Jews rose by about 180,000 and their share of the total population from 17 percent to 27 percent.

Census data yielded information not only about population figures, but also about the age pyramid, birth and death rates, health conditions, marriage practices, and other matters—information that offers important clues as to the social and cultural norms and patterns followed by individual groups within "Palestinian" society. According to the 1922 census, around 40 percent of the population was younger than 15 years. In all religious communities the average age stood at 20 years. While Muslims and Christians registered a slight surplus of men, the Jews did not. Birthrates are of special interest, as they reflected not only prevalent social and cultural norms, but also political motives.[27] In 1922–25, the birthrate lay at a high 4.6 percent. It was highest among the Muslims (5

TABLE 1
Demographic Development under the British Mandate

Religion	1922*	1931*	1946*
Muslim	640,798	777,403	1,175,196
Jewish	94,752	176,648	602,586
Christian	76,194	93,029	148,910
Other	8,515	10,314	15,657
Total	820,259	1,057,214	1,942,349

*estimated totals at end of year
Source: McCarthy (1990): 35.

[27] The following data on birth and death rates are taken from Himadeh (ed.) (1938), pp. 12–16. See also Metzer (1998), pp. 32–52.

percent, the highest rate in the world) followed by the Christians (3.6 percent) and then the Jews (3.5 percent). They did not change substantially until the end of the Mandate in 1948. Demographic data also provides insights into the condition of women: In 1931, 32 percent of Arab girls and women 15–19 years old were married, as opposed to 11.5 percent among the Jews. For ages 20–29, the respective shares were 80 and 64 percent. Only for women ages 30–39 did they become roughly equal (87 and 85 percent). Muslims, in particular, tended to marry quite young. According to one statistic covering the years 1936–41, 34 percent of the girls were younger than 15 on their wedding day, and 52 percent younger than 17. On the average, an Arab mother would give birth to seven children, of whom only some survived. Read in conjunction with reports on school attendance and gainful employment (the latter must be distinguished from unpaid domestic and fieldwork), this gives an idea of the living conditions of Arab women. The proportion of Arab women and girls classified as "employed" in the official statistics (which was 8 percent of those over 10 years old and 9 percent of those over age 15) was very low by international standards, and not just in comparison with the Jewish Yishuv (25 to 27 percent); only in Mexico was it even lower.[28]

Mortality rates also differed by religion, especially among infants and children. They were decisively influenced by medical and sanitary standards (not least those of water quality and sewage disposal), and unlike birthrates they clearly declined over the years. Among the Arab population, mortality rates for girls were generally higher than for boys. Life expectancy differed significantly between Jews and Arabs, particularly between Jews and Muslims. From 1933 to 1935 it stood at 61 years for Jews and 42 for Muslims, and from 1939 to 1941 the difference was 64 and 47 years (47 years was incidentally not very low by international standards, but was poor in comparison to the Jewish community). Education and health indicators were weakest among the Muslims.[29]

---

[28] Ibid., pp. 38, 119–20. For female work and employment, see also Fleischmann (2002), pp. 51–62, who highlights the negative role of British attitudes to female work and education in addition to Arab ones. For Palestinian Arab family life and the condition of women in the late Ottoman and Mandate periods, see notably Tucker (1998), Moors (1995), and Fleischmann (2002), chs. 2 and 3; for narrative sources, memoirs, and memories, see Slyomovics (1998) and Enderwitz (2002), ch. 6. See also note 30 below.

[29] Among Jews, the death rate in the period from 1931 to 1935 fell from 1.5 to 0.9 percent in 1922–25 (here the youth of many immigrants must have played a role). Among Christians, it fell from 1.6 to 1.5 percent, and among Muslims from 2.7 to 2.5 percent. In the same period, infant and child mortality rates fell among Jews from 12.3 to 7.8 percent, among Christians from 14.4 to 13.6 percent, and among Muslims from 19 to 16.6 percent. See Himadeh (ed.) (1938), pp. 17–19. On life expectancy, see Metzer (1998), pp. 43–47.

Correlated with education and health ("human capital," as economists would say), the social profile of the three religious communities also displayed glaring differences in the 1920s and 1930s, and not least between Christians and Muslims. This can be seen from occupational statistics.[30] In 1931 the vast majority of Muslims lived from agriculture, especially grain farming (64 percent of Muslims as opposed to 18 percent of Christians and 15 percent of Jews). Industry and trade employed 29 percent of Jews and 25 percent of Christians, but only 10 percent of Muslims. Among the technical and liberal professions, Jews made up 10 percent, Christians 8, and Muslims only 1.5. The differences were less marked in commerce, where 22 percent of Jews and 13 percent of Muslims were occupied. The salaries and wages of Jewish workers and employees were consistently higher than those of Arabs, who on the average also worked longer hours (8–10 hours on the average compared with 8). Unemployment among Arabs was estimated at 7–10 percent, as opposed to 2–4 percent among Jews.

Urbanization

During the Ottoman period, Palestinian society was mostly agrarian in character. This changed gradually under the British Mandate.[31] In 1922 two thirds of the population lived in rural areas, and the remaining one third (264,000 people) in the twenty-three cities and municipalities of the Mandate area. By 1931 the share of the urban population had risen to 37 percent (387,000 people), while that of the rural population had fallen to 63 percent. In 1935 the urban population already stood at 43 percent (539,000), and the rural at 57 percent. Thus, the early 1930s witnessed a remarkable process of urbanization. In the same period, about 67,000 nomads were registered. Again the religious communities involved in this process differed markedly. Interestingly enough, the greatest difference lay not between Muslims and Jews, but rather between Muslims and Arab Christians. In 1922, 77 percent of Muslims lived in rural areas (73 percent in 1935); in stark contrast, 75 percent of Arab Christians resided in cities in 1922 (and 79 percent in 1935).

[30] Himadeh (ed.) (1938), pp. 31–36; Metzer (1998), pp. 117–37, and ch. 5, esp. p. 142. Metzer discusses wages, salaries, and unemployment (pp. 123–28) and offers an assessment according to the criteria of the Human Development Index for 1939 (p. 57). Nadan (2006) challenges many of Metzer's conclusions; for salaries and wages in what he calls the "ethnonational" labor market, see pp. 4–7, and ch. 3, esp. pp. 146–51. For a brief, but instructive discussion of peasant income, or rather the chronic deficits therein, see Benvenisti (2000), pp. 96–97.

[31] Himadeh (ed.) (1938), pp. 12–16; Metzer (1998), pp. 7–9. For British urban and agricultural policies, see Y. Miller (1985) and El-Eini (2006).

Among the Jews, the share of urbanites decreased from 82 to 73 percent. This appears to be mainly due to the rapid spread of rural settlements, which expanded into large centers without achieving the legal status of cities; examples include Hadera, Petah Tikva, Rehovot, and Rishon le-Zion.

Jewish immigration and the development of a Jewish economic sector had great effects on population density and distribution in the various regions, which in its turn had a notable impact on the Arab economy and society.[32] Under the Mandate, the economic and demographic center shifted more decisively toward the coastal region. Even in the mid-1930s the majority of the population lived in the mountainous and hilly country, yet population density there was significantly lower than along the coast (76 people per square kilometer in 1931, compared with 118 in the coastal region). The Negev remained thinly settled: Even in the 1930s, its population density stood at only 4 people per square kilometer, while in most other parts of the country it rose from 71 to an estimated 93 people per square kilometer in the years from 1931 to 1936 alone. Hence, the nationwide average of 40 (in

TABLE 2
Population Density and Distribution by Geographic Region

Region	Area (km^2)	Population		Pop. Density (per km^2)	
		1922	1931	1922	1931
1. Coastal Plain	2,928	209,830	344,137	71	118
2. Plain of Acre	316	15,225	18,405	48	58
3. Esdraelon	351	10,629	12,504	30	36
Jezreel	65	2,521	5,566	39	86
4. Mts. of Judaea	6,005	335,133	457,619	56	76
Dsrt. of Judaea	1,051	11,483	10,922	11	10
5. Galilee	2,083	85,472	109,568	41	52
6. Jordan Valley	681	8,329	11,995	12	18
Hula Valley	262	3,306	14,023	—	54
7. Beersheva	12,577	75,254	5,182	—	4
Palestine (total)	26,319	757,182	1,035,821	29	40

Source: Himadeh (ed.) 1938: 6.

[32] Himadeh (ed.) (1938), pp. 4–6, 14–15; K. Stein (1984), pp. 3–4, 185–87.

1931) or 51 (in 1936) people per square kilometer does not adequately describe the situation.

The varying degrees of spatial separation between communities within these regions was of great political significance, which table 2 does not show.[33] In the shadow of mounting tension, separation between the communities grew more marked throughout the 1930s, until it finally prevailed by the end of the Mandate. As a rule, villages were not mixed, but were either Arab or Jewish or, in certain areas, Druze. Even so, spatial separation was diminished by the fact that Arab and Jewish settlements often lay close to one another. Within the Arab community, Muslims, Christians, and Druze (who would sometimes be classified as Arabs, and sometimes not) frequently lived together in villages, though often enough in separate neighborhoods. If a village was designated as "Christian" or "Druze," this usually signaled the majority population. Among the cities, Jaffa, Haifa, Safed, Tiberias, and Jerusalem were mixed (that is Arab and Jewish). Jews formed the majority in Jerusalem, and gradually became the majority in Haifa too, while Jaffa remained predominantly Arab. Gaza, Acre, Nazareth, Baisan, Jenin, Nablus, Hebron, Bethlehem, and Beersheva—where almost 60 percent of Arab city dwellers lived in 1922—were considered purely Arab, even if they numbered some Jewish residents as well. Growing segregation (based largely on political developments) was reflected in official statistics: In 1922 only 22 percent of Jews lived in "purely Jewish" municipalities, by 1946 it was over 50 percent.

[33] Metzer (1998), pp. 7–9, and *Survey of Palestine* (1946), pp. 140–64. The mixing and unmixing was to assume special relevance in the bloody confrontation of 1947–49; see below, chapter 13.

Chapter Nine

"TWO PEOPLES IN ONE LAND"

OF ALL COMMUNITIES IN PALESTINE, the Zionist "new Yishuv" was certainly the most self-contained, and very much centered upon itself. In everyday life, contact with others was kept to a minimum. The school and educational system was almost exclusively Jewish, as was cultural life. Economically speaking, the Jewish and non-Jewish communities did not develop fully autonomously (land, labor, and trade created important interconnections), yet were to some degree separate from one another. Politically speaking, Jews and Arabs viewed one another warily, if not with hostility. And yet, up to the 1930s, Zionist activists were less concerned with the Arab majority in the country than with British policy in London and Jerusalem, as well as with intra-Jewish and intra-Zionist issues. For this reason, it would be wrong to focus solely on interactions between Jews and Arabs, even though, in political terms, relations between the two were of the greatest import.

BUILDING A NEW SOCIETY: THE JEWISH YISHUV

Looking at Jewish society in Mandate Palestine, there is a certain danger of equating all Jews with Zionists, neglecting the "old Yishuv" in favor of the "new," and of considering only the Zionists within this new Yishuv. By the same token, urban society tends to get neglected in favor of a rural society that is taken to be thoroughly Zionist, and indeed to embody the very spirit of Zionism. Finally, due to the sociopolitical dominance of Ashkenazi Jews, it is easy to overlook the Sephardic and Middle Eastern communities, which in the midthirties made up nearly one quarter of the Jews living in Palestine.[1] These tendencies reflect the political focus of most studies dealing with the period, and the projection of later political developments onto earlier ones. Even so, there is no doubt that the Zionists were the most dynamic element within the Yishuv: young, highly-motivated people on a mission, however poorly

[1] According to Himadeh (ed.) (1938), p. 9, the composition was as follows in late 1936: 76.7 percent Ashkenazi, 14.1 Oriental Jews (of which 4.4 percent came from Yemen, 2.2 from Iran, 1.3 each from Iraq and Kurdistan, 0.5 from Bukhara, and 4.4 from elsewhere), and 9.2 percent Sephardic.

they might be living. This was true not only of the rural pioneers and settlers, but of urban laborers as well. "Without a doubt," a German observer wrote in the 1930s:

> The Jewish people form a pyramid of their own. . . . Two thirds of the city of Jerusalem are made up of terribly poor living quarters, built from the metal of petroleum canisters, from lathes, from roofing felt, penetrated by the heat and by the fearful cold of the winter, mud paths that lie full of rubbish, orange peels, and rags. Alongside these are pleasant lower middle class districts, with clean houses in the front and great covered terraces in the back. Yet even age-old Jewish misery, Jewish poverty produces not only students of the Talmud-Tora schools, students of ancient yet unworldly wisdom, but new Jews such as the freshly arrived immigrants, the construction workers with horn-rimmed glasses on their noses who speak only Hebrew, chauffeurs who work only collectively, and the crowds of craftsmen of every kind.
>
> They all bring the atmosphere of Canada to the Holy City. It is not just the rubble and the construction sites, nor the office building towering over the old Arab one. Rather, it is those cheerful youths who do gymnastic exercises on the Sabbath, and play their soccer games, that move through the streets, arms interlinked, not exactly quietly, not very considerately. They do not want to devote themselves to holy studies, nor do they long for the bourgeois bridge club. What they want—cheerful Jews—is to build their own country, by Jews for Jews.[2]

In accordance with the spirit of "auto-emancipation," the Zionists succeeded in forming institutions of Jewish self-government, and in creating a wide range of political, economic, and cultural activities within the Mandate framework, and occasionally even against the express wishes of the British Mandate authorities. One pillar of social and economic development was the Zionist Committee, later transformed into the Palestine Zionist Executive and ultimately the Jewish Agency; another was the Jewish labor movement known as Histadrut. Together they exerted considerable control over Jewish immigration and settlement; they founded their own school and health systems, and provided pensions for the elderly and for those in need. In addition to their own credit institutions, they created a number of business companies that by the 1940s extended from the Jewish construction company Solel Boneh to the shipping line Zim. Against widespread assumptions, Zionist activities were not confined to the rural sector: Land acquisition

---

[2] Tergit (1996), p. 46. Bernstein (2000), Introduction and ch. 1, offers a sophisticated analysis of Jewish "self-segregation," which however did not amount to isolation or insulation.

was one important field of their activities, but by no means the most important.

In April 1918, even prior to the end of World War I and the British conquest of northern Palestine, a Zionist Commission under Chaim Weizmann had arrived in Palestine. The commission representing the Zionist Organization in London (also chaired by Weizmann) was recognized by the British as an advisory body to facilitate contact with the local Jewish community. From its offices in Jerusalem, the Zionist Commission (renamed Palestine Zionist Executive in 1921) quickly assumed the role of actual spokesman for the Jewish Yishuv.[3] Under Article 4 of the draft mandate, provision was in fact made for a "Jewish agency," which was to advise the Mandate government in all matters "affecting" Jewish interests in Palestine. This provision brought the difficulty of distinguishing between Jews and Zionists into sharp relief: The Zionist Commission represented an *international* political body that endeavored to act as the representative of the Jewish community *in Palestine* (against some resistance from this very community). Among the Yishuv itself, an Assembly of Delegates (*asefat ha-nivharim*) was elected in 1920. Its executive organ, the National Council (Vaad Leumi, *va'ad le'umi*), met regularly with the high commissioner. At this time, more than 90 percent of the local Jews were represented in this body, excepting only non-Zionist Orthodox groups such as Agudat Israel, which only joined the Zionist-dominated national institutions in the 1930s. Orthodox circles in the Sephardic, Oriental, and Ashkenazi communities fought stubbornly against the right of women to vote, but to no avail. In Orthodox families (similar to what often happened among Muslim families and no doubt among many Arab Christian ones, too), the men voted on behalf of the women, if they did not boycott the elections altogether.[4] Since the political institutions representing the Jewish Yishuv were financed by donations and member contributions, their autonomy vis-à-vis the Mandate authorities was assured.

The Third Aliya (1919–23) did much to strengthen the Zionist left in the country.[5] By the same token, it sharpened tensions between Jews and Arabs as well as within the Jewish community itself, especially within

---

[3] Stoyanovsky (1928), pp. 87ff.; *Peel Report* (1937), pp. 172–74; *Survey of Palestine* (1946), vol. 2, ch. 22; Wasserstein (1978), pp. 24–25, 133–36; Metzer (1998), pp. 4–5. For local reactions, see also Porath (1974), pp. 30–39.

[4] For Agudat Israel, see Mendes-Flohr/Reinharz (eds.) (1995), pp. 565–66, and Salmon (2002). On the female vote, see the brief account in Naor (1998), pp. 93, 114, 133.

[5] Wasserstein (1978), pp. 136, 139. For Ahdut Haavoda and the ideology of Labor Zionism, see Shimoni (1995), ch. 5, and Mendes-Flohr/Reinharz (eds.) (1995), pp. 585–89. For Jewish credit and banking under the Mandate, see Metzer (1998), pp. 112–16. For immigration, see below, note 10.

its highly politicized Zionist wing. The political spectrum became increasingly diversified: In 1919 one of the parties of Labor Zionism, the Marxist Po'alei Zion, entered a coalition with other groups to form the United Labor Movement (ha-Tnu'a le-Ahdut ha-'Avoda, or more simply: Ahdut Haavoda). In December 1920 Ahdut Haavoda and the leftist Young Worker (ha-Po'el ha-Tza'ir, Hapoel Hatzair) joined to establish the General Federation of Hebrew Workers in Eretz Israel, or Histadrut for short. Under the leadership of David Ben-Gurion (1886–1973), Yitzhak Ben-Zvi (1884–1963), and Berl Katznelson (1887–1944), the Histadrut became the driving force in the local Jewish economy and society. Starting with some 4,400 members in 1920, it already numbered 27,000 by 1930. As early as 1921 the Histadrut opened its own credit institution (Bank ha-Po'alim), and from 1925 its own daily newspaper, Davar, which quickly surpassed the other Jewish dailies in circulation.

In 1925 Vladimir Ze'ev Jabotinsky (1880–1940) founded the Revisionist Party—in Paris, not in Palestine. Its ultimate aim was the creation of a "Jewish state within its historic boundaries," that is to say, on both banks of the Jordan River, entailing a "revision" of the 1922 Treaty amendment that had excluded Transjordan from the Mandate obligation to promote a Jewish national home. If possible, this revision was to be brought about through cooperation with the British, but if necessary against their opposition, too. All else was to be subordinated to this goal, including the socialist aspirations of the Zionist left.[6] The Revisionist movement met with considerable success in Europe. Beginning in the late 1920s, it expanded into Palestine, where Revisionist youth groups (Betar) were founded in many places. Betar, an acronym for Brith Yosef Trumpeldor, referred not only to the hero of Tel Hai, who was killed in March 1920 in an Arab attack on his kibbutz (in the Jewish Yishuv and later in the state of Israel, the so-called battle of Tel Hai achieved the status of a national myth). It also evoked the Betar fortress, the main stronghold of the Bar Kokhba revolt of A.D. 132–35. Like other European and Arab paramilitary movements of the time, Betar cultivated a military spirit and sported uniforms; their shirts were brown. At the same time, illegal paramilitary units were formed, among them the Hagana ("defense" in Hebrew), which recruited its members among the

---

[6] Shapira (1992), esp. pp. 98–109, and 154–62; Shimoni (1995), ch. 6; Mendes-Flohr/ Reinharz (eds.) (1995), pp. 594–97. Former members of the Jewish Brigade joined together in 1919 in their own unit, "The First Judaeans," which numbered five thousand soldiers and officers in 1919–20. Shortly after, it was dissolved by the British who feared political difficulties; Naor (1998), pp. 84, 87, 93. On Tel Hai (which still stood under French military control in 1920, so that the Balfour Declaration did not apply to it), cf. the heroizing account in Naor (1998), pp. 93–94, and the critical treatment in Shapira (1992), pp. 98–109, and Zerubavel (1995), esp. chs. 3 and 9.

armed guards of the Jewish settlements and the former Jewish (Hebrew) Brigade.

On January 1, 1928, the Knesset Israel, as the official representative of the Jews in Palestine, was officially constituted, though it continued to be rejected by ultra-Orthodox (*haredi*) Jews. In a meeting in Zurich in 1929, the so-called General Zionists led by Chaim Weizmann finally succeeded in establishing a Jewish Agency for Palestine (the so-called expanded Jewish Agency), with its headquarters in Jerusalem. For the first time, non-Zionists were to be represented on an equal basis with Zionists. One of the major aims of this measure, taken at a time of economic crisis, was to integrate non-Zionist circles with abundant capital and to promote investment in the Jewish Yishuv.[7] The involvement of prominent figures such as Albert Einstein and Léon Blum won respect for the new Agency. It also underscored the international character of the organization, which saw itself as the representative of the Jewish people as a whole and not just of its Zionist members. The expanded Jewish Agency was recognized in August 1930 by the Mandate authorities as representative of the Jewish community in Palestine. It was also granted the right to allocate immigration permits (so-called certificates) for workers and other immigration candidates without sufficient financial means. The Jewish Agency transferred this task to the Histadrut, which took care to consider applicants in view of both their practical skills and political convictions. The powerful position of the Jewish Agency aroused suspicion, and not just among Arab nationalists. In the eyes of British observers, too, it formed in actual fact a kind of parallel government:

> Speaking generally, it may be said that the Jewish Agency has used to the fullest extent the position conferred on it by the Mandate. In the course of time it has created a complete administrative apparatus. This powerful and efficient organization amounts, in fact, to a Government existing side by side with the Mandatory Government.[8]

Nonetheless, the growing tensions within the Jewish community could neither be resolved nor hidden—tensions between the old and the new Yishuv, between religious and nonreligious Jews, socialists, liberals, and conservatives. The same was true for tensions between the local and the international Zionist movement personified respectively by David Ben-Gurion and Chaim Weizmann. Violent disputes arose over the appropriate strategy for realizing the Zionist project. Put simply, it was a question of whether priority should be attached to num-

---

[7] Wasserstein (1978), pp. 159–60; Shimoni (1995), chs. 3 and 4.
[8] *Peel Report* (1937), p. 174.

bers, financial means, or political convictions, and how the collective forms of settlement and labor should be assessed against "bourgeois" private initiative.

Change through Immigration

In 1922 some 76,000 Jews were registered by the British authorities, following the return to Palestine of many who fled or were deported during World War I, and the influx of a modest number of new immigrants. By the end of the 1920s, the total had risen to 165,000. The number of Jewish agricultural settlements increased from fifty-five to one hundred. The 1920s also witnessed some of the most extensive land purchases in Marj Ibn Amir (Jezreel) and Wadi Hawarith south of Haifa, densifying Jewish settlement especially in the fertile plain of Marj Ibn Amir, which, however, still included large tracts of swamp. Here, the first kibbutzim were founded in 1921, named Nahalal and Tel Yosef, followed in 1924 by the Orthodox Polish settlement Bnei B(a)rak, underlining the fact that not all Jewish rural settlements were Labor Zionist in character. The spectrum of rural forms of life and production grew increasingly diverse, ranging from settlements made up of private family farms (*moshava*) to rural cooperatives (*moshav*) combining private and communal property, to the collective kibbutzim that allowed no private property. In addition, there were the citrus plantations, which for the most part were privately owned. The private sector largely predominated. The greatest landowner was not the Jewish National Fund, but rather the Palestine Jewish Colonization Agency (PICA), founded by Baron James de Rothschild in 1924. Unlike the JNF, the PICA did not regard the land as the eternal trust of the Jewish people, and it did not exclude Arab workers; by the second half of the 1920s it held around 55 percent of all Jewish-owned land.[9]

Jewish immigration ran unevenly, even within the greater waves commonly numbered the Third Aliya (from 1919 to 1923) and the Fourth (from 1924 to 1931).[10] From 1920 to 1923, around 8,000 Jewish immigrants arrived in Palestine per year, while in both 1924 and 1926 it was 13,000, and in 1925 a total 33,000—almost as many as during the entire Second Aliya. Yet in 1927 it was only 2,300 and in 1928 no more than 800. High emigration rates during these years actually resulted in a net decline in the Yishuv: In 1926 and 1927, 74 percent of the new

[9] Metzer (1998), pp. 101–102; for Jewish land acquisition, see below.
[10] For official immigration, cf. Himadeh (ed.) (1938), pp. 21ff; Mossek (1978), pp. 170–71; Metzer (1998), ch. 3, esp. table 3.2; also K. Stein (1984), p. 65.

immigrants (*'olim*) re-emigrated from the country, from 1928 to 1931 it was 38 percent, and from 1919 to 1923 it was 21 percent. Only in 1924 and 1925 did the figure fall below 10 percent. Both immigration and emigration were caused by a combination of political and economic factors: Only a limited number of Jews responded to World War I and the revolutionary changes in Russia by emigrating to Palestine, which under the given circumstances presupposed a high commitment to Zionist ideals. Even the Zionist organizations did not advocate mass immigration, which they would have been unable to control and handle. In view of an official policy that linked immigration to the "economic absorptive capacity" of the country, the Jewish organizations involved had to prove the possibility of gainful employment for able-bodied applicants without sufficient financial means who entered via so-called Workers' Certificates. This was possible only within the Jewish economic sector, as yet barely developed. While the criterion of economic absorptive capacity left some leeway for negotiation, it actually set narrow limits for immigration in these early years.

The United States, always the leading destination for European emigrants of all religions and nationalities, toughened its immigration laws in 1921 and 1924, and introduced fixed quotas linking new immigration to a specific percentage of naturalized citizens of the same origin (for example, Polish immigration could not exceed 3 percent of naturalized Americans of Polish origin). At the same time, policies of economic and financial austerity in Poland served as an additional push factor.[11] The high immigration figures for 1925 can be explained primarily by these developments, which had little to do with the situation in Palestine itself. They did of course affect local conditions, stimulating an intense but brief economic boom that gave way to recession in 1927, even prior to the world economic crisis starting in 1929. The high rate of return emigration during the years from 1926 to 1931, and the sharp downturn in immigration figures in 1929, appear to have been closely linked to the economic crisis in Palestine as well as to the unrest at the Wailing Wall in 1928 and 1929.

Numbers are one thing—the social and political profile of the immigrants is another. If the immigrants of the early 1920s were predominantly young, male, unmarried, and highly motivated, the arrivals starting in 1925 also included many Jewish middle-class families who were not subject to the official quotas as they disposed of independent financial means.[12] While nearly half of the Jewish immigrants still arrived by

---

[11] Metzer (1998), pp. 61ff., 66, and table 3.1 show the total Jewish emigration from Europe for the years 1920–39, thereby placing the Aliya to Palestine in its larger context.

[12] Mossek (1978), appendix 7, p. 171, offers a breakdown according to the data of the

way of the Workers' Certificates, the share of "capitalists" (the official term in use), rose to about one quarter (16 percent in 1922–23 and 32 percent in 1924–26). With their middle-class lifestyle, habits, and interests, they began to slowly transform Jewish society in Palestine, much to the dismay of the socialist Zionist pioneers. Their interests were represented by the Association of Hebrew Industrialists and Employers, founded in 1921. The great majority of the immigrants of the Fourth Aliya, both "workers" and "capitalists," settled in the cities. Within two decades Tel Aviv, first founded in 1909 as a garden city, changed beyond recognition. While the greater part of the capital flowed into midsized family enterprises, shops, and restaurants, the cornerstone was also laid for modern industry. Among the largest enterprises was the Anglo-Palestine Electricity Company, founded by Pinhas Rutenberg in 1923, which monopolized the local power market, beginning with the electrification of Tel Aviv. Those Arab communities that refused to buy their electrical power from a Jewish company had to make do with kerosene lamps for their houses, businesses, and streets.[13]

Overall, the 1920s offered no straight path to the creation of a Jewish national home or, as it was sometimes put, a Jewish "Commonwealth" in Palestine. The crisis of the late 1920s affected the urban areas especially hard. Unemployment rose significantly when in 1927 Solel Boneh, the contracting company of the Histadrut, was forced to declare bankruptcy. During the same years the Yishuv witnessed numerous labor struggles between socialist workers and Jewish employers, real estate and landowners, who in many places monopolized the right to vote in the municipal assemblies. Under the banner of the "conquest of labor," the Histadrut fought tenaciously against the employment of Arab workers in agriculture, construction, and industry, Jewish as well as public (that is, financed by the Mandate); Petah Tikva and other places saw violent clashes between Zionist activists, Jewish employers, and Arab workers in 1927. Yet in some of the urban industrial strikes, Jewish and Arab workers stood side by side, overcoming their political differences and wide disparity in background, living conditions, and mentality.[14] A joint Arab-Jewish union of railway workers was founded in 1923,

---

Zionist Executive's Immigration Department; see also Metzer (1998), pp. 72–83, esp. table 3.4. For capital formation, Metzer (1998), pp. 103–16.

[13] Munayyir (1997), pp. 20–21, shows this in connection with Lydda; for Rutenberg, see also LeVine (2005), pp. 201–202, 211.

[14] Lockman (1996); LeVine (2005), ch. 4; Metzer (1998), pp. 6–7, 128–37. Bernstein (2000), chs. 1 and 2, highlights the disparities in background and mentality separating Jewish from Arab workers: Jews formed a real proletariat, whereas Arabs were mostly migrant peasant workers, that is to say temporary, seasonal, or casual laborers of peasant background.

though it never attracted more than five hundred members and remained the only mixed union. The Palestine Arab Workers' Society (PAWS), also founded among workers of the Palestine Railway based in Haifa in 1925—which quickly expanded to include other economic sectors—was purely Arab. Under the impact of the recession, the Histadrut in 1927 set up the Palestine Labor League (PLL), again in Haifa, to attract Arab workers so as to enhance their own bargaining position against the employers. Yet the PLL was organized separately and was merely affiliated with the Histadrut, which remained the exclusive domain of the Jewish working class until well beyond Israeli independence.

CULTURE MATTERS: JEWISH OR HEBREW?

The Jewish Yishuv may have been small in numbers, but it was highly diverse, colorful, multilingual, and indeed multicultural—granted the proviso that all Jews in Palestine shared a common bond of Jewishness. Here as elsewhere, diversity entailed the potential for friction. There were the well-known political differences that in many cases reflected generational conflicts. There was the great conflict over language, in which supporters of the exclusive use of Modern Hebrew (Ivrit) agitated against the use of all other languages, whether Yiddish, German, Russian, French, or Arabic. There was the dispute over rest on the sabbath which some Labor Zionists did not observe, while at least as many others did. Finally, there were complaints by Oriental and Sephardic Jews against discrimination by the Ashkenazi Jews, who had attained political, social, and cultural predominance during the period of Zionist immigration. One important conflict line divided the advocates of "cultural Zionism" from the supporters of a "Hebrew revival." "Cultural Zionism," as represented by Ahad Haam ("One of the people," the pen name of Asher Hirsch Ginzberg, 1856–1927) and his followers, aimed at a *Jewish* renewal in Palestine/Eretz Israel and the diaspora that could or could not be accompanied by nationalist ideas. If Herzl was concerned with the problem of the *Jews* (*Judenfrage*), Ahad Haam worried about the fate of *Judaism* in the face of secularization and assimilation.[15] The "*Hebrew*" revival, on the other hand, was by definition nationalist, looking for inspiration to the heroic past not only of Solomon, David, and Joshua, but also of the Maccabees and the Jewish fighters who fell at Masada. The distinction between Jewish and Hebrew was largely

[15] On Ahad Haam, see Shimoni (1995), pp. 104–12; on the National-Religious trend within the broader Zionist movement, see ch. 4; also Salmon (2002). The data for cultural and recreational institutions are taken from Naor (1998).

blurred by translation into European languages, in which both *yehudi* and *'ivri* were usually rendered as "Jewish." Conflict between the two camps was intense, and crossed the fault line dividing the secular from the religious or Orthodox.

The modern "Hebrew" sector quickly expanded to reach the arts, culture, sport, and entertainment. Even before World War I had ended, in July 1918, the cornerstone was laid for a Hebrew University on Mt. Scopus, which was opened in 1925, a few months after the Technion in Haifa. The Hebrew University gave young Jews the possibility of acquiring a first-class modern (that is, nonreligious) education in their own country. Shortly after the war, in December 1918, the first Hebrew-language film was made. In 1919 the newspaper *Haaretz* (*ha-'aretz*) was published, which later became one of the most respected dailies in Israel. In 1921 a Jewish writers' union was formed in Tel Aviv, and in 1924 it was organized nationwide. Theater companies were set up, and in 1923 even an opera (also in Tel Aviv), which opened with a performance of Verdi's *La Traviata*. In Jerusalem the cornerstone was laid for the Rockefeller Archeological Museum in 1929. The passion for sport also took hold in Palestine, and in some instances it bridged the communal divide: The Palestinian Football Association, founded in 1928, included an Arab team from Jerusalem along with several Jewish clubs.

Gabriele Tergit, who lived in Palestine from 1933 to 1938 and left us with a highly perceptive travel account, described three varieties, or ideal types, of Jewish life in Palestine to illustrate its diversity: the citizen, the worker or pioneer, and the scholar. All could be found in Jerusalem with its various quarters and suburbs, ranging from bourgeois Rehavia at one end to the ultra-Orthodox Mea Shearim at the other:

Out there lie the colonies: Jews at the plow, Jews with the scythe, broad-shouldered, long-legged, wearing short pants, with naked arms, and they speak Hebrew.

Out there lies Rehavia. A modern suburb of affluent Jews who could live anywhere, elegant clothing, fine food, tasteful homes, lawyers, doctors, merchants, and they speak Hebrew.

Out there are the more modest suburbs: . . . Young fellows, red-faced, healthy, and coarse, they read the Davar, the Hebrew workers' newspaper.

But in the middle of this new country lies an island of eternal Judaism, of two thousand year-old Judaism: the ghetto of Jerusalem, Mea Shearim. Wall-like buildings, and gates, always prepared for attack. Prayer house after prayer house. Life nothing but an interruption from prayer and the study of the Talmud. A miserable small market, with stall after stall, grey cheese, salted herring, olives, sweets, unappealing pastries. . . . Small houses with dilapidated wooden staircases leading to a covered balcony

on the first floor, bordered with vines, pomegranate flowers covering the
filth. . . .

By day, an area in need of renovation, of dirt and misery. But by night,
the republic of scholars. They sit by their oil-lamps, and in the white pages
and the black letters they encounter life. They converse with the wisest of
all times and discourse with the most eloquent.[16]

Social distinctions were as relevant to Jewish society as they were to
Arab society. They were simply based on different criteria:

Rehavia is a city of officials and academics. And so it is. The normalization
of the Jewish people has produced the Jewish official: narrow-mindedness,
importance of career and salary, patriotism, chauvinism, and arrogance.
One gives parties, one attends parties, has farewell teas, attends farewell
teas, gives little speeches, holds receptions, and goes about dressed in dinner jackets when the temperature is 104 degrees. For the English also wear
dinner jackets. There is the good family and the not so good family and
the very good family. There are numerous social yardsticks. The first yardstick is one's place within the Zionist Organization, which is a matter of
income as much as of power. The second yardstick is how long one has been
in the country—the Mayflower is not specific to America. The third yardstick
is the place of origin. Russia is very good, Poland less so, Russian Poland is
better than Galicia, and at the very rear range since 1933 the German Jews.
The English-speaking world is *hors de concours*. . . . A Zionist official with
an Eastern European Jewish grandmother, living in Rehavia, no longer has
any problems. The Jewish question is buried. One knows everything.[17]

It was precisely the bourgeois lifestyle of good Jewish society in Rehavia, Haifa, and rising Tel Aviv that the Zionist pioneers rejected. They
hoped that physical labor would lead to the "normalization" of Jewish
Luftmenschen and the "restructuring" (*Umschichtung*) of the Jewish
people. They acted from a sense of conviction: The Aliya might turn all
new immigrants into "ascenders," but only physical labor could redeem
them.

Those who despise Tel Aviv demand, like God himself, that the people
should wander for forty years through the desert before reaching the Promised Land. Like all professional ideologues possessed by some idea, they
call for a new generation. They want no cities, and place moral value on
the use of a tractor.[18]

---

[16] Tergit (1996), pp. 36–39.

[17] Ibid., pp. 44–45.

[18] Ibid., p. 65. For the idealization of peasant and Bedouin life, see also Benvenisti
(2000), p. 59.

As diverse as they may have been according to origin, opinions, and lifestyle, the members of the "new" Yishuv did not get along with those of the "old": "There is no bridge between Rehavia and the Wailing Wall."

> The Jews of Palestine do not like the praying, Talmud-studying, dirty, and poor ghetto Jews, partly because they lived for decades on donations. They want the naked-armed, forceful, tough young people of the colonies. They want the smith and the carpenter, the postman and the policeman. They want the people in its natural stratification, beyond the gates, beyond the walls.[19]

ADAPTATION AND RESISTANCE: ARAB POLITICS, 1918–30

"The Politics of Notables"

When British rule was established in Palestine, people there could not know whether it would last or have any deep effects on the existing situation. Hence they adopted a strategy of caution to protect their own position against all eventualities. For the broad mass of the population it was primarily a question of recovering from the losses of the war years that left little room for political activism. For the local elites, the fall of the Ottoman Empire and British occupation marked a turning point. For one thing, they lost important positions that had previously secured their status and influence: above all, tax farming, which ceased to exist under the British, and the supervision of land allotment and registration, which they had exercised in the framework of various administrative and advisory bodies. The connections to Istanbul that they had cultivated at considerable expense were now useless. Under British occupation new structures of communication and new political hierarchies emerged that tended to further strengthen the position of Jerusalem and its elite. The status of Jerusalem was enhanced in spite of the perceptible shift of economic activity toward the coast, where a new economic and cultural center formed for both Arabs and Jews in the urban agglomeration stretching from Jaffa to Tel Aviv.[20] More toward the north, Haifa developed rapidly in the 1930s, largely on account of its port, its industries, and the Palestine Railway linking Palestine to Egypt and Iraq, for which Haifa hosted a repair facility. By contrast, Nablus lost the eco-

---

[19] Tergit (1996), p. 44. The emphasis on the body, more specifically the naked arms and legs of young men and women, comes out strongly in the relevant literature. It also fueled friction with local Arab society, as the unrest of the 1920s and 1930s was to show.

[20] Vashitz (1983), Seikaly (1998), pp. 185ff., and Bernstein (2000), chs. 2, 5, and 6, illustrate the radical changes of the Mandate period using the example of Haifa. For Jaffa and Tel Aviv, see LeVine (2005); for Nablus, Graham-Brown (1982).

nomic importance that it had maintained into the early twentieth century, and was even deprived of its rank as a district capital. Yet it remained a center of political activity, as the events of the 1930s would show.

Despite certain racist stereotypes, which were neither confined to Palestine nor particularly pronounced there, the British followed a policy of "indirect rule." The strategy to use local elites as mediators between the authorities and the broader populace had proven especially effective in India. In Palestine as elsewhere, the British privileged people from "good families" who were seen as "natural leaders" of their respective communities, comparable in a way to the British landed gentry.[21] Early in 1917, before the Levant was even conquered, the military secret service in Cairo had compiled a three-volume handbook (*Vademecum*) of local leaders and notable families. In essence, the British policy of notables amounted to a consolidation of existing social hierarchies, even if they had not necessarily existed for a long time, giving effect to status quo policies that the British were unwilling or unable to maintain in other domains.

The British policy of notables did not make the position of the local elites any easier. Their primary concern was to remain "in play" in a situation of considerable uncertainty, defending their position against threats from above and below while preserving their local influence, all without offending the British. This called for caution and circumspection. Their dilemma was obvious: Many members of the Arab elite were not entirely averse to a British mandate—provided it were a mandate without Zionism. More than a few hoped to influence the British in favor of Arab interests (and hence their own). However, the British denied the Arabs any recognized political representation for as long as they refused to accept the Mandate Treaty. Yet to cooperate with the British in the given framework entailed acceptance not only of the Mandate, but also of the Balfour Declaration, and hence the negation of the Arab right to national self-determination. Arab participation in the Mandate system thus did not offer the prospect of gaining influence as it did for the Jews, but, rather, looked as if it would be an act of surrender. The traditional function of the notables to mediate "top-down," restraining the common people (and this language was widely used), was still in demand. "Bottom-up," however, the elite found itself lacking in effective means of influence and pressure to wring concessions from the British or the Zionists. This reinforced the lack of parity between Jews and

---

[21] Y. Miller (1985), pp. 36ff., 51ff., 71ff.; also Muslih (1988), pp. 155–56; Lesch (1979), p. 59. On the handbook, see Wasserstein (1978), p. 14; Nafi (1998), p. 54, and chapter 7 above.

Arabs regarding their abilities not only to articulate their own interests vis-à-vis the outside world, but to pursue those interests in the face of opposition, even if by nonviolent means.

The Arab dilemma was well known to the British, as indicated in July 1937 by the *Peel Report*:

> A national self-government could not be established in Palestine as long as it would be used to frustrate the purpose of the Balfour Declaration. Even so, the crux was plain enough to Arab eyes. It was the Balfour Declaration and its embodiment in the draft Mandate and nothing else which seemingly prevented their attaining a similar measure of independence to that which other Arab communities already enjoyed. And their reaction to this crux was logical. They repudiated the Balfour Declaration. They protested against its implementation in the draft Mandate. . . . And they refused to co-operate in any form of government other than a national government responsible to the Palestinian people.[22]

However, the Arab elite's strategy of refusal was largely confined to the national level that was also most visible at home and abroad. It was barely practiced at the municipal level, and hence was not part of any comprehensive policy of noncooperation.[23] In the municipal elections of 1927 and 1934, for instance, Arabs participated along with Jews. For the purposes of daily life and interaction between the two communities that were so strictly segmented in many domains, municipal elections were of special importance. They were organized according to confessional proportion, which in Jerusalem assigned places to four Muslims, two Christians, and six Jews, but were configured in such a way that Jews must also vote for Muslim candidates, and vice versa. Despite their pointed acts of noncooperation at the national level, the local elites essentially followed a pragmatic strategy—pragmatic at least in their own eyes, if not in those of their Zionist adversaries. Even after 1920, when the chances of Arab unification under Faisal appeared slim, they still placed some hope in British justice and fair play.

THE MUSLIM-CHRISTIAN ASSOCIATIONS

Between 1917 and 1920 over forty political associations numbering thousands of members were formed, attracting predominantly members

[22] *Peel Report* (1937), pp. 55–56.

[23] Porath (1974), pp. 157–58; Y. Miller (1985), pp. 43–46. In 1926 elected bodies replaced the city councils; the right to vote in municipal elections was premised on property qualifications, since the British (like the Ottomans before them) supposed that only property holders would have a "sense of civic responsibility"; Wasserstein (1978), p. 152. On

of the Arab middle and upper classes. They did not act as political parties, nor did they advance a well-defined program beyond the struggle against Zionism. Among the most important new groups were the Muslim-Christian Associations as well as the Literary Forum and the Arab Club, which had forerunners in the pre–World War I period. Scholars have sought to correlate specific options and organizations with distinct generational groups to make sense of the confusing tangle of clubs, unions, and parties. According to this interpretation, the older generation, socialized under the Ottoman Empire, was distinguished for its cautious and conservative attitude (as displayed by the Muslim-Christian Associations), while a younger generation, no longer rooted in an Ottoman worldview, adopted radical nationalist positions.[24] While not without a certain logic, this model is too schematic: In actual fact, there were younger people involved in the Muslim-Christian Associations, while the Literary Forum and the Arab Club counted a number of members from the older generation.

The first Muslim-Christian associations had formed in early 1918 in Jerusalem and Jaffa—the old center of urban life in Arab Palestine and one of the new ones, respectively. A few months later, they were formally constituted as Palestinian Muslim-Christian Associations (MCA, *al-jam'iyyat al-islamiyya al-masihiyya al-filistiniyya*).[25] Similar expressions of Muslim-Christian solidarity occurred in both Syria and Egypt, where the newly formed national Wafd movement advocated "the unity of cross and crescent." The public involvement of Christian Arabs, who despite their strong role in trade, education, and the liberal professions had long remained aloof from politics, was something new in Palestine.[26]

---

the 1934 municipal elections in Jerusalem, cf. Porath (1977), pp. 62ff.; for Haifa, Seikaly (1998), pp. 193–207, 232–34. For different evaluations of local administration, see Stoyanovsky (1928), pp. 245ff.; *Survey of Palestine* (1946), pp. 128–39; al-Hut (1981), p. 133; El-Eini (2006), ch. 1.

[24] Muslih (1988), pp. 158–63. Nafi (1998), pp. 50ff., is critical.

[25] Porath (1974), pp. 31–34, 287; slightly differing data in al-Hut (1981), pp. 80–87, 186–87. The Islamist Salih (1989), pp. 99–103, finds fault with these associations, which he describes as largely under British control. For Syria, cf. Gelvin (1998), pp. 181–86. Steppat (1974) documents an interesting forerunner of Muslim-Christian cooperation—an urban Community of Solidarity (*'ammiyya*) of Muslims and Christians that formed in Nazareth in 1854 to provide protection against external danger.

[26] Porath (1974), pp. 293–94; Muslih (1988), p. 158; for background information, see Abu Jabir (2004). For Haifa, see Seikaly (1998), p. 165. The figures are taken from Himadeh (ed.) (1938), pp. 9–11, 30, and McCarthy (1990), pp. 30–38. In the nineteenth century, Christian emigration had increased. According to al-Hut, as cited in Nafi (1998), p. 64, Christians made up 21 percent of the notables despite comprising only 11 percent of the population in 1918–34. For Atatürk and the Missionary Congresses of 1924 and 1928, cf. Nafi (1998), pp. 75–76, 214–17; Kupferschmidt (1987), pp. 247–48; Salih (1989), pp. 137–40. For the Syrian uprising, see Provence (2005). Generally speaking,

At the beginning of the 1930s, around 91,000 Christians lived among 760,000 Muslims. About 40 percent of the Christians, or 40,000 people, belonged to the Orthodox Patriarchate of Jerusalem (commonly referred to as Greek Orthodox, although a minority belonged to the Russian Orthodox Church). The Catholics (Latin Christians) numbered just under 19,000, most of them Arabs. The Greek Catholics (Melkites) totaled around 13,000, and Arabic-speaking Anglicans and Lutherans around 5,000. In the various administrative and advisory bodies of the Tanzimat era, Christians (most of them Orthodox) were well represented, and possibly even overrepresented within the framework of the proportional system. They were also active in the Chamber of Commerce and in philanthropic and literary associations, and from the outset played an active role in the vocally anti-Zionist local press. But the Italian invasion of Tripolitania created an anti-Christian mood in the Ottoman Empire after 1911, which intensified during World War I. Muslim enthusiasm for Kemal Atatürk's war of liberation awakened fresh anxieties among Palestinian Christians, some of whom felt solidarity with the Greeks who fought against the Turkish independence movement in Anatolia. The nationalist uprising in Syria in 1925, during which Christian villagers were harassed, raised fresh fears. On the other side, two Christian World Missionary Congresses, held in Jerusalem in 1924 and 1928, provoked the Muslims, creating apprehensions among the Christians that relations with Muslims could be damaged through the activities of foreign missionaries. In this context, any political initiative expressing the common concerns of Muslims and Christians under British rule was of considerable importance.

As mentioned earlier, Arab Christians lived almost exclusively in the urban areas. Many felt threatened by the immigrant Jews, both socially and economically. For them, the dangers of massive Jewish immigration and the creation of a Jewish national home proceeded not only from the rural Jewish settlements that captured public attention. Trade, industry, and the liberal professions, where Jews were strongly represented, played a major role as well. Yet the measures taken to deal with this challenge were not uniform. Like their Muslim counterparts, Christian Arab notables initially tended to adopt a friendly policy toward Britain, without abandoning their anti-Zionist stance. The Orthodox Patriarchate of Jerusalem, dominated by Greek clerics rather than Arabs, was in search of a new protecting power after the downfall of the Czarist Empire, and in principle was pro-British and opposed to Faisal. The Nahda Urthuduksiyya, the Orthodox revival movement of the late nineteenth

---

British and Zionist reports on Christian-Muslim friction have to be used cautiously, as they often tend to project their own prejudices and/or political interests onto the situation.

century, as well as its successors, took a very different position: They represented the Arabic-speaking community and viewed themselves as Arab nationalists, giving new expression to the age-old division between the Greek clergy and the Arab congregations that had already erupted in 1860 and 1908.[27] Many Arabic-speaking Orthodox Christians saw themselves as oppressed by more than one party in the postwar period— the British, the Jews, *and* the Greeks.

The Muslim-Christian Associations brought together local notables and religious dignitaries of the Christian and Muslim communities, gradually expanding to include village sheikhs of the mountain areas and the Karmel region near Haifa. In the immediate aftermath of World War I, they called for Palestinian autonomy under British protection, opposing any unification of Palestine with Syria. Their political ideas and activities moved along traditional lines in that they relied on petitions and other means of persuasion, generally directed "bottom-up" toward the Mandate authorities. The MCA employed no new methods of political activity "top-down," let alone a strategy of mass mobilization, which would first be used by other groups at a later time. Little wonder, then, that the British viewed the Muslim-Christian Associations favorably. In the initial phase, they may even have enjoyed active British support as an Arab counterweight to the evolving Zionist organizations.[28]

In 1919 the Muslim-Christian Associations had an estimated three thousand members and supporters in the whole of Palestine, though the share of active members quickly declined.[29] Although they did elect a board, the MCA remained a loose association of local groups without a national hierarchy. While they quickly established themselves in the interior mountains and the Karmel region, winning influential village sheikhs for the movement, they were less successful in the more recently established and socially less stratified villages of the coastal plain and Galilee. In Haifa, which since the close of the nineteenth century had seen tensions between Muslims and Christians as the latter outdid the former both socially and economically, separate Muslim and Christian associations formed in 1918–19, though they frequently acted in unison. In Nablus with a Christian community so tiny that it was difficult to recruit even one member, a Muslim-Christian Association was active from 1919 to 1931. Muslim-Christian Associations were also created in

---

[27] Al-Hut (1981), pp. 187–88, reports on the foundation of various Orthodox clubs beginning in 1924. See also Porath (1974), pp. 295ff.; Tsimhoni (1978). For financial reasons, the Patriarchate sold large plots of land to Jews, provoking strong criticism among the Orthodox community; see Katz/Kark (2005); more data in Abu Jabir (2004).

[28] Porath (1974), pp. 32ff., 38; al-Hut (1981), pp. 81–82; Muslih (1988), pp. 160–62.

[29] Porath (1974), pp. 276ff., 283ff. By 1921 only 650 members seem to have been left; see ibid., pp. 105ff. On Haifa, see Seikaly (1998), pp. 160–81.

Gaza in 1920, and in 1922 in Nazareth with its Christian majority, which until then had not witnessed any political activism at all. A purely Muslim organization was established in Tiberias, but no longer heard from after 1923. The movement was rather weak in Hebron, a city represented for the first time at a MCA Congress in 1923. Various competing groups were active in Safed, Baisan, Ramallah, Ramla, Lydda, Tulkarm, Jenin, and Acre. The Bedouins of Beersheva proved resistant toward all attempts at organization.

In the early 1920s, the most important intellectual and political associations in the country were still the Literary Forum (*al-muntada al-adabi*) and the Arab Club (*al-nadi al-'arabi*), which also included Muslims and Christians, but had a somewhat younger clientele than the MCA. Women did not figure in any of them. Charitable associations, while in essence not apolitical, did not openly engage in political activities. The same is not true for the Arab press that began to slowly develop, often in close connection to political or clan-based organizations.[30] The Literary Forum, founded in 1909 in Istanbul, had attracted numerous members in the Arab provinces. Despite its pro-Ottoman leanings, it was caught up in the turmoil of war, and had to halt its activities following the execution of its chairman in 1915. It was reestablished in 1918–19 in Jerusalem with the prominent participation of several members of the Nashashibi family, and remained especially active in that city. While the Nashashibis were (at least later) widely identified with a pro-British attitude, the Literary Forum proclaimed the warlike slogan "we live and die in the name of the Arabs" (*bismi l-'arab nahya wa-bismi l-'arab namut*), advocating political union with Syria under Faisal and a determined struggle against Zionism. The Arab Club, founded in 1918 in Jerusalem with the motto "Our land belongs to us!" (*arduna lana*), followed similar lines. The Arab Club built on a predecessor organization that had been active in Damascus, Aleppo, Jerusalem, and Nablus and had close connections with the al-Fatat organization.

Unlike the Muslim-Christian Associations, these groups did not attempt to merely transmit their views "upward" in the form of petitions and meetings with British military and civilian officials. Rather, they wished to carry them to the Palestinian public, and to mobilize it in their favor. To this end, they not only engaged in journalism, issued manifestos, and staged demonstrations, but also appeared at mosques, churches,

---

[30] For women and charitable associations, see Fleischmann (2003), ch. 4. For the press, see ibid., pp. 66–73; R. Khalidi (1997), chs. 6 and 7, and Ayalon (2004); al-Najjar (2005) contains factual errors and is to be used with caution. For the Literary Forum and the Arab Club, see al-Hut (1981), pp. 84–89; Nafi (1998), pp. 35–36, 68, 141–42, and 182, note 7; Muslih (1988), pp. 164ff., 174, 220; Gelvin (1998), pp. 64–86. Porath (1974), pp. 74–79, is partly obsolete. See also chapter 7 above.

and religious celebrations. They were also the first to make use of sports activities, theater productions, and school events. But their impact was limited by shaky finances. The post–World War I period also saw the rise of the several militant secret societies, such as the Association of Brotherhood and Virtue (*jam'iyyat al-ikha' wa-l-'afaf*) active in Jerusalem around 1918. Their main targets appeared to be Arabs who cooperated with Jews—sold them land or bought it for them—and their members seem to have come from a more modest background compared to the MCA or the Literary Forum with their elitist bias.[31] None of these groups appears to have been explicitly Islamic in orientation.

In the subsequent years, the various groups and associations sought to consolidate their forces and to gain support for their ideas from both the Arab population and the Mandate authorities. The MCA organized a number of conferences on Palestinian soil, while the pro-Syrian activists held their meetings in Damascus. In early 1919 a first Palestinian-Arab Congress met in Jerusalem, attended by twenty-seven deputies from various Palestinian cities, including a number of representatives of the Muslim-Christian Associations.[32] The main theme was the rejection of both Zionism and French claims to Syria. Following heated debates and considerable confusion, a majority passed a resolution in favor of merging with an independent Syria, to be created with British assistance, and sent this resolution to the Paris Peace Conference. Coordinated action was required in June 1919 when the King-Crane Commission arrived in Palestine to determine the will of the Syrian population to be transmitted to the Peace Conference. As the year 1919 reached its end, calls to resist the British and the Zionists grew stronger throughout the country, and the first attempts at nationwide organization were made.[33] The Arab defeat in the battle of Maisalun in July 1920 marked a turning point. French rule put an end to the Syrian option. This compelled Palestinian nationalists to adopt a narrower focus, requiring closer union between the various Palestinian regions and their inhabitants than existed so far.

Unrest in Palestine

In the early Mandate period, Arab politics were by and large nonviolent. Political demands were mostly voiced through diplomatic channels, such

[31] Muslih (1998), pp. 170–74, 220ff.; also al-Hut (1981), pp. 89–90. According to Porath (1974), p. 79, the *jam'iyyat al-ikha' wa-l-'afaf* had two hundred members at the beginning of 1919, including lower-class people; see also ibid., pp. 129–31.

[32] Al-Hut (1981), pp. 195–200; Muslih (1988), pp. 162, 178–90; also Porath (1974), pp. 79–85. For the King-Crane Commission, see chapter 7 above. A second meeting was not permitted by the British authorities who feared unrest; al-Hut (1981), pp. 82, 123–24.

[33] Muslih (1988), pp. 112–13, 198–200; Porath (1974), ch. 2, esp. pp. 93ff.; Khalidi (1997), ch. 7.

as talks and negotiations with the British administration, supplemented with petitions and occasionally accompanied by demonstrations, boycotts, and strikes. The first anniversary of the Balfour Declaration was marked with protest rallies in Jerusalem, which the British had conquered only shortly before (the Zionist Commission for its part held a parade to celebrate the occasion). When in late February 1920 the military administration officially announced that the Balfour Declaration would be put into effect, thousands of protesters marched through Jerusalem, Haifa, Jaffa, Bethlehem, Bait Jala, and other locations in peaceful and orderly fashion. In Haifa, for example, following Friday prayers in the great mosque, a train of people set out toward the Catholic church, where representatives of various Christian communities had gathered, so as to display a unified front of Muslims and Christians. As on many similar occasions both earlier and later, they presented the military authorities with a petition in protest against the establishment of a national home for the Jews.[34] Violent demonstrations occurred a few days later, on March 8, 1920, following the news of Faisal's coronation, which nourished the hope that Palestine might still become part of an independent Arab kingdom. Palestinian society as a whole remained quiet, though. In April 1920, reports of an attack against a British military unit by Bedouins from Hawran in southern Syria and the region around Baisan, which was allegedly meant to unleash a nationwide uprising on behalf of Faisal, remained without noticeable effect. The country as a whole seemed peaceful, Arab resistance was barely coordinated, and a national movement was at best in the making.

April 1920: The Nabi Musa Riots

The shock came unexpectedly: On April 4–5, 1920, Jerusalem witnessed severe riots in connection with the Nabi Musa festival (*mawsim al-nabi Musa*), leading for the first time to deaths and severe injuries. In the nineteenth and early twentieth centuries, pilgrimage to the shrine (*maqam*) of Moses (whom the Muslims regard as one of their prophets), situated about seven kilometers southwest of Jericho on the road to Jerusalem, was one of the most significant religious events in Palestine. Unusual for a Muslim festival, the pilgrimage was timed to coincide with a major Christian festival, Orthodox Easter, suggesting an element of competition that may have been introduced at the time of the Crusades. Yet by the nineteenth and twentieth centuries competition was no longer its distinguishing feature, and like other popular festivals, especially those held in honor of a saint, it attracted Christians as well as Mus-

---

[34] Porath (1974), pp. 95–97, 100; al-Hut (1981), pp. 119–20.

lims.[35] Its most important ritual element was circumcision. All in all, it was a merry occasion, complete with music, song, and dance, attended by families and groups of friends; if they were needy or could make a justified claim for assistance, they were fed and housed by the administration of the religious endowment supporting the shrine. The tomb of Moses is known to have been visited as early as the 1150s, and was highly sought after as a place of burial. The complex of buildings erected over the grave can be traced to the late twelfth or early thirteenth centuries; various reconstructions and renovations are also documented. In the modern period, the annual pilgrimage was mostly made by inhabitants of the districts of Nablus and Hebron and the villages around Jerusalem, meaning that the majority of pilgrims were peasants, fieldworkers, and their families. Up to the outbreak of the Arab revolt in 1936, its "constituency" continuously expanded in both social and geographical terms. Beginning in the eighteenth century, the administrators of the Nabi Musa Waqf (a family endowment) were the distantly related Jerusalem families of Yunus and al-Husaini, who saw to it that their native city played an important role in the festivities. No less important than the growing role of Jerusalem notables was the gradual politicization of the event. Even before 1914 it brought together residents of several rural districts, thus creating a feeling of unity and community beyond the local level. Still, it appears that in the Ottoman period the festival was not connected with any political demonstrations (though it was heavily guarded and protected by Ottoman soldiers). The situation changed after World War I: Beginning in 1919 there were first reports of political speeches held during the procession. In 1920 a few pilgrims even carried banners with the slogan "Palestine is part of Syria."[36]

In 1920 the festival fell in the same week as both Orthodox Easter and Passover, and Jerusalem was crowded with pilgrims. Prayer at al-Aqsa Mosque was part of the pilgrimage, and on their way to the mosque, many pilgrims would cross the Jewish Quarter in Jerusalem. On April 4, 1920, violence erupted against its Jewish inhabitants after a number of Muslim dignitaries, from Mayor Musa Kazim al-Husaini to the young Amin al-Husaini, had given political speeches calling for resistance to the Balfour Declaration. Amin al-Husaini is said to have

[35] On the Nabi Musa festival, cf. Friedland/Hecht (1996); Canaan (1927), pp. 193–214; for a description by a Jewish observer, cf. Kaiser (1992), pp. 490–92. I have not seen Kamil J. Asali, *Mawsim al-nabi Musa fi filastin. Tarikh al-mawsim wa-l-maqam* (Amman 1990).

[36] Canaan (1927), pp. 197, 204–205. Flags and other symbols are discussed in al-Hut (1981), p. 212. The Nabi Musa endowment was made subject to the Waqf Ministry in 1913. The British placed it under the control of the Supreme Muslim Council in 1921; Kupferschmidt (1987), pp. 116–18, and Reiter (1996), pp. 13–14, 135–36.

Figure 11. The shrine of Nabi Musa. Anonymous photograph, c. 1900.

shown the crowd a picture of Faisal and to have called out: "This is your king!" The mood was agitated, and tension was further fueled by the provocative entry of a group of Zionist youths and by the gunshots of British soldiers trying to scatter the crowd. In the riots that followed, nine people were killed (5 Jews and 4 Arabs) and around 230 were seriously injured, most of them Jews.[37] Most inhabitants of the Jewish

[37] Segev (2000), ch. 6; Lesch (1985), pp. 101–104; Verdery (1971), pp. 276–77, 281; Wasserstein (1978), p. 108. In a textbook case of "tunnel vision," al-Hut (1981), pp. 120–22, ignores the Jewish victims. Salih (1989), pp. 165–71, confirms the role played by Amin al-Husaini, the later mufti of Jerusalem. With different assessments, see al-ʿAsali (1991a), pp. 21ff., and Mattar (1988), pp. 16–17. For Jewish reactions, cf. Shapira (1992), pp. 109–26.

Quarter were members of the old Yishuv, who for the most part had no sympathy with Zionism. Yet the Arab assailants made no distinction between Jews and Zionists, and attacked precisely those who were least able to defend themselves. The outbreak of violence caused general dismay, and the explanations given for its causes and effects proved highly revealing. The British military court and commission of inquiry charged with analyzing the events viewed the riots as an expression of political and racial tensions, and not so much of religious antagonism. Zionists by contrast tended to portray the Arab attacks not as politically motivated, but rather as the expression of anti-Semitism.

The Riots of May 1921

The riots of May 1921, which cost around one hundred human lives, including Jews and Arabs in almost equal numbers, were of a very different character.[38] They broke out when during the May Day parade supporters of the Communist Party (officially called Socialist Workers' Party, and commonly known as Mopsi after its Hebrew acronym), which at that time was exclusively Jewish, marched from Jaffa in the direction of Tel Aviv and, on their way, clashed with demonstrators of the Zionist Ahdut Haavoda. When the police shot in the air to disperse the crowd, Arab onlookers thought Jews were shooting at them. The communists were finally driven into the mixed Jewish-Arab Manshiyya Quarter of Jaffa, where they entered into a fight with local Arabs who now moved to attack Jewish stores and institutions in Jaffa. This included an immigrants' hostel run by the Zionist Commission that housed both men and women and was therefore regarded by many local Arabs as a hotbed of vice. The (Arab) police did not intervene to stop the violence. Armed Jewish units retaliated, beating and killing Arabs and looting their property, leading to new and intensified protests and riots, which abated only after a state of emergency was imposed on May 3. At the end of these three days, nearly 60 people had been killed (43 Jews and 14 Arabs) and more than 180 injured (134 Jews and 49 Arabs). The Jews, then, suffered greater losses than the Arabs. Among those killed was the well-known writer Josef Chaim Brenner, creating another martyr for the Zionist cause similar to Josef Trumpeldor. Leaders of both sides—including the prominent sheikh Sulaiman al-Taji al-Faruqi—sought in vain to calm their people. Aroused by the events in Tel Aviv and Jaffa, Arab peasants and Bedouins attacked the Jewish

---

[38] LeVine (2005), ch. 4, esp. pp. 109–20; see also *Peel Report* (1937), pp. 51–54; Verdery (1971), pp. 279–80, 284. Al-ʿAsali (1991a), pp. 28–33, tells a different story; Salih (1989), pp. 172–78, is even more one-sided.

agricultural settlements in Hadera, Petah Tikva, and Rehovot, as well as the Jewish residents of Tulkarm and Qalqilya from May 5 to 7. In all of these places they met with armed resistance, so that they suffered great losses as well. By May 7, official reports listed around 48 Arabs and 47 Jews killed, and 146 Jews and 73 Arabs injured. The actual number of victims may have been still higher. Jerusalem, which in the previous year had been the site of violence, remained calm over the entire period—possibly due to the restraint exercised by the newly elected Mufti, Hajj Amin al-Husaini, who thus gave the British a visible sign of his willingness to cooperate. Yet on the fourth anniversary of the Balfour Declaration, on November 2, 1921, there was fresh unrest in Jerusalem leading to 8 casualties, which again did not seem to be colored by religion.

The clashes of May 1921 were of a new order. Apart from isolated attacks, the Jewish settlements had been able to develop undisturbed in the four decades between 1880 and 1920. The outbreak of violence came completely unexpectedly for both the British and the Jews. The (illegal) Jewish security forces, forerunners of the Hagana, had wrongly assessed the security situation and, shortly before, had transferred a secret arsenal of weapons from Tel Aviv to certain settlements in northeastern Galilee that seemed to be threatened. To all appearances, the riots were unplanned, uncoordinated, and in no way religiously inspired. In its report published in October 1921, the Haycraft Commission (named after its chairman, chief justice of the Supreme Court of Palestine, Sir Thomas Haycraft) highlighted the Arab sense of being economically threatened. It also mentioned Zionist "overbearing" and "arrogance," which it held responsible for fueling tensions.[39] Racial antagonism, anti-Semitism, and Islam seemed to the Commission of lesser importance. Instead, it referred to the "Bolshevik" aims and convictions of the Eastern European immigrants.

Here the British found themselves in rare agreement with Arab leaders and Muslim activists, who also warned of the "Bolshevik peril" emanating from eastern European Jews, and of the subversion of custom and propriety that the free-spirited pioneers brought into the country— especially their women. Along with the motifs of fear, resentment, and outright hatred, the moral dimension merits attention: Not surprisingly, it was tied to the themes of female honor and (im)morality, so basic to the perception of the Jewish Other, notably in socially conservative Arab circles, both Muslim and Christian. The differences in behavior, dress, and customs between European Jewish immigrants and local Arabs were all too obvious. They could be witnessed in the city as well as the coun-

---

[39] Haycraft Report cited from *Peel Report* (1937), p. 52. For Zionist arrogance and overbearing, see also chapter 8 above, esp. notes 14 and 15.

tryside, especially of course among the socialist pioneers, and particularly among women. "For centuries, Arab Palestine has remained the biblical Palestine," wrote Gabriele Tergit in the 1930s, picking up a familiar theme, "[but] the Jewish Palestine is Russian." She continued:

> The Arab woman covers herself. Even the fellah woman, whose face is uncovered, works in a long dress, she wears a colorful embroidered garment, colorful necklaces, bracelets around her arms, coins around the head. The Jewish woman works in the field with naked thighs, short pants, and a blue worker's blouse, with a Slavic kerchief on her head, sometimes with lipstick on her mouth, and during pauses in her hard work she smokes a cigarette.[40]

The British certainly noticed Arab disapproval of the "liberated" lifestyle of many Jewish immigrants. In this connection, the Peel Commission noted that:

> Finally, the Arabs had observed with dislike and disquiet the attitude and behaviour of many among the younger immigrants. It was natural enough that young Jews, escaped from the miseries and dangers of Eastern Europe, tasting freedom for the first time, feeling "at home" at last in a land they claimed as theirs by right, should give rein to their high spirits, and freely reflect in dress and behaviour the unconventional standards of the younger post-war generation in other parts of the world; but it was no less natural that such conduct should be regarded with distaste, if not opprobrium, by Arabs trained in the stricter school of Islam. They detected, too, in some of those young newcomers an arrogance which seemed to suggest that they felt themselves to be members of a superior race, destined before long to be masters of the country.[41]

At the same time the unrest showed how far the segmentation of society had already progressed, how few the exchanges of opinion and information between Arabs and Jews were, how great accordingly the effect of rumors and suspicions, and how differently the same phenomenon could be perceived by different people. British observers noted the deep division of society, with all its negative and positive effects. As for the

---

[40] Tergit (1996), p. 22. Sherman (1997), p. 28, comments on the "extreme minimalism of their dress." See also a caricature from *Filastin*, July 25, 1936, in LeVine (2005), p. 138.

[41] *Peel Report* (1937), pp. 51–52; see also p. 54. Salih (1989), p. 178, expresses himself along similar lines: "Hence Islamic sensibilities, directed against the Jewish occupation of the holy land of Palestine, and against libertinage, moral corruption, and communism, played an influential role in this revolution, even if they were not its only cause." See also Porath (1974), pp. 56–60; Mossek (1978), pp. 19ff. For contemporary Arab literature, see al-Osta (1993), ch. 1, esp. pp. 24ff., 43–51.

unrest of May 1921, the Haycraft Commission remarked: "It is all very well to say that there has been peace for a generation between Arab [sic] and Jews. It was the sort of peace that exists between two bodies of men who have little or nothing to do with one another."[42]

The British were eager to calm the situation, and therefore yielded to certain Arab demands, though without making any fundamental concessions concerning the Mandate Treaty and Arab representation. The first high commissioner to take his post at the helm of a civilian government in July 1920 (the Nabi Musa riots had occurred under military administration) perceived the dilemma of British policy all too clearly. Sir Herbert Samuel, a cousin of Sir Edwin Montagu, came from an assimilated British-Jewish banking family and was known as a committed Zionist.[43] Not surprisingly, he was greeted with enthusiasm by local Zionists. Yet the Arab community also received him with respect. Driven by the liberal conviction that some sort of understanding must be possible between the conflicting parties, Samuel sought a "rational" compromise (which by necessity had to be an asymmetrical one). Certain gestures of goodwill eased his entry into office. Zionists were permitted to raise their flag and thus in a literal sense "show their colors," and they were also allowed to publicly sing their anthem. In accordance with the Mandate Treaty, Hebrew was adopted as a third language in official communications. Land sales were once again permitted so as to give fresh impetus to the rural economy, and Jewish immigration was once more authorized. At the same time, pardons were granted to a number of Arabs arrested during the riots of April 1920. Press censorship was also lifted. The severe unrest of May 1921, during which Jerusalem was conspicuous for its quiet, were unexpected by Samuel and made a deep impression on him.

In June 1922 the Colonial Office published a new policy statement. The so-called Churchill Memorandum officially stated that the Jews were in Palestine "as of right and not on sufferance." But it also introduced the criterion of the "economic capacity" of Palestine "to absorb new arrivals" (later usually abbreviated to "absorptive capacity") as the yardstick for regulating Jewish immigration, which had already been unofficially applied for a number of years.[44] Evidently linked to the "wel-

---

[42] Cited from *Peel Report* (1937), p. 52.

[43] For Herbert Samuel, see Wasserstein (1978), pp. 73ff., 103ff.; Porath (1974), pp. 126, 145.

[44] Text of the Churchill Memorandum in Stoyanovsky (1928), pp. 76–77, and *Survey of Palestine* (1946), pp. 87–90. On immigration policies, see Mossek (1978), chs. 2–4, and pp. 152–55; on economic absorptive capacity, ibid., p. 59, and ch. 7. It was later expanded to include a political and psychological dimension that no longer focused on economic data, but rather on the will of the Arab majority (how many new Jewish immi-

fare" argument used by both the British and the Zionists to justify immigration in the face of Arab protest, the concept was as problematic as it was contested. It should however be remembered that as a result of limited finances, even the Zionist organizations had an interest in immigration controls for all those without independent financial means. Contrary to widespread belief (especially among Arabs), the Zionists therefore did not press for immigration "at all costs." The point under dispute was who would establish the criteria of selection and who would carry them out—the British authorities or the Zionists? While British repression hurt relations with the Arabs, Samuel's attempt to respond to the May riots by suspending Jewish immigration damaged his standing with the Zionists, among whom Chaim Weizmann had been his chief contact. There was occasional talk of Palestine as a "second Ireland."

Among the most important measures taken by the high commissioner were his permission to create a Supreme Muslim Council, and his appointment of Hajj Amin al-Husaini as mufti of Jerusalem in 1922. Other political institutions set up by the Arabs were denied official status. At the third Palestinian-Arab Congress (the second congress scheduled for May 1920 had been banned by the British military authorities) held in December 1920, an Arab Executive Committee was formed (AEC, often simply Arab Executive or AE; *al-lajna al-tanfidhiyya al-'arabiyya*). It was headed by Musa Kazim Pasha al-Husaini (1853?–1934), the new chairman of the Muslim-Christian Associations who had been dismissed as mayor of Jerusalem in the wake of the Nabi Musa riots.[45] Like the Muslim-Christian Associations, the Arab Executive included both Muslims and Christians, even if it was dominated by Muslims. It sought the recognition of the British authorities, which was denied them on the grounds that they were "nonrepresentative" and hence lacking in political legitimacy. Beyond this, it was burdened with financial difficulties. A Constitution (Palestine Order in Council) prepared by the British in August 1922 envisioned a Legislative Council, to be elected in February and March of 1923 representing Jews as well as Arabs.[46] However, the Arab Executive decided to boycott the elections because the British authorities made it illegal to call into question the Mandate Treaty and the Balfour Declaration included in it. In early 1922 Arab leaders had already defined their position:

> Whilst the position in Palestine is, as it stands to-day, with the British Government holding authority by an occupying force, and using that authority

---

grants was the Arab majority willing to accept in Palestine?). A comparison of Palestine and Ireland is found in Bowden (1977).

[45] Porath (1974), pp. 125ff., 274ff., 291–92; al-Hut (1981), pp. 123–24, 139–45.

[46] *Peel Report* (1937), pp. 54–58; Wasserstein (1978), ch. 6; Verdery (1971), pp. 284–85.

to impose upon the people against their wishes a great immigration of alien Jews, many of them of a Bolshevik revolutionary type, no constitution which would fall short of giving the People of Palestine full control of their own affairs could be acceptable.[47]

Here, the "Bolshevik threat" posed by immigrant Jews was clearly addressed. In the campaign for an election boycott, the mosques, local muftis, and preachers played an important role, declaring it a religious duty of Muslims not to vote under such conditions. Even the high commissioner's idea of establishing an Arab Agency parallel to the Jewish Agency, to advise the British concerning Arab affairs, came to naught. If previously the Arab leadership had been responsible for inadequate political representation, later attempts to find a recognized voice for all Arab Palestinians were foiled by the Zionists: Not without cause, the Zionists feared organized resistance to Jewish immigration, Jewish land purchases, and the development of the Jewish homeland.[48]

---

[47] Cited from *Peel Report* (1937), p. 54.

[48] Al-Hut (1981), pp. 165–69; Porath (1974), pp. 153ff.; Wasserstein (1978), pp. 112ff., 122ff. For Islamic activists, see Porath (1974), pp. 153–54, and Salih (1989), pp. 131–32.

Chapter Ten

THE MUFTI AND THE WAILING WALL

ARAB RESISTANCE TO THE BRITISH MANDATE and the Zionist enterprise took various forms, and was not from the beginning expressed in religious or nationalist terms. In the late 1920s, however, a gradual Islamization took place, as clearly discernible in the unrest of September 1928 and August 1929. In parallel, religious figures and institutions emerged as spokesmen of the Palestinian people, or at least of its Muslim part. And yet, not all political demands and activities took on a religious hue. The riots of May 1921 showed no specifically Islamic overtones, and the same held true for a number of later clashes. Positions were often ambiguous and therefore could be interpreted in different ways; they could change over time and be combined in various ways. Individual groups and figures were in touch with one another. For that reason, political camps were as a rule not sharply defined, and much was still in flux.

We do not know all that much about how Islam was actually lived and practiced in Mandate Palestine.[1] It would seem that belief in God as such was for most Muslims (as for most Christians) a given, something not to be questioned, but at the same not something to deeply think about. At the turn of the century, there were about three hundred mosques and shrines of saints in the later Mandate area. Religious festivals were popular, from the birthday of the Prophet to the various birthdays of a saint (*mawlid* or *mawsim*). An annual average of two hundred to five hundred Muslims made the pilgrimage to Mecca (*hajj*). The merchant-cum-scholar best known from Shi'i Iran also existed in Sunni Palestine, and the link between mosque and bazaar, representing the fusion of the commercial with the religious ethos, could be witnessed among the Nablus traders and soap manufacturers of the nineteenth century. Yet, there was no significant movement of reform and renewal among the Palestinian *'ulama'*, whose contribution to intellectual life in the country was rather limited. The abolition of the caliphate in the Turkish Republic in 1924 found no strong echo in Palestine. In the twentieth century, Islam first gained wider notice in the shape of *political* Islam.

---

[1] Canaan (1927); Kupferschmidt (1987), ch. 10, esp. pp. 222–29; Benvenisti (2000), ch. 7; see also chapter 3 above.

In many parts of the Muslim world, Islam played a key role in the anticolonial struggle—not just Islam as a religion with its specific set of beliefs and practices, but also its representatives and institutions, first and foremost the religious scholars and (some of) the Sufi brotherhoods (who were not as clearly distinct from one another as is often believed). In the nineteenth century, jihad movements were active in many parts of the Muslim world, fighting to liberate their country or community from foreign occupation in the name of Islam.[2] In certain cases, the anticolonial struggle took a nationalist flavor from the very beginning. In Syria, for instance, Arab resistance against foreign occupation and the French Mandate invoked a "national jihad" (*jihad watani,* with *watani* referring to the homeland, *watan,* not the nation). Not only in Iran, but also in Iraq, Egypt, Syria, and Palestine, mosques (and churches) were often the point from which political gatherings or demonstrations started and to which they returned, and the national cause was sometimes presented as "the cause of Islam." In Mandate Palestine, religious authorities ranging from muftis to simple village preachers played a greater role in politics and society than one would suppose from the nationalist literature that tended to belittle their role.[3]

Several elements should be distinguished when studying the gradual Islamization of Arab politics in Palestine: the role of religious officeholders and dignitaries in the Muslim community; the figure of the Mufti of Jerusalem, al-Hajj Amin al-Husaini, and the role of the Supreme Muslim Council; the function of the Nabi Musa festival; and finally, the significance of the Haram al-Sharif, with the Dome of the Rock and al-Aqsa Mosque, as concrete symbols of the national and/or the Islamic cause.

HAJJ AMIN AL-HUSAINI, MUFTI OF JERUSALEM

The rise and fall of the Mufti of Jerusalem, al-Hajj Muhammad Amin al-Husaini (1895?–1974), has been the subject of intense debate, scholarly as well as public.[4] His involvement with National Socialism has been especially controversial, and for many observers it was enough to place him in permanent discredit. In the present context, however, it is his significance for Palestinian politics and society in the Mandate era

[2] R. Peters (1996). For Syria, cf. Gelvin (1998), pp. 32–33, 186–88.

[3] See, e.g., Porath (1974), pp. 41–42, 152–54; Salih (1989), pp. 117–22, 203–204. For biographies, cf. Manna' (1998).

[4] For his involvement with National Socialism, cf. Höpp (1999) and Höpp (ed.) 2001; Gensicke (1988); Elpeleg (1993); Krämer (2006). His memoirs (*mudhakkirat*) are of limited value in this context.

that matters: Amin al-Husaini succeeded in transforming the Islamic holy sites in Jerusalem into *the* symbol of collective resistance against Zionist designs, thereby giving a religious coloring to its various expressions, and making the Palestinian cause known well beyond Palestine itself.

In March 1921 the incumbent mufti of Jerusalem, Kamil Effendi al-Husaini, died. British High Commissioner Herbert Samuel (who had only been in office for a few months) recommended Kamil's younger half-brother Muhammad Amin as his successor. Although Amin lacked formal qualifications for the office, the young man had much to recommend him: He belonged to one of the "great families," he already enjoyed some popularity, and from an early age he displayed political talent. The Husainis traced their ancestry to Husain b. Ali, the grandson of the Prophet Muhammad (hence "al-Husaini"), and from this lineage derived considerable prestige. One ancestor is said to have come from a small village near Jerusalem and to have settled in the city around 1380. Since at least the mid-eighteenth century, the Husainis belonged to the most prominent families of Jerusalem.[5] Origin, education, and wealth (consisting largely in landed property) predestined them for high office in the Ottoman religious and administrative hierarchy. Already in the early seventeenth century, a Husaini held the office of Hanafi mufti of Jerusalem—a fairly high-ranking position in the Ottoman religious hierarchy even if the city and its subprovince were of little political significance at the time. In the eighteenth century, other family members occupied the respected position of shaikh of the Haram and chief of the descendants of the Prophet (*naqib al-ashraf*). Though these positions later went to members of other families such as the Alami, Jarallah, Budairi, and Khalidi, with the Khalidis frequently holding the office of *kadi* of Jerusalem, the Husainis were able to once again rise to social preeminence among the Jerusalem notables in the late eighteenth century. Some served in the religious hierarchy, while others joined the ranks of the administration. Since 1856 they held the office of mufti of Jerusalem uninterruptedly. Several family members served as mayors of Jerusalem or sat in the Ottoman Parliament. Under the British occupation, Musa Kazim al-Husaini served as mayor of Jerusalem until being dismissed from office following the unrest of April 1920, when he was replaced by his rival Raghib al-Nashashibi. Like his father and grandfather before him, Kamil al-Husaini served as mufti of his native city.

[5] For the Husaini family, cf. Manna⁽ (1998); Mattar (1988), pp. 6–7; Porath (1974), pp. 184–87. It should be emphasized that the name signaled descent from Muhammad's grandson al-Husain, or the claim thereto; not all Husainis belonged to the same family, no matter how extended. The Husainis in Gaza, for instance, were apparently not related to their namesakes in Jerusalem.

Born in 1895 or 1896, Muhammad Amin al-Husaini was a mere twenty-six years old when his elder half-brother died. He already had an interesting career behind him that showed him to be a man of political talent.[6] As the son of the incumbent mufti of Jerusalem, Tahir al-Husaini (d. 1908), Muhammad Amin was from early on groomed for the tasks of a religious officeholder. Yet in terms of education he was essentially an effendi, wearing the tarbush (fez), as was typical of the Ottoman bureaucracy, the social elite, and middle class, not a scholar educated in Islamic law and the religious sciences. Amin first donned the turban of the religious scholar in 1921 while preparing to succeed his brother in office. The honorary title of "hajj(i)" by which he was commonly addressed in Arabic, was earned by a pilgrimage to Mecca he made in 1913 in the company of his pious mother, Zainab. Amin attended a Qur'anic school (kuttab), an Ottoman secondary school (rüsh-diyye), and the secondary school of the Catholic Frères in Jerusalem—a remarkable course of studies, but not atypical for his time and milieu. Beginning in 1912 he studied briefly at al-Azhar University in Cairo and at the Dar al-Da'wa wa-l-Irshad, then under the direction of Rashid Rida, the student of Muhammad Abduh and prominent Salafiyya reformer. Yet by 1913 he had already returned to Jerusalem and, shortly after, transferred to the military academy in Istanbul, where the outbreak of World War I interrupted his education once again—this time for good.

Amin entered the Ottoman army as an officer, serving far from the front in Anatolia. Around 1916, however, he joined an Arab secret society that advocated Arab rights as well as greater autonomy within the Empire. These political interests were not altogether new: His father had chaired a committee of Jerusalem notables established in 1897 to keep a watch on land sales to Jews, so that Amin must have been acquainted from early on with the "Zionist danger." During his time in Cairo he had already taken part in founding an anti-Zionist association of Palestinian students. While still an officer in the Ottoman army, he severed his allegiance to the sultan. In 1917, during sick leave in Jerusalem, he was recruited by the British for the troops of Emir Faisal. Serving first as their recruiting officer in the British-occupied parts of Palestine, he then fought against the Ottomans in the territories east of the Jordan. Returning to Jerusalem after the war, he was elected president of the Arab Club (al-nadi al-arabi), which at that time advocated union with Syria. Unlike most members of his social class, Amin al-Husaini ventured beyond the urban milieu and endeavored to enlist the peasantry

---

[6] Mattar (1988), pp. 7–21; Khalidi (1997), ch. 4; for his role in the Nabi Musa riots, see above, chapter 9. See also *Peel Report* (1937), pp. 176–81.

in the Arab cause, the struggle against Zionism, and unity with Syria. In 1920 he took part in a series of demonstrations against the Balfour Declaration and on behalf of King Faisal. The British military authorities accused him of having given a "provocative" speech during the unrest of April 1920 and sentenced him to ten years in prison. He was able to flee to Damascus, however, and, following the collapse of the Arab government under Faisal, managed to escape into Transjordan. He was pardoned in August 1920 by the high commissioner and returned to Jerusalem a few months later.

What, then, recommended Amin al-Husaini for the office of mufti of Jerusalem, in spite of his obvious lack of proper qualification? Above all, the British hoped to cultivate him as a promising young man from an elite family who in the tense atmosphere of the early Mandate years could credibly defend a policy of "reason and moderation" against all forms of "extremism," a policy that would ultimately serve British interests.[7] In the election for the office of mufti held in April 1921, Amin al-Husaini finished only fourth, behind respected scholars from equally good families (Husam Jarallah, Khalil al-Khalidi, Musa al-Budairi). At that point, petitions in his favor started pouring in from throughout the country, organized not just by the Arab Club and the Husaini family eager to secure the position for one of their own, but also by Christian congregations and notables—a clear indication of the prestige enjoyed by his family and of his standing as a national figure. The opposition of Raghib al-Nashashibi, incumbent mayor of Jerusalem and bitter enemy of the Husainis, proved fruitless. Shortly after the riots of May 1921, the British notified Amin al-Husaini of his appointment. Unlike his deceased older brother, he did not officially receive the title of "Grand Mufti" (al-mufti al-akbar) but was appointed mufti of Jerusalem and Palestine (mufti al-quds wa-l-diyar al-filistiniyya).Yet from an early date, the more important-sounding title of "Grand Mufti" caught on and became attached to his name, at least in Western sources.

THE SUPREME MUSLIM COUNCIL

In his new position Amin al-Husaini benefited from the fact that after the fall of the Ottoman Empire, he was no longer subordinate to the

---

[7] Porath (1974), ch. 4; Mattar (1988), pp. 21–27; also Monk (2002), pp. 52–56. Even before the death of his brother, Amin al-Husaini prepared for his succession by exchanging his tarbush for a turban and allowing his beard to grow; Monk (2002), pp. 22–23, and al-Hut (1981), pp. 203–204. Kamil al-Husaini (who succeeded his father in 1908) had done much to maintain calm following the entry of the British. The British showed their gratitude by granting him the title of "Grand Mufti," previously unknown in Palestine

religious and judicial hierarchy in Istanbul, whether the *sheih ül-islam* as head of the Ottoman religious hierarchy (*ilmiyye*), or the ministers of justice and of *awqaf*. This gave him immediate control over the local Sharia courts and religious endowments. Yet it was only the creation of a Supreme Muslim Council under his chairmanship that confirmed al-Husaini's status as head of the Muslim community, allowing him to emerge as the dominant figure in Palestinian Arab politics.[8] For most of the time, British Mandate authorities pursued a policy of nonintervention in the religious affairs of the local population, especially the Muslim majority. The presence of millions of Muslim subjects in various parts of the British Empire (first and foremost India), as well as the Balfour Declaration and the Mandate Treaty suggested as much. To this end, the British decided in December 1921 to establish a Supreme Muslim Sharia Council (SMC, *al-majlis al-shar'i al-islami al-a'la*) to administer the religious affairs of the Muslim population, in large part independently of the Mandate administration. (A similar body formed by Austria-Hungary in Bosnia-Herzegovina in 1908 may have served as their model here.) Shortly thereafter, in January 1922, Amin al-Husaini was named its chairman with the newly created title of "head of the religious scholars" (*ra'is al-'ulama'*). As subsequent years were to show, the Supreme Muslim Council, which strictly speaking represented the local Muslim community only, remained the only spokesman of the Arab population recognized by the Mandate authorities, which accorded it a status similar to the Jewish Agency in the latter's representation of Jewish interests in the country. The Arab Christians remained without an officially recognized mouthpiece.

Legally speaking, the Supreme Muslim Council was tied to the Mandate administration. The judges and other employees of the Sharia courts were appointed by the SMC, but paid with public funds, while the far more numerous personnel of the religious endowments were financed by these endowments themselves. This gave the Supreme Muslim Council control over considerable funds and a high degree of autonomy vis-à-vis the British. To demonstrate its distance from the Mandate administration, the SMC established its headquarters within the precincts of the Haram al-Sharif.[9] In his capacity as chairman, Amin al-Husaini

---

(presumably in imitation of the situation in Egypt, where there was a "national mufti," *mufti al-diyar al-misriyya*). In a break with precedent, they simultaneously appointed him *kadi* of the district of Jerusalem, and thus gave him control over both the Sharia courts in charge of personal status matters, and the administration of the Islamic religious endowments. Following the flight of the Mufti in 1937, the office remained vacant until 1948.

[8] Kupferschmidt (1987), chs. 1 and 3, esp. pp. 13, 26, 31ff.; Porath (1974), pp. 194–207; Mattar (1988), pp. 27–32; also *Peel Report* (1937), pp. 174–81.

[9] Kupferschmidt (1987), pp. 26–28, 58–63, 139–44, 227. On the schools (*rawdat al-*

controlled the religious endowments and related institutions (which included several schools and a small institute of higher education, a hospital, a library, a small museum, and a number of scholarships) as well as the Sharia courts. He also controlled access to all religious posts and offices in the Palestinian Muslim community. The SMC ran an orphanage for approximately 170 to 250 children. Operating under the motto "knowledge and work" (al-'ilm wa-l-'amal), it was connected with a vocational school that also ran a print shop. This print shop, as well as a private newspaper (al-Jami'a al-'Arabiyya), proved extremely useful in spreading the views of the SMC. In short, the Mufti had considerable personal and financial means at his disposal, as well as an extensive patronage network. The religious endowments, which the SMC controlled as the legal successor to the Ottoman Waqf Ministry, were of prime importance here.[10] Predictably, control over the awqaf also led to repeated conflict within the Muslim community, as the SMC was accused by the Mufti's opponents of illegally diverting some of the income of local endowments to Jerusalem. Although the British more than once considered withdrawing control over the awqaf from the SMC, this never happened. Instead, in 1932 they redefined income drawn from agricultural endowments to the SMC's advantage, a move aimed primarily at securing the good conduct of the Mufti.

Provided with these resources, Amin al-Husaini set out to promote Jerusalem as a holy city of Islam. Its most distinguished sites had visibly decayed over the past centuries of Ottoman rule, and were damaged anew in a severe earthquake in 1927.[11] As one would expect, work began with the renovation of the Haram al-Sharif including the Dome of the Rock and al-Aqsa Mosque, an endeavor that attracted great attention in the Muslim world, particularly in the Hijaz and in India. The Mufti pursued a deliberate strategy of internationalizing the Palestine issue, which eventually bore fruit in the 1930s. In late August 1928, the restoration of al-Aqsa Mosque was celebrated with great ceremony, and work was completed in 1929. At the same time a small museum of Islamic art and a library for Islamic religious literature were opened on the premises of the Haram. Religious sites and institutions in other parts of Palestine were restored and renovated, too. The SMC also devoted itself to the Nabi Musa festival and other religious events, which in the spirit of Salafiyya reform were successively "cleansed" of "unorthodox"

---

ma'arif in Jerusalem and kulliyat al-najah al-wataniyya in Nablus) and the orphanage, see also Tibawi (1956), pp. 59–60; Salih (1989), pp. 153–54; al-Hut (1981), p. 208.

[10] On the awqaf, cf. Kupferschmidt (1987), pp. 66–77; Reiter (1996), chs. 1 and 2.

[11] Kupferschmidt (1987), pp. 129, 188, 237–40; Mattar (1988), pp. 29–30; Reiter (1996), p. 163.

practices and increasingly adapted to serve national causes.[12] Still, there were no further political incidents after 1921.

THE MUFTI AND THE "OPPOSITION"

In his first years in office, Amin al-Husaini focused on consolidating his position against his Arab critics and rivals. These were found not only among the Nashashibis and their supporters, but also in certain cities and areas of Palestine, above all in the north. Among contemporaries they were known simply as "the opposition," whatever their base of power or individual interests.[13] The Nashashibis had entered relatively late into the ranks of the Jerusalem elite, and frequently competed for posts with the Husainis and other families. Often enough, such competition took the form of a zero-sum game, with the gain of one family entailing losses for the other. So when Musa Kazim was removed from his position as mayor of Jerusalem, he was replaced by Raghib al-Nashashibi (who in 1934 was forced to yield this post to Husain al-Khalidi who then joined the Husaini camp). As a result, the Nashashibis, or at least some of their prominent members, drew closer to the British, while the Husainis distanced themselves more strongly (but not completely) from the Mandate authorities. The Mufti also had critics and rivals among the *'ulama'*, preventing him from totally dominating the field of religion. Given these conflicts, it was perhaps not surprising that the rivals should accuse each other of collaborating with the enemy. And in fact, there are indications that the opponents of Amin al-Husaini received material or other support from the Zionists. These rivalries also had repercussions beyond the narrow confines of Palestinian politics. Hashemite ambitions for regional dominance were of crucial importance here, as represented by Abdallah b. al-Husain, the (decidedly pro-British) emir of Transjordan. The Supreme Muslim Council belonged to the small number of Muslim institutions that, in 1924, recognized Abdallah's father Husain b. Ali as caliph. The Nashashibis, too, maintained

---

[12] Kupferschmidt (1987), pp. 232–36; Porath (1974), pp. 101, 205ff.; al-Hut (1981), pp. 211–13; Salih (1989), pp. 152–54; Friedland/Hecht (1996), pp. 99–100, 108–109. With the outbreak of the Arab uprising in 1936, the significance of the pilgrimage to the shrine of Nabi Musa steadily decreased, especially after the flight of the Mufti in October 1937. The Hashemites had no interest in promoting an independent religious center in and around Jerusalem. Not until early 1987 were pilgrims again allowed to visit the shrine by the Jerusalem Awqaf Administration (controlled by Jordan). This should perhaps be seen in connection with the so-called Jordanian solution as envisioned by the Israeli-Jordanian agreement of 1986.

[13] Porath (1974), ch. 5; Porath (1977), pp. 61ff.; Wasserstein (1978), pp. 217–18; Nashashibi (1990). For Haifa, see Seikaly (1998), pp. 153–54, 185ff.

contacts in the Arab world outside of Palestine, including Emir Abdallah himself.[14]

Contrary to his later reputation, the Mufti started office by cultivating good relations with the British. Despite his policy of Islamizing Arab politics and by the same token politicizing religion, there were no further bloody incidents during the Nabi Musa festival or other religious events after he assumed office. On the whole, Palestine seemed calm and peaceful. With the exception of an impressive strike during the visit of Lord Balfour (who had arrived as guest of honor for the opening of the Hebrew University in March 1925), hardly any resistance against the Mandate or the Zionists was recorded. Even plain criminality seemed largely under control; Bedouin incursions were repelled, and in general the land was "pacified." Before departing Palestine, the high commissioner, Sir Herbert Samuel, expressed his satisfaction with the situation:

> The spirit of lawlessness has ceased; the atmosphere is no longer electric; there have been no more raids from Trans-Jordan; all the brigands have been hunted down and either shot, executed or imprisoned. . . . For some time past Palestine has been the most peaceful country of any in the Middle East.[15]

Though the Jewish population continued to grow very fast, from 93,000 in 1922 to 154,000 in 1927, and Jewish-owned land increased to around 1 million dunam, Zionism seemed to many Arab Palestinians to have been weakened, if not altogether finished. Significantly, they tended to pay more attention to Jewish immigration than to Jewish land purchases, which continued quietly but steadily, and had far greater mid- to long-term effects on the Arab population than the immigration of a few thousand European Jews. Immigration of course has always been easier to register than the continual expansion and densification of Jewish settlement. In the mid-1920s the Nashashibis took a daring turn away from their previous attitude of noncooperation, and openly endorsed Arab participation in elections and political advisory bodies; in 1927 the Arab Executive Committee followed suit. In June 1928 the Seventh Palestinian Congress proposed elections for a Legislative Council, an initiative supported by the British high commissioner. The outbreak of new unrest in September 1928, followed by the serious riots of August 1929, brought the process to a temporary halt. In early 1935

---

[14] For the Hashemite connection, see Porath (1977), pp. 72–75; Wilson (1987); Shlaim (1990); Gelber (1997); for Husain's recognition as caliph, see also Porath (1974), pp. 160–61; Kramer (1986), ch. 8, and below, note 34.

[15] Cited from *Peel Report* (1937), p. 187. For what follows, see also Porath (1974), ch. 6; Porath (1977), pp. 20ff. Naor (1998), p. 134, shows the black flags raised by Arab demonstrators against Lord Balfour's visit on the occasion of the inauguration of the Hebrew University in 1925.

British Parliament turned down the proposal of creating a Legislative Council representing the local population, contributing to the outbreak of the Arab uprising in 1936.

ESCALATION AT THE WAILING WALL: 1928

The riots of 1928 and 1929 broke out at the Wailing Wall, one of the sites holy to both Jews and Muslims, though in quite different ways. The "Wailing Wall" (in Hebrew *ha-kotel ha-ma'aravi*, Western Wall), a 28-meter-long part of the enclosure wall of the Temple of Herod, became a symbol of the religious claims (and complaints) of Jews and Muslims.[16] To the Jews it was holy as the last remnant of the Temple, while the Muslims regarded it as the outer limit of the "holy district" (*al-haram al-sharif*), to which, according to pious legend, Muhammad had tethered his mount, Buraq, during his night journey and ascent to heaven; hence also the Arabic name for this part of wall: *al-buraq al-sharif*. Shortly after the battle of Hittin (1187), Saladin's son and successor converted the adjacent zone into a *waqf* for the benefit of Maghrebi pilgrims and scholars (also known in Jerusalem as Moghrabis), who had taken up residence there; the largest *waqf* was named after an important mystic, Abu Madyan Shu'aib, who had died in Tlemcen in 1197. In 1922 supervision of the Abu Madyan *waqf* passed from the Ottoman Waqf Ministry to the Supreme Muslim Council. We will not understand the ensuing events if we forget that, for centuries, only a narrow alley separated this sensitive site from the neighboring residential area. Incidentally this fact lends some credibility to reports that the residents of the Moghrabi Quarter threw their garbage at the Wailing Wall—a further link in a chain of narratives reaching back to the time of the Muslim conquest that relate the degradation of the sacred Temple area and its later cleansing of garbage and waste (photographs from the late nineteenth century period show no waste in front of the Wall, though). The open square in front of the Western Wall was created only in 1967, when after their conquest of the Old City the Israelis tore down the Moghrabi Quarter. Hence, events unfolded in the narrowest possible space, adding fuel to the existing tension.

The level of latent tension present at this site can be gathered from a report by Nahum Goldmann on his first trip to Palestine, undertaken in 1914 when he was eighteen years old:

---

[16] Porath (1974), ch. 7, esp. pp. 260, 272. On the Abu Madyan *waqf* and other "Maghrebi" endowments in Jersualem, see Reiter (1996), pp. 55, 137; Kupferschmidt (1987), pp. 104, 110, 118. Elmendorf (1912), table 83; Gidal (1982); Ben-Arieh (1984), esp. pp.

Figure 12. Jews praying at the Wailing Wall. At the left edge of the photo is the wall that bordered the narrow alleyway before the Wailing Wall until it was torn down by the Israelis in 1967. Anonymous photograph, c. 1900.

The great wall all of a sudden became for me the symbol of our eternal existence . . . and these stones appeared to me to announce the promise of our eternal future: like them, which none is able to remove, which endured despite all destructions through the centuries, so too will their people exist to all eternity. . . .

As I stand sunk in these thoughts, sensing an inward calm, my soul once again filled with consolation and hope and faith, there suddenly rings out behind me the offensive, grunting cry of a donkey. In great shock, I turn

371, 373, or Osman (1999), pp. 98–99, 108, have good photographs of the narrow space before the Wailing Wall.

around to see an Arab driving two donkeys through the alleyway. In the first moment I was seized with such rage that I could have struck this stupid, hulking fellow dead to the ground.

After brief consideration, he thought better of it:

The alley is a public passage, and it is ridiculous to request such tender consideration of this barbarian that he should make a detour in order to spare those who are praying. We are guilty, we Jews. What kind of a people are we, that we are able to endure such things?[17]

In the course of the nineteenth century, the Western Wall had been gradually elevated among wider Jewish circles to a site of commemoration and particular sanctity, which was popularized in many forms. The Jewish national movement invested it with national significance. As early as 1836, Zvi Hirsch Kalischer, one of the forerunners of Zionism, had suggested to Baron Meyer Anschel Rothschild in Frankfurt that he purchase the Temple Mount and all of Palestine from Muhammad Ali, whose troops occupied the country at the time.[18] In response to repeated clashes, demands, and accusations, the Ottoman authorities attempted in 1840 to establish the rights of both parties. These were set down in 1911 by the Jerusalem district council as the "status quo," which the British were obliged to preserve under Article 13 of the Mandate Treaty, expressly guaranteeing the immunity of the Muslim holy sites. Both before and after 1918, several attempts were made to acquire the Wall by purchase or to exchange it for a different endowment property, which was difficult but not entirely impossible under Islamic law.[19]

Among Muslims these endeavors prompted the fear that the Jews planned to rebuild the Temple—a manifestation of the old topos of threat to the holy sites, which had previously been part of the Jewish repertory. The fears were fanned by rumors: Already in the early 1920s reports were spreading that pictures had been discovered in Jerusalem showing al-Aqsa Mosque or the Dome of the Rock crowned by a Star of David, or the crown of Zion, or a Zionist flag. References by Zionist leaders and their European sympathizers to the Zionist endeavor as tantamount to rebuilding the Temple, when taken literally rather than metaphorically, appeared to point in the same direction.[20] And pictures and

---

[17] Nahum Goldmann, *Erez Israel. Reisebriefe aus Palästina 1914. Rückblick nach siebzig Jahren* (Darmstadt 1982), pp. 27–28, cited from Kaiser (1992), pp. 149–50.

[18] For Kalischer, cf. Salmon (2002), pp. 20–21, and chapter 5 above.

[19] Under Ottoman rule, the status quo safeguarding religious rights and sites originally only concerned Christian not Jewish ones; cf. Stoyanovsky (1928), pp. 292ff.; Wasserstein (1978), pp. 109, 224; for the Temple Mount and the Wailing Wall, see also Porath (1974), pp. 258–62; Ben-Arieh (1984), pp. 141–54, 308–14, and 371–75.

[20] For conflicting accounts, cf. Porath (1974), pp. 206–207, 262–64, 366; Kupfer-

Figure 13. Postcard from Jerusalem, late nineteenth century. The card signals the reconstruction of the Jewish Temple on the Temple Mount. The Temple, the floral decorations, and the Wailing Wall are shown in color, while al-Aqsa Mosque, the Dome of the Rock, and their environs are left in gray. (Source: Mordecai Naor, *Eretz Israel*. Cologne 1998, p. 97.)

postcards did exist showing a reconstructed Jewish Temple on the Temple Mount, be it next to al-Aqsa Mosque or the Dome of the Rock or in their place, as did city maps indicating the site of the Jewish Temple. What mattered beyond all disagreement over the exact details was that people widely believed that a Jewish conspiracy was at work to destroy al-Aqsa Mosque and the Dome of the Rock and to rebuild the Jewish Temple in their place—and the Mufti was studiously promoting this as a concern of the Muslim community at large.

On September 24, 1928, the Jewish Day of Atonement (Yom Kippur), first clashes occurred after Jewish worshippers had brought a portable screen before the Western Wall in order to separate men and women during prayer.[21] This contravened not just established custom but the

schmidt (1987), pp. 237–38; Mattar (1988), pp. 25, 40–42; Segev (2000), p. 305; for a labored analysis of the meanings of (re)presentation, see Monk (2002), chs. 6 and 7; fortunately, he also shows a number of the incriminating images.

[21] With certain variations in detail, see Porath (1974), ch. 7; Segev (2000), ch. 13; Mattar (1988), ch. 3; also al-Hut (1981), pp. 220–21, 231–33; Salih (1989), pp. 179–85; Kolinsky (1993), ch. 3, esp. pp. 160–62. See also *Peel Report* (1937), pp. 65–68. A contemporary Jewish caricature depicts the scene as British soldiers remove the chairs and benches; cf. Naor (1998), p. 151. In May 1931 an international commission of inquiry

status quo as established in 1911. The Temple district was at that time under renovation: August had seen celebrations at the conclusion of the first phase of work, and the Muslim public in Palestine and beyond was reawakened to the sanctity of the site. Hence, the British forcibly removed the screen as well as the chairs and benches that had been brought with it, despite passionate resistance of the Jewish worshippers. Just how sensitive the British considered the situation to be can be seen from the fact that in November 1928, the colonial secretary personally confirmed the Ottoman status quo before British Parliament. On November 19, 1928, it was set down in an official policy statement. The events, which had taken place on the holiest day of the Jewish year, at the holiest place of Judaism, provoked strong reactions even among nonreligious Jews. Leading spokesmen including the Vaad Leumi demanded that the British Mandate government not only protect the rights of Jewish believers, but that they buy or even expropriate the Abu Madyan *waqf*, including the Western Wall. These appeals were preceded by attempts to create facts on the ground through the sale or exchange of property in the immediate vicinity of the wall. The issue was discussed at the Zionist Congress in July and August 1929. Joseph Klausner, a leading (if controversial) historian and sympathizer of Vladimir Jabotinsky's Revisionist movement, founded a Committee for the Defense of the Western Wall. A nationalist newspaper even urged that the Temple be rebuilt.

In the meantime, the Muslims did not remain inactive. Already in the final days of September 1928, they decided to create a Committee for the Defense of the Noble Buraq Wall (*lajnat al-difa' 'an al-buraq al-sharif*). In early November 1928 a General Muslim Congress met in Jerusalem with the Mufti as acting chair.[22] Numbering almost seven hundred participants from all over Palestine and neighboring Arab countries, the Congress resolved to create a Society for the Protection of al-Aqsa Mosque and the Islamic Holy Sites (*jam'iyyat hirasat al-masjid al-aqsa wa-l-amakin al-islamiyya al-muqaddasa*). The resolutions stressed the exclusive right of Muslims to the Noble Buraq/Wailing Wall as a "holy Islamic site." They were prepared to grant the Jews the right

---

presented their report, which confirmed Muslim ownership of the Wall and the Abu Madyan *waqf*, as well as the right of Jews to hold prayer there. They were allowed to continue bringing lamps, a washbasin, and a container of Torah scrolls, as well as a stand and a table for their prayer books and scrolls. However, they were not permitted to bring chairs, benches, dividing walls, curtains, or rugs, as they were liable to give the impression of permanence (or, as the Muslim side put it, to transform the square into a synagogue); see al-Hut (1981), pp. 231–33; Kolinsky (1993), pp. 160–62.

[22] Monk (2002), chs. 6 and 7; for restoration work in the late Ottoman and Mandate periods, see also Tütüncü (2006), pp. 109ff.

to visit the Wall, but not to bring with them any solid or mobile ob-
jects—whether it be books, Torah scrolls, candles, stools, chairs, or barriers. This reflected the fear that the Jews might not only transform the
area in front of the Wailing Wall into a site of prayer, but that beginning
with the Wailing Wall they would lay claim to the entire Temple Mount,
so as to replace the Muslim holy sites with the rebuilt Temple. From
1929 onward, the Supreme Muslim Council intensified construction
work on the Haram al-Sharif in order to demonstrate their exclusive
claims to the Temple Mount. The appointment of a person to make the
daily call to prayer, and the performance of Sufi rites (*dhikr*) directly
next to the Wailing Wall served the same purpose. Not without reason,
Jewish believers felt disturbed in their prayer.

August 1929

Tensions escalated in the summer of 1929.[23] Against the wishes of the
Jewish authorities, who sought to avoid further clashes and appealed to
the Jewish population for calm, a large demonstration took place in Tel
Aviv on August 14, the eve of the Ninth of Av (Tish'a be-Av), the fast
day when Jews commemorate the destruction of the Temple. On August
15, about three hundred revisionist youths marched with raised flags to
the Western Wall, where they sang the "Hatikvah" and reclaimed the
Wall for the Jews ("The Wall is ours."). Allegedly, a few of them also
insulted the Prophet, Islam, and the Muslim community at large; according to the same rumors, some of them turned violent. On the following
day, a Friday, the Muslims celebrated the birthday of the Prophet (*mawlid* or *mawsim al-nabi*). During Friday prayer, appeals were made that
Muslims defend the holy sites allegedly under threat from the Jews. In
response to these appeals, about two thousand Muslims marched to the
Wailing Wall shouting "God is great," "the Wall is ours," and "death
to the Jews." Upon reaching the Wall, they burned the scraps of paper
containing the wishes and prayers traditionally stuck by Jews into its
cracks. Another incident showed how tense the situation had become by
that time: An Arab hit a Jewish boy who had accidentally kicked a soccer ball into an Arab woman's vegetable garden. When the frightened
woman started to scream, the man rushed to her defense. The boy died
of his injuries, and Jewish residents took revenge by stabbing an Arab

---

[23] Differing accounts in Mattar (1988), pp. 45–49; Kupferschmidt (1987), pp. 80, 82,
235, 239; Kolinsky (1993), pp. 42–70 (detailed but biased); Segev (2000), pp. 309–27;
also al-Hut (1981), pp. 221–24; al-'Asali (1991a), pp. 124–36; Salih (1989), pp. 185–91.
For Haifa, see Seikaly (1998), pp. 208–209. Naor (1998), pp. 156–58, shows photos and
caricatures.

Figure 14. The faithful at the Dome of the Rock. Anonymous photograph, c. 1900.

youth. The burial of the Jewish boy was marked by anti-British and anti-Arab protests.

One week later (on August 23, 1929), rumors that Jews planned an attack on al-Aqsa Mosque and had already killed a number of Arabs, led to an explosion of violence. Apparently goaded by militant preachers and activists, thousands of Muslims from the city and the neighboring villages came to Friday prayer on the Temple Mount. Many of them were armed with sticks and clubs, some with knives and daggers, a few with rifles and pistols (in the clashes of the next few days, even swords were used). Notified by the British police commander, the Mufti hurried to al-Aqsa Mosque, but was unable to calm the situation. At about the same time, several Arabs were murdered in the Jewish neighborhood of

Mea Shearim. Violence escalated. An undefined Arab "mob," which also included a few Christians, marched beyond the city walls and entered several Jewish neighborhoods; in the Yemin Moshe quarter they encountered armed resistance. News of these events spread like wildfire. After hearing reports that Arabs had been murdered in Jerusalem and that the Haram was in danger, Muslims attacked the Jewish quarter in Hebron, killing and raping men, women, and children, and looting Jewish property. Most of their victims were members of the old Yishuv, few of whom sympathized with political Zionism, though many were close to the ideals of religious Zionism. What appears to have caused alarm among the Arab populace was the establishment in 1924 of an Orthodox yeshiva that quickly attracted large numbers of students from Europe and the United States (some 265 in 1929), who again were mostly non-Zionist or even anti-Zionist, but who with their Western clothes and habits looked like Zionists to local Arabs. Shocking as the assaults were, they were not a pogrom (the persecution of Jews carried out under government auspices); the majority of Jews in Hebron were saved by their Arab neighbors.[24] At the same time, a number of kibbutzim were attacked and six of them completely destroyed. British police barracks in Nablus were similarly attacked, where the angry crowd sought to obtain the same weapons that the Jews already seemed to possess. In Jerusalem, Haifa, and other places, a Jewish "mob" avenged itself on the Arabs, killing men, women, and children, and lynching passersby; in Jaffa, an imam and six other people were murdered in a mosque, and the mosque itself was burned to the ground. In Jerusalem the Ukasha shrine in the Jewish Zikhron Moshe neighborhood was severely damaged. One week after Hebron, the Jewish community of Safed, still the most important center of the old Yishuv, was attacked and at least six of its members killed.

During the weeklong violence, at least 250 people (133 Jews and 116 Arabs) were killed and another 570 injured. It would seem that most of the Jewish casualties were killed or injured by Arabs, whereas the majority of the Arabs fell victim to British countermeasures. The Jewish community in Hebron was evacuated; a minority returned in 1930–31, only to be evacuated again in April 1936, shortly before the outbreak of the Arab strike and revolt. In the following days, many Jewish shopkeepers, merchants, and businessmen abandoned their businesses in mixed areas and resettled in purely Jewish neighborhoods, whether outside the Old

---

[24] Segev (2000), ch. 14, esp. pp. 314–26; Wagner (2002), esp. pp. 24ff., and ch. 6. The Slobodka Yeshiva (originally located in the Slobodka district of the Lithuanian city of Kovno) was part of the pietist Musar movement, founded in the 1840s in Lithuania to counter secular influences, including Jewish Enlightenment (Haskala), and later, socialism

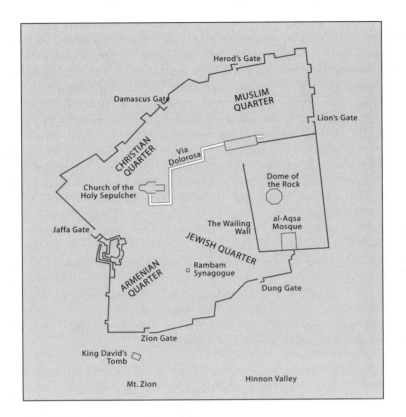

Map 6. The Quarters of Jerusalem

City in the case of Jerusalem, or in Tel Aviv in the case of Jaffa, reinforcing the spatial and social separation of Jews and Arabs. The Zionist organizations adapted their strategies of land purchase and settlement to the changed conditions, and in the following years concentrated on plots of land that were located in strategically favorable positions, not isolated and for that reason more easily defended against attacks.[25]

While many Jews had been protected by their Muslim or Christian neighbors, the effects of the violence were nonetheless devastating. Both before and afterward, landlessness and a rural exodus were identified as the primary causes of Arab hostility toward Jewish immigrants. Yet the

---

and Zionism; for a brief introduction, see Mendes-Flohr/Reinharz (eds.) (1995), pp. 396–38.
[25] K. Stein (1984), pp. 174ff.; for reactions among the Jewish community, see also Shapira (1992), ch. 5. On spatial segregation, see chapter 9 above.

Arab "mob" attacked not only Jewish settlers, but also Jewish city dwellers who were by no means all sympathetic to Zionism, and many of whom had been their neighbors for years, if not generations. The Mufti argued that the Jews were the aggressors.[26] The Arab Executive Committee initially distanced itself from the acts of violence. Yet the harsh measures of the British, who employed the police, army, and air force, and imposed collective punishment on entire villages and neighborhoods, created widespread bitterness among the Arab population. Those men who were sentenced to death before the British courts, and those who were actually executed in June 1930, were celebrated as heroes, martyrs, and victims of imperialism. Donations for their families were collected in other Arab countries. The literature referred to the riots of 1929 as the "Buraq revolution" (*thawrat al-buraq*) and honored its Arab victims as "martyrs" (*shuhada'*).[27] In September 1930 an Arab National Fund (*sunduq al-umma*) was created on the model of the Jewish National Fund (Keren Kayemet le-Israel), though in terms of achievements the two could not compare.[28] Given the general mood, the Arab Executive Committee was no longer able to maintain its posture of detachment. This in turn called British policy into question, for either the notables were responsible for the unrest or they were unable to control it. Both possibilities were equally disturbing.

A White Paper and a Black Letter

In this situation, the British employed the tried and true method of setting up a commission of inquiry. Under the leadership of Sir Walter Shaw, it prepared a thorough report published in March 1930 that recommended (much to the dismay of the incumbent Labor government of Ramsay MacDonald) a strict limitation on land sales and Jewish immigration.[29] MacDonald was unhappy not only for political reasons, but for economic ones as well. The British mandates and colonies were meant to be financially self-supporting, and from a financial point of view, a substantial Jewish presence in Palestine seemed advantageous, given that the Yishuv made a greater contribution to tax revenues than the Arabs (though rising conflict between Jews and Arabs also caused

[26] Wasserstein (1978), p. 234.
[27] *Peel Report* (1937), p. 189; Kolinsky (1993), pp. 84–91; Y. Miller (1985), pp. 8–9. For an Islamist interpretation, see al-ʿAsali (1991a), pp. 163–65.
[28] Porath (1977), pp. 16–69, 39ff.; Reiter (1996), pp. 190–91; al-ʿAsali (1991a); Nadan (2006), pp. 13, 287.
[29] *Peel Report* (1937), pp. 68–78; K. Stein (1984), pp. 80–114; Kolinsky (1993), chs. 4, 7, and 8.

increasingly higher expenditures on security).[30] It was therefore resolved to constitute a new commission under Sir John Hope-Simpson to investigate in greater detail the issues of land, immigration, and the development potential of the Palestine Mandate. Hope-Simpson's findings, published in August 1930, largely substantiated the recommendations of the Shaw Report. Both reports left their mark on the so-called Passfield White Paper of October 1930 (Statement of Policy of His Majesty's Government on Palestine, named after the incumbent Colonial Secretary Lord Passfield, formerly Sydney Webb, the well-known Fabian thinker and author—and one of the few anti-Zionist colonial secretaries). It recommended that Jewish immigration be suspended so that the standard of living of the Arab peasants could be maintained at the current level. The White Paper's contention that no further cultivable land was available for new immigrants proved especially controversial—evaluation of soil quality was and remained a political issue of the first rank.

The Passfield White Paper, greeted by most Arabs as a sign that the British had returned to fairness and justice, provoked outrage in Zionist circles. Even before the publication of the Hope-Simpson Report, large parts of the Jewish population in Palestine went on strike to protest the anticipated halt to immigration.[31] Under strong domestic pressure, especially from Conservative opposition circles, Prime Minister Ramsey Mac-Donald distanced himself from the white paper in a "letter of clarification" to Chaim Weizmann that covered the issues of immigration and land purchases. MacDonald assured Weizmann that His Majesty's Government viewed the Mandate not only as an obligation toward the population of Palestine, but also toward the Jews in the world at large. Among Arabs the letter quickly became known as the "Black Letter." A few years later the Peel Commission summarized the problem in remarkable fashion:

In this stark contradiction between Arab aspirations and British obligations lay and had always lain the one insurmountable crux. The rate of Jewish immigration might rise or fall, Jewish land-purchase might be extended or restricted, "Black Letters" might follow on "White Papers", but all these factors, though they were certainly important, were only subsidiary factors. They might add fuel to the flames or dampen them down. But the Mandate itself, of which these other factors were only applications or interpretations, had lighted the fire; and the Mandate itself, however applied or interpreted, was bound to keep it burning—

---

[30] In 1928 Jews made up 17 percent of the total population but contributed 44 percent to the tax revenue; K. Stein (1984), p. 87; also *Survey of Palestine* (1946), pp. 570–80.
[31] K. Stein (1984), pp. 93ff., 115–32.

except on the old original assumption that the two races could and would learn to live and work together.[32]

There was little evidence of this at the time, and in the British view it was the Arabs who lacked the decisive will to cooperate or reach an understanding with the Jews.

In view of mounting tensions and repeated outbreaks of violence, a pattern of British behavior began to form. It held until the late 1930s, and then changed not so much through local developments as through the need to confront European fascism, which threatened to have an impact in the Arab world as well.[33] The basic features were as follows: Arab disaffection with the British Mandate administration in general, and Jewish immigration in particular, would lead to outbreaks of violence, carried out mostly by peasants and the urban poor, and leading to injuries and deaths among Jews (and not only Zionist Jews, who in many cases did not hesitate to retaliate). Whenever the level of violence rose too high to be controlled by the available means, London would set up a commission of inquiry. The commission would quickly determine that Arab disaffection was essentially politically motivated, and that the Balfour Declaration and the Mandate based upon it were completely unacceptable to the Arabs. In the best tradition of British fair play, the commission would then make suggestions designed to address Arab grievances without damaging the spirit and letter of the Mandate Treaty, including the Balfour Declaration. But what could "fairness" mean when faced with the irreconcilable commitments to both parties and their exclusive claims? This phase would be followed by a period of intense lobbying in London, in which the Zionists (or more generally the Jews) were better positioned due to their easy access to British decision makers. The word "appeasement" was used frequently, referring to concessions not be offered to the Arabs. Following lively debate in Parliament, a white paper would be published that in some instances (Shaw, Hope-Simpson, or Peel) would follow the recommendations of the commission of inquiry. The Arabs would regularly reject the white paper, while the Zionists would adopt a flexible attitude accepting something less than their ultimate demands. The Arabs could not afford such flexibility, since this would have signified recognition of the Mandate including the Balfour Declaration. Rather, they called for the unconditional recognition of their claims. As the strategy of rejection was not based on effective leverage either locally or in London, Washington, or Geneva, it was no match to Zionist strategies that in spite of the irritation they might occasionally cause, were on the whole much more sophisticated and effective.

[32] *Peel Report* (1937), pp. 76–77.
[33] Verdery (1971), pp. 275–76.

INTERNATIONALIZING THE PALESTINIAN ISSUE

The Mufti emerged from the unrest of 1928–29 as the hero and leader of Arab Palestine who succeeded in awakening interest in the Palestinian cause not just in the surrounding countries, but as far as Iran and India. This was doubly important, for it also made the influential India Office aware of the Palestine issue. A precedent was set when the leader of the Indian Khilafat (caliphate) movement, Muhammad Ali, brother of the well-known Muslim writer and activist Shawkat Ali, was buried on the grounds of al-Aqsa Mosque following his death in January 1931.[34] In June 1931, Husain b. Ali was buried there, the former sharif of Mecca, king of the Hijaz and "all Arab lands," who in 1924 had had himself proclaimed caliph (though few were prepared to recognize his claim). Al-Haram al-Sharif appeared to be developing into a kind of "pan-Islamic pantheon." In December 1931 the Mufti convened a General Islamic Congress in Jerusalem.[35] Funded mainly by the Supreme Muslim Council, the conference attracted around 145 participants from numerous Muslim countries, among them such prominent figures as Shawkat Ali representing the Indian Khilafat movement, Rashid Rida, Shakib Arslan, and the Indian poet and reformer Mohammed Iqbal. Only Kemalist Turkey and Saudi Arabia sent no representatives. Not everyone was happy with the meeting, though: Some Muslim leaders feared that the caliphate issue would be brought up once again, as was indeed the aim of Shawkat Ali. The plan to create an Islamic university in Jerusalem, as envisioned in the final resolution, met with little sympathy at al-Azhar University in Cairo; lack of funds assured that such an institution could not be created. The participants called for a boycott of Jewish products, the promotion of agricultural enterprises in Palestine, and other measures to strengthen the Arab economic sector. For the time being, however, these appeals remained without practical effect.

[34] Kupferschmidt (1987), p. 194. See also Nafi (1998), pp. 95–103; Mattar (1988), pp. 56–57. Ayyad (1999), pp. 98ff., reports on first international contacts in 1921. Husain "accepted" the title of caliph in March 1924 from a gathering of loyal adherents. However, he was not recognized as such by the majority of Muslims, including the Indian Khilafat movement. In Palestine itself there were also protests. Among the few exceptions was the Supreme Muslim Council, who hoped for Husain's support in their dealings with Great Britain. In view of strong resistance, Husain gave up the title in June 1924; see Porath (1974), pp. 160–61; Kramer (1986), ch. 8. For the Khilafat movement, see Jacob M. Landau, *The Politics of Pan-Islam. Ideology and Organization* (Oxford 1994), and Azmi Özcan, *Pan-Islamism: Indian Muslims, the Ottomans & Britain (1877–1924)* (Leiden 1997).

[35] Kramer (1986), chs. 8 and 11, esp. pp. 123–41; Kupferschmidt (1987), pp. 209–18; Mattar (1988), pp. 58–65; Salih (1989), pp. 205–16. Al-Thaʿalibi (1988) provides a detailed account of the General Islamic Congress.

Chapter Eleven

FROM UNREST TO UPRISING

THE JEWISH COMMUNITY, and the Zionists in particular, were determined to use every opportunity the Mandate offered to press for the rapid creation of their "national home." The impatience some of their representatives displayed, their single-mindedness and arrogance provoked considerable ill will, and not only among British officials. Yet more was at stake than politics widely defined. Most of the European immigrants—whether committed Zionists or not—set out to create something new, to break with tradition, and to demonstrate to themselves and others their will to achieve. They wanted to prove their "competence," a competence often denied to Jews in Europe outside the spheres of business and finance. The pioneers (*halutzim*) in the rural settlements were the purest embodiment of this will and determination, but not the only ones. Urban workers were imbued with the same spirit.

The differences between Jews and Arabs were not all based on ideology, and they did not have to be expressed in political terms. The differences were visible and tangible, easily discerned from clothing and architecture, from forms of conduct and economic organization in urban enterprises and rural settlements alike. Poultry farming provided one example, as vividly described by Gabriele Tergit in the 1930s:

> There the Arab takes the harvest away on camel and donkey. Here the Jew delivers it in a truck. There the *fellaha*, the peasant woman herself takes her wares to the city in a basket on her head to offer them for sale. Here there is the Jewish sales organization, which takes standardized wares to the city to sell them in specialty stores.
>
> Among the *fellahin*, the hens run around in the yard behind the wall. On Jewish land, one sees the hen-stalls of corrugated iron, scientifically tested. There lives the colorful rooster, here the white laying race. There a tiny egg is produced, here the model agricultural product. . . .
>
> There is Allah, and here is success. There are the thorns, and here is the experimental field. There is the Orient, and here not Europe, but rather a mixture of Russia and America.[1]

---

[1] Tergit (1996), p. 24. Poultry and animal husbandry in general have been studied very seriously; see *Survey of Palestine* (1946), pp. 332–33, 380–81; Metzer (1998), pp. 150–54; Nadan (2006), pp. 97–108; El-Eini (2006), ch. 2, esp. pp. 139–40.

Arab society offered a very different picture. Most Arabs, men as well as women, Muslims as well as Christians and Druze, had a different attitude not only to the Mandate, but also to innovations in social, cultural, religious, and political life.[2] The very confrontation with Zionism and the Zionists tended to reinforce conservative instincts that aimed to "protect" Arab Muslim and Christian "identity" and "culture" against the twofold threat of British colonialism and Zionist designs. This made innovations difficult—as difficult as among the "old Yishuv," which also fought against the new, secular spirit of the Zionist champions of a Hebrew renewal. Outside relatively narrow urban circles, social habits and values remained remarkably conservative, especially concerning family matters and female codes of behavior. Few were inclined to rethink conventional norms of thought and conduct, commonly thought to be grounded in religion. In the political realm, uncertainty prevailed at first. Uncertainty produced critiques of the new situation created by the Mandate, but no strategy of coordinated resistance. In contrast to the Jewish community, Arab society in Mandate Palestine had an elite, but no leadership.[3] The result was an unfortunate combination of accommodation and resistance, by which the new state of affairs was not accepted but not fundamentally altered either. Perhaps it was this sense of deep unease that contributed to the (false) impression of utter stagnation in the "Arab sector," contrasting with the creative ebullience of the "Jewish sector," which by and large worked to the disadvantage of Arabs. In the course of the 1930s, this changed considerably.

LAND AND LABOR: THE CONSOLIDATION OF THE JEWISH YISHUV

Up to 1928–29, the 1920s were comparatively peaceful, and the Jewish Yishuv was able to expand and organize in unspectacular but continuous fashion. The 1930s brought about a marked deterioration of Arab-Jewish relations, mainly caused by Jewish immigration and extensive Jewish land purchases, which made the Arab community feel more threatened than before. Ramsay MacDonald's "Black Letter" of February 1931 put a provisional end to the policy of limited Jewish immigration. Shortly thereafter, the persecution of Jews in Europe lent a new quality to immigration: Anti-Semitism in Poland, and the Nazi seizure of power in Germany in 1933, pushed ever larger groups of Jews toward Palestine. The Jewish Agency engaged even more intensely to build up a

---

[2] For more nuanced analysis, see Bernstein (2000) and Fleischmann (2003) dealing with workers and women, respectively. For literacy and the press, also Ayalon (2004).

[3] Pappe (2004), p. 81.

Jewish homeland there. In the short period between 1931 and 1936, the
Jewish population more than doubled, from 175,000 to 370,000 people,
bringing up its share of the total population from 17 to 27 percent.
From 1926 to 1932, an average of 7,200 Jews entered Palestine legally
each year. In both 1933 and 1936, the number was 30,000; in 1934,
42,000; and in 1935, 62,000—altogether more than 164,000 people in
just four years. In addition to legal immigration, illegal immigration rose
sharply. Most Jewish emigrants appear to have chosen Palestine for political reasons, since alternate destinations were available: The American
immigration quota, for example, was not filled from 1932 to 1935 (although the fact that the United States was still in the grips of the Depres-
sion may have played a role here). In the early 1930s, the Jewish Yishuv
developed in every respect, and the urban economy boomed. Immigration strengthened the middle class disposing of private capital, which
mostly engaged in private business and settled in the cities. Between
1931 and 1936, Tel Aviv grew from 46,000 to 140,000 residents, while
the Jewish population of Haifa increased from 16,000 to 40,000 (out of
a total population of a little under 100,000). Construction, industry,
commerce, and the banking and service sectors developed at a fast pace.[4]

The share of Jewish enterprises in industrial output rose between 1922
and 1932 from 50 to 60 percent, reached 72 percent between 1933 and
1939, and during World War II finally attained 80 percent.[5] Industry
was mostly of medium size, and relatively diversified, including food,
metal, wood, and construction materials, textiles, and leather. Big industrial companies were still rare, and mainly based in and around Haifa:
The cement factory Nesher employed around four hundred workers and
employees. The oil and soap factory Shemen was one of the greatest
enterprises in the country and offered strong competition to traditional
Arab soap production in Nablus, Jenin, and elsewhere. Potash works
and a power plant were later added. In 1924 the first "Levant Fair" was
held in Tel Aviv, which was also attended by companies from neighboring Arab countries. At the same time, Jewish land purchases were intensified, dozens of new settlements created, and the profitable citrus plantations expanded (more on this below).

As before, development was not restricted to economics and politics.
In April 1930 the (Jewish) National and University Library opened its
doors on Mt. Scopus in Jerusalem. In Tel Aviv, the Great Synagogue
was dedicated after eight years of construction, and one year later, the
Dizengoff Museum followed suit. In 1933 the cornerstone was laid for

---

[4] Metzer (1998), p. 69.
[5] The following data are from Himadeh (ed.) (1938), pp. 19–31, and Metzer (1998),
ch. 5. On the Levant Fair, see Schlör (1999), pp. 161–69; LeVine (2005), p. 326, note 78.

TABLE 3
Immigration and Emigration, 1920–36

Year	Registered Immigrants		Registered Emigrants	
	Jews	Non-Jews	Jews	Non-Jews
1920 (Sep.–Dec.)	5,514	202	a	a
1921	9,149	190	a	a
1922	7,844	284	1,451	1,348
1923	7,421	570	3,466	1,481
1924	12,856	697	507[b]	604[b]
1925	33,801	840	2,151	1,949
1926	13,081	829	7,365	2,064
1927	2,713	882	5,071	1,907
1928	2,178	908	2,168	954
1929	5,249	1,317	1,746	1,089
1930	4,944	1,489	1,679	1,324
1931	4,075	1,458	666	680
1932	9,553	1,736	a	a
1933	30,327	1,650	a	a
1934	42,359	1,784	a	a
1935	61,854	2,293	396	387
1936	29,727	1,944	773	405

a. The statistics do not register emigrant ethnicity (or "race," as the source puts it).
b. July–December
Source: Himadeh (ed.) 1938: 24.

the later Weizmann Institute in Rehovot, and in 1934, construction work started. The Habima theater group settled in Palestine in 1931, and in 1935, it moved into its own building. The year 1932 witnessed the premiere of the first Hebrew-language feature film, and in 1935, the first sound film was shot in Palestine. In 1931 the first Maccabi Games, the "Jewish Olympic Games," were attended by athletes from twenty-one countries. To reach a wider audience, the Jewish Agency published an English-language newspaper, the *Palestine Post*, in 1932. With so much modernity, one is surprised to see photographs of a man in a horse-drawn carriage, blowing the ram's horn (shofar) to announce the beginning of the Sabbath by the orders of the Tel Aviv city council.[6]

On the political level, too, the Jewish Yishuv continued to evolve. In January of 1930 Ahdut Haavoda and Hapoel Hatzair joined to form the Eretz Israel Workers' Party (*mifleget po'alei be-eretz yisrael*, or Mapai after its Hebrew acronym) to secure the influence of the labor movement over the local and international Zionist organizations. In later years it would develop into one of the largest Jewish parties to rule the State of Israel until Menachem Begin's premiership in 1977. The Zionist movement was further strengthened when, under the impact of the unrest of 1929, the Orthodox Agudat Israel formally abandoned its former policy of strict opposition to Zionism. At the same time the Revisionist movement under Vladimir Ze'ev Jabotinsky posed a greater challenge to Labor Zionism: It demanded not just a "revision" of the 1922 exclusion of Transjordan from the Palestine Mandate, but the establishment of a Jewish *state* (and not just a "national home") in Eretz Israel. Tensions peaked in 1933 with the murder of Chaim Arlosoroff, who, as head of the political division of the Zionist Executive and the Jewish Agency, had negotiated the Haavara Agreement with the German Reich, which allowed for the "transfer" (Hebrew *ha'avara*) of Jewish property, facilitating the emigration of German Jews to Palestine. Although his murder was never entirely cleared up, Revisionists were widely held responsible.[7] Revisionist influence grew within the World Zionist Organization, too, until the majority of Revisionists seceded in 1935 to form their own international organization. The first congress of the New Zionist Organization held in Vienna hosted the representatives of 713,000 registered Revisionist voters (more than the 635,000 voters for the Nineteenth Zionist Congress, held in August and September 1935 in Lucerne).[8] These figures help to correct the idea that being radical "dissenters," the Revisionists must also have been numerically weaker than the Zionist mainstream. Despite all these differences, the National Socialist takeover in Germany ultimately led to greater unity and cooperation among the

[6] Naor (1998), p. 176.

[7] Hence, the assassination of Yitzhak Rabin was not the first political murder within the Jewish Yishuv (in 1924, Dr. Jacob de Haan, leader of the anti-Zionist Agudat Israel, had been murdered, again under unclear circumstances). For Arlosoroff, cf. Shimoni (1995), pp. 216–21, and Naor (1998), pp. 177–83. See Black (1984) for the Transfer (Haavara) Agreement, which was highly controversial in political terms. It is frequently cited by Arabs in order to blame the Zionists for collaboration with the Nazis, of which the Arabs themselves have been accused, especially when the Mufti moved to Berlin in 1941; see also Krämer (2006), and above, chapter 10, note 4.

[8] Shimoni (1995), ch. 6, and pp. 366–69; Smith (1996), pp. 79–80.

TABLE 4
Economic Growth, 1922–47

	Annual Growth Rate	
	Arabs	Jews
Population	2.8%	8.5%
GDP	6.5%	13.2%
Per Capita Income	3.6%	4.8%

Source: Metzer 1998: 16.

competing parties within the Jewish Yishuv, which now stood under growing pressure.

LAND AND HONOR: THE CRISIS OF ARAB SOCIETY

Though the Arab economy experienced no expansion comparable to the Jewish one in the 1930s, it did not stagnate.[9] To be sure, the Arab economy was overshadowed by the rapidly expanding Jewish sector, which benefited from a steady influx of financial and human capital (people with contacts, skills, and "know-how") that the Arabs could not match. Yet by regional and international standards the Arab economy showed considerable progress. While the Arab population grew at an average rate of 2.8 percent per year due to unusually high birthrates among Muslims, the gross domestic product increased by 6.5 percent. (Admittedly, it had started from a very low level, below that of Egypt, though China, for example, was even poorer).

Despite this record of achievement, it was the comparison with the Jewish Yishuv that counted politically, not with neighboring Arab countries, Thailand, or Bolivia. The comparison was unfavorable: In the two years between 1931 and 1933 (that is, *before* the massive increase of Jewish immigration in 1935), the Arab share of GDP fell from 57 to 43 percent and then remained at this level. Jewish per capita income was two to five times higher than the Arab rate. Arab productive industries still largely focused on food and raw materials: Grain mills, tobacco, soap production, and the processing of olive and sesame oil made up 80 percent of commercial production. The rural exodus to the urban cen-

[9] Metzer (1998), ch. 5, esp. pp. 14–27 (see also table 1.1) and the Appendices, esp. tables A.22 and B.1. Nadan (2006) comes to different conclusions; see esp. p. xxviii, chs. 2–4, 7, and Conclusions.

ters of Haifa, Jaffa, and Jerusalem took on growing proportions. The best chances of employment were offered either by the booming construction industry, which benefited from investment in the infrastructure of the Mandate authorities and the influx of Jewish immigrants, or by the citrus plantations operated by both Jews and Arabs. All in all, the situation was difficult and perceived by many as threatening.

LAND AND LAND SALES

The land issue was of crucial importance for the economy, politics, and society of Palestine in general, and for Arab-Jewish relations in particular.[10] In the 1930s, the majority of Muslims (63 percent) still lived in the countryside, compared to a mere 22 percent among Arab Christians. The upswings and downswings of the Arab economy depended primarily on agriculture and more specifically on the harvests, which were extremely bad in 1928 and 1938, but especially good in 1934, 1935, and 1937 (so that fat and lean years stood in close proximity). Still, Arab agriculture experienced steady growth in the Mandate years at a rate of around 6 percent annually. Land ownership was relevant not only economically, but socially and politically as well. While historically, honor, prestige, and authority could be derived from diverse criteria and personal qualities, they were now founded primarily on landed property. Nationalist myths elevating the land and those working it to the very epitome of Palestinian identity increased its symbolic value. Among both Jews and Arabs, a similar kind of blood-and-soil mythology evolved, expressed in song and dance and poetry, and (at least among the Jews) in iconography.[11] Given the real and symbolic value of land, statistical data concerning land transfers, and even more so land sales to Jews, is sensitive and contested. Here no less than with population figures, a "political arithmetic" was at work that could significantly limit the usefulness of the data. Nothing was neutral or innocent here, nothing merely a technical question: Even the evaluation of soil quality and the fertility of a given plot or area gained a political dimension when considered in light of the "absorptive capacity" of the Palestinian economy. Criteria such as "cultivable land" could give rise to years of controversy. For this reason, even the most detailed statistics should be viewed with caution, and the figures provided be taken as indicators of certain trends rather than confirmed facts.

[10] K. Stein (1984), esp. chs. 1 and 2. Nadan (2006), ch. 1; also Smith (1996), pp. 83–87, 94–95; Metzer (1998), pp. 145–54.

[11] For the Jewish Yishuv, see Shapira (1992); Arbel (ed.) 1996; Benvenisti (2002); for Arab society, see, e.g., Enderwitz (2002); for both, Slyomovicz (1998).

Quantitative data on land acquisition and transfers are of limited meaning unless the geographic location of the individual plots and estates, as well as their previous owners and uses are taken into account: Is it a question of wasteland or fallow fields (*mawat*) that were previously neither cultivated nor otherwise used (for example, as seasonal grazing land)? Did the land need to be drained or irrigated (desert, steppe, marshes)? Did it lie on the plains or in hilly land, close to the roads or isolated, was it easy to defend from adjacent land? Were the previous owners small farmers, tenant farmers, or great landowners? Were there a number of different owners involved? Was it part of a *waqf*? Did the previous owners live on the land, or were they absentee landlords? Did the land sale involve any restriction of rights, especially of water and pasturage rights, as established by custom and possibly even fixed in writing?

During the entire Mandate era, the trade in land and real estate was lively. According to some estimates, around 70 percent of the transactions occurred *within* either the Arab or Jewish community, and 30 percent *between* the two.[12] Not all transfers were established in writing and entered into land registries: There was always room for informal business. According to the (incomplete) statistics for the years 1878 to 1936, only 9.4 percent of the 681,978 dunam legally acquired in this period by Jews were sold by local farmers. More than two thirds were sold by great landowners who had acquired the land in the second half of the nineteenth century. Among those great landowners, 52.6 percent were (former) Ottoman citizens who did not reside in Palestine, and were hence considered "foreign" absentee landlords; 24.6 percent were local Arabs, including members of the great urban notable families, from the Nashashibis and Husainis in Jerusalem to the Shawwa family in Gaza ("local" absentee landlords). The sales were economically motivated and the gains high (prices and profits augmented dramatically in the years 1932–37 and again 1942–45). Jewish purchasers were as a rule prepared to pay a price above market value and the expected yields. High demand caused steep increases in land prices, especially in the 1930s. As the land acquired by Zionist organizations like the Jewish National Fund became the unalienable property of the Jewish people, and was at least in principle removed from the market (in theory, even tenants could

[12] Shafir (1989), pp. 41–42; Nadan (2006), pp. 12–25; Metzer (1998), pp. 85–103, esp. table 4.1 with price indices. According to Metzer, pp. 89–90, "Arab foreigners" (the term is my own) made up 74 percent of land purchasers during 1920–32 and 19 percent during 1933–47. On the question of "cultivable land," see Stein (1984), pp. 4 (table 4) and 105ff.; Nadan (2006), pp. 71–79. An Ottoman dunam (often spelled dunum) was equivalent to 919.3 square meters until the British introduced the metric dunam of 1,000 square meters in 1928.

only be Jews), cultivable land tended to become a scarce commodity in certain areas.

Unlike immigration, Jewish land purchases developed uninterruptedly under British rule. In October 1920 the British once again permitted land transactions, having banned them in November 1918 when it was discovered that the Ottoman authorities had removed a great part of the relevant documents, or even destroyed them (some were later returned or found).[13] Size alone did not determine the sociopolitical impact of land transfers, as a chronological survey will reveal: Legal land sales to Jews amounted to 500,000 dunam in the 1920s, over 300,000 in the 1930s, and another 200,000 dunam in the period from 1940 to 1947. What mattered was the character of the land transferred and Arab perceptions of these transfers. The 1920s witnessed several extensive Jewish purchases in the coastal region and the fertile valleys leading to the hilly country, which were then still sparsely settled: Large tracts of land were bought in 1921 and 1924–25 in the plain of Marj Ibn Amir (Jezreel Valley) from the Beiruti Sursuq family and a number of other owners, followed in 1929 by a particularly important purchase in Wadi al-Hawarith (south of Haifa in the Tulkarm area) from the Tayyan family, also of Beirut. Already in the 1920s, more than a quarter of all land purchased by Jews was sold by local landowners and peasants, not by "foreign" absentee landlords.[14]

In the 1930s, various factors combined to change the character of land sales, the way they were perceived, and therefore their sociopolitical impact.[15] Starting in 1929, an increasing number of local landowners began to sell; by 1933 they accounted for a majority of sellers. In the northern and central plains, even fellahin now sold land to Jews. For 1928–32 their share was estimated at 18 percent, for 1933–36 at 22.5 percent. Large purchases occurred in 1934 and 1935, and even after 1936, when political tensions exploded in the Arab uprising, Arab peasants and landowners were prepared to sell land to Jews—provided it was discreetly done. At that time, Jewish land purchases were not so much limited because Arab owners were unwilling to sell, but rather because Jewish purchasers lacked sufficient funds. Another factor changed in the course of the 1930s: Up to the late 1920s, it was mostly a question of uncultivated land (though it could be used in other ways, notably as pasturage), so that the number of Arab peasants, tenant farmers, fieldworkers, shepherds, or Bedouins who were affected remained

---

[13] K. Stein (1984), ch. 2, esp. pp. 23–24, as well as chapter 7 above. See also Owen (ed.) (2000), ch. 4, and Naor (1998), pp. 115, 128, 140–41.

[14] K. Stein (1984), ch. 2, esp. pp. 66–67 and 81.

[15] Ibid., esp. pp. 37, 69, 103, 120ff., 131, 173–87; Nadan (2006), ch. 1.

relatively small. This changed to the extent that land was now sold in more densely settled zones. A variety of factors help to explain this shift: For one, following the unrest of 1928 and 1929, Jewish buyers endeavored more systematically to acquire contiguous plots of land or to rearrange the lots, so as to improve the defense of individual settlements if need be. Second, given dramatic price rises for land bordering on existing Jewish settlements, Jewish authorities decided, in some instances, to buy land even in regions where previously hardly any Jews had lived. As a result, Jewish land purchases and settlement were gradually expanded into the central hills and mountains, the Hula Valley, the area around Tiberias and Baisan in the north, as well as Gaza and Beersheva in the south. In the years 1930–35, 62 percent of all Jewish land purchases were still concentrated along the coast, 18 percent were in the Jordan Valley, 10 percent in the plain of Marj Ibn Amir, and a mere 3 percent in the central hills and mountains. Plans for larger land purchases in Transjordan and Syria failed due to the political opposition of Arab Palestinians—not the lack of willingness to sell on the part of local Arab owners.[16] The gravest problem resulted less from land sales as such (which could make economic sense for both individual sellers and the Arab economy as a whole) than from their political consequences. It is no accident that we speak of a "political economy."

Credit and Debt

The most important motive for Arab landowners and peasants to sell land (even if this meant selling it to Jews) was to obtain capital, or cash. The same held for tenants, fieldworkers, and shepherds, who in return for cash were prepared to either leave the land or renounce their traditional rights to it.[17] Sales were not always prompted by simple lust for profit, and not in all cases did they imply landlessness, land flight, or expulsion. Owners with more than the subsistence minimum might decide to sell a plot, so as to invest the capital in the remaining land and utilize it more intensively through irrigation and other measures. This was especially true of citrus cultivation, which was highly profitable though dependent on volatile world markets (80 to 90 percent of the harvest was exported abroad). It rapidly expanded in the 1920s and

[16] K. Stein (1984), ch. 6, esp. pp. 173ff., 192–202; Porath (1977), p. 85; for Transjordan, see also Wilson (1987), ch. 7.

[17] K. Stein (1984), pp. 59, 64, 68, 100–102, 142, 178ff. On citrus cultivation, see Metzer (1998), pp. 145–48, 163–64, 220–25; Reiter (1996), p. 191. Nadan (2006), pp. xxviii, 9ff., and chs. 2–4, cautions against overestimating profitable investment, especially in citrus growing, as a result of Arab land sales.

1930s in both the Jewish and Arab economic sectors. In 1922 citrus groves and plantations comprised 29,000 dunam, and in 1931, 107,000; by 1935, the area had more than doubled to 250,000 dunam. The rate of citrus farming among overall agricultural production rose from 11 percent in the mid-1920s to around 40 percent in the late 1930s. In 1935 Palestinian *shamuti* oranges already made up 20 percent of all worldwide citrus exports. Citrus cultivation played a lesser role in Arab agriculture, but even there it steadily expanded. However, improvement and expansion required considerable capital investment, as citrus and olive plantations only began to show a profit after a number of years, capital that small farmers had no chance of obtaining.

The greatest problems for the Palestinian economy and society lay in the indebtedness of the peasants—which compelled many of them to sell, turning growing numbers into landless peasants—and in the expulsion of tenant farmers, fieldworkers, and Bedouins that resulted from land transfers. Again one must guard against oversimplifications. When purchases were made by the Jewish National Fund, non-Jews were theoretically excluded from further occupancy and use of "Jewish land." However, it can be shown that during the crisis of 1926–27, sales and return sales from Jews to Arabs actually occurred, and at reduced prices.[18] Land was also not only sold to Jews; Arab landlords too would expand their properties, as they had done since the mid-nineteenth century. Within the Arab sector, landed property was distributed in highly unequal fashion. Arab landlords too would expel tenant farmers and fieldworkers, or block customary forms of use through the enclosure of grazing land and other measures. Buyers and sellers could hope to avoid trouble if they expelled tenants, fieldworkers, and shepherds *before* the transfer, or persuaded them to renounce their traditional rights against monetary payments. Society as a whole could not evade the problem.

Nor could the problem of debt be traced back to Zionists machinations. It dated back to the nineteenth century, and was worsened in the 1930s through a series of natural catastrophes (earthquakes, locust plagues, and drought), crop failures due to mice and worms, and more systematic tax collection—even though the British reduced certain Ottoman taxes with a view to improving the condition of the peasantry so as to foster sociopolitical stability.[19] The chronic lack of cash and capital

[18] Porath (1977), p. 91. For what follows, see Y. Miller (1985), pp. 81ff.; Porath (1977), pp. 105–106. On land distribution, see Metzer (1998), pp. 96–99.

[19] K. Stein (1984), pp. 19–20, with the statistics for 1931, as well as ch. 5 on the problem of landlessness. Nadan (2006), pp. 28–29, and ch. 5. Nadan stresses the fact that the Islamic ban on interest (*riba*) had little or no effect on local moneylending practices, pp. 247–48. For credit and debt, see also Porath (1977), pp. 86ff.; Metzer (1998), pp. 110ff.; Benvenisti (2002), pp. 96–97. For locusts, mice, and worms, see El-Eini (2006), ch. 3.

proved to be the chief obstacle to a steady expansion of Arab agriculture, as well as the chief problem of the peasant household, which additionally suffered from high birthrates. Quite often, peasants were compelled to buy on credit if specific payments fell due before the harvest
could be sold, or if weather or other factors prevented it from being
sold, or to be sold at a fair price. Still, seed, work tools, livestock, or
clothing had to be purchased irrespective of the profits realized. With an
average interest rate of 30 percent (it could be as high as 50 percent, or
occasionally as low as 10 percent), this drove peasants into debt, and
forced emergency land sales. Most creditors and usurers were not Jews
or foreigners, but rather local Arab moneylenders, traders, merchants,
landowners, and 'ulama', including women. According to British statistics, by 1931 almost one third of Arab villagers had no land of their
own, while more than a quarter had too little for subsistence, and were
thus dependent on additional income.

The Mandate authorities registered these developments with growing
concern. But until the unrest of 1929, when the various commissions of
inquiry identified the land question as the decisive factor in the outbreak
of violence, they did little to remedy the situation.[20] In October 1920
they had allowed land transfers to resume, not least to prevent landlessness and flight from the land, which were perceived as dangers to internal security. The primary aim was to keep the peasants on the land and
to preclude instability and criminality, and indeed the very rise of a "social question." The order limited the size of land transfers, and at the
same time established that the tenants affected should not be compen-
sated financially, but with land. Later modified and amended, it remained without effect. The Passfield Memorandum of 1930 openly addressed the problem of landlessness as a politically explosive issue, but
offered the peasants no substantial assistance. Drastic measures were
first proposed in the White Paper of 1939, yet due to the outbreak of
war they were not implemented.

PALESTINE AS A MUSLIM *WAQF*

The social problems that resulted from the fragmentation of landhold-
ings, overuse, debt, and impoverishment were not new. But during the
1930s they gained in force and intensity. Among the rural population
there was a growing sense of existential threat; urban nationalists
pointed to the political danger emanating from Zionism, or from the

[20] K. Stein (1984), pp. 50ff., 188ff.; Metzer (1998), pp. 90–94; Owen (ed.) (2000), ch.
4; Nadan (2006), pp. 25–35; El-Eini (2006), ch. 4.

Jews more generally.[21] In the 1920s, Jewish land purchases were rarely discussed in Palestinian politics. Attention was focused instead on the Mandate, the Balfour Declaration, and Jewish immigration. This changed after 1929, presumably caused by increased Jewish purchases of cultivated land from Arab landlords, affecting growing numbers of Arab peasants, tenant farmers, fieldworkers, and shepherds. Arab landlords found themselves trapped between their nationalist convictions (to the extent that these existed) and economic interests, between the common good and personal profit. There were some parallels here with the Jewish farmers of the late nineteenth and early twentieth century who had to make a choice between cheap Arab labor and more expensive Jewish labor. As profitable and even sensible as land sales may have been in economic terms, they were compromising from a national point of view. They could not but damage the reputation and credibility of the Arab elite. The German consul, to give just one example, made no secret of his contempt for the Arab nationalists who, as he put it, agitated against Jewish immigration by day and by night sold their land to the Jews.[22]

Arab society was very much aware of these developments. From the 1930s onward, the Muslim-Christian Associations and the Arab Executive, supported by the local Arabic-speaking press, sought to mobilize the peasantry against land sales. They appealed to them to sell no land to the Jews and also to not leave land that had already been sold. In fact, numerous conflicts arose between Arab tenant farmers, fieldworkers, and Bedouins and the new Jewish owners, bringing the issues of land and expulsion into public consciousness. The Mufti and the Supreme Muslim Council intervened more vocally in the dispute. Sociopolitical, national, and religious concerns began to fuse ever more closely, giving rise to an argument that was not entirely new, but would remain powerful well beyond the 1930s: Accordingly, conflict with the Jews was not just over the holy sites of Islam in Jerusalem, the Haram al-Sharif with al-Aqsa Mosque and the Dome of the Rock, but rather over the land of Palestine (*ard filastin*) as a whole, which the Jews sought to appropriate and tear away from Islam. The land of Palestine was not just holy to Muslims, it was *entrusted* to them by God as an endowment and for this reason was nonnegotiable. The sale of land to Jews was

---

[21] Porath (1977), pp. 87, 91ff. K. Stein (1984), esp. pp. 49–50, 142–46, as well as pp. 67ff. On pp. 228–29, he lists names of prominent Arab landowners and activists who sold land to Jews between 1918 and 1945. See also Y. Miller (1985), pp. 18–19. The thesis that land was primarily if not exclusively sold by "foreigners" and absentee landowners, and that the Palestinian peasantry was thus largely innocent of these unpatriotic acts, is defended by several Arab authors including Salih (1989), pp. 217–19.

[22] Porath (1977), pp. 87, 91ff.

both sin and high treason, illegitimate in terms of both religion and politics. What was at stake was not just the Muslims living in Palestine—these were mere trustees of the endowment. Islam was at stake and the community of Muslims at large. What we find here is a mirror image of the Zionist understanding of Eretz Israel as Jewish land, based on divine promise and requiring the "redemption" of this land. We also find a reflection of the argument put forth by British politicians who dismissed the wishes of the local population arguing that Palestine was not merely about its local inhabitants, but about the Holy Land, the solution of the Jewish question, and indeed human history.

The notion of Palestine as an endowment, translating a political issue into religious language, was neither unique nor entirely new (incidentally, the term "*waqf*" itself was seldom used in this connection, yet the terminology employed was largely derived from the relevant provisions of Islamic law).[23] In the final resolution of the Islamic World Congress held in December 1931, the Hijaz Railway, whose Damascus Station had fallen under French rule in 1920, was called a *waqf*, partly because it was financed through Muslim donations. The Hijaz Railway served mainly to transport pilgrims from Damascus to Mecca and Medina. Via a connecting line that led from Haifa through the plain of Marj Ibn Amir (Jezreel) to Baisan, Palestine was connected to the rail network as well. In January 1932 the participants in a Conference of Arab Youth spoke of Palestine as a "holy land" and asserted that the sale of any part of this land must count as high treason. At the beginning of 1933, a speaker in Safed warned his audience about selling out "our holy land" to the Jews. Village sheikhs and preachers denounced land sales as sin and high treason; in December 1934 a large assembly of village notables adopted the same terminology. In October 1933 the prominent Muslim reformer Rashid Rida (1865–1935) condemned the sale of land in Palestine and its environs to the Jews or the British, and indeed to anyone belonging to the *dar al-harb* (the "abode of war," that is territories not under Islamic rule), as a betrayal of God and his Prophet, though again without explicitly designating Palestine as a *waqf*:

> Whoever sells a piece of Palestinian soil and its surroundings to the Jews or the English acts like someone who sells them the Aqsa Mosque and the homeland at large, for that is the purpose for which they buy the land—that, and to endanger the Hijaz [i.e., the holy sites of Islam in Mecca and

---

[23] Kupferschmidt (1987), pp. 127, 210–11, 240–54; al-Hut (1981), p. 226; K. Stein (1984), p. 182; Salih (1989), pp. 217–26; also Seikaly (1998), p. 76, note 5. A similar fusion of religion and politics occurred when Muslims who adopted the citizenship of the respective colonial power were threatened with exclusion from the Muslim community (*takfir*), as happened for instance in French-occupied Tunisia.

Medina]. Ownership of this land (*raqaba*) is like a man's ownership of his own body. In accordance with Islamic law it is a good that belongs to all Muslims for them to benefit from it, not private property. The sale of Islamic land to a non-Muslim foreigner (*harbi*) is null and void and a betrayal of God and his Prophet and the entrusted good of Islam. I need not recall here the punishment that awaits those who commit this betrayal [commonly classified as apostasy, which under Islamic law is punishable with death, as well as with grave sanctions under civil law]. Rather, I suggest to all those who believe in God, his holy book, and his messenger . . . to proclaim this immutable Islamic provision throughout the country, together with the appeal to have no dealings with the traitors who persist in their treachery.[24]

Muhammad al-Husain Al Kashif al-Ghita (1877/78–1954), one of the most prominent Shi'i scholars of Najaf in Iraq, expressed himself in a similar vein, when asked for a legal opinion by a Palestinian Muslim: Selling the "holy land" to the Jews, assistance with such sales, and even silent approval of them amounted to acts of war (*muharaba*) against God and his Prophet—one of the most serious crimes, and subject to the death penalty according to Islamic law.[25] By contrast, Kashif al-Ghita merely demanded that the traitors be ostracized, and their names be made public by all associations and newspapers, as people who had deviated from Islam (*al-khawarij min al-islam*). Indian scholar Mohammed Suleiman al-Qadiri al-Chishti (in Arabic Jashti), a leading member of the Association of Indian Ulama (Jam'iyyat Ulama-i Hind), used similar arguments in a fatwa:

> Those Muslims who today sell the holy land of Palestine to the Jews or who provide assistance to this abominable deed, although they know that the Jews only buy the land in order to drive the Muslims out of this holy land, and to erect the Temple in place of al-Aqsa Mosque, and to found a Jewish state, stand before God as enemies of Islam who have abandoned themselves to unbelief. . . . Their punishment is none other than the fires of hell.[26]

---

[24] Cited from al-Hut (1981), p. 741. In Arabic, the relevant passage reads:

wa-hiya bi-hadhihi tu'add shar'an min al-manafi' al-islamiyya al-'amma la min al-amlak al-shakhsiyya al-khassa wa-tamlik al-harbi li-dar al-islam batil wa-khiyana li-llah wa-li-rasulihi wa-li-amanat al-islam.

[25] Kashif al-Ghita (his statement was not explicitly described as a fatwa) translated from al-Hut (1981), pp. 740–41. On Kashif al-Ghita (the family, Al, bears the honorific of the "lifter of the veil"), see Kramer (1986), pp. 132–33; Kupferschmidt (1987), p. 198.

[26] Translated from al-Hut (1981), p. 742.

In January 1935 Amin al-Husaini finally published his own fatwa, stating that according to Qur'an 33:72 (which does not refer to any specific territory), Palestine was a good entrusted (*amana*) to all Muslims. The fatwa was read aloud at a conference of some three hundred '*ulama*', who met in the Aqsa Mosque at the invitation of the Supreme Muslim Council. It was then printed and distributed throughout the country. The participants also issued a collective fatwa of their own. Referring to the pronouncements of the Mufti and other authorities from Chishti to Kashif al-Ghita, they condemned as traitors, infidels, and apostates, the sellers, brokers, and intermediaries who in "this holy Islamic land" (*hadhihi l-bilad al-islamiyya al-muqaddasa*) sold their land to the Jews, threatening them with social ostracism and the denial of a Muslim burial, because they contributed to driving the Muslims out of their homeland and to the destruction of the mosques and other holy sites of Islam, and because they took the Jews as friends—all familiar Qur'anic references to the enemies of Islam.[27] A little later, an association of '*ulama*' was founded who, after the well-known Qur'anic exhortation "to promote virtue and prevent vice," called themselves Central Society for the Promotion of Virtue and the Prevention of Vice (*jam'iyyat al-amr bil-ma'ruf wa-l-nahy 'an al-munkar al-markaziyya*). The aim was to keep an eye not only on land sales, but also on immoral behavior in general (unseemly clothing, inadmissible intermingling of men and women, indecent scenes in literature, film, and the theater).

The credibility of the notables and the religious establishment, many of whom secretly sold land to the Jews, was limited, the more so since they offered little help to the impoverished peasants.[28] An Arab Bank founded in 1930 and an Arab National Fund (*sunduq al-umma al-'arabiyya*) established in 1931 provided little assistance. The activities of the National Fund fell far short of expectations: After a few transactions in the years 1932–35, they came entirely to a halt following the uprising in 1936. The Supreme Muslim Council, too, was only active for a short time, although control of the Islamic religious endowments provided it with considerable funds. In the wake of 1929, the SMC proclaimed the objective of "rescuing" (*istinqadh*) Muslim land—a concept corresponding to the Zionist goal of "redeeming" the land (*ge'ulat ha-adama*). In any case, growing indebtedness of Arab peasants after 1930 also caused the Council's income to drop, as the tithe represented an important

---

[27] Al-Hut (1981), pp. 739–42, contains the concluding fatwa of the conference, as well as a Christian Orthodox statement dating from February 1935, which threatens real estate brokers and those who sell land with excommunication. See also Kupferschmidt (1987), pp. 242–53. For the *amr bil-ma'ruf*, see Michael Cook, *Commanding Right and Forbidding Wrong in Islamic Thought* (Cambridge 2000).

[28] Kupferschmidt (1987), pp. 45–53, 245–47; Porath (1977), pp. 93ff.

source of income for the rural *awqaf* that it controlled. The SMC did advocate a number of practical measures to preserve Arab land: One was to transform private property into religious endowments (family *waqf*s) so as to block its transfer, another to purchase land with *waqf* funds if its owner saw himself compelled to sell. Yet others were to acquire shares in communal *musha'* land, which made further sale very difficult, and to extend credit to cultivators in financial straits. Yet all practical initiatives seem to have subsided by the summer of 1935.

New Voices

The failures and setbacks in the pursuit of national interests could not but weaken the position of the notables whom the British actively sought to cultivate. In Palestine as in the surrounding Arab countries, new political actors appeared on the stage, accompanied by a broader political mobilization of what in Arabic is called "the street," and in Western sources easily becomes "the mob," under whose influence the prevailing patterns of political action and organization were gradually transformed. The rural exodus altered the relation between city and countryside. As the coming years would show, the experiences of former peasants and fieldworkers as they entered the cities had an impact on village society and rural patterns of organization as well. The idea of nationalism began to take root in urban as well as rural society. Limited though the social base of the national movement remained, the emotional power of the national idea was continually gaining in strength. New organizations formed, frequently in declared opposition to the notables. Some, like the Young Men's Muslim Association, adopted an Islamic orientation; others made no explicit references to religion; only a tiny fraction openly declared themselves secular. For the most part politics remained a male business, yet the first female voices were to be heard, too, especially among the urban elite. Women had long been involved in social work and charity among the poor. From the late 1920s onward, they occasionally made their appearance in politics. A visible sign of the new spirit was an Arab Women's Congress, held in Jerusalem in 1929 with some two hundred participants. In November 1929 the Arab Women's Association (AWA, later Arab Women's Union) was founded in Jerusalem with branches in many parts of the country.[29]

The "Black Letter" of February 1931 enhanced Arab disillusionment with British policies. The first appeals for a policy of noncooperation and of civil disobedience were heard, to be combined with a boycott of

[29] Fleischmann (2000), chs. 5 and 6; Mogannam (1937), pp. 67–92.

British and Jewish institutions, goods, and services. In March 1933 even the Arab Executive began to advocate such a strategy.[30] On October 13, 1933, a general strike was declared to be accompanied by demonstrations throughout the country. Police dispersed the demonstrators by force, causing deaths and injuries in Jerusalem. More dramatic still were developments in Jaffa two weeks later: In the course of broad protest involving thousands of Palestinians as well as two Arab delegations from Transjordan and Syria, the police shot dead at least twenty-six protestors (according to other reports it was thirty) and wounded an additional two hundred. The harsh policy of repression provoked angry protests that were directed almost exclusively against the British; only in Haifa, Jews and Jewish establishments were assailed, too. For the first time, Arabs began to make extensive use of firearms and dynamite. The British added press censorship to their extensive range of police measures, which already included collective punishment of Arab villages and neighborhoods suspected of involvement in the unrest. Also injured in the October 27 demonstration in Jaffa was Musa Kazim al-Husaini, president of the Arab Executive, who died a few months later, in March 1934. With his death, this organization quietly came to an end, paralyzed by internal rivalries.

In the 1930s, more and more young people began to appear on the political stage. Again, this was not an entirely new phenomenon, for in the nineteenth and early twentieth centuries, a number of new groups and associations had called themselves "young," or were designated as such by outsiders, among them the Young Ottomans, the Young Turks, and the Arab group al-Fatat. In the 1930s, youth organizations spread in many places around the world; in Syria, Lebanon, Iraq, and Egypt political and paramilitary groups formed, from "Young Egypt" (Misr al-Fatat) to the "Blue Shirts," and the "Steel Shirts." In Palestine itself, the Zionist pioneers (halutzim) and the Revisionist Betar organization (whose repertory of images had much in common with the iconography of socialist realism and fascism) demonstrated to their Arab countrymen and women the power of youth, commitment, and idealism.[31] At the beginning of the 1930s, 60 percent of the Palestinian population was younger than fifteen years. Yet among the political establishment, only the Mufti could still be considered young.

[30] *Peel Report* (1937), pp. 82–92, 193–94; Porath (1977), pp. 34–35, 40ff.; Kolinsky (1993), pp. 172–84. For a different account, see Salih (1989), pp. 202–203.

[31] Y. Miller (1985), pp. 116–17; Gelvin (1998), pp. 111, 199–201; for the paramilitary youth movements, cf. Krämer (2006). For the pioneers, Betar, and Zionist iconography cf. Shapira (1992), ch. 2; Arbel (ed.) 1996; for a powerful statement of the claims of youth, see Ha-Shomer ha-Tza'ir, "Our Worldview," dated January 17, 1927, in Mendes-Flohr/Reinharz (eds.) (1995), pp. 577–79.

Among the associations that proliferated in this period was the Young Men's Muslim Association, YMMA (*jam'iyyat al-shubban al-muslimin*) which, originating in Egypt, became active in Palestine in 1927–28. Though it declared itself to be apolitical, it had a definite political impact. The YMMA aimed not only at spreading education, art, and the scouting spirit, but also at improving Muslim representation in government and the administration. Given the heavy Christian presence in the administration, this aim was bound to put an additional strain on intercommunal relations, which were already growing more tense in light of the Islamizing tendencies.[32] In July and September 1931, participants in two YMMA conferences in Nablus spoke publicly of the need for armed resistance against the Zionists. In January 1932 a National Congress of Arab Youth voiced pan-Arab demands and, from its original base in Jaffa, later opened branches in various parts of the country. Even the Palestinian Boy Scout Movement, established by the British to promote among Arab youth the virtues of cleanliness, order, and exercise in fresh air, became attracted to nationalism. Coordinated since January 1936 under a national umbrella organization, it became especially active during the strike of 1936.

New political parties entered public view in the early 1930s, though they remained of marginal importance. The Arab Independence Party (*hizb al-istiqlal al-'arabi*) was founded in August 1932 by Awni Abd al-Hadi and in the two years of its existence, took a pan-Arab line. Unlike the Mufti, but also unlike the majority of notables both inside and outside the Arab Executive who hoped to fend off the Zionist danger with British help, it attacked not only the Zionists, but also the British Mandate authorities. In their view, the British were the prime enemy of Arab Palestinians, and the Mandate itself the decisive obstacle on the path to Arab self-determination: If the Mandate fell, then the Zionist project would also collapse. The Istiqlal Party propagated a strategy of noncooperation and refusal to pay taxes to the Mandate administration, but it also took an interest in the plight of Arab peasants and workers.[33] More remarkable than its program was the fact that the party recruited

[32] Porath (1974), pp. 300–303; Porath (1977), pp. 109, 119ff., 127; Y. Miller (1985), pp. 114ff.; Kupferschmidt (1987), pp. 224–25; al-Hut (1981), pp. 188–91; Salih (1989), pp. 157–62. For Haifa, cf. Seikaly (1998), pp. 191–92, 227. Photographs from the 1930s show the boy scouts wearing a curious combination of uniform shirts, ties, kaffiyeh, shorts, and kneesocks (usually in a checkered pattern); see, for instance, Naor (1998), p. 191. More on dress below, chapter 12.

[33] Nafi (1998), pp. 170–73; Muslih (1988), pp. 132ff., 143; Porath (1977), pp. 51–52, 123–28. They stood within the tradition of the Istiqlal Party active in Syria in 1918–19. For their Islamic orientation, see Schleifer (1979), pp. 76–77. For Awni Abd al-Hadi's participation in land sales to Jews, see K. Stein (1984), pp. 161–62, 231.

most of its members (there were never more than sixty) not from Jerusalem, but from northern towns like Nablus and Haifa, and was identified with none of the great families. Compared with the notables and their "parties," the Istiqlalists were radical, but thoroughly respectable. In ideological terms, they tended toward the left, yet they were ready and able to translate national demands into an Islamic language, or at least to furnish them with Islamic overtones. The party as a whole was short-lived, but had long-term effects. Some of its former members later joined Hajj Amin's camp, while many remained politically active as individuals (in addition to Awni Abd al-Hadi himself, these included Izzat Darwaza, Akram Zu'aitir, and Ahmad al-Shuqairi).

More conventional than the Istiqlal were the competing "parties" of the Jerusalem notables, which were essentially loose associations of individual families and their clients, and were generally perceived as such. They neither formulated a clearly defined program nor engaged in regular activities beyond the publication of statements, petitions, and at best of newspapers. Nor did they address broader segments of the population. They were commonly divided into the camps of the Mufti (majlisin, derived from al-majlis al-islami al-a'la or Supreme Muslim Council) and the "opposition" (al-mu'arada, mu'aridin), with a regional base of support in Haifa, Nablus, Nazareth, and Hebron.[34] The case of Nablus, where the spirit of resistance against any kind of external interference—whether it be the Sublime Porte in Istanbul, the Jerusalem elite, the British Mandatory, or the Zionists—was always strong, serves to show that any explanation falls short that proceeds from a simple distinction between radicals (ostensibly led by the Husainis) and moderates (embodied by the Nashashibis). Rather, what we see are residents of towns and subregions, especially in the north, warding off any attempt by the Mufti to act on their behalf and dominate Arab politics in the name of the national cause.

The National Defense Party (hizb al-difa' al-watani) was largely seen as the party of the Nashashibi family. It emerged in December 1934, when Raghib al-Nashashibi was defeated in the Jerusalem municipal elections and not reelected as mayor.[35] The inaugural meeting in Jaffa was attended by some one thousand participants, among them some of the richest Arab landowners and entrepreneurs in the country, including numerous Christians. The National Defense Party could count on the support of two newspapers, Mir'at al-Sharq (Mirror of the East) and Filastin, which upheld the line of "positive politics" vis-à-vis the Man-

---

[34] Morris (1987), pp. 12, 15; also Survey of Palestine (1946), pp. 30–32.

[35] Porath (1977), pp. 62–71, 75–79, 143–59; al-Hut (1981), pp. 660ff. Also Nashashibi (1990).

date, advocating participation in a Legislative Council to be established. As a countermove, the supporters of the Mufti formed the Palestinian Arab Party (al-hizb al-'arabi al-filastini) at a meeting held in Jerusalem in March 1935 attended by some 1,500 participants. To demonstrate their ecumenical character, they elected Jamal al-Husaini, a cousin of the Mufti, as president, and the Greek-Catholic entrepreneur Alfred Rok from Jaffa as vice president. Religious dignitaries were strongly represented, as were a number of rural notable families. In addition to Jerusalem and other cities, the party was also able to open branches in rural areas. In February 1936 they founded a youth section, Firaq al-Shabab, later renamed al-Futuwwa, that adopted as their motto: "Freedom is my right, independence my goal, Arabism my principle, Palestine my land alone. I bear witness to this, so help me God." Jews were thereby denied any political claim to Palestine.

In June 1935 the Arab-Palestinian Reform Party (hizb al-islah al-'arabi al-filastini) was formed to defend the interests of the Khalidi family, which in the twentieth century repeatedly occupied the office of mayor of Jerusalem, but otherwise had little political influence. At the same time, several of its members were highly regarded as literary figures and scholars, foremost among them Yusuf Diya al-Khalidi (1842–1906) and his nephew Ruhi al-Khalidi (1864–1913).[36] Ostensibly pan-Arabist, the party was in fact "moderate" and advocated unification of Palestine with Transjordan (after the annexation of the West Bank, Husain al-Khalidi became Jordanian prime minister for a short time in April 1957). The National Defense Party, the Reform Party, and the National Bloc (al-kutla al-wataniyya, founded in October 1935, and not to be confused with the Syrian party of the same name, which achieved local significance only in Nablus) were "moderate" competitors, critics, and opponents of the Mufti. Yet they were too much at odds with one another to form an effective and cohesive "opposition."

Already in the 1930s, certain members of the established families made greater efforts to reach beyond their own circles to other strata of urban and rural society.[37] In 1934 Fakhri al-Nashashibi tried to mobilize workers in Haifa and Jaffa for the national cause. Massive Jewish immigration, combined with the policy of "Hebrew" labor, increased competition for jobs and in 1934–35 led to numerous clashes between Jewish employers and their Jewish and Arab employees, in which Jews and Arabs sometimes acted in solidarity. Yet the Palestine Communist Party,

[36] On the Khalidi family, who traced their genealogy to Khalid b. al-Walid, one of the most famous commanders in the early Muslim conquests, see Khalidi (1997), ch. 4; Manna' (1998).

[37] On communism and the labor movement, see Bernstein (2000); Lockman (1996); Tahbub (1982); Flores (1980).

founded by former members of the Socialist Workers Party in 1922, had great difficulties establishing itself. Until 1929 it was almost exclusively Jewish, and even when it decided to devote greater attention to Arab peasants and Bedouins, its influence remained weak. It gained only a few Arab members in the urban milieu, and in the Arab villages it showed no presence at all.

Izz al-Din al-Qassam

Among the new associations that emerged in the 1930s, there were a number of militant secret societies, which in some ways resembled those that had been active during World War I. Unlike the established notables, great families, and parties, and also unlike the Supreme Muslim Council, they advocated armed struggle (jihad) against the Zionists and the Jews.[38] In October 1929 an Islamic organization known as the Green Hand (al-yad al-khadra) was active in the hills around Safed: It had about twenty-five members who regarded themselves as mujahidin, and attacked Jewish settlements and British targets. In 1931 they were liquidated by the British. In 1932 a group of similar name was reported to operate in the Hebron area. The Holy War Organization (munazzamat al-jihad al-muqaddas), which despite its Islamic name also had a few Christian members, was founded in early 1931 by Abd al-Qadir al-Husaini, a son of Musa Kazim al-Husaini and collaborator of the Mufti. By the end of 1934, it is reported to have given military training to some four hundred youths. It played a role in the Arab revolt of 1936–39 and in the fighting of 1947–49. In 1935 a group figuring as the Young Rebels, or Avenging Youth (al-shabab al-tha'ir) operated in the region of Tulkarm and Qalqilya. It was and remains controversial to what extent the Mufti supported these individuals and organizations, even if covertly.[39] Though important as an indicator of social and political change, they remained of local significance only.

Not so the group that formed at the same time around Izz al-Din al-Qassam (1882?–1935), one of the first representatives of the Islamic Salafiyya reform movement to actively engage in social work and mili-

---

[38] Porath (1977), pp. 130ff.; Lachman (1982), pp. 56ff.; Kupferschmidt (1987), pp. 253–54.

[39] Lachman (1982), pp. 57–59, postulates this without evidence; according to Mattar (1988), p. 67, he advocated political means and refused to support military resistance. Porath (1977), pp. 118, 132, cites remarks claiming that in the middle of 1934, Hajj Amin thought that the time for armed resistance to the British was not yet ripe, but nonetheless assumes his clandestine support for Abd al-Qadir and other underground organizations.

tant action, or armed jihad against foreign occupation. Izz al-Din al-Qassam has attracted considerable interest in scholarly circles as well as among a broader audience. Yet he left no writings, and reports from his comrades in arms, followers, and other contemporaries are often contradictory.[40] Important aspects of his life story remain unclear, and even his year of birth is disputed, with estimates differing by as much as a decade. Izz al-Din was probably born in 1882 in the northern Syrian village of Jabla near Latakia, the son of a Qur'anic schoolteacher and Sufi sheikh of the Qadiriyya order. For eight years he studied at al-Azhar University in Cairo, where he may have made the acquaintance of Muhammad Abduh and his student Rashid Rida. The claims by some of his supporters that he actually studied with Abduh and Rida may have served primarily to enhance his religious and intellectual standing. Whether formally their student or not, Qassam proved himself quite early to be politically active. Around 1904 he returned to Jabla, where he worked as prayer leader (*imam*) and Qur'anic schoolteacher. Following the Italian invasion of Libya in 1911, he sought to mobilize the local population in a jihad against the Italians but was prevented by the Ottoman authorities from entering military action. After Latakia was occupied by French troops in October 1918, he joined the guerrillas fighting in the Syrian mountains. Condemned to death by a French military court, he and a few companions fled via Beirut to Haifa, then a gathering point for Syrian and Lebanese nationalists.

Haifa, since 1905 the administrative headquarters of the Hijaz Railway, was at this time an expanding industrial and port city whose character was rapidly changing as a result of the influx of landless peasants from the surrounding countryside. We have a lively description of Haifa in the 1930s, when the port was modernized and the pipeline from the oilfields of northern Iraq completed:

> Haifa is the northernmost town in Palestine, the one furthest from the Orient, and furthest from the desert. . . . Haifa rises from the sea to the mountaintop. Down below are the port, the Arabs, the Old City, the commercial center. Half way up, a Jewish middle-class town. On the mountain top, the residential area of the most affluent. On the plain, mostly small-scale housing estates and a factory town. . . .
>
> Haifa is the frontier. It is Europe, global politics, working class district, rich suburb of villas, petroleum and cement factory, suburb of the grand social experiment of the Kwuzah [a form of kibbutz], it is high-rise building and naval base.[41]

---

[40] See Schleifer (1979); Salih (1989), pp. 229–317; Nafi (1997), and—with very different assessments—Lachman (1982), pp. 59ff.; Porath (1977), pp. 132–39.

[41] Tergit (1996), pp. 53–55. I have inverted the order of the citations, beginning with p. 55 and ending with p. 53.

In the Arab Old City, situated close to the new Jewish quarters of the middle and upper classes, Izz al-Din al-Qassam was quickly able to establish himself as a teacher and preacher.[42] In 1925 he was appointed imam of the newly constructed Istiqlal Mosque, which apparently was not subordinate to the Supreme Muslim Council, or at least not directly (the name "*istiqlal*," independence, suggests as much). In May 1928 he took part in founding the Haifa branch of the Young Men's Muslim Association, which gave him access to wider social circles; in 1934 the YMMA elected him their local head. His appointment as marriage registrar (*ma'dhun*) of the Haifa Sharia Court in 1930 allowed him to extend his field of action to rural Galilee and the district of Jenin.

Like Hasan al-Banna and the Egyptian Muslim Brotherhood, Qassam and his supporters tied Islamic reform to militant nationalism. Both al-Banna and Qassam called for individual reform and a reform of practiced religion, so that individual change and communal action would go hand in hand and reinforce one another. Like other Muslim activists before and after him, Qassam understood jihad as the quest for a godly life (*al-jihad fi sabil allah*), and thus did not reduce it to politics, let alone armed struggle. This did not prevent him from preaching violence, and from practicing it. In light of the threatening situation in Palestine, he declared armed struggle the individual duty of Muslims (*fard al-'ain*) and propagated the ideal of the martyr who would sacrifice himself for the cause of Islam.[43] Qassam advocated a type of Islam that was definitely political—and he lived it. The combination of Sufi leanings and commitment to a reformed Islam purified of alien and "popular" influences, fighting not only against magical practices and the cult of shrines, but also against "deviants" and "heretics," was not unusual among Islamic activists of his time; Hasan al-Banna operated along similar lines.

More unusual was Qassam's combination of reformist preaching with active social work (though not in comparison with the Egyptian Muslim Brothers who strongly engaged in both). Qassam devoted himself to the plight of migrant and casual workers, primarily impoverished peasants who were employed in the railroads or construction, especially when in the early 1930s a deep-sea port, an oil pipeline, and an oil refinery were built in Haifa. He also turned to the fellahin in the rural hinterland of Haifa. Qassam did not just remain in the mosque and the school, but went to coffee houses, clubs, and even, as some of his critics noted, to

[42] Salih (1989), pp. 248–54. On the Istiqlal Mosque, see also Seikaly (1998), pp. 191–92; on Haifa in general, see pp. 219ff.; also Bernstein (2000); Gelvin (1998), pp. 19–20.

[43] Schleifer (1979), pp. 71ff., 79. Salih (1989), esp. pp. 241–44, 265–74, places great value on Qassam's armed Jihad. For the Egyptian Muslim Brothers, cf. Richard P. Mitchell, *The Society of the Muslim Brothers*, new ed. (Oxford 1993), and Brynjar Lia, *The Society of the Muslim Brothers in Egypt: The Rise of an Islamic Mass Movement 1928–1942* (Reading, 1998); see also Mayer (1983).

suspicious establishments with an equally suspicious clientele from hash-ish dens to brothels. Qassam knew how to make his message understood by his audience, and to express social concerns and national aspirations in familiar Islamic language. More than that, he was credible: With him, doctrine (insofar as it existed) and personal conduct seemed to be one. He praised the ascetic lifestyle of the Sufis (*zuhd*) and propagated an uncompromising moral view, demanding the strict fulfillment of reli-gious duties and a simple life among simple people. He advocated piety, struggle, and sacrifice, and to a large extent he lived these moral princi-ples. Qassam exerted moral authority, and he was filled with pious con-fidence. Yet he was apparently no dour moralist, a feature that certainly helped to enhance his popularity.

Sheikh Izz al-Din did not restrict himself to political activities in a narrow sense. Rather, along with religious instruction proper, he would also give reading and writing lessons in evening schools and rural coop-eratives. In parallel with these activities, however, he began to prepare for active resistance, emphasizing the necessity of armed jihad in his Friday sermons, and cautiously recruiting followers to whom he gave clandestine military training. As a starting point for recruitment, he, like other Islamic activists before and after him, made use of mosques. First preparations for armed struggle may date back as far as 1925. His con-nections to the Mufti are unclear and disputed; on the whole, the latter seems to have remained noncommittal.[44] The significance of Qassam and his men for Palestinian resistance to British occupation and the Zionist project must not be overestimated, since they were not the only secret militant organization to operate in the country. Here as elsewhere, there has been a tendency to collapse diverse phenomena and activities in one individual and to make Izz al-Din al-Qassam the quintessential Islamic fighter and martyr of his time.

By 1935 Qassam is reported to have attracted several hundred volun-teer fighters (*fida'iyyun*), who underwent paramilitary training under the motto "This is jihad, victory or martyrdom" (*hadha jihad, nasr aw is-tishhad*). Estimates range from two hundred to one thousand men.[45] In a conscious link with the Sufi tradition, his early supporters called them-selves "sheikh" and grew a beard, but later gave up this practice to be less conspicuous. The center of activities of the Qassamites, as they be-came known to their contemporaries, lay in northern Palestine, with a few members coming from other parts of the country as far south as

[44] Salih (1989), pp. 250, 255–60; Porath (1977), pp. 137–38, and, again with a different assessment, Lachman (1982), pp. 74–77; see also note 39 above.

[45] Salih (1989), pp. 246–312 (citation on p. 267); Lachman (1982), pp. 64–65, 77; Schleifer (1979), p. 74.

Gaza. Although some may already have carried out first attacks against Jewish settlements in the years following 1929, the group only decided in late November 1935 (possibly in order to preempt impending discovery and arrest) that the time had come for an uprising.[46] Following the "Cement Incident" of October 1935, in which arms and ammunition for the Jewish Yishuv were discovered in the port of Jaffa, Qassam and a small band of twenty-five supporters moved to the Jenin area to mobilize the peasants for armed struggle. To acquire weapons and ammunition, Qassam had sold his house, and his companions at least some of their furniture and their wives' jewelry. On November 20, 1935, Qassam and a number of his fellow fighters were killed in a clash with a British patrol near the village of Ya'bad, making him one of the first Islamic activists to "bear witness" for his faith and the Palestinian cause. With his "act of martyrdom," Izz al-Din al-Qassam attained immediate status as a cult hero. His funeral in Haifa was attended by thousands of mourners; his grave in Balad al-Shaikh quickly became a site of pilgrimage.[47]

In Palestine Qassam's brand of activism, culminating in his act of martyrdom, was new, drawing admiration and imitation far beyond religious circles. His death did not end his movement or his idea, as the Arab revolt would show. The fact that he left behind no writings made it all the easier for diverse groups and individuals from Fatah to Hamas to appropriate his legacy: Nationalists appealed to Qassam as the "first commander of the Palestinian revolution," and Islamists claimed him as one of their own. Unlike the Palestinian notables—but also unlike the Mufti—Qassam served far beyond his death as a role model, and as a source of inspiration.

[46] Salih (1989), pp. 308–12; Schleifer (1979), pp. 61, 79; Porath (1977), pp. 134ff.; Lachman (1982), pp. 69–71.

[47] Salih (1989), pp. 310–27; Schleifer (1979), pp. 61, 78–79; Lachman (1982), pp. 72–74, 87; Porath (1977), pp. 137–38. On martyrdom in the Syrian context, cf. Gelvin (1998), pp. 175–81. For comparisons between Qassam and Josef Trumpeldor, cf. Swedenburg (1995), p. 12. For his image in Palestinian memoirs, cf. Enderwitz (2002), pp. 238–42.

Chapter Twelve

THE ARAB UPRISING, 1936–39

THE ARAB UPRISING that began in April 1936 and lasted intermittently until the early summer of 1939 resulted from several crises that had begun to mount in the preceding years and finally reached the breaking point.[1] In 1935 Jewish immigration was higher than ever: More than 62,000 legal immigrants were recorded, almost twice as many as during the entire Third Aliya. Land purchases reached 73,000 dunam. In mid-October 1935, a great quantity of weapons and ammunitions was discovered in the port of Jaffa, concealed in a cement shipment to a Jewish businessman in Tel Aviv. It was not the first weapons seizure of its kind, and those responsible for the operation were never officially identified. But among the Arab community, the "Cement Incident," as it became known, enhanced existing fears of a massive arming of the Jews that the Arabs would not be able to match. On the international scene, tensions were on the rise following the Italian invasion of Abyssinia (Ethiopia). At the same time, developments in Syria, Iraq, and Egypt demonstrated what could be achieved in a colonial setting through pressure and negotiating skill. The Syrian population held a general strike in January 1936 to enforce their demand for independence. Meanwhile, Egypt and Iraq had become nominally independent (although the British retained military control and the right of intervention); even the emir of Transjordan enjoyed considerable room for maneuver.

Any comparison between Palestine and its neighboring countries, whose populations could hardly be described as "more ready" for self-government and indeed independence, could only be sobering. While Arab Palestinians were growing more aware politically and also better organized, the framework of the Mandate gave them no recognized political representation. The Arab Executive had ceased to function after the death of Musa Kazim al-Husaini in March 1934. New attempts to establish some sort of recognized representation met with failure. In December 1935 the incumbent high commissioner, Sir Arthur Wauchope, announced that in accordance with the recommendations of the Passfield White Paper, a Legislative Council would be formed, made up of Muslims, Jews, and Christians. The Council would be granted control over

[1] Porath (1977), pp. 140ff., 159ff.; Y. Miller (1985), pp. 11–12; Kolinsky (1993), pp. 113–16.

immigration and land purchases. This step was opposed by the Zionists, who feared any recognized Arab representation as long as the Jews formed a minority in the country. It was also opposed in London. British Parliament rejected Wauchope's recommendation at the very moment when Arab politicians either had agreed to participate in such a body within the Mandate framework (as with Raghib al-Nashashibi and other "opposition" figures) or had privately hinted at changes in their previous strategy of noncooperation (as with Hajj Amin al-Husaini and his followers). British policy seemed to confirm the notion of an all-powerful Zionist, or Jewish, lobby in Europe and America. In this situation, the Arab leaders did not have many options: petitions, talks, and negotiations in London, Geneva, and Jerusalem had proven fruitless. There did remain civil disobedience, strike, and boycott—all of which had been practiced with great success in Egypt and Syria, while in Palestine itself they had so far been tried without the desired results.

EDUCATION, COMMUNICATION, AND MOBILITY

Palestinian society in 1936 was no longer what it had been in the immediate post–World War I period. The social and economic changes of the 1920s and 1930s, in particular the expansion of education (however limited among the Muslim community), had produced a new class of men and also some women who were actively engaged in politics. In the cities, at least, they were able to use new forms of communication. This is not to say that the traditional sites of meeting and coordination had lost their importance: private homes, coffee houses, public baths (the *hammam* was especially important for contacts among women), mosques, and churches. The same is true for the traditional occasions that would bring people together: circumcisions, weddings, and burials, pilgrimages, and the birthdays of saints and of the Prophet. Schools played a significant role in the spread of national ideas. By the mid-1930s, all sorts of clubs and associations had formed in addition to the existing political parties, including welfare organizations, women's associations, the bar association, chambers of commerce, trade unions, sports clubs, the boy scouts, the Young Men's Muslim Association, the YMCA and other Christian youth groups, and so forth. While most of them were primarily apolitical in nature, they still had a political impact. In addition to a lively Arabic press (not always financed or controlled by specific people, families, or parties), the cities also had cinemas and theaters that created support for the national cause, just as among the Jewish community. Gradually, at least in the urban milieu, a "civil soci-

ety" evolved that now had the means to articulate and exchange opinions that had been unknown to political activists during World War I.

   This was a result of improvements not only in education, but also
in infrastructure, communication, and the spread of information. The
transportation system had expanded rapidly since the war.[2] Although
camels, donkeys, and mules still played an important role in the transport of goods, the rail and road network had been steadily enlarged to
connect the larger towns and Jewish settlements. It became less common
that roads linking individual villages and smaller settlements to the
larger road network needed to be partly financed or constructed by local
residents. Along with the horse and carriage (which had by no means
vanished in the 1930s), there was an increasing number of trucks, buses,
taxis, motorcycles, and cars, especially on those roads that could be used
throughout the year. Even so, cars remained a luxury item that only few
members of Arab society could afford, partly because of high car and
fuel taxes. One of the first was Raghib al-Nashashibi, who after the war
had acquired a large green American limousine that he annually replaced
with a new vehicle. In 1923 there were twenty-one private cars registered within the Mandate territory (here the statistics do not distinguish
between Arabs and Jews). By 1924 the number had risen to 274 cars,
going up to 774 in 1930, 1,688 in 1933, and a total of 6,369 cars in
1936. In the same period the number of motorcycles rose from 79 to
2,637. Buses, taxis, and cars also provided the most important means of
access to neighboring Arab countries for those not traveling by sea. In
1937 an international airport opened in Lydda (Lod). It replaced Gaza
airport, and greatly shortened the travel time for passengers and mail
deliveries to Cairo, Baghdad, and the rest of the outside world. (The
Jewish population had its own airline, Aviron, funded by the Jewish
Agency and the Histadrut.) But even those who owned no car or had no
access to buses, taxis, trucks, or railways retained a measure of mobility:
Palestine was small, distances were relatively short, and the streets safe
almost everywhere. Any place could be reached by horse, mule, or donkey, or on foot.

   In parallel to the transportation system, the postal and telegraph net-
works were steadily expanded. First established in Ottoman times, they

[2] Data taken from Himadeh (ed.) (1938), ch. 6, esp. p. 332 (motor vehicles), and p. 342
(telephone connections); Nashashibi (1990), p. 16; El-Eini (2006), ch. 1. Useful maps are
found in Kolinsky (1993); for the nineteenth century, see Philipp/Schaebler (eds.) (1998).
Naor (1998), p. 171, reports on the enthusiasm of Jewish youth for motorcycles. In 1933
a number of Jewish firms joined to form the bus company Egged. A small car like the Fiat
Topolino cost around sixteen months' salary for a Jewish worker or employee; Naor
(1998), p. 202. In 1927 there were thirty-three telegraph offices in Palestine, in 1935 fifty-

were now made accessible to some of the larger villages and settlements. The telephone network was created in 1920, and in later years spread to all towns and larger settlements. In 1933 international telephone connections with Europe were installed. In 1931 a total of 486 private telephone lines were registered nationwide. By 1933 their number had risen to 2,500, to reach 12,200 in 1935 and 20,400 in 1936. As a result of these investments, information and news traveled much faster, benefiting government and opposition alike. In March 1936 just weeks before the uprising, the Palestine Broadcasting Service went on the air, broadcasting daily programs in the three official languages of Arabic, Hebrew, and English. In the same year, the Muslim Friday sermon was broadcast from al-Aqsa Mosque for the first time. In a number of villages, public loudspeakers were set up to transmit government announcements to those who had no radios of their own.

In addition to the religious feasts and celebrations, from the *mawlid* of Nabi Musa to the *mawsim* of Nabi Salih, which were slowly acquiring a political character, new memorial days were introduced that were explicitly national in character.[3] Beginning in 1918, annual demonstrations and parades were staged on November 2 to protest the Balfour Declaration ("Balfour Day"). Beginning in the late 1920s, various locales marked the anniversary of the Battle of Hittin in 1187, when Saladin defeated a Crusader army and paved the way for the Muslim reconquest of Jerusalem. This was not unproblematic, since it risked driving a wedge between Muslims and (Arab) Christians, a risk only reduced when Hittin was reinterpreted as a symbol of the struggle between "East" and "West." Beginning in 1930, May 16 was celebrated as "Palestine Day." Traditionally, Sufi shrines and brotherhoods, guilds, villages, and neighborhoods had their characteristic banners that were displayed on public processions and other festive occasions. These were now brought out for parades and national events along with the new Arab flag (supposedly designed by T. E. Lawrence, better known as "Lawrence of Arabia"), which had been used during the Arab Revolt of 1916. While there was no Arab anthem comparable to the Zionist "Hatikvah," the various processions, parades, and demonstrations were notable for their drumming, singing, and chanting. The Haram al-Sharif in Jerusalem provided a symbol radiating well beyond Palestine throughout the Arab and Muslim world. The Mufti had obvious leadership

---

six. For the radio broadcast from al-Aqsa, see Kupferschmidt (1987), p. 236, note 82. But see also Benvenisti (2000), ch. 2.

[3] For celebrations in memory of Hittin, see Kupferschmidt (1987), p. 236, and Salih (1989), pp. 152–54; for Palestine Day, Kolinsky (1993), p. 67.

qualities, though he remained controversial even within Arab ranks. (The same incidentally was true of Herzl. But Herzl had been dead for thirty years, making it so much easier to idealize him as a hero comparable to Moses.) Izz al-Din al-Qassam and his followers offered an alternative to the diplomatic course taken by the notables, encouraging at least a small number of local Arabs to pursue armed struggle.

IMAGES OF THE ENEMY

Above all, the Arab movement had enemies (or at least opponents) that were very much alive and visible: the British who occupied the land, and the Zionist Jews who wished to make it their own. This raises the question of perceptions, and the extent to which it was (and still is) possible to distinguish between Jews and Zionists on the one hand, and between anti-Zionism, anti-Judaism, and anti-Semitism on the other. Some Zionists tried to discredit Arab resistance to their goals as an expression of anti-Semitism that they claimed was rooted in Islam itself. Arab resistance was thus depoliticized, transposed onto a racist plane tied to religion, and robbed of moral legitimacy. However, the Zionist interpretation (anti-Zionism equals anti-Judaism equals anti-Semitism) misses the point: It is itself politically motivated, and must be understood as such. True, manifestations of European-style anti-Semitism were not entirely lacking in Palestine and the Arab world in the interwar period. Following his escape from Palestine in 1937, the Mufti would ally himself to Nazi Germany and support its anti-Semitic policies.[4] Yet the Arab population of Palestine and its political elite (whether the older generation or the new one that had risen to prominence between the two world wars) did not follow him in this direction.

Arab resistance to Zionist policies was political in character, aiming to defend Arab social, economic, cultural, and political interests. It was not based on racial conflict, and neither did it reflect racist concepts rooted in Islam.[5] It must be said, though, that the distinction between political conflict and religious antagonism was not always easy to draw. Even in the 1930s, language and iconography occasionally betrayed the imprint of anti-Semitic stereotypes that would become more widespread in the Arab and Muslim world from the 1950s onward. (The hook-

---

[4] His involvement with Nazism has attracted much attention; for serious research as opposed to mere polemics, see Gensicke (1988); Mattar (1988), ch. 8; Elpeleg (1993); Höpp (1999) and (2001); Krämer (2006). For Arab public opinion, see also Porath (1974), pp. 58–62, 97; Höpp et al. (eds.) (2004), esp. the contribution of Wildangel (2004).

[5] For a brief survey, cf. Krämer (2006); also Wild (2002) and (1985); Nicosia (1985); ʿAbd al-Ghani (1995); for poetry and literature, see Wild (1984) and al-Osta (1993).

nosed, claw-fingered Jew in a kaftan depicted then and there closely resembled the typical Arab in contemporary European caricatures, if we replace the kaftan with the Arab *jalaba*, and the hat or kippa with the kaffiyeh.) The idea of a Jewish conspiracy was spreading fast, responding as it did to the situation Palestinian Arabs themselves experienced. After all it was "the Jews" who had succeeded more than once in foiling Arab plans to gain official recognition for a political body representing their interests and to see them considered in London, Paris, Geneva, or New York. The *Protocols of the Elders of Zion*, the notorious anti-Semitic forgery, which was translated into Arabic in the 1920s, seemed to lend scientific credibility to the conspiracy theory. Many Arab readers regarded the *Protocols* as genuine, especially since they were recorded in a European document (many believe in its authenticity even today). But in the 1930s, anti-Semitic views were still confined to the margins; they were not part of an elaborate racial theory, and above all were not advocated by the political leadership. Anti-Semitism had no roots among Arab Muslims comparable to the deep-seated stereotypes and prejudices partially based on Christian teachings, that Jews faced in Europe. In a Muslim Arab context, the image of the Jew carried much less religious and historical baggage. In religious terms, Jews were not as central for Islam as they were for Christianity. What is more they were never the only non-Muslim minority living in a Muslim majority society. In more than one way, the Jews were nothing special.

Anti-Zionism and a general hostility toward Jews were more difficult to keep clearly separate. But how could it be otherwise? Zionism spoke in the name of the Jewish people at large, not of a political party or the Jewish Yishuv in Palestine. The Zionist Commission and the Jewish Agency were international *Jewish* organizations through which even non-Zionist Jews became involved with the Zionist cause. When faced with pious believers from Eastern Europe, Yemen, or Bukhara, who lived in Safed, Tiberias, or Mea Shearim, with no national claims to Palestine as the Jewish homeland, it was easy to perceive them simply as Jews. It was easy to integrate them into local society as members of a religious minority—silent and unobtrusive, as was expected of them. Such interaction moved within the established pattern of Muslim/non-Muslim relations, as exemplified in the Ottoman *millet* system. The pious Jews of the old Yishuv did not challenge the existing order. They only wished to live, and seek redemption, after their own fashion. It was also not difficult to identify the Zionists (whether new immigrants or natives of Palestine) who in the name of God and history proclaimed the right of the people of Israel to the land of Israel—one could confront them on the political level precisely by denying these claims. But how should an "ordinary Arab" classify someone like Albert Einstein, who, without making Aliya himself, joined the expanded Jewish Agency, which championed the Zionist objective of creating a national home for the Jews in Palestine? How could one distinguish between the Jew and the Zionist here? Until the 1960s, this was done rarely or never. Chaim Weizmann, Menachem Ussishkin, or David Ben-Gurion spoke of a Jewish state, they spoke for the Jewish people, and they addressed the Jewish people all over the world. Muslim and Christian Arabs did the same. For them it was "the Jews" who wanted to take Palestine away from them, to desecrate the holy sites of Islam, and possibly even to rebuild the Temple there. No sharp distinction was thus made between Judaism and Zionism. In a similar way, reference was usually made to "the English," not to the "West" or "imperialism," which in later times came to be seen as the embodiment of all evil.

If the difference between Zionists and Jews had been clear and unequivocal, and if it had been recognized as such by local Arabs, the Jews of Hebron and Safed would not have been assaulted in 1929. The fact that the killings occurred in places where Muslims and Jews had lived together as good neighbors, *next to* one another if not *with* one another, where Jewish land purchase was insignificant, and where socioeconomic transformation could not be called traumatic, showed how poisoned relations had already become by the late 1920s. It also shows how baseless rumor ("the Jews have attacked the Haram," "the Jews are slaughtering Arabs," "the Jews want to occupy the mosque of Hebron") was able to prompt massive violence. Though the violence remained localized, it caused great shock among all parties, enhancing the feelings of anxiety and mistrust in a situation where there existed few open channels of communication (and indeed, not many secret channels either), and hardly any "confidence-building measures" between the two communities.

BOYCOTT AND RESISTANCE: 1936–37

The Arab uprising of 1936–39 was multifaceted and not exclusively inspired by national ideas.[6] Several major phases can be distinguished: It began in the cities with a combined strike and boycott that lasted from April to November 1936. In the summer of 1936, it was accompanied by armed resistance, especially in the rural regions of central and northern Palestine. The intervention of Arab leaders from neighboring countries put a provisional end to the fighting, and the British formed yet another commission of inquiry. The Partition Plan proposed by the Peel Commission in July 1937, far from calming the situation, caused

---

[6] For an overview, see Kalkas (1971); Y. Miller (1985), pp. 11–12.

another outbreak of fighting, this time more violent than before. Only in the late autumn and winter of 1938–39 was the uprising finally suppressed, as the Munich Agreement with the German Reich allowed the British to send additional troops to Palestine. Beginning in early 1939, general peace and calm prevailed. By the outbreak of World War II, Arab Palestine was again "pacified."

STRIKE IN THE CITIES

As is so often the case, the immediate trigger of the revolt (as distinct from its underlying causes) was a road attack whose actual details can no longer be reconstructed. On the night of April 15, 1936, a group of armed men (probably followers of the late Izz al-Din al-Qassam, acting under the name of Qassam Brethren, or Ikhwan al-Qassam) ambushed a convoy on the road between Nablus and Tulkarm, and murdered two Jewish passengers.[7] The following night, two Arabs were killed near Petah Tikva. The memorial service for the Jewish victims in Tel Aviv led to anti-Arab demonstrations and assaults upon individual Arabs and Arab property, which in turn provoked Arab strikes and demonstrations in neighboring Jaffa, as well as in Tulkarm, Nablus, and other places. From April 19 to 21, 1936, "national strike committees" formed in almost every Arab town from Gaza to Nablus to protest the events in Tel Aviv. Their members were mostly Arab businessmen, lawyers, doctors, teachers, and students, men but also some women, who despite their lack of political experience felt compelled to act. It seems that they acted on their own initiative without taking orders "from above," whether from the Supreme Muslim Council, Hajj Amin al-Husaini, or one of the notable families. However, "spontaneous" and "autonomous" do not necessarily mean isolated and uncoordinated: Everywhere, debate and action focused on the same themes and demands, while the telegraph, telephone, train, bus, car, motorcycle, and horse permitted rapid communication between individual locales and actors.[8] The strike and boycott were accompanied by marches, demonstrations, and mass assemblies. On April 25, 1936, several hundred women protested on the streets in Gaza, which until then had been little involved in national politics. Similar activities followed not only in Jaffa, Haifa, and Jerusalem as

[7] *Survey of Palestine* (1946), p. 35; Kalkas (1971), pp. 239ff.; Porath (1977), pp. 136–37, 162ff., 172–73; Salih (1989), pp. 331–40.

[8] Kalkas (1971), pp. 241–54, 269; Porath (1977), pp. 164–65, 180, 192ff.; for the Mufti, see esp. Mattar (1988), chs. 5 and 6; Salih (1989), pp. 389–96. Fleischmann (2003), pp. 123–36, and Swedenburg (1995), pp. 176–77, underline the active role of women in the strike. Naor (1998), pp. 193ff., shows interesting illustrations.

traditional centers of female activism, but also in Jenin, Hebron, and Beersheva where such were relatively new. In many schools, teachers and students, male as well as female, went on strike.

Under pressure "from below," Arab leaders were stirred to action too. Their dilemma was obvious: They knew that strikes could harm the Arab cause and their own interests if they turned into general unrest, yet British repression and Jewish countermeasures only sharpened popular anger, compelling them to adopt a more uncompromising stance. For a brief period, old rivalries were set aside. On April 25, 1936, members of the existing political parties (but not the various secret societies or the Arab Women's Association) joined together to form an Arab Higher Committee (AHC, *al-lajna al-'arabiyya al-'ulya*). Chaired by the Mufti, it was to coordinate action and represent Arab interests to the British authorities. Arab demands and grievances were basically unchanged since the Mandate had been first established: a halt to Jewish immigration as the precondition for negotiations over the future of the country; a ban on land sales to Jews; and the creation of a national government, that is to say an Arab one.

The Mufti stood at the head of this movement of resistance without formally involving the Supreme Muslim Council as the recognized representative of Muslim interest in Palestine. The general strike went together with a boycott of British and Jewish goods, services, and institutions. In the name of noncompliance, taxes were withheld in early May—a measure with limited effect, as the government mainly collected indirect taxes. In any case, the strike could not be uniformly enforced on a national level: Arab railworkers for instance did not initially participate in the strike, so that the British were able to move troops and material without hindrance. Workers and employees of Haifa Harbor, which only a short time before had been developed into the sole deep-sea port of Palestine, did not join the strike either, even though the Palestine Arab Workers' Society as well as the Palestine Labor League affiliated with the Histadrut had their strongest base there. Peasants were at this stage little involved in the action, yet producers of cash crops suffered heavy losses, as they were not able to sell their perishable goods on time. At the same time, it proved difficult to adequately supply the strikers and the Arab population as a whole. In this situation, women played their classic role as supporters of families in need, of jailed strikers, resistance fighters, and their relatives; they also served as intermediaries between individual groups, families, and locations. More confounding to the British, but entirely in line with tradition, they actively encouraged their men to defend their honor and their homeland. Some help was also forthcoming from other Arab countries, especially Syria.

Given the existing imbalance in economic strength and viability, the strike and boycott were double-edged swords, as the Arab economy was more dependent on the Jewish economy than the reverse. Excluding land sales, the Arab economy exported more than half its goods and services to the Jewish sector in 1935, amounting to some 14 percent of its share of the Gross Domestic Product. On the Jewish side, the Arab market absorbed only 26 percent of its exports, amounting to 7 percent of its GDP. If we include land sales, the rate of imports from the Arab sector to the Jewish one and vice versa was almost equal (20 percent and 18 percent respectively).[9] The Arab economy supplied mostly agricultural and industrial products such as construction materials, (unskilled) labor for the citrus plantations and the construction industry, as well as real estate and rented space in the "mixed cities"; more important, however, were the land sales. By contrast, the Jews mostly provided semifinished and finished products as well as services. In 1935 around 12,000 Arabs (5 percent of Arab wage earners) were employed in the Jewish sector, more than half of them in agriculture, especially in citrus groves; the remainder worked in construction, industry, and services (by comparison, 32,000 Arabs were employed by the Mandate authorities, while 211,000 were either self-employed or working for Arab employers). Large-scale loss of revenue resulting from the strike and boycott was necessarily felt by both sides, especially since the Jewish economy could not easily replace Arab labor, goods, and services with imports from abroad. Yet they succeeded. Though this was certainly not intended, the Arab uprising actually reinforced the existing trend toward self-reliance as expressed in the concepts of "Hebrew labor" and the "conquest of labor" attached to it (though it was never achieved in the unskilled sector). As early as May 1936, the Mandate government granted permission to build a ("Jewish") port in Tel Aviv that would make the Yishuv independent of the port at Jaffa, contributing to its decline (again self-sufficiency was not fully attained as the workforce was mostly Arab). In spite of significant losses, the strike did not bring the economy to a complete standstill. Though the Levant Fair in May 1936 attracted only half as many people as in the previous year, this still amounted to 320,000 visitors.

As the strike progressed, its base was appreciably widened through the inclusion of existing and newly formed associations of students, women, and other groups, chambers of commerce, and trade unions. Arab employees of the Mandate administration, from mayors to postal

---

[9] Metzer (1998), pp. 20, 130–33, 167–75 (esp. table 5.0); Nadan (2006), pp. 36–38. On the Levant Fair, see Kalkas (1971), p. 262. On the Jaffa port, see LeVine (2005).

officials to the police, rallied behind the demands of the Arab Higher Committee. This posed difficulties for prominent men like Jerusalem mayor Husain al-Khalidi and the Mufti himself, since in a broad sense they, too, were government employees. For this reason they opposed participation in the strike by state employees, and instead encouraged declarations of solidarity and salary contributions. Throughout the first two months of the strike, the Mufti acted in decidedly moderate fashion.

For his part, the British high commissioner resisted all demands to move beyond the state of emergency that had been declared at an early stage, and to impose martial law.[10] Yet the measures taken by the British against the strike activities became increasingly harsh. Along with press censorship, they included house searches without warrants, night raids, preventive detention, collective punishment, caning and flogging, deportation, the confiscation or destruction of the homes of actual or presumed rebels, and in some cases even the torture of suspects and prisoners. Massive force was used to break up demonstrations, causing numerous casualties. In time-honored fashion, the authorities initially blamed the unrest on communist agitators on the one hand, and Italian and German agents on the other, and in April 1936 they arrested a number of well-known communists (most of them Jews). The situation was worst in Jaffa, from where the unrest had initially spread. In June 1936 the old city of Jaffa was largely destroyed by the Royal Air Force, a measure crudely packaged as a program of urban improvement.

REBELLION IN THE COUNTRYSIDE

By June and July 1936, the cities were largely under British control. As a result, the center of resistance shifted to the countryside, especially to the so-called triangle of Nablus, Jenin, and Tulkarm, changing the character of the uprising. While urban activities were essentially directed against the Mandate, the inhabitants of the hilly country pursued a variety of goals: They defended their autonomy, their property, their land, and their honor (with land and honor, al-ard and al-'ird in Arabic, being closely connected). They settled old disputes, and moved not only against the British and Zionists, or the Jews more generally, but also against members of the Arab urban elite, rural landowners, and rivaling clans.

Even previously, Palestinian peasants had not just passively accepted their loss of land, status, and income. Their reactions ranged from flight

---

[10] Kalkas (1971), pp. 249–54, 263ff. For Jaffa, cf. Gavish (1990), pp. 315–19, and the aerial photos that give evidence of the destruction; also LeVine (2005), pp. 112–13. Sher-

to robbery and banditry, as described by Eric Hobsbawm in his classic study of the "social bandits" of the nineteenth century.[11] While organized resistance to oppressive landlords and the authorities was not part of their traditional repertory, passive resistance was, a resistance commonly described as "laziness," "obstruction," "apathy," or "foot-dragging" in the written sources. Beginning in the 1870s there were isolated incidents of armed resistance against Jewish settlers, but also against native landowners. Such incidents now acquired a new relevance and significance. The 1930s saw a growing mobilization of peasants. Returning school graduates played an important role in this context, especially in the triangle of Nablus, Jenin, and Tulkarm just mentioned.[12] Patriotic poems were of special import and reached the great majority of those who could neither read nor write. Access to the nationalist Arabic-language press was not entirely blocked for them, as the articles were read aloud by others in public places such as village guest houses, coffee houses, mosques, churches, or at private gatherings. Even radios and telephones were gradually becoming more available in the countryside.

In addition to the antiquated cudgels, clubs, knives, swords, and daggers that the peasants had used in 1928–29 in Jerusalem, Hebron, and Safed, they also possessed rifles and pistols acquired in one way or another following the Ottoman withdrawal. Smuggling routes over the Syrian and Transjordanian borders as well as theft and arms trafficking (primarily from British arsenals, involving British personnel working in them) provided them with new supplies. In a few instances, bombs, machine guns, and anti-aircraft guns were also put to use after 1936.[13] During the course of the summer, the rebels succeeded in bringing large parts of the Palestinian mountains under their control. They interrupted telephone and transportation lines and even took control of several large settlements in the plains. There seems to have been no comprehensive plan and no joint leadership; most of the rebel groups operated on a local basis, without a wider network of contacts, or an agenda of well-defined goals.[14] Individual members of the great families such as Fakhri Abd al-Hadi, Abd al-Qadir al-Husaini, and Anwar al-Shuqairi, son of the mufti of Haifa, as well as a number of local notables, landowners,

---

man (1997), ch. 3, is of special interest; Enderwitz (2002), pp. 105–107, refers to Arab memoirs.

[11] Hobsbawm (1979); also Adas (1981); Swedenburg (1988), pp. 467ff., 493–97. For the nineteenth and early twentieth centuries, Khalidi (1997), ch. 5, and chapter 6 above.

[12] Swedenburg (1988), pp. 485–86; Porath (1977), pp. 64, 130; for literacy and access to information, see again Ayalon (2004).

[13] Porath (1977), pp. 183ff.; also *Tegart Papers*; Sherman (1997), ch. 3.

[14] Swedenburg (1995), p. 178, 184; Fleischmann (2002), pp. 125–36; for the Ikhwan al-Qassam, see Salih (1989), pp. 361–88.

and academics played a certain role in organizing the resistance. But most of the local "commanders" were peasants, workers, and in a few cases Bedouins. The Ikhwan al-Qassam, whose deeds were glorified in speech and writing, and who were widely celebrated as role models, were actively involved, too. There even seems to have been a group of Qassam Sisters (*rafiqat al-Qassam*), though little is known about their activities. By contrast, the active involvement of peasant women in support of activities including arms smuggling and occasionally even in physical combat is well attested.

Despite British fears, the unrest did not spread to Jerusalem; no clashes occurred on the Temple Mount or at the Wailing Wall. Still, the familiar accusations against the Jews were voiced: Rumor had it that the Jews were planning attacks against the holy sites, against Muslims, and indeed against Islam itself, while the British stood by doing nothing. The rebels (usually *thuwwar* in Arabic, the plural form of *tha'ir*) often referred to themselves as mujahidin. Yet jihad had long since become synonymous with the struggle for national liberation, so that the religious significance of the term (struggle on the path of God, *al-jihad fi sabil allah*) had become obscured. Even a Christian (and theoretically even a Jew) could thus be a mujahid. Christians who had lost their lives for the sake of the national cause were accordingly called "martyrs" (*shuhada'*) no less than Muslims, and not merely "casualties"—like the Zionists, Jews, and British.

In the countryside as much as in the cities, the uprising resorted to nonviolent as well as violent means.[15] Violence was directed primarily at British institutions, from police stations to the railway system, with the aim of preventing British supplies and reinforcement through the destruction of tracks and materials. Roads were damaged by mines, vehicles blocked by chunks of rock and scattered nails, and telephone and telegraph lines were cut. The pipeline of the Iraq Petroleum Company (IPC), first opened in 1935, was repeatedly damaged and the flow of oil interrupted. Snipers were positioned at strategic points to shoot at patrols, vehicles, and passersby. One author recalls how, as a young man in his hometown of Lydda, he helped tear up railroad tracks (Lydda Junction was the most important railway node in the country) and hurled stones at the British soldiers, who employed brute force against children and adults—the prototype of the Intifada youth who became known after 1987 as the "children of stones." Violence was also directed at Jewish institutions, settlements, neighborhoods, and individuals. Peo-

---

[15] Kalkas (1971), p. 243; Porath (1977), pp. 178ff.; Swedenburg (1995), pp. 171ff. and 215, note 31. Al-Radiʻi (1982) provides statistics on the actions. For Lydda and the stone throwing, cf. Munayyir (1997), pp. 23–25.

ple were murdered, fields laid waste, fruit and olive trees cut down, and livestock killed in order to harm or actually drive out the Jewish settlers. As early as April 1936, migrant workers from the Syrian Hawran had burned down the Yemenite Quarter in Jaffa. Many Jews fled from locations with mixed populations, reinforcing the spatial separation between Jews and Arabs. But the early phase also witnessed acts of violence directed against Arabs, ranging from intimidation to the occasional murder of strikebreakers.

Reactions to the uprising in the Arab world were initially marked by reserve, despite an energetic propaganda campaign by the Mufti. The earliest success was in Iraq, where a Committee for the Defense of Palestine was created.[16] But for the Arab governments, there was always one crucial factor on which their policies hinged: relations with Great Britain, or France. The Palestinian question only came second. The same was not true for growing segments of the Arab public, which was becoming more actively involved with Palestine, not least because of the uprising itself. In Egypt in particular, members of the Azhar University and the Muslim Brotherhood sent declarations of solidarity and even some material assistance. Indian Prime Minister Pandit Nehru expressed his support for the Palestinian Arabs. Support was not just moral. In August 1936 Fawzi al-Qawuqji (1890–1976)—a former officer in the Ottoman army of Lebanese origin, hero of the 1925 Syrian uprising against the French, and an ex-officer of the Iraqi army—entered Palestine with around 190 volunteers to fight on the side of the rebels. "To fight on the side of" is perhaps the wrong way of putting it, as the operation quickly ran into difficulties when the local guerrilla and militia leaders refused to submit to Qawuqji, who as a professional officer and renowned fighter for the Arab cause naturally wished to assume command over all armed units.[17]

In June 1936 efforts were stepped up to involve Arab mediators in the conflict. The British hoped that their clients in Transjordan, Egypt, Iraq, and Saudi Arabia would bring a moderating influence to bear on the Palestinian leaders, who evidently were no longer up to fulfilling the classic function of notables—to calm and to mediate. At the same time, local leaders including the Mufti himself could use Arab intervention to justify ending the rebellion to their own people, even without having forced significant concessions from the British or the Zionists. The policy of internationalization can thus be read as another expression of the hope that outsiders would bring about what the locals themselves were

[16] Kalkas (1971), pp. 254–60; Porath (1977), pp. 199–201; Mayer (1983); Nafi (1998).
[17] Arnon-Ohanna (1981), pp. 234–36; Porath (1977), pp. 188–92; also Provence (2005), pp. 95–100.

incapable of achieving. Arab politicians were supposed to pressure the British to pressure the Zionists to pay heed to Arab interests—a notion that survived well beyond the 1930s. Arab leaders had their own reasons for responding to the invitation. Emir Abdallah in particular still hoped to create a Greater Syria under Hashemite rule and to regain the position his father and his brother Faisal had lost through the machinations of the British, the French, and the Saudis.[18]

It was not only the policy of harsh repression that visibly weakened Arab resistance in the late summer of 1936. The citrus harvest was approaching, and prices had soared since the Spanish Civil War had eliminated Spanish competition. In September 1936 the Arab Higher Committee lodged a formal request with neighboring Arab governments for mediation to facilitate an end to the strike. On October 9 Emir Abdallah of Transjordan, King Ghazi of Iraq, King Sa'ud, and the imam of Yemen made a corresponding appeal to the Palestinians, which was adopted by the Arab Higher Committee. On October 12 the strike was officially ended. Qawuqji and his fighters received free passage to Syria.[19] Initially, it looked as if calm were restored. In December 1936 Arturo Toscanini conducted the first concert in the newly opened Tel Aviv concert hall.

The Peel Plan

With the uprising apparently ended, London appointed yet another commission of inquiry, chaired by William Robert Wellesley, Earl Peel, to inquire into the underlying causes of the disturbances and to make suitable policy recommendations. The Royal Commission arrived in Palestine in November 1936, was boycotted by the Arabs until shortly before its departure in January 1937, and published its report on July 7, 1937.[20] Once again, the Commission established that irrespective of all economic and social issues, the problem was essentially political, deriving from the Balfour Declaration and the Mandate and their unconditional rejection by the Arab side. The Commission explicitly described the resistance not as mere "disturbances," but as a rebellion:

> The underlying causes of the disturbances, or (as we regard it) the rebellion, of 1936 are, first, the desire of the Arabs for national independence:

[18] On Abdallah, cf. Porath (1977), pp. 72–75, 195, 202–11, 226–27; Wilson (1987), ch. 7; Shlaim (1990); Gelber (1997).

[19] Kalkas (1971), pp. 269–72; Porath (1977), pp. 213–14. On harvest times for summer and winter crops, olives, citrus and other fruits, see Dalman, vol. I, 2 (1928), esp. pp. 403–20, 550–67.

[20] The most important source is the *Peel Report* (1937) itself; see further Biger (2004), ch. 7; El-Eini (2006), ch. 5, esp. pp. 314–31.

secondly, their antagonism to the establishment of the Jewish National Home in Palestine, quickened by their fear of Jewish domination. . . . Among contributary causes were the effect on Arab opinion of the attainment of national independence by Iraq, Trans-Jordan, Egypt, Syria and the Lebanon; the rush of Jewish immigrants escaping from Central and Eastern Europe; the inequality of opportunity enjoyed by Arabs and Jews respectively in placing their case before Your Majesty's Government and the public: the growth of Arab mistrust: Arab alarm at the continued purchase of Arab land by Jews: the intensive character and the "modernism" of Jewish nationalism: and lastly the general uncertainty, accentuated by the ambiguity of certain phrases in the Mandate, as to the ultimate intentions of the Mandatory Power. . . .

We have found that, though the Arabs have benefited by the development of the country owing to Jewish immigration, this has had no conciliatory effect. On the contrary, improvement in the economic situation in Palestine has meant the deterioration of the political situation.[21]

The *Peel Report* was both thorough and extensive, running some four hundred pages, and it contained something new. The Commission stated that in the existing circumstances, the British Mandate could no longer be maintained and would need to be replaced by new treaty arrangements. The shortcomings and failures of British policy were openly addressed:

The application to Palestine of the Mandate System in general and of the specific Mandate in particular implied the belief that the obligations thus undertaken towards the Arabs and the Jews respectively would prove in course of time to be mutually compatible owing to the conciliatory effect on the Palestinian Arabs of the material prosperity which Jewish immigration would bring to Palestine as a whole. The belief has not been justified, and we see no hope of its being justified in the future.[22]

The "welfare argument" was buried once and for all. For, as the Commission had already established, the Palestine government ultimately failed to discharge the "contradictory obligations" (!) of the Mandatory by "holding the balance" between Jews and Arabs. The situation had reached a deadlock.[23] Unlike British politicians of the immediate post–World War I period, who had perceived the Arabs of Palestine as "people" but not "a people," the Peel Commission no longer hesitated to recognize both Jews and Arabs as "national communities." Conflict between these communities had proven irreconcilable:

---

[21] *Peel Report* (1937), p. 363.
[22] Ibid., p. 370.
[23] Ibid., pp. 363–64. Cf. chapter 8 above.

An irrepressible conflict has arisen between two national communities within the narrow bounds of one small country. About 1,000,000 Arabs are in strife, open or latent, with some 400,000 Jews. There is no common ground between them. The Arab community is predominantly Asiatic in character, the Jewish community predominantly European. They differ in religion and in language. Their cultural and social life, their ways of thought and conduct, are as incompatible as their national aspirations. These last are the greatest bar to peace. Arabs and Jews might possibly learn to live and work together in Palestine if they would make a genuine effort to reconcile and combine their national ideals and so build up in time a joint or dual nationality. But this they cannot do. The War and its sequel have inspired all Arabs with the hope of reviving in a free and united Arab world the traditions of the Arab golden age. The Jews similarly are inspired by their historic past. They mean to show what the Jewish nation can achieve when restored to the land of its birth. National assimilation between Arabs and Jews is thus ruled out. In the Arab picture the Jews could only occupy the place they occupied in Arab Egypt or Arab Spain. The Arabs would be as much outside the Jewish picture as the Canaanites in the old land of Israel. The National Home, as we have said before, cannot be half-national. In these circumstances to pretend that Palestinian citizenship has any moral meaning is a mischievous pretence. Neither Arab nor Jew has any sense of service to a single State.[24]

Rarely had it been stated so bluntly. The Royal Commission formally abandoned the idea of creating a common state for Arabs and Jews, whether organized binationally or otherwise. There was no talk of "missed opportunities" to seek a compromise and achieve reconciliation, only the sober recognition of failure and the sense that, as bad as things were, they could yet become worse. A "cantonization" along Swiss lines was considered but ultimately dismissed, as the commission felt that it entailed too many risks. Rather, the Royal Commission recommended a partition of the Mandate territory into an Arab Area and a Jewish State, plus a third zone along a corridor from Jaffa to Jerusalem (including Bethlehem) with the most important holy places to remain under a redefined British Mandate. Within this "sacred trust of civilization" (which had originally served to legitimize the Mandate), the Balfour Declaration would no longer apply.[25] In spite of its strategic value,

---

[24] *Peel Report* (1937), pp. 370–71.

[25] Ibid., ch. 12 (pp. 380–96); Biger (2004), pp. 190–208; El-Eini (2006), pp. 320–31. In accordance with the plan, the Arab area (or state) would have received the subdistricts of Nablus, Ramallah, Jericho, Hebron, Gaza, and Beersheva, while the Jewish state would have received those of Haifa, Acre, Safed, Tiberias, and Nazareth. Meanwhile, the subdistricts of Jaffa, Ramla, Tulkarm, Jenin, and Baisan would have gone partly to the Arab

Haifa was not to be part of this British enclave. The Arab Area was allocated 70 percent of the Mandate territory, stretching from Jabal Nablus in the north to the southern tip of the Negev, as well as the coast around Gaza. But rather than gaining independence, the Arab Area was to be merged with Transjordan, which, as will be remembered, had originally been part of the Palestine Mandate and was only severed from it in 1922 as a separate territory to which the Balfour Declaration would not apply. By contrast, only 20 percent of the total surface of the Palestine Mandate was allocated to the Jewish state (Galilee, Marj Ibn Amir south of Nazareth, as well as the coast from the Lebanese border to the south of Tel Aviv). But this 20 percent contained many of the most fertile lands and was significantly more than the land then in Jewish possession, which comprised only 6 or 7 percent of the Mandate territory. The Jewish state would support the Arab state (that is Transjordan enlarged by the Arab Area) with a subvention to make up for the loss of tax revenue previously contributed by the Jews living in that part of the country. The British treasury would provide an additional grant.

While the proposed Arab Area would include around 90 percent of the Arab population then living in Palestine, the British estimated that about 225,000 Arabs would either come under Jewish rule or would need to be resettled. In this connection, the so-called transfer option was aired, which had occasionally been discussed even previously.[26] The *Peel Report* referred to the "population exchange" Greece and Turkey had agreed upon after the Greco-Turkish War of 1922, stipulating that around 1.3 million Orthodox Greeks and 400,000 Muslim Turks (or rather, people defined as Greeks or Turks according to various criteria) were to be "compulsorily removed" under the supervision of the League of Nations. The operation had, as the report put it, been difficult but ultimately successful ("Now the ulcer has been clean cut out"). The Commission realized that a similar operation would be much more difficult in the case of Palestine, which was so much smaller than either Greece or Turkey, the more so since the "exchange" would involve not only people, but also land. In this respect, they were counting on the generosity of the British taxpayer. On the other hand, however, the creation of two separate states would make it possible to finally get rid of the problematic provision linking Jewish immigration to the (economic, political, and psychological) absorptive capacity of the country and its (Arab) residents.

---

area and partly to the Jewish state, with those of Jerusalem going partly to the Arab area and partly left under a British mandate.

[26] *Peel Report* (1937), pp. 389–92 (citation on p. 390). For population "transfer," see below, note 29, and chapter 13.

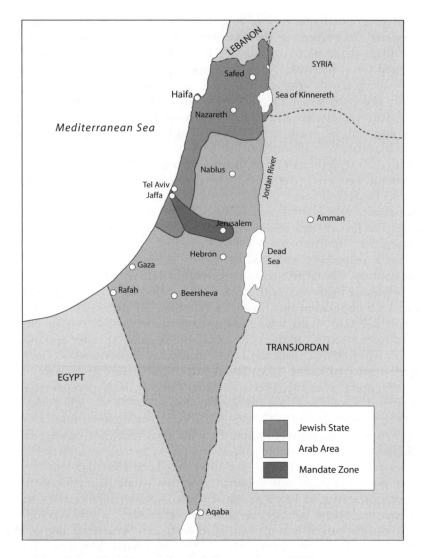

Map 7. Partition Plan of the Peel Commission (1937)

In the view of the Commission, the sacrifice demanded of the Arabs was certainly great, but not too great. For by giving up one piece of territory ("this small notch" of which Lord Balfour had spoken in 1920), they rendered outstanding services not only to the Jews faced with persecution in Europe, but to humanity at large:

Considering what the possibility of finding a refuge in Palestine means to many thousands of suffering Jews, we cannot believe that the "distress" occasioned by Partition, great as it would be, is more than Arab generosity can bear. And in this, as in so much else connected with Palestine, it is not only the peoples of that country that have to be considered. The Jewish Problem is not the least of the many problems which are disturbing international relations at this critical time and obstructing the path to peace and prosperity. If the Arabs at some sacrifice could help to solve that problem, they would earn the gratitude not of the Jews alone but of all the Western World.[27]

This statement was made after the Nazis had initiated their policy of persecution (to speak of a "Jewish Problem" is distorting the facts) but before the Holocaust, of which first reports began to reach the world in 1942. Under these circumstances, British hopes that it might be possible to confine Jewish immigration to a relatively small area with limited resources may not have seemed entirely unfounded. Yet it did nothing to change the fact that the British evidently expected the Palestinian Arabs to make up for European crimes.

The response of those affected was not quite as original as the proposals made by the Peel Commission. On the Arab side, it met with total rejection (at least at first, and at least officially); on the Jewish side, it was met for the most part with qualified approval. The Permanent Mandates Commission in Geneva endorsed partition, opposed immediate independence, and suggested either "cantonization" or two separate mandates.[28] Arab protests were especially vocal in northern Palestine, and more particularly in Galilee, which was to be allocated to the Jewish state. The Arab Higher Committee called for a rejection of the partition plan and demanded the creation of an Arab state in all of Palestine. The partition plan galvanized Arab public opinion well beyond Palestine itself. Participants at a conference held in Bludan (Syria) in September 1937 sharply condemned it. Palestinian and Syrian nationalists consulted, concerning the resumption of armed struggle. Militant organizations in Syria, among them the paramilitary Steel Shirts (al-qumsan al-hadidiyya), declared their solidarity with the Palestinians. In Iraq the Committee for the Defense of Palestine became newly active, with the press and numerous 'ulama' participating in lively fashion. In Egypt growing numbers of students, religious scholars, and Islamic activists from al-Azhar to the Muslim Brotherhood became involved with the Palestine issue, as did members of the secular opposition. The Egyptian Women's Association under Huda Sha'rawi organized a solidarity conference in Cairo. And yet, rejection of the partition plan was not as

---

[27] *Peel Report* (1937), p. 395. See also chapters 8 and 13.
[28] *Survey of Palestine* (1946), pp. 41–42; Porath (1977), pp. 228ff., 231ff., 274ff.

unanimous as it appeared. Within Palestine, the Nashashibis favored partition, and Emir Abdallah was very much inclined to accept it. After all, it promised to considerably strengthen his position if the Arab Area were to be annexed to Transjordan. To the great disappointment of the Mufti, even the Syrian National Bloc spoke in favor of the plan.

On the Jewish or, to be more precise, the Zionist side, the response was mixed.[29] David Ben-Gurion and Chaim Weizmann thought it advisable to accept partition in principle, but demanded that borders be renegotiated in favor of the proposed Jewish state. Ben-Gurion was fascinated by the opportunities a "mass transfer" of Arabs would offer to the Jewish Yishuv—opportunities ranging from the "redemption of the soil" to the "conquest of labor" to the security of the Jewish state. To him, a transfer seemed not only useful, but also humane, and advantageous for Jews and Arabs alike. At the Twentieth Zionist Congress in Zurich, Ben-Gurion declared that the transfer of (this part of) the Arab people *to their own land* and the settlement of *empty tracts of land* (he was thinking of Iraq and Transjordan), corresponded to an important humane and Zionist ideal. But the issue was still too "hot" to be openly discussed. In the records of the Congress, the relevant discussions are in fact missing. In his testimony before the Royal Commission, Vladimir Jabotinsky had expressed "the profoundest feeling" for the Arab case. It was reasonable, and it deserved respect. But the Jewish case was simply more pressing. "We have got to save millions, many millions," he argued, and "when the Arab claim is confronted with our Jewish demand to be saved, it is like the claims of appetite versus the claims of starvation."[30] Hardly could this argument be put more tersely.

British reaction was also divided. The Cabinet adopted the partition plan on the assumption that the Zionists as well as the Arab governments would agree to it. So did the Colonial Office. The Foreign Office on the other hand, expecting Arab resistance, was strictly opposed to partition. In this delicate situation, the prime minister recommended that the League of Nations discuss a possible partition of the Mandate area.

RADICALIZATION

Far from showing a way to settle the conflict, the *Peel Report* provoked a new and more violent wave of resistance that did not subside until the

---

[29] Galnoor (1995); also Morris (2004), pp. 45–49; Morris (2001), pp. 39–48 (43–44). Masalha (1992) gives a different assessment. For Jewish reactions to the Arab uprising more generally, see Shapira (1992), ch. 6.

[30] Quoted from Mendes-Flohr/Reinharz (eds.) (1995), pp. 610–11.

approach of World War II. On September 26, 1937, the acting district commissioner of Galilee, Lewis Andrews, was assassinated in Nazareth with his escort.[31] The Mandate government reacted by dissolving the Arab Higher Committee (which had condemned the murder) and the national strike committees. They arrested leading Palestinian politicians and deported them to the distant Seychelles. They also dismissed Hajj Amin al-Husaini from his office as president of the Supreme Muslim Council (he had already fled into the Haram al-Sharif, which the British did not dare to enter), took control over the religious endowments away from the Supreme Muslim Council and thereby deprived it of the greater part of its income. Hajj Amin managed to escape to Lebanon, where the French authorities briefly arrested but then released him. From his residence near Beirut he went to Iraq after the outbreak of war in September 1939, and after the abortive coup of Rashid Ali al-Gailani of April 1941, he finally fled to Berlin where he put himself at the disposal of the Nazi war effort.[32] The dissolution of the Arab Higher Committee signified the de facto abandonment of the British policy of notables.

Leadership of the Arab revolt definitely passed into other hands: to local leaders, groups, and committees with a local base of support who neither could nor wished to be united under a supreme command. When the general strike was ended in October 1936, the armed groups were not disarmed. In the second phase of the uprising beginning in October 1937, they succeeded in expanding the scope and scale of their activities as well as their social base, attracting growing numbers of members and sympathizers.[33] Resistance was initially centered in Galilee and the triangle of Nablus, Jenin, and Tulkarm, and gradually extended into the rural areas near Jerusalem and Hebron, where the Holy War Organization was active. The coast and the plains, where most of the Jews and Jewish settlements were found, and where the Mandate government had greatest control, were less involved. Hence, the rebels were for the most part not those peasants and Bedouins that were immediately confronted with Jewish immigration and colonization, but rather residents of those areas that had traditionally defended their autonomy, and whose geographic and social environment allowed them to do so.

The rebels had no unified leadership, no coordinated strategy, and no detailed program. Some groups acted as village militias, while others

---

[31] For what follows, cf. Lachman (1982), pp. 81–82; Porath (1977), p. 233; Salih (1929), 342, (proudly) attributes the murder to the Ikhwan al-Qassam.

[32] Mattar (1988), pp. 82–83; Elpeleg (1993), pp. 48ff., and Gensicke, Höpp, and Krämer cited above, note 4. The British also did not dare to enter the Haram in the ensuing years, even though rebels were hiding there; cf. the *Tegart Papers*.

[33] Porath (1977), pp. 235–36, 242ff.; Arnon-Ohanna (1981); Swedenburg (1995); for a heroic mode, see Salih (1989), pp. 340–88.

represented individual families and clans (*hamula*); some were part of a structured but mobile organization under the command of a leader of their own that remained active over an extended period of time. These bands had the military training of modern guerrillas; they wore uniforms, and were equipped with handguns and explosives. From the villages they obtained food, lodging, money, and weapons. Other groups consisted of civilians who worked by day and took action by night. Some are better described as youth gangs ("the young men," *al-shabab*, traditionally played an important role in urban and village neighborhoods, which were to become even more important during the Intifada). In others, sober heads of families came together. A small number of rebels had a criminal background. Some commanders were recognized as leaders by more than one group, such as Abd al-Rahim al-Hajj Muhammad, Yusuf Sa'id Abu Durra, Arif Abd al-Raziq, or Hasan Salama. In this way their influence spread beyond the local level without ever reaching a "national" dimension.

From his refuge in Lebanon, the Mufti tried in vain to impose centralized control on the rebels through an Office of the Arab Revolution in Palestine (*diwan al-thawra al-'arabiyya fi filastin*) based in Damascus. His failure was widely taken to be yet another sign of the factionalism and fragmentation weakening Arab society and politics. Yet it had its obvious advantages, too, as it created flexibility and allowed for continued action even if individual persons or groups were apprehended by the authorities. Women played an important role in this phase of the revolt, because, under the cloak of a conservative code of conduct, they could move about more easily than men: Even the British could not easily carry out body searches of women who struck them as suspicious, or hinder their movements in the city, marketplace, bath, or on visits to relatives, all occasions that could be used to deliver food, arms, ammunition, and news. The revolt reached its peak in the summer and autumn of 1938 with more than ten thousand men and women involved, most of them members of the peasantry and the urban middle and lower classes, but also a considerable number of Bedouins.

By contrast, there were few Christians among the activists and leaders of the revolt. This may have had to do with mounting tension between Muslims and Christians, fostered by Muslim suspicions that the Christians received better treatment from the British, while the Christians felt threatened by the growing signs of Islamization—a classical pattern of mutual fears and perceptions that had been in place well before the uprising.[34] Some of the Christian villages were unwilling to cooperate with

[34] Porath (1977), pp. 247–48, 260–73. By contrast, Fleischmann (2002), ch. 5, makes repeated reference to Christian women active in the strike and rebellion.

the rebels even under pressure. In the winter of 1936 there were calls for a boycott of Christian businesses, which were strongly condemned by the Mufti and the Supreme Muslim Council. The partition plan made for renewed solidarity, as the Arab Christians living in Galilee were no less affected by it than their Muslim neighbors. Yet in the second phase of the uprising, new tensions arose over the role played by the Druze.[35] The majority of Druze lived in Syria and Lebanon, but a minority resided in a number of villages in Galilee and the Karmel region. Until 1936 they remained neutral in relation to Muslims and Jews. After that, most of them sided with the Jews, as one of their most important leaders (Sultan al-Atrash, who in 1925 had led the revolt against the French in Syria) was favorably disposed toward them. Living in exile in Transjordan from 1934, al-Atrash maintained contacts with the Jewish Agency. Beginning in December 1937, there was even open agitation against the revolt among the Druze of Lebanon. Their hostility, like that of the Maronite Christians, can be explained in large part by their mistrust of Arab nationalism and its heavy dose of Sunni Islam. In 1938 Druze villagers who refused to join the revolt were attacked by the rebels, and many were actually killed or injured. A peace agreement in January 1940 was unable to heal the wounds: During the war of 1948–49, most Druze cooperated with the Jews.

Though in itself of limited importance, one act of symbolic politics will help to illustrate how complex the situation really was. When the rebels, who for the most part were peasants, tenants, or fieldworkers, took a number of Palestinian towns in 1938–39 (including the Old City of Jerusalem, which they briefly held in October 1938, excepting only the Jewish Quarter), they sought to make their victory visible through the classic instrument of a dress code imposed from above.[36] In August 1938 all Arab men were ordered to wear the kaffiyeh (also known as *hatta* in Arabic), which was worn by most Bedouin tribesmen and in some areas of Palestine by peasants as well, but not by the urban middle and upper classes who commonly wore the fez or tarbush. The kaffiyeh was a cotton cloth, usually white, fixed firmly to the head with a dark cord ('*iqal*). It was only in the 1950s that the gray-and-white chessboard

---

[35] Parsons (2000), ch. 1; for the Syrian uprising, see Provence (2005).

[36] On the politics of head coverings, including the kaffiyeh and the veil, cf. Swedenburg (1995), pp. 30–37, 151, 174ff., 181–94. For Palestinian costume, see Stillman (1979); Völger et al. (eds.) (1987). For wider comparison, see Kreiser (2005); Faroqhi/Neumann (eds.) (2004); Lindisfarne-Tapper/Ingram (1997); Norton (1997); Quataert (1997). For pictures and photographs, see Landau (1979); Graham-Brown (1980); W. Khalidi (1984); Howe (1997), or Osman (1999). For the Jewish Hashomer, see Shapira (1992), pp. 71–72, Shilony (1998), pp. 150–56, and the photo in Naor (1998), p. 55. For Edwin Samuel, Naor (1998), pp. 95.

pattern became generally known as "typically" Palestinian. The Bedouins east of the Jordan could be recognized by the red-and-white chessboard pattern, which was also worn by the troops of the Arab Legion and Emir Abdallah himself. One motive behind forcing city dwellers to wear the kaffiyeh was surely practical, as the rebels hoped to avoid being too conspicuous in an urban setting. But at the same time they tried to impose upon the effendis (in the name of national unity) a type of head covering that was historically identified with the rural lower classes.

Still, the "politics of headgear" was not as simple and straightforward as it might seem. The only unambiguous item was the hat, worn by Europeans and hence by many Jews of European origin, including their rabbis, while the Zionist pioneers and workers preferred the proletarian peaked cap. In Turkey Kemal Atatürk had prescribed the hat in the 1920s as a sign of Western modernity. In Palestine, by contrast, the Arab elite, irrespective of their political preferences and their degree of Westernization, remained faithful to the Ottoman tarbush, or else (as was increasingly the case in the interwar period) went about bareheaded. They did not wear a hat. Sultan Mahmud II had prescribed the fez to his officials in 1829, even before the Tanzimat reforms, as a sign of Ottoman loyalty and solidarity. From there it gradually spread to the urban effendis, replacing a variety of head covers that were differentiated by color, form, and material, allowing observers not only to distinguish between various professions and status groups, but also to identify the Muslims and different groups of non-Muslims among them. The dress code imposed by the sultan thus served the purpose of homogenizing the subject population, not yet under nationalist auspices but rather under dynastic ones.

As for the kaffiyeh, it was by no means the one and only form of head wear traditionally worn by Palestinian peasants and Bedouins, as claimed by the nationalists. Historical drawings and photographs show a great variety of head coverings worn by various population groups in different regions even after the Tanzimat reforms: simple felt caps, bulky turbans, tightly wound turbans (like the one worn by the Mufti), as well as the fez or tarbush. At the same time, to wear the kaffiyeh was not identical with being an Arab nationalist. While it is true that during the Arab Revolt of 1916, Faisal's troops did wear Bedouin kaffiyehs of the Hijazi variety (with a different cord than was usual in Palestine), so did the camel-mounted troops of the Ottoman army (the British camel troops wore broad-brimmed hats in the style of the Canadian border police) and the Jewish watchmen of the Hashomer, who around the turn of the century dressed in rather peculiar style complete with kaffiyehs, jumpers, and boots: half dashing Bedouin, half Russian Cossack. In the

1930s, the Palestinian boy scouts also donned the kaffiyehs, combined with uniform shirts, ties, knee-length shorts, sturdy footwear, and sometimes tartan kneesocks. Even Edwin Samuel, son of the first high commissioner, was photographed wearing a kaffiyeh at his wedding to Hadasa Garsovsky in 1920. In the 1930s, then, the kaffiyeh still stood for many different things: status, profession, political conviction, romanticism, or a concept of rugged masculinity.

It was essentially the same with the veil (*hijab*), which the rebels tried to impose upon women, including Arab Christian women. Here too, a status symbol was charged with political meaning, and transformed into a national symbol of high moral significance. Again, tradition was less uniform than is often assumed.[37] Until World War I, the veil was more widespread among women of the urban middle and upper classes than among peasants and Bedouins: Peasant women could not afford to be obstructed by a veil during their housework or fieldwork, while the Bedouin women traditionally did not wear it at all. What was customary was a white cloth (*mandil*) similar in function to the kaffiyeh, which covered the head, the shoulders, and sometimes also the upper body, while leaving the face uncovered. In the first instance, then, the veil covering the face was a status symbol distinguishing the upper classes from the lower, a sign of female modesty and family honor. As a rule it was worn only by those women who did not have to perform physical labor. It had little to do with freedom, or a lack of freedom, in the legal or political sense; what it did affect was freedom of movement. In the interwar period, at least in the more open milieu of Jaffa and Haifa, some women of the urban upper and middle classes started to take off the veil, and not only during demonstrations against the Balfour Declaration and the Mandate. Urban society in Nablus, Gaza, and Jerusalem remained largely conservative. After all, women were able to demonstrate even while wearing the veil. Yet the female members of the Jerusalem aristocracy on certain occasions also liked to present themselves as ladies, fully dressed in European style and with their faces uncovered. Islamic scholars and activists, from the Mufti and the Society for the Promotion of Virtue and the Prevention of Vice to Izz al-Din al-Qassam, spoke out strongly against these signs of Westernization (in the conservative view, the female Jewish pioneers walked about half naked). They spoke out against the symptoms of moral decadence, and in favor of strict moral standards as exemplified by the veil. Their conservative attitude was shared by the rural rebels, who used their newly acquired

[37] In addition to the titles cited in note 36 above, see Fleischmann (2002), chs. 2 and 5, esp. pp. 58–59, 76–80, 133–36; see also above, chapter 9, note 19.

power to put their own vision of morality and decency into effect. In a communiqué issued in October 1936, one of the most influential guerrilla leaders, Abd al-Rahim al-Hajj Muhammad, declared:

> It has reached the attention of the Central Command that some effeminates (*mukhannathun*) who resemble men are going around in the streets bareheaded, forgetting what we previously announced about the requirement to wear the *kufiyya* and the *'iqal*. It also came to our attention that some women eager to imitate Western (*afranji*) dress are neglecting the order to veil. To all these persons we address this warning, reminding them of the penalties awaiting them if they continue in their recklessness.[38]

The dress code was never fully imposed. The members of the All Palestine Government, formed in 1947, all wore the tarbush (only the Mufti continued to wear a turban), while the women took off their veils in growing numbers. This was indeed the long-term trend. By contrast, the tarbush just barely outlived World War II, while in the post–World War II period the kaffiyeh turned into the symbol of Palestinian resistance.

Some measures revealed the rebels' marked sense of social justice and equality; not always was it combined with national sentiment.[39] In the regions under their control, they proclaimed a moratorium on debt to remedy one of the most immediate causes of rural impoverishment, prevented tax collectors and creditors from entering villages and neighborhoods, and declared all rent payments to be abolished. (Arab) landlords, businessmen, and moneylenders were not pleased. Their disaffection mounted when certain rebel leaders introduced their own courts, which were ostensibly based on the Islamic Sharia and accompanied by an intelligence network designed to uncover and intimidate "enemies of the revolution." Violence was thus directed not only against British, Zionist, and Jewish targets more generally, but also against Arab effendis and notables and all those who were not prepared to support the rebels, including simple peasants, Bedouins, and the urban poor. In many instances, money, food, and weapons were extorted by means of coercion and intimidation. A number of people were accused of collaboration with the Jews and assassinated. Many fled to safer areas. Almost inevitably, social and political objectives mixed with personal animosities, clan feuds, and sometimes with common criminal intent.

In the second phase of the uprising, Jews (hard to distinguish in this context from Zionists) passed from self-defense to selective acts of retaliation and terrorism. The paramilitary Hagana (literally "defense"),

---

[38] Cited from Swedenburg (1995), p. 182.

[39] See with varying assessments Porath (1977), pp. 265ff.; Arnon-Ohanna (1981), pp. 244–46; al-Hut (1981), pp. 401–406; Swedenburg (1995), pp. 34, 153ff.

which had secretly evolved since World I, became increasingly stronger, partly through the assistance of the British security forces.[40] Among Arabs this confirmed the fear that the Jews would be armed by the British to pursue their objectives by force. As early as May 1936, the British allowed the formation of armed Jewish units to serve as police auxiliaries, which included thousands of members and even possessed armored vehicles. In 1936–37, mobile armed groups were formed to protect Jewish settlements and institutions. At the same time, the first fortified Jewish defense settlements were built (the so-called fence-and-watchtower settlements, *homa ve-migdal*), which could be defended more easily in case of attack. In 1937 the militant underground group Etzel (or IZL, the Hebrew acronym of Irgun Tzva'i Le'umi, National Military Organization) split off from the Hagana to protest the official policy of restraint (*havlaga*). In November 1937 they carried out the first terrorist acts against Arab buses, cafés, markets, and other public places, which would be stepped up during the 1940s. In July 1938 bombs placed in the Haifa fruit market caused the death of 74 Arabs and injured 129.

In 1938 mixed British-Jewish counterinsurgency units (Special Night Squads) were formed under the command of a Scottish officer, Orde Charles Wingate. Their purported task was to guard the pipeline of the Iraq Petroleum Company, which had been completed in 1935. Their chief purpose, though, was to fight the Arab insurgents. Cooperation with the British security forces was not limited to the training, equipment, and logistical support the Hagana fighters received, but also included intelligence and espionage work, in which Arab-speaking Jews could be very useful to the British, many of whom did not speak the language and knew little about the country. Though already dissolved in 1939, the Special Night Squads made a significant contribution to the military training of Hagana members. Cooperation did not prevent conflict, however. Once the British began to seize ships with illegal Jewish immigrants and either interned the passengers in camps or shipped them back to Europe, Etzel and the Hagana made their first attacks on British installations, from radio stations to military barracks, causing military as well as civilian casualties.

In the second phase of the rebellion, the British adopted even harsher methods than before.[41] In March 1938 Sir Harold MacMichael replaced Sir Arthur Wauchope, who had come to be seen as too soft and too

---

[40] *Survey of Palestine* (1946), p. 45; Kalkas (1971), pp. 260–61; Shapira (1992), ch. 6; Sherman (1997), ch. 3; Naor (1998), pp. 193–213, with numerous illustrations.

[41] Porath (1977), pp. 252ff.; for similar practices used by the French in Syria, see Provence (2005), p. 26. According to Morris (1987), p. 57, the number of those who temporarily fled the country was forty thousand. Fakhri al-Nashashibi was assassinated in Baghdad in 1941.

friendly with the Arabs, as high commissioner. In June 1937 the British imposed the death penalty for unauthorized possession of weapons, ammunition, and explosives. This order was directed primarily against the Arab rebels, since many Jews at this time had permission to carry weapons and store ammunition for defense purposes. Between 1937 and 1939, more than 112 Arabs were hanged in the main prison of Acre, mostly for illegal possession of weapons. Moreover, the houses of families that were suspected of supporting the rebels ("terrorists") were blown up—a practice later adopted by the Hagana and eventually by the State of Israel. Collective punishment was imposed on entire villages and neighborhoods, and frequent curfews were enforced. Roads were built in remote places so as to increase control over the rural areas. By the same token, the acts of revenge taken by the insurgents against real and presumed collaborators and traitors served as models for later generations of Palestinian fighters. Caught between the rebels and the British, who cared little about individual responsibility, ordinary people came under mounting pressure. Many of the wealthier Arabs fled to neighboring countries—a time-honored practice that would produce devastating results in 1947–49. Some joined the Arab Peace Corps (*fasa'il al-salam*) formed in late 1938 under the leadership of Fakhri al-Nashashibi to fight the rebels with British assistance. In some instances, so-called Village Leagues turned to their Jewish neighbors for help.

After the Munich Agreement of September 1938, which seemed at the time to have removed the danger of a German attack on Britain, the British transferred additional troops and police to Palestine. Faced with overwhelming military might, organized Arab resistance collapsed early in 1939.

DIPLOMACY: FROM THE ROUND TABLE TO THE MACDONALD WHITE PAPER

Diplomatic efforts continued in parallel with military action.[42] Already in March 1938, with the Arab revolt quickly spreading all over the country, a commission of inquiry was formed under Sir John Woodhead. It submitted its report in November 1938, suggesting a modified partition plan. A white paper published in the same month dismissed any partition of Palestine, as suggested by the Peel and Woodhead Commissions, as "impracticable." It recommended a continuation of the

---

[42] El-Eini (2006), pp. 331–44; also Porath (1977), pp. 280, 288–90; Smith (1996), pp. 103–104.

Mandate and invited Jews and Arabs to a conference in London. The St James Conference of February and March 1939 was in fact conducted at a "round table," though the Arab delegates refused direct discussion with the Zionists, so that the British had to act as mediators. The Arab delegation included several members of the Arab Higher Committee under Jamal al-Husaini (with the exception of the Mufti himself) and the Nashashibi faction, as well as representatives of the Arab states of Egypt, Iraq, Saudi Arabia, and Yemen; Transjordan was equally represented. Lebanon and Syria, by contrast, had not yet attained independence from France. In the context of the deliberations, the Husain-McMahon correspondence was again discussed, with the result that the British had to acknowledge that certain passages were unclear. However, they were not prepared to submit to Arab demands that the correspondence be considered a formal treaty binding under international law. Given that no consensus could be reached concerning immigration, partition, and statehood, the conference ended without agreement on March 27, 1939 (shortly before, the German Reich had broken the Munich Agreement and invaded Czechoslovakia). Talks with the Arab governments were continued beyond the formal ending of the conference.

The MacDonald White Paper issued by Colonial Secretary Malcolm MacDonald, a son of Ramsay MacDonald, and published on May 17, 1939, put forth a number of new ideas: a fixed limit on Jewish immigration of 75,000 people during a period of five years, after which further immigration would be permitted only with Arab "acquiescence"; a restriction of Jewish land purchases to specific areas; and finally, a binational Arab-Jewish state that would become independent within ten years and enter into a new treaty relationship with Great Britain. In addition to the criterion of economic absorptive capacity, the question of political absorptive capacity would also be considered in the future—a suggestion already made by the Peel Commission, only to be abandoned by that commission in favor of a partition of the Mandate region. A key passage of the White Paper reads as follows:

> It has been urged that the expression "a national home for the Jewish people" offered a prospect that Palestine might in due course become a Jewish State or Commonwealth. . . . But, with the Royal Commission [the Peel Commission], His Majesty's Government believe that the framers of the Mandate in which the Balfour Declaration was embodied could not have intended that Palestine should be converted into a Jewish State against the will of the Arab population of the country.[43]

[43] Cmd. 6019 cited from *Survey of Palestine* (1946), pp. 90–91; see also pp. 90–99; Porath (1977), pp. 288–89.

At first glance this was a great success for the Arab side, a success that could be attributed to the Arab revolt in Palestine itself. Yet at the back of it stood the rise of fascism in Europe and the threat of war, which it was feared might endanger the British position in the Near and Middle East. Europe and the protection of imperial interests were still of paramount importance to British policy makers.[44] Ever since the Italian invasion of Abyssinia in October 1935, British officials saw their control of the eastern Mediterranean under threat. This enhanced the strategic importance of Palestine and of Haifa in particular, as an important element of the British communications and air-defense systems. In Haifa the British had completed the modern deep-sea port in 1933 and finished laying the pipeline to the northern Iraqi oilfields in 1935, reducing their dependence on the Suez Canal. In light of changed strategic and political conditions, the attitude of the Arab governments—which were now in a position to expect more concessions, including concessions on the Palestine issue—gained in weight. Some British observers warned of a policy of "appeasement" merely designed to keep the Arabs quiet.

All in all, the White Paper was a failure: It enraged the Zionists without satisfying the Arabs. Both rejected it. Interestingly enough, some Palestinian Arabs (including prominent nationalists) saw the White Paper in a more positive light than did the Arab leadership and most of the rebels. The Zionists roundly refused to accept a link between Jewish immigration (which had taken on vastly greater significance as a result of Nazi persecution in Europe) and Arab consent. The British, Chaim Weizmann tersely remarked, were not in Palestine with the consent of the Arabs either. David Ben-Gurion, who fully understood the Jewish predicament, said of the impending war that "in this war the Jews would fight with the British as though there were no white paper, and would fight against the white paper as though there were no war."[45] Subsequently, the Zionists increasingly turned toward the United States, as the rising power with a larger Jewish population (the so-called Biltmore Program of 1942 would serve as a first indication of this shift). In the wake of the Arab revolt of 1936–39, the Palestine issue was internationalized even further, drawing in the Arab countries on one side and the United States on the other.

By the outbreak of World War II, Palestine was "pacified." The Arab uprising had produced mixed results. The first phase had strengthened the Mufti and the Arab Higher Committee, and weakened their opponents both inside and outside the Nashashibi camp. But Arab economy and society had suffered greatly: Over the three years of the uprising,

---

[44] *Survey of Palestine* (1946), p. 54; Porath (1977), pp. 277ff., 291–93.
[45] The citations from Weizmann and Ben-Gurion are taken from Smith (1996), p. 105.

several thousand Arabs had been killed and wounded, and many houses, fields, and orchards had been destroyed. The strike, boycott, and armed revolt had ultimately weakened the Arab economy and strengthened the Jewish sector with its plethora of institutions, and deep concern with self-reliance. In 1936 Jews already made up almost a third of the population. In Haifa and Jerusalem they were a majority, while Tel Aviv was entirely Jewish. The most important industries were owned by Jews; in the trade and banking sectors they were significantly better placed than the Arabs. Wherever Arab laborers, employees, craftsmen, or farmworkers went on strike, Jews endeavored to take their place—a matter of the greatest importance to the Jewish Yishuv at a time of massive immigration. Construction of the Tel Aviv port provided the clearest example of this determined effort to achieve self-reliance. No less important was the creation of the Hagana, which developed into a sort of unofficial military force. The economic, political, and spatial separation of the communities became ever more pronounced.

Among the Arab community, the uprising left a deep mark and long-lasting effects. It was mostly remembered as a national struggle against the British and the Jews, and memories were consciously cultivated by its participants and later generations. But it had always been more than an expression of national protest against British occupation and Zionist designs. It had also expressed social protest against inequality and injustice within Arab society itself, which were at most indirectly linked to Zionism and imperialism. This suggests a comparison with the so-called national revolution in Egypt in 1919, or with the 1834 uprising against the Egyptian occupation of Palestine, but also with the Intifada that was to follow decades later, in which social grievances and national aspirations again intertwined in complex ways, not always without friction. British concessions contained in the MacDonald White Paper could be regarded a short-time victory at most. What counted in the long run was the decisive weakening of Arab leadership at a time when the Jewish Yishuv was growing daily stronger (though it was primarily due to the persecutions in Europe rather than to events in Palestine itself). The imbalance with regard to economic performance, social cohesion, political organization, and not least military capacity would become evident after World War II.

Chapter Thirteen

TRIUMPH AND CATASTROPHE: FROM
WORLD WAR II TO THE STATE OF ISRAEL

WORLD WAR II BROUGHT VERY DIFFERENT EXPERIENCES to Arabs and
Jews in Mandate Palestine. The economic situation improved percep-
tively once British troops, whose demand for goods and services boosted
the local economy, were stationed there. At the same time, knowledge
was spreading of the existential threat to European Jewry, and possibly
even to the Jews of the Near East, if the Axis powers were to continue
their advance across North Africa and to conquer Palestine. For the
Yishuv, worries about the fate of the Jews in both Palestine and Europe
overshadowed all other events and considerations. The threat to European Jewry strengthened the resolve, and not only among committed
Zionists, to keep Palestine open as a refuge ("safe haven") for the Jews
of Europe and to create not just a Jewish national home, but a Jewish
state, as recommended by the *Peel Report* but rejected by the Passfield
Memorandum. Under these circumstances, the wishes and interests of
Palestinian Arabs counted for little. Yet it was not the war that acted as
a turning point, but rather the ensuing partition of the Mandate territory. The creation of the State of Israel put relations between Arabs and
Jews on an entirely new footing—and not just in Palestine.

PALESTINE IN WORLD WAR II

During World War II it was again the "larger context" that mattered to
the belligerent parties rather than Palestine itself. The war began with
the German invasion of Poland on September 1, 1939. On September 3,
Great Britain and France declared war on the German Reich. Between
April and June 1940, the Wehrmacht conquered Denmark, Norway,
Belgium, Luxembourg, the Netherlands, and most of France. In late June
1940, the Axis-friendly Vichy government took power in Paris. In the
air war over England in August and September 1940, however, the British were able to fend off German attacks. The war entered a new phase
in June 1941, when Hitler broke his 1939 pact with Stalin and ordered
German forces to invade the Soviet Union, opening a second front in

Europe. During the first half of 1942, German troops were advancing on all fronts.

With the fall of France, the war had already come closer to Palestine.[1] Beginning in June 1940, Vichy loyalists controlled not just Algeria, Morocco, and Tunisia, but also Syria and Lebanon. Although they pursued no anti-Jewish policy in Syria and Lebanon, so close to Palestine and its Jewish Yishuv, the possibility could not be excluded that they would do so in the future. Impressed by German victories, fascist Italy (which had since occupied Rhodes as well as Libya) entered the war on the German side on June 10, 1940. This threatened British control of the Mediterranean, the very base of its superiority in the Near and Middle East. In 1940 and 1941 the Italian air force repeatedly bombed Palestinian cities, including Tel Aviv and Haifa, resulting in hundreds of deaths. The British established their Middle East Supply Centre in Cairo, underscoring the strategic importance of the port of Suez and the Suez Canal. Palestine served as a strategic hinterland and a training ground for troops. Haifa, its only deep-sea port, endpoint of the road to Baghdad, and terminus of the oil pipeline from northern Iraq, gained additional importance when an oil refinery began operations there in June 1940, supplying the British Mediterranean fleet with its most important source of fuel. In April 1941 the Wehrmacht conquered Yugoslavia and Greece, where strong British forces had been stationed. At the same time, Iraqi Prime Minister Rashid Ali al-Gailani, then hosting the refugee Amin al-Husaini, staged an uprising against the British military presence in his country. Al-Gailani then sought German military assistance. The Royal Air Force suppressed the rebellion with the support of the Arab Legion from Transjordan (Emir Abdallah had sided with the British at the beginning of the war, so that no danger loomed from this direction). The Mufti fled to Iran, Italy, and finally to Berlin.

As the Vichy government had allowed German aircraft to land in Damascus en route to Iraq, the British took action. In May 1941 British troops with the support of Free French units under General de Gaulle and smaller groups of Hagana fighters (including Yitzhak Rabin, Yigal Allon, and Moshe Dayan, who lost an eye in this operation) marched from Palestine into Syria and Lebanon, which they occupied completely by July. This signified the end of Vichy rule there, but not the end of the French Mandate. Under British pressure, de Gaulle did promise independence to Syria and Lebanon, but broke his promise once the Vichy administration was ended. Prior to the takeover, British Foreign Minister Sir Anthony Eden had tried to win the Arab nationalists over by declar-

---

[1] For vivid description, see Segev (2000), ch. 21; for the Mufti and Gailani, see Mattar (1988), ch. 7.

ing British support for Arab unity and Syrian independence. It was not until 1946 that French troops finally withdrew from Syria and Lebanon.

Despite the successes in Iraq, Syria, and Lebanon (even Abyssinia had been liberated from Italian occupation in April 1941 by indigenous and British forces), the military situation appeared quite threatening to British interests in early 1942. True, the Japanese attack on the American base at Pearl Harbor in December 1941 led to American entry into the war on the side of the Allies, but Japan conquered Singapore, the largest British naval base in the eastern hemisphere ("east of Suez"). The German advance in Russia still seemed unstoppable. In North Africa, the German-Italian Afrika Korps under Field Marshal Rommel marched from Tunisia to the vicinity of Alexandria, threatening both Egypt and the Suez Canal, always one of the "lifelines" of the Empire. In Egypt protestors took to the streets chanting "Forward, Rommel!" On February 4, 1942, the British ambassador forced the king to install a pro-British government under the Wafd Party, which since the "revolution" of 1919 had lost a good deal of its former prestige and power, but which unlike many nationalist politicians and the king himself was not suspected of pro-Axis sympathies. The real turn in the war came at the end of 1942. In the Pacific the Americans won the upper hand against the Japanese; at Stalingrad in 1942–43, the Wehrmacht suffered a devastating defeat; at al-Alamain in November and December 1942, the British brought the German advance in North Africa to a halt. The immediate danger of a fascist takeover in the Near East was dispelled.

RECOVERY IN THE ARAB SECTOR

Palestine itself obtained mixed results from the Allied war effort and the war itself, which unlike World War I never fully entered the country. Enemy propaganda was intense: Radio Bari broadcast an Arabic-language program beginning in 1935, in which the Mufti participated from 1941 onward, that appealed to the Arabs to rise against Great Britain and France on the side of the Axis powers. Still, the Arab population in Palestine remained calm.[2] This was partly due to, as it were, negative causes: As a result of the 1936–39 revolt, the traditional urban leadership had been largely eliminated, the Arab Higher Committee dissolved, and the infrastructure of resistance destroyed; many of the prominent politicians were exiled, deported, or jailed, and the rural leaders were

[2] For detail, see Wild (1985); Nicosia (1985); 'Abd al-Ghani (1995); Höpp et al. (eds.) (2004); Krämer (2006). For the Mufti's commitment to the Nazi war effort, see above, chapter 12, note 4.

demoralized, imprisoned, or executed. Hundreds of thousands of Allied soldiers were stationed in the area. At the same time, the concessions of the MacDonald White Paper had created a more positive mood. A few nationalist leaders signaled their endorsement of the White Paper, which the Mufti and his supporters continued to reject.

Economic prosperity stimulated by the war also helped.[3] While the citrus market collapsed due to the disruption of civilian imports and exports, causing great loss to citrus planters and the workers they employed, their loss was set off by gains in the economy as a whole. More goods could now be produced locally and thereby "substituted" for foreign imports, affecting above all food supplies. In the course of the war, agricultural production rapidly expanded. In the Jewish sector this happened mostly through the cultivation of new land. In the Arab sector it occurred mainly through additional manpower, which reduced unemployment, and through the expansion of irrigation, which raised productivity. The troops stationed in the country, and the Allied war effort at large, offered an additional stimulus to the local economy. The British systematically developed their supply lines, building new roads and rail connections, and establishing bases, dockyards, and military airports. The demand for food, industrial commodities, and services also benefited Arab peasants, craftsmen, and businessmen who had suffered economically during the Arab revolt. In more than one respect, the British troops behaved differently from the Ottoman army during World War I: For one, Palestinians were not conscripted into the military. There was no large-scale confiscation, deforestation, or financial exploitation. The land was also free of hunger and epidemic disease, despite the rationing of food that began in January 1942, imposing hardship on parts of the urban population. By contrast, the peasants benefited from inflation, which reduced their debt burden. As a result, banks were more disposed to grant them loans, which in turn lessened their dependence on private moneylenders and usurers. In economic terms, then, the war years were good years for many ordinary Palestinian Arabs.

THE YISHUV IN THE SHADOW OF THE HOLOCAUST

If it were only a matter of economics, conditions would have been equally favorable for the Jewish Yishuv.[4] After three difficult years, 1942 saw an upturn in the Jewish economic sector. Owing to war-related demand and the high educational level within the Yishuv itself, new

[3] *Survey of Palestine* (1946), pp. 365–68; Metzer (1998), pp. 111, 153–54.
[4] Metzer (1998), ch. 5.

branches of industry developed, such as mechanical engineering, chemical and pharmaceutical products, optical and electronic equipment. When the Germans occupied the Netherlands, the diamond-cutting industry shifted to unoccupied foreign countries, including Palestine; by 1943 it employed 3,500 people. The construction of settlements was resolutely pursued, often in the form of fortified fence-and-watchtower settlements, even in remote and exposed sites in the hilly uplands (such as the so-called Etzion Block near Hebron), as well as in the Negev. Even land purchases were continued, within certain limits. In 1939 a new daily newspaper appeared, *Yedi'ot Aharonot* (*Latest News*), that met with large success. Theaters continued to stage plays (especially patriotic pieces based on ancient and modern Jewish history), while Arab and Jewish teams faced off in soccer matches. Yet political developments in Europe pushed a different issue to the fore: the rescue of European Jewry, which according to the Zionists had only one safe haven—Palestine, or rather Eretz Israel. The plight of European Jewry stood at the back of their relentless struggle against any limitations on immigration, land sales, or settlement, a struggle directed more than ever against the British, who refused to grant unrestricted immigration and settlement. The British were concerned with the stability not only of Palestine, but of the wider Arab world: They were afraid of driving the Arabs into the arms of the Axis powers, which until the end of 1942 seemed poised to invade and conquer the Middle East. Jewish conflict with the Mandate power had already occurred prior to the MacDonald White Paper of May 1939. In 1938 the leadership of the Yishuv had resolved to expand illegal immigration, even though other countries were available for Jewish emigrants and the American immigration quotas were left unfilled. In 1939 close to 40 percent of Jewish immigrants arrived in Palestine illegally (11,156 out of a registered total of 27,561); during the war, legal immigration came more or less to a standstill.[5]

The British made serious attempts to deter illegals: Ships carrying them were not permitted to enter the ports; authorities in transit countries were asked not to allow the ships to continue their voyages. Captured illegals were put in camps, deported to the island of Mauritius, or even sent back to Europe. The *Patria*, a French vessel enlisted by the British to take more than 1,700 illegal Jewish immigrants to Mauritius, sank in the harbor of Haifa in November 1940 when the Hagana tried to prevent the ship from departing by means of a bomb attached to its hull. The attempt went awry, some 250 refugees drowned and the rest

[5] Ibid., pp. 69–83; Smith (1996), p. 114. On the *Patria* and *Struma*, see Friling (2002), pp. 332–38; Sherman (1997), ch. 4. Naor (1998), pp. 220 and 229, show the "Wanted" poster.

were interned by the British in the Atlit camp and many ultimately deported to Mauritius. In December 1940 some 230 refugees died when the *Salvator* sank in the Marmara Sea. The greatest disaster occurred in February 1942 when the *Struma* sank in the Black Sea with 769 Rumanian Jews onboard, possibly struck by a Soviet mine or torpedo; for two months, the Turkish authorities had refused to let its passengers disembark in Istanbul while attempts were made to repair its defective motor. On the walls of buildings in Palestine, placards appeared that accused High Commissioner Harold MacMichael of murder ("Wanted for Murder!"). The tragedies strengthened the resolve of the Zionist leadership to pursue their own course against all obstacles.

Military training and supply of the Jewish community was becoming ever more important under these conditions, and service under the British flag contributed to this end.[6] From the beginning of the war, Jewish leaders tried to form Jewish units within the Allied armies to fight against the Axis powers under the blue-and-white star of David. The British military rejected this demand. Nevertheless, the leaders of the Yishuv called for general mobilization and appealed to fighting-age men (and women) to enlist as volunteers in the British army. The appeal was answered by tens of thousands of men, and thousands of women as well. But only in September 1944 was a Jewish Brigade formed with 5,000 actives; when in 1945 it was sent to the European front, the war was almost over. The Hagana pursued a policy of cooperation with the British and, wherever possible, used it to their own advantage. Legal action took the form of military and intelligence service cooperation, which the British were more than willing to accept given the excellent linguistic skills, knowledge of the land, and personal contacts Jewish agents possessed. Illegal methods included arms smuggling that was supported by more than a few members of the British army, most of them Jewish. The Hagana built up its organization at every possible level. It founded an illegal radio station, Kol Israel (Voice of Israel), as well as its own news service, Shai, and its own underground newspaper. In May 1941 it organized so-called Storm Troops (*pelugot mahatz*, or Palmach for short) in view of the growing threat of German entry into Palestine. Trained and equipped with British assistance, these troops formed the nucleus of a standing Jewish army. In 1944 the Palmach established its first defense village in Lower Galilee.

Given their ongoing disputes with the British, the leaders of the Yishuv simultaneously looked for support in other quarters, and found

---

[6] Segev (2000), ch. 21; Naor (1998), entries for 1939–45, esp. p. 238. A Women's Auxiliary Corps was set up in 1942 and soon numbered four thousand members. Women were also recruited into combat units and deployed as paratroopers behind Allied lines in Europe.

it in the United States. During World War I, Jewish Americans had already provided humanitarian aid to the Yishuv. By contrast, American politicians had taken no special interest in Palestine or the Zionist project. This changed in May 1942, when at the initiative of Chaim Weizmann a Zionist conference was held at the Biltmore Hotel in New York. In its concluding declaration, the conference demanded, among other things, that

> the gates of Palestine be opened; that the Jewish Agency be vested with control of immigration . . . and that Palestine be established as a Jewish Commonwealth integrated into the structure of the new democratic world. Then and only then will the age-old wrong to the Jewish people be righted.[7]

The conference demanded not the creation of a Jewish national home or state *within* Palestine, but rather the transformation of Palestine into a Jewish state of an undefined nature. This was a significant step, and was soon followed by deeds: the multiplication of Zionist associations in the United States; an intense advertising and fund-raising campaign, which received even greater response as the first news of the Holocaust reached the outside world; systematic lobbying among American politicians, including President Roosevelt; and the founding of pro-Zionist Christian organizations, which in the tradition of nineteenth-century philo-Semitism advocated a restoration of the people of Israel to the land of their fathers.

There remained the difficult issue of the fate of Jewish refugees and displaced persons. Despite reports of the Holocaust, American politicians were not prepared to increase immigration quotas to alleviate the plight of European Jewry. At the same time, Zionist leaders insisted on directing the refugees exclusively toward Palestine, so as to establish the necessity of building a safe haven there for the Jews of the world—the sole safe haven in the world. This was obviously a circular argument: The Jews threatened with extermination must take refuge only in Palestine, which for this reason must open its doors to unlimited Jewish immigration, and which therefore must be developed into the Jewish national home. The goal was to establish facts on the ground to counter the MacDonald White Paper of 1939 with its idea of a binational state and limitations on Jewish immigration and settlement. The costs of this strategy were potentially high, given that it risked the lives of those refugees who did not make it to Palestine but who were not accepted elsewhere. It also left little room for the Arab population.

---

[7] Cited from Mendes-Flohr/Reinharz (eds.) (1995), pp. 617–19 (618). For what follows, including the question of refugees, cf. Smith (1996), pp. 117–19; also Merkley (1998).

Within Palestine, the British took energetic action against the arming of the Yishuv, once the danger of a German invasion appeared to have been dispelled. This intensified conflict with those activists who were prepared to pursue their goals by force of arms if need be ("direct action," as the British called it).[8] For a short period following the defeat of the Arab revolt, Jabotinsky's Irgun (also known as Etzel) had attacked British targets. After the outbreak of war, they changed their strategy and enlisted in the Allied ranks in the struggle against Nazi Germany. One small group, however, refused to follow this decision. Under the leadership of Abraham Stern, they founded in June 1940 an organization known as Lehi (*Lohamei Herut Yisrael*, Fighters for the Freedom of Israel, among them future Israeli Prime Minister Yitzhak Shamir), which continued its attacks on British targets. Stern was shot dead by a British patrol in February 1942, and a number of his comrades were arrested. While the dispute continued within the Zionist leadership as to what course should be taken—a dispute linked to the conflict between Chaim Weizmann, the moderate pro-British "father" of the Balfour Declaration, and the rising star David Ben-Gurion—the militant underground began to organize in late 1943 and early 1944. Survivors of the Stern Gang escaped from a British prison camp and resumed their terrorist activities. In the meantime, in December 1943, newly immigrated Betar activist Menachem Begin (another future prime minister of Israel) took over leadership of Irgun/Etzel (Jabotinsky himself had died in New York in August 1940). Irgun and Lehi were united in their aims: the creation of a Jewish state within the borders of the Maccabees, which would extend well beyond the Mandate area to include Transjordan as well as parts of southern Lebanon and Syria. This was not the Jewish state "from the Nile to the Euphrates" that may have existed briefly under Solomon, and that was occasionally identified as the ultimate Zionist goal. But it was considerably more land than stood under Jewish control at the time. Irgun and Lehi were not entirely in agreement as to strategy, but the gap between them was visibly narrower than that between either of them and the Hagana (although there existed connections here as well, through individual people and specific actions).

Both groups continued their attacks against British military, police, and civilian institutions. Lehi went even further: Several attempts to assassinate High Commissioner MacMichael failed. But in early November 1944, they murdered Lord Moyne, the British minister resident in the Middle East, in Cairo. Moyne was a close friend of Churchill's, who did not abandon his pro-Zionist attitude in the wake of the killing, but

---

[8] Segev (2000), chs. 21 and 22; for Radical Revisionism, see also Shimoni (1995), ch. 6, and pp. 369–72.

who did now begin to advocate energetic measures against Zionist terror. Under British pressure, the Hagana took action in 1944–45 against
the underground organizations (the operation became known as "the
hunting season").[9] British reprisals did not end the terror, as would
quickly be seen after World War II.

WITHDRAWAL FROM THE MANDATE

On May 8, 1945, the German Reich surrendered, followed by Japan on
August 15. Great Britain emerged from the war decisively weakened,
forcing it to readjust its foreign and security policies with the aim of
securing the Empire's strategic lines of communication while dramatically reducing the costs of overseas engagement. Naturally, this reorientation affected Palestine, whose strategic importance had already been
reexamined in 1942–43 in light of the existing political situation.[10] In
July 1945 Prime Minister Churchill suffered an unexpected election defeat. The new Labor government under Clement Attlee seemed to be
entirely committed to the Zionist project. In April 1944 the Labor Party
had not only endorsed the creation of a Jewish state in Palestine, but
also the "voluntary" transfer of the Arab population out of Palestine.
And yet, after their electoral victory, they pursued the quota policy of
the MacDonald White Paper and worked to prevent illegal Jewish immigration by all possible means. A letter from U.S. President Truman in
August 1945, in which he asked for the immediate admission to Palestine of 100,000 Jewish refugees, did not affect British policies. (An Anglo-American Commission of Inquiry took up the demand in 1946, linking it to the lifting of restrictions on Jewish land purchases.)

The British refusal to accept Truman's proposal led to an additional
surge in anti-British attacks and acts of sabotage in the autumn of 1945.
It was not only the "extremists" of Irgun and Lehi who joined the "Hebrew resistance movement," but also members of the Hagana, and it
was broadly supported (though not in every detail) by leading Yishuv
politicians such as David Ben-Gurion.[11] The British government declared
a state of emergency and concentrated close to 100,000 troops in Palestine to combat Jewish armed struggle, which in many respects resembled
the Arab uprising of 1936–39. British civilian and military installations,

[9] Segev (2000), pp. 455–58.

[10] M. Cohen (1978); Smith (1996), pp. 125–35; Morris (2004), pp. 54–56; El-Eini
(2006), pp. 344–64; also *Survey of Palestine* (1946), pp. 70–71, and 80.

[11] Smith (1996), pp. 135–39; Segev (2000), ch. 22, esp. pp. 471–82. He also analyzes
the moral dilemma faced by the British in their fight against Jewish armed resistance and
terrorism.

especially arsenals, bridges, roads, railways, train stations, the oil pipe-line, and port facilities were attacked, and British civilians and military personnel were assassinated. With the help of the so-called Second Aliya Bureau, the Hagana intensified its efforts to promote illegal immigration and accelerate the construction of settlements. Arabs played at most a secondary role in this phase, whether as enemies or as victims: It was not they who stood in the path of the immediate creation of a Jewish state, but rather the British. On June 29, 1946, during Operation Aga-tha, better known as "Black Sabbath," the British searched for terrorists, weapons, and ammunition, which led to mass arrests. Many Jewish leaders were interned for a number of months in the Latrun camp. Things came to a head on July 22, 1946, when the Irgun blew up the southern wing of the King David Hotel in Jerusalem, headquarters of the British general staff. Ninety-one people perished in the rubble, with dozens more injured.

In the winter of 1946–47, it became clear that Britain would no longer be able to sustain its involvement in the Mediterranean region. (British involvement pertained not only to Palestine but, as part of the general anticommunist containment strategy, also included financial and military aid to Turkey and Greece.) On February 25, 1947, Foreign Minister Bevin announced his government's resolve to hand over the problem of Palestine to the newly founded United Nations.[12] The United Nations Special Committee on Palestine (UNSCOP) visited Palestine during June and July of 1947 in order to gain a sense of the situation. As usual, the committee received comprehensive testimony from the Zi-onists but was boycotted by the Arabs. The fate of the *Exodus 47* (actu-ally named the *President Warfield*) highlighted the drama of the situa-tion for the members of the Committee, and at the same time damaged the reputation of the British, when in July 1947, it was turned away with its 4,500 passengers from Haifa and sent back to southern France, and ultimately to Hamburg in the British-occupied zone.

In its report, published on September 1, 1947, the UNSCOP members opted unanimously for an end to the British Mandate. A majority sup-ported partition into separate Jewish and Arab states, as well as the creation of a neutral enclave in Jerusalem. Hence, it essentially followed the recommendations of the Peel Commission, but as to the details, it recommended a rather different map in light of the changed conditions of land ownership and settlement. At the end of 1946, the total popula-tion of Palestine was estimated at around 1.94 million, including 1.33 million Arabs (1.18 million of them Muslims and 149,000 Christians),

[12] Biger (2004), pp. 208–19; El-Eini (2006), pp. 365–69; Segev (2000), ch. 23; also Sherman (1997), ch. 5; for a sharp critique, see W. Khalidi (1997).

603,000 Jews, and 16,000 "Other."[13] The Jewish share was thus barely a third. Jewish property had grown to about 11 percent of cultivable land and 20 percent of the land already cultivated. Despite the limitations imposed by the Passfield White Paper, a further 145,000 dunam were acquired between 1939 and 1946—almost 10 percent of the total that came into Jewish possession prior to 1948. Nearly half of it was owned by the Jewish National Fund, which made long-term lease agreements with kibbutzim, communal settlements (*moshavim*), and individual Jewish settlers. The settlements, numbering about 280, were concentrated along the coast, in eastern Galilee, the plain of Marj Ibn Amir (Jezreel), and the Hula Valley. In more scattered fashion, it had also expanded to the vicinity of Jerusalem and to the northern Negev. Around 23 percent of the coastal plain and 30 percent of the northern valleys were now owned by Jews. The N-shape recommended for settlement by Arthur Ruppin in 1907 had thus become a reality. UNSCOP took these conditions into account insofar as, unlike the Peel Commission, it assigned those parts of Galilee densely settled by Arabs to the proposed Arab state. Arab territory, especially north and east of Jerusalem, in western and Upper Galilee as well as near Hebron (the so-called Etzion Block), also contained a number of Jewish settlements, planting the seeds for future conflict.

However, the potential for conflict was far greater on the other side—for the proposed Jewish state, with its 55 percent of the land area, not only contained considerably more land than was then owned by Jews, but was also home to 350,000 Arabs along with its 520,000 Jews. Both territories, each composed of three segments touching one another only at narrow points, were tiny. Even at a first glance, the proposed solution was fraught with risk.

On November 29, 1947, the United Nations General Assembly voted on Resolution 181, with 33 in favor of the partition plan, 13 opposed, and 10 abstentions (including Great Britain). The Jewish population of Palestine received the decision enthusiastically, while the Arabs were appalled. At the beginning of December, the British government announced that it would end the Mandate at midnight on May 14, 1948, and would withdraw its forces from Palestine by August 1. No formal arrangements were made as to how power would be handed on or to whom. While the Jews had functioning institutions of self-government, the Arabs did not.

---

[13] Biger (2004), pp. 213–19; W. Khalidi (1997). For demographic data (as always contested), see also McCarthy (1990), pp. 35–38; for land sales and settlement, see Morris (1987), pp. 28, 179; Metzer (1998), pp. 86, 99–103. Smith (1996), pp. 136–37, provides a map of Jewish settlements. See also Rashid Khalidi, "The Palestinians and 1948: the

TABLE 5
Regional Distribution of Population in Mandate Palestine

	1931		1944	
	Arabs	Jews	Arabs	Jews
Coastal Plain				
Central and Northern	23.8%	58.6%	25.3%	75.2%
Southern	10.1%	0.4%	11.2%	0.5%
Central Mtns.				
Jerusalem Region	11.5%	31.4%	12.2%	18.1%
Other	32.3%	0.1%	29.0%	0.0%
Northern Valleys	1.3%	1.6%	1.6%	1.7%
Galilee	11.5%	3.5%	11.4%	2.2%
Jordan Valley	3.7%	4.4%	4.2%	2.3%
Negev	5.9%	0.0%	5.1%	0.0%
Total	100.1%	100%	100%	100%

Source: Metzer (1908): 8.

PARTITION ON THE GROUND

The partition of the Mandate territory by the international community (which at that time was still limited in numbers) was a milestone in Palestinian history. But for the time being it existed only on paper, waiting to be translated into reality on the ground. Palestinian Arabs were firmly opposed to partition and the foundation of a Jewish state on territory that they considered their exclusive homeland. For them it was unacceptable that the Arabs of Palestine should have to atone for the guilt of Europe, which had first discriminated against "its own" Jews, then persecuted them, and finally sought to annihilate them, only to end with the grand compensatory gesture of offering them land that did not belong to them in the first place. Arab politicians recognized the suffering that had been visited upon the Jews—by Europeans, not by Arabs. Injustice in one case they argued could not be remedied by injustice in another. In October 1944 the assembled Arab heads of state drafted the Alexandria Protocol, which served as the basis for the later Arab League. In this document, they stated:

---

underlying causes of failure," in Rogan/Shlaim (eds.) (2001), ch. 1; for a nuanced picture of Arab opinion, see Flapan (1987), pp. 55–79.

The Committee also declares that it is second to none in regretting the woes that have been inflicted upon the Jews of Europe by European dictatorial states. But the question of these Jews should not be confused with Zionism, for there can be no greater injustice and aggression than solving the problem of the Jews of Europe by another injustice, that is, by inflicting injustice on the Palestine Arabs of various religions and denominations.[14]

The Arabs did not enter the ensuing conflict entirely unprepared, but they were insufficiently coordinated. On one side stood the Palestinians, divided into a variety of groups and factions, and with very little military experience and organization; on the other stood the neighboring Arab states, which also pursued no unified course. In Palestine, wartime prosperity had made it possible to establish new enterprises, organizations, and institutions, which strengthened the Arab sector in economic, social, and cultural terms.[15] The educational system was expanded due to Arab expenditures far greater than what the Mandatory was prepared to invest. There was an increasing range of clubs and associations from sports to charity, attracting men as well as women, Muslims as well as Christians. Cultural life was active, with cinemas and theaters offering entertainment at least to urban audiences. Step by step, political life was reconstituted too. Former members of the Istiqlal played an important role in this process, such as Awni Abd al-Hadi, who with the assistance of the newly revived Arab National Fund sought to halt land sales to Jews. Nor were the established notables entirely finished. In the early 1940s, the Arab Palestinian Party, close to the Husaini family, returned to the stage under the leadership of Emile al-Ghuri. The Nashashibis and their clients were also active. Arab society seemed to recover from the 1930s, which makes it all the more striking that in the usual depiction of the ensuing events, it hardly figures at all.

The new element was the Arab League, founded in March 1945 with its headquarters in Cairo, but unable to unite its rival member states in any effective way.[16] The governments of Egypt, Syria, and Saudi Arabia mistrusted the intentions of Emir Abdallah, who for years had sought to extend his domain beyond his poor and tiny emirate (known from 1946 as the Kingdom of Transjordan). The path to Greater Syria was through Palestine, with which he continued to maintain economic, cultural, and family ties. Abdallah also kept close contacts with the Nashashibis, who would not end their rivalry with the Husainis even under

[14] Cited from Smith (1996), p. 125.
[15] Khalaf (1991), pp. 36–37; Fleischmann (2003), ch. 7; for armed bands and militias, see Morris (2004), pp. 28–30.
[16] See Wilson (1987), chs. 8 and 9, as well as the contributions of Shlaim, Gerges, and Landis in Rogan/Shlaim (eds.) (2001); also Khalaf (1991), ch. 8, esp. pp. 189ff.

increased pressure. The same was true for the other side, including the Mufti. Jordanian relations remained strong with Iraq, also ruled by a member of the Hashemite family. With the possible exception of Emir Abdallah, all parties were united in the aim to prevent the Jews from taking possession of the territory granted them under the United Nations partition plan. And yet their highest priority was to make sure, in the coming conflict, that none of their rivals would gain more than they did themselves. It was a first indication of the pattern that was to character-ize Arab-Israeli as well as inter-Arab relations for decades: For the Arab governments it was never just a question of facing their Jewish oppo-nents, but of struggling for hegemony within the Arab camp as well. Nothing showed this more clearly than the war of 1948.

In November 1945 the Arab League established a new Arab Higher Committee (al-hai'a al-'arabiyya al-'ulya) to represent the Palestinian people, a body largely made up of followers of the Mufti (and not to be confused with the Arab Higher Committee, al-lajna al-'arabiyya al-'ulya, dissolved by the British in 1937).[17] Yet in October 1947, they rejected the Mufti's suggestion to form a Palestinian government in exile, which would possibly have allowed him to direct the further course of action and to enhance both his own international status and his position within the Arab League. King Abdallah wanted to play the key role in Arab politics, and the Mufti and the Arab Higher Committee were his com-petitors. Leading representatives of the Arab League also feared the Mufti's lack of flexibility, worrying that he would complicate relations with Britain and stand in the way of a possible agreement with the Jews.

PRELUDE TO WAR: NOVEMBER 1947 TO MAY 1948

Fighting began immediately after UN Resolution 181 became known.[18] The violence was later said to have been triggered by an Arab attack on two buses on the road between Petah Tikva and Lydda on November

---

[17] Morris (2004), pp. 31–32; also Wilson (1987), chs. 11 and 12; Shlaim (2001); on Qawuqji, Shlaim (2001), pp. 85–86; Provence (2005), pp. 95–100. In spite of his known involvement with the Nazis, the Mufti was not discredited in Arab eyes, and was able to escape to Cairo after the war; cf. Gensicke (1988) and Elpeleg (1993). However, he found his influence over Arab politics and more particularly Palestinian politics much reduced; see Mattar (1988), ch. 9; Höpp (1999).

[18] Morris (2004), 28–35, and ch. 3. For the "trigger" and the first wave of violence, see also Segev (2000), pp. 500–18; Khalaf (1991), pp. 190ff. For Salama, see also Munayyir (1997). For the role of women, see Fleischmann (2003), pp. 201–10. For al-Husaini and his role in the 1936–39 uprising, including his training in Germany, see Salih (1989), pp. 396–400, who also deals at length with the Muslim Brothers; see also ibid., pp. 433–51, 464–78.

30, 1947, in which seven Jewish passengers were killed and several others injured. The incident was in fact "only" one in a chain of violent acts committed by one side or the other. In protest of the partition resolution, the Arab Higher Committee called for a three-day general strike on December 1. Just as at the beginning of the Arab uprising in April 1936, national committees were formed in most cities, towns, and large villages to organize Arab resistance. In several areas, armed units were formed similar to those of 1936–39, made up of peasant and urban militias and a mobile guerrilla force equipped with rifles and pistols—many of them obsolete—and a limited number of machine guns. Their infrastructure, funds, and medical support were quite insufficient. Amin al-Husaini, who was still banned from entering the country, made attempts to influence events from abroad. His most important ally was perhaps Abd al-Qadir al-Husaini, who had already fought in the uprising of 1936–39 and owed his reputation to more than his connection with the Mufti. Abd al-Qadir led one contingent of the so-called Army of the Holy War (*jaish al-jihad al-muqaddas*) that was active primarily in the area around Jerusalem. Another militia operated under Hasan Salama, another veteran of the uprising, in the region between Ramla and Lydda.

In accordance with the Arab League's decision in favor of indirect intervention, Arab volunteers entered Palestine in January 1948. At least theoretically, they were part of Fawzi al-Qawuqji's Arab Liberation Army (ALA, actually "Rescue Army," *jaish al-inqadh*). Qawuqji himself, who was familiar with the terrain from the time of the Arab uprising, arrived in Palestine in March 1948. At its peak, the ALA included around five thousand men. It was pieced together in motley fashion, had little military experience, and was poorly equipped. At least in theory, it stood under the Arab League's military High Command under General Isma'il Safwat, an Iraqi officer who had his headquarters in Damascus. Qawuqji was a sworn enemy of the Mufti and his men. Relations were tense between local militias, supporters of the Mufti both inside and outside of the Holy War Army, and the Arab Liberation Army. In many places, local inhabitants sought to keep the fighters away to avoid Jewish attacks and retaliation.

In the first weeks and months of fighting, the initiative lay mostly with the Arabs. They were able to take control of a good portion of the highways and connecting roads; (West) Jerusalem with its 100,000 Jewish residents was especially affected. Attacks by Arab guerrillas against Jewish settlements, neighborhoods, institutions, and businesses, and Jewish travelers, buses, cars, and convoys were answered with similar acts of violence. Jewish "extremists" inside and outside the Hagana attacked Arab settlements, villages, and Bedouin encampments, contributing to the general climate of fear and intimidation. In January 1948 the Irgun blew up the municipal office of Jaffa (Serail). Unemployment, inflation, supply shortages, and rising criminality sharpened the sense of crisis among the Arab population. Already in these first months of fighting, approximately 75,000 Arabs fled their homes. It was for the most part members of the well-off middle and upper classes who left the "mixed" cities of Haifa, Jaffa, and Jerusalem, but there were also peasants and Bedouins from the villages around Jerusalem and Baisan and from the coastal plain between Tel Aviv and Hadera, where Arabs and Jews had lived in close proximity. They fled into the hilly uplands and into neighboring Arab countries, where they initially found sanctuary with friends and family. They had done much the same thing during the uprising of 1938–39.

The Yishuv found itself in considerable distress. And yet, from a Zionist point of view, the "unmixing" of the population had its positive effects: By February 1948, as David Ben-Gurion remarked, Jerusalem was more Jewish than it had been at any time since its destruction by the Romans in A.D. 70. What had happened in Jerusalem might well be repeated in other parts of the country. Great changes stood ahead, not all of them disadvantageous to the Jews.[19] Deeds followed words: a few days later, Ben-Gurion ordered the Hagana High Command to clear the Arab Quarter of Jerusalem and settle Jews there instead. After the murder of an Arab woman, a Hagana-owned truck drove through the streets of the suburb of Talbiya, announcing over a loudspeaker that its Arab residents must leave, "or else be blown up with your possessions." The Arabs fled indeed, soon followed by the residents of other Arab neighborhoods and villages close to Jerusalem. Intimidation, terror, and expulsion triggered a flood of refugees in the coastal plain as well. On February 5, 1948, the Hagana carried out the first systematic destruction of an entire town in Caesarea, whose Arab and Jewish residents had previously lived in harmony. The refugees and the expelled population spread their fear of Jewish attacks to those with whom they found refuge: "Flight fever" swept the country.[19] Despairing efforts by the Arab Higher Committee to urge the Arab residents of Jerusalem, Haifa, and Jaffa to stay, whether by means of personal appeals, printed flyers, threats, or punishments, remained without effect. During this phase, there is no evidence for the later assertion that the Arab leadership itself had called upon Palestinian Arabs to flee.

[19] Morris (1987), pp. 52ff.; Flapan (1987), pp. 81–118; for Jerusalem, see also Tamari (ed.) (1999).

PLAN "D": APRIL TO MAY 1948

In April 1948 the Hagana shifted from its initial policy of "active defense," which included harsh "retaliatory strikes," to an offensive strategy. Their aim was to secure the connecting routes between Jewish settlements, and to maintain free access to Jerusalem. Under Plan D, they overcame heavy resistance and pressed into those zones granted to the Jews under the UN plan of partition but not yet occupied by them militarily; additionally, they sought to gain control of further regions in which Jews lived in great numbers. The goal was to establish a contiguous Jewish territory that could be defended from an attack by the Arab states, which was expected to occur following the end of the British Mandate on May 14.[20] Plan D, dated March 1948, envisaged the "pacification" of the zones in question, which meant nothing less than the capitulation, elimination, or expulsion of their Arab inhabitants, as well as the destruction of their houses, villages, and businesses. But the desired "clearing" or "cleansing" of "Jewish land " presupposed the expulsion or liquidation not only of those Arab residents who opposed Jewish rule, hindered it, or adopted a "provocative" attitude toward it, but also of those who lived in strategically important zones—whether close to the desired boundaries of a Jewish state, or near the key connecting routes within Jewish territory itself. Still, it seems that during this period a mass exodus of Arabs was neither intended nor expected by either the Arabs or the Jews.

The guerrilla warfare of the first phase was replaced in April by "conventional" warfare, as the Hagana undertook the systematic conquest of strategic sites and regions. The object was primarily to conquer land, whether the local residents took up arms or not.[21] The Jewish troops

---

[20] Plan D dates from the first half of March; Morris (2004), ch. 4; English translation in W. Khalidi (1988). Morris's original thesis, found in (1987), chs. 3 and 5, and (2001), that mass expulsion was the result of war actions rather than a preconceived strategy of "transfer" and expulsion was contested by a number of senior researchers, including W. Khalidi (1988), Masalha (1992), N. Finkelstein (1995), and Pappe (1999) and (2004). In response, Morris corrected his earlier assessment and added an important chapter on the idea of transfer in Zionist thought and practice before 1948 to his *The Birth of the Palestinian Refugee Problem Revisited*, published 2004 (ch. 2). However he did not change his evaluation of Plan D; see p. 266, note 1. The controversy still centers on the question of whether the mass expulsion, or ethnic cleansing of 1948, was preconceived and indeed an integral part of Zionist ideology, in line with previous concepts of "transfer," or whether, rather, it resulted from wartime circumstances.

[21] The ensuing events are highly contested, now as ever; for varying perspectives, cf. Smith (1996), pp. 139–45; Morris (1987), pp. 93–94, 156, and 304, note 19; Morris (2004), ch. 3; for Haifa and Balad al-Shaikh, see Morris (2004), p. 100–102. For Jewish armament, see Smith (1996), p. 116, and Sherman (1997), pp. 158–62.

were not only highly motivated: They could also draw on superior mo-
rale, education, and equipment, the latter upgraded and improved by
arms shipments from Czechoslovakia with the permission of the Soviet
Union. While the Arab Liberation Army did have some heavy weapons,
artillery, and a few tanks, they were at this stage not equal to their
opponents. In April 1948 Abd al-Qadir al-Husaini, one of the most capable Palestinian military leaders, fell in battle. In addition to "conventional" warfare, both sides made use of every conceivable means of violence, which they justified as legitimate means of self-defense, even those
that fell under the usual definition of terrorism. Lehi and Irgun returned
to those forms of action for which they were already known in World
War II—and Irgun, at least, with its two to three thousand members,
was no mere splinter group. They placed bombs in crowded public
places, in Arab markets, cafés, restaurants, and schools. At the end of
December 1947, a bomb killed six people and injured some fifty others
in the Haifa oil refinery, whereupon an angry Arab mob murdered
thirty-nine Jewish workers and seriously injured an additional eleven.
Revenge came two days later, when Hagana members dressed as Arabs
entered the Arab village of Balad al-Shaikh and shot around sixty Arab
men, women, and children while also blowing up dozens of houses.

The spiral of violence and retaliation was set in motion, drawing in
both sides. The massacre of Dair Yasin of April 9, 1948, became for the
Arabs the supreme symbol of Zionist evil until it was replaced in the
1980s by the massacre in the Palestinian refugee camps of Sabra and
Shatila, carried out by Lebanese militias under the eyes of Israeli
troops.[22] The villagers of Dair Yasin, located in the immediate vicinity
of Jerusalem, had entered into an agreement of nonaggression with their
Jewish neighbors. They were attacked in a joint action by Lehi and Irgun
fighters who were assisted by Palmach fighters. The raiders raped and
murdered over one hundred men, women, and children, and then pa-
raded the survivors through the streets of West Jerusalem. While the
leadership of the Yishuv apologized, sending a letter of condolence to
King Abdallah(!), the Irgun openly announced its deeds over loudspeakers in Arab residential areas. Revenge came on April 13, when Arabs
ambushed a Jewish convoy on its way to Hadassah Hospital on Mount

[22] Morris (1987), pp. 38, 113–15, 193; Morris (2004), pp. 237–40; for the dispute over
the number of victims, Morris (2004), note 566; Benvenisti (2000), pp. 114–17. Hasso
(2000) stresses assaults on women (and by the same token, violation of male honor, 'ird)
as a major element of the massacre and the impact it made on the Arab community.
Despite protests from Jewish intellectuals from Martin Buber to Akiva Ernst Simon, a new
settlement, Givat Shaul Bet, was established for Jewish immigrants in summer 1949 on
the site of the destroyed village; Morris (2004), p. 393. I have not seen Walid Khalidi's
Dair Yasin: al-jum'a 9/4/1948 (Beirut 1998).

Scopus in Jerusalem, murdering seventy-eight people including a number of doctors and nurses, and wounding many others. On May 13, 1948, nearly all of the 130 inhabitants of the Jewish settlement of Kfar Etzion in the Hebron area were massacred after they surrendered to Arab forces.

Earlier, leading Zionists had already spoken in favor of "encouraging" Arabs to flee (perhaps by "teaching them a lesson" with the destruction of houses, gardens, fruit and olive groves) and preventing their return. This amounted to more than expulsion; it also entailed their dispossession.[23] Not only Lehi and Irgun, but also the Hagana, made systematic use of the massacre of Dair Yassin, and similar atrocities, as a means of intimidation. This strategy did not miss the mark. The decision to remain in the "holy land" of Palestine, as demanded by the Arab resistance and national movements since the 1930s ("steadfastness," *sumud*, later became a key concept of the Intifada), or to flee in hopes of returning soon thereafter, lay in most cases with local leaders, families, and communities. Arab leaders abroad, from the Mufti to the Arab Higher Committee, could do little in this respect. This became evident in mid-April 1948 when the Hagana conquered the first "mixed" city in the country, Tiberias, whose Arab and Jewish notables had signed a nonaggression agreement in the preceding month. The Arab residents fled the city.[24] Developments in Haifa were far more dramatic. Out of its original 70,000 Arab inhabitants, 20,000 to 30,000 had fled since December 1947. The rest followed when their civilian and military leaders abandoned their posts on April 21–22, even before the city had been captured by the Hagana. In mid-May, a mere four thousand Arabs continued to live in Haifa under wretched conditions. On April 25, 1948, Jaffa came under attack. Here Irgun took the initiative, viewing this Arab enclave as a "cancer" in the Jewish body politic and as the "scourge" of neighboring Tel Aviv, their actual stronghold.[25] The attack was designed to create mass panic and a mass flight. It was successful in both respects, especially since the Hagana simultaneously "cleansed" the surrounding Arab villages, even though the local British garrison intervened in favor of the Arabs. The first to flee, after heavy defensive efforts by the local Arab militias, were once again the local leaders. From an original fifty to sixty thousand residents, only four to five thousand still remained by mid-May 1948. David Ben-Gurion saw the Arab mass exo-

---

[23] Morris (2004), chs. 2–5, and above, note 20; Fischbach (2003). On *sumud*, see also R. Khalidi (1997), pp. 177–209.

[24] British units stationed in the city took some of the refugees to Nazareth and over the border into Jordan; Morris (2004), pp. 181–86; for Haifa, see pp. 186–211; for Jaffa, pp. 211–21.

[25] Cited from Morris (1987), p. 95; Morris (2004), p. 212.

dus as the proof of "who is really bound to this land and for whom this land is nothing but a luxury, to be easily abandoned."[26] As he saw it, God and history identified the Jews as the (sole) legitimate proprietors of Eretz Israel; by fleeing, the Arabs had disqualified themselves.

Between the beginning of April and the middle of May, the Hagana, assisted by the Irgun and Lehi, executed Plan D: Beyond the zones granted to the Jews in the UN partition plan, they conquered the cities of Jaffa, Haifa, Acre, Safed, Tiberias, and Bet Shean. Even before the outbreak of the first Arab-Israeli War, some 300,000 Arabs had already fled the country, almost half of the eventual total who either fled or were driven out of Palestine between 1947 and 1949.[27] The majority were city dwellers, including the greater part of the Arab elite. A few hours before the British Mandate officially ended on the night of May 15, 1948, David Ben-Gurion read aloud the Declaration of Independence of the State of Israel in Tel Aviv (not Jerusalem!). The next day, the Soviet Union became the first state to formally recognize the State of Israel.

OPEN WAR: MAY 1948 TO SPRING 1949

The Arab League had already made plans for military invasion in April 1948. On the night of May 15, Arab troops moved against the Jewish state, entering from Egypt, Jordan, Syria, Lebanon, and Iraq, supported by small Saudi and Yemeni contingents. The Egyptian air force bombed Tel Aviv and other towns in the Jewish-controlled areas. Contrary to the agreed battle plan, the national forces operated largely independently of one another. The military headquarters under Iraqi General Nur al-Din Mahmud was unworthy of the name, and King Abdallah did not succeed in making himself commander in chief of the Arab army. In terms of hard data, from troop strength to equipment, the frequent claims that 1948 represented a battle between David and Goliath, the bold young hero against the better-armed giant, are unfounded. At most, it was a battle between David and other Davids, of whom a few were decisively smaller and weaker than David himself. The Yishuv had emerged from the Arab uprising and World War II stronger than ever. The Hagana (known from May 1948 as the Israeli Defense Forces, *tzva hagana le'umit*, or Tzahal for short) had more than 35,000 trained men and women in the army, air force, and navy, supplemented by large

---

[26] Cited from Morris (2004), pp. 168–69; for a slightly different wording, cf. Morris (1987), p. 95.

[27] Morris (2004), pp. 262–65; slightly higher figures in Pappe (1999), pp. 50–52. Text of the state proclamation in Mendes-Flohr/Reinharz (eds.) (1995), pp. 629–30.

numbers of volunteers. In mid-July 1948, the Israeli army numbered 65,000 men and women, and in December 1948 more than 96,000. They had at their disposal an efficient infrastructure and logistical network, a well-developed intelligence service, and modern equipment. Morover they could rely on sophisticated structures of civic organization, ranging from rural settlements to strong labor unions. Most of all, they could count on the unconditional support of the Jewish community. Faced with an Arab invasion bent on destroying the State of Israel, Palestinian Jews were a "community without choice."[28]

Israel was opposed by states that had just emerged from colonial rule, and even those states that had been nominally independent for a longer time were closely tied to France or Britain in matters of their defense and foreign policies.[29] Tens of thousands of British soldiers were still stationed in Egypt, nominally independent since 1922, under the Anglo-Egyptian Treaty of 1936. Suez was the most important British base in the Mediterranean and the Middle East; the Egyptian army itself had no military experience whatever. Iraq, "independent" since 1932, stood in a similar relation to Great Britain. Lebanon was nominally independent since 1943, and Syria since 1946—hence, their preparatory phase for national independence was not much different from the one of the Yishuv. Even after attaining independence in 1946, Jordan submitted to de facto British control of its finances and military. What is more, the five participating Arab states did not send their full armies into Palestine, but only smaller units. Taken together, they mobilized 25,000 soldiers at the outbreak of war—less than the Jewish forces even in terms of sheer manpower. Most of the soldiers were poorly trained and armed; they were disorganized, and were sent to the field without functioning supply systems. In May 1948 Egypt contributed about 10,000 men, Jordan 8,000, Iraq 4,000–6,000, Syria 1,500–2,500, and Lebanon fewer than 1,000. The Arab Liberation Army at this time numbered around 4,000 irregulars. Over the course of war, the number of Arab regular soldiers increased considerably, but in terms of motivation, education, and equipment they could not measure up to the Israeli army. Only Jordan had an effective military force, which had developed out of the

[28] Flapan (1987), pp. 119–52, 187–99; Rogan/Shlaim (eds.) (2001); Morris (2004), pp. 14–17, and note 21 above.

[29] Rogan/Shlaim (eds.) (2001), chs. 4 and 5, as well as the map on p. xiv. Lebanon could not be treated in this anthology for political reasons. (One especially delicate question was and remains Maronite cooperation with Israel.) For a brief reference, see pp. 8ff. See also Khalaf (1991), pp. 172–78, 192–96. Relations between Transjordan, Great Britain, and the Zionists/Israel are well researched; for an overview of the scholarly literature in English and Hebrew, see Shlaim (2001); also Wilson (1987); for Glubb Pasha, cf. Morris (2003).

British-created Arab Legion and still stood under the command of former British officer John Bagot Glubb Pasha. Yet it was the Jordanian forces that failed to adhere to the joint battle plan, attempting instead to conquer the area the UN had granted to the Arabs. They were at least partly successful in this effort. There was heavy fighting near Jerusalem and Hebron (where Jewish settlers were concentrated in the so-called Etzion Block), areas that were not assigned to the Jewish state under the UN partition plan. On May 28, 1948, the residents of the Jewish Quarter of Jerusalem surrendered to the Arab Legion. Still, Jordanian forces made no efforts to conquer Jewish territory or even to attack it.

At the outbreak of war, "objective" facts, then, seemed to lie in Israel's favor. But "subjective" perceptions were entirely different: Among the Jewish community, the sense of existential threat so shortly after the Holocaust was powerful and very real. Arab politicians, grotesquely misreading the situation, declared that they would quickly do away with the "Zionist gangs" (due to their greater knowledge of military realities, Arab military experts judged the situation quite differently). Seen from Cairo, Riyadh, or Damascus, the danger was not so much "the Jews" as the expansionist intentions of King Abdallah, which not only disturbed the Arab balance of power, but endangered their own position as well. Every attempt at coordinated action failed as a result of inter-Arab rivalry.[30] In the first phase of war, the Israeli army was able to halt the Arab advance until an armistice went into effect on June 11, overseen by a UN peacekeeping mission. These initial weeks, in which Israel saw itself threatened on all fronts, were decisive for contemporary perceptions of the war and later memories of it. It was at this time that the image of a struggle between David and Goliath, of the few against the many, established itself. The Jordanian army had taken the Old City of Jerusalem; one part of the Egyptian force had advanced to within twenty kilometers of Tel Aviv, while the other, strengthened by volunteers from the Muslim Brotherhood, had reached Hebron and Bethlehem ("Arab" territory); Iraqi units stood in the triangle of Nablus, Jenin, and Tulkarm; the Syrian contingents were positioned north of Lake Tiberias and in the northern Jordan Valley; only the Lebanese incursion into northern Galilee had been repelled.[31]

In mid-June, despite considerable international pressure, the Israeli government resolved to prevent a return of Arab refugees who were

---

[30] See Gerges and Landis in Rogan/Shlaim (eds.) (2001).

[31] Shlaim (2001), pp. 89–90. On the ensuing fighting, cf. Morris (1987), chs. 5 and 6. For the Christians and the Druze, see Morris (1987), pp. 198ff. and 224–36; with a broader scope, see also Morris (2004), pp. 24–26, 416–21, 508. For Lydda, whose resi-

thereby dispossessed of their property.[32] The decision was taken amid great confusion at a time when Israeli victory could not be predicted. Europe too had witnessed massive displacements of population after the war, mostly as a result of coercion or violence. Still, it was a momentous decision to take, and it was to have lasting effect. The Israeli army also used the ceasefire to upgrade their armaments. The Egyptians broke the ceasefire on July 8, one day before it expired. In the second phase of the war that ran to July 18, the Israelis were thus able to fight from a position of greater strength. Within ten days, they conquered large parts of the region between Ramla and Lydda, so valuable agriculturally, thereby securing the lines of communication with Jerusalem as well as parts of western and Lower Galilee, which had been assigned to the Arabs in the 1947 partition plan after being allotted to the Jews in 1937. In the process, they also took the cities of Nazareth and Shafa Amr, where many of the "internal" Arab refugees had previously found sanctuary. During this period an additional 100,000 Arabs were driven from their homes, with an important distinction evident in Galilee: While the majority of Muslims were either expelled or fled before the Israeli advance, many Christians as well as most Druze (who often, though not always, had made arrangements with Israeli commanders in advance) stayed in place. Israeli military leaders and politicians distinguished somewhat crudely between hostile Muslims, passively friendly Christians, and actively friendly Druze, even if this distinction was not consistently observed. Preferential treatment was the reward for an attitude ranging from neutrality to active collaboration.[33] The Israelis not only permitted friendly Druze to remain in their villages, but also to gather their harvest and

---

dents were largely expelled, see Morris (2004), pp. 430–34; Busaylah (1981) and Munayyir (1997), ch. 3, offer alternative accounts, from Arab eyewitnesses of the time.

[32] Josef Weitz, an early advocate of a transfer, had already spoken of the desirability and necessity of a "retroactive transfer." At the beginning of June 1948, he recommended a plan of action that Ben-Gurion was not prepared to support unconditionally (at least not in writing): The plan involved preventing the return of Arab refugees, their field work and more specifically the harvest, destroying their houses, rapid settlement of Jews in the abandoned sites, neighborhoods, and houses (so as not to allow any "vacuum" to arise), active propaganda against any return of Arab refugees, and help in settling them "elsewhere." See Morris (1987), chs. 4 and 5, esp. pp. 134–35, 163, 166–68, 170–79; Morris (2001); Morris (2004), chs. 2, 5, 6. On the ensuing campaign of ethnic cleansing and dispossession, see also Pappe (1999) and (2004), ch. 4; Benvenisti (2000), pp. 124–31; Fischbach (2003).

[33] In early summer 1948, a part of the Druze battalions of the Arab Liberation Army, which came mostly from Syria, joined the Israeli forces. Shortly thereafter, the Israeli army recruited from their ranks a so-called Minority Unit, which also included some Circassians (Arabic-speaking Muslims who were not ethnic Arabs) and Bedouins. In October this unit took part in Operation Hiram in Galilee. For collaboration of Druze civilians with Israeli military personnel, cf. Parsons (2000), esp. pp. 77–86; Morris (2004), pp. 416–18.

even to move about the country, providing them with significantly better conditions than those available to Muslim and Christian Arabs.

The ceasefire of July 18, 1948, did little to calm the situation. Even so, Israel developed its civilian infrastructure. In July it introduced its own currency and printed stamps (both of them still without the official state name), and in September it founded a supreme court. At the same time, international pressure to reach a peaceful agreement mounted. With American and British backing, Swedish UN mediator Count Folke Bernadotte demanded a right of return for the Arab refugees, the internationalization of Jerusalem, as well as territorial concessions. His aim was to prevent any great imbalance between the two sides and the corresponding danger of later irredentism. In September 1948, he was murdered by Lehi. Arab disunity starkly contrasted with Israeli state-building. To prevent Abdallah's feared land grab, the Arab League in September 1948 resolved to establish an All Palestine Government (*hukumat 'umum filastin*) based in Gaza, which the Egyptians had previously occupied.[34] Without adequate financial and military means, and without a functioning state apparatus, its claim to govern "all Palestine" was doomed to failure. In October 1948 Jordanian forces moved against the Mufti's loyalists in the Holy War Army, who stood in the way of Jordanian control of Arab Palestine. The guerrillas were disarmed and disbanded.

On October 15, 1948, the Israelis broke the armistice and pressed into the Egyptian-occupied Negev, not so much for economic reasons as for strategic and historical ones. The military operation was initially called Ten Plagues, evoking the ten plagues with which God had punished Pharaoh. In a bloody campaign (Operation Hiram), Israeli forces conquered the remaining parts of Galilee, which were defended by the Arab Liberation Army along with Syrian and Lebanese troops.[35] They also seized more than a dozen villages in southern Lebanon. As a result of these campaigns, an additional 100,000 to 150,000 Arabs were either expelled or fled. When a new armistice went into effect on October 31, the Israel army had conquered 77 percent of the former Mandate area. In January 1949 it entered the Sinai, but withdrew under international

---

[34] Shlaim (2001), pp. 96ff.; Shlaim (1990); Shabib (1988).

[35] Morris (2004), ch. 8. Here as in his earlier study (2001), pp. 48–57, Morris illustrates with the example of Operation Hiram (October 28–31, 1948) the deliberate use of atrocities (mass shootings of able-bodied men as well as women and children, rapes, mutilation of corpses, etc.) and expulsions that were designed to cleanse this part of Galilee of Arabs. For the campaign into Sinai, see Morris (2004), ch. 9. For the campaign of ethnic cleansing, see also Benvenisti (2000), ch. 4. Among the Egyptian troops caught in the Faluja salient was young officer Gamal Abd al-Nasir; cf. Rogan/Shlaim (eds.) (2001), pp. 98ff., 158.

pressure. The ceasefire of January 7, 1949, was not broken again by either side. It inaugurated the long state of "neither peace nor war" between Israel and its neighbors. As successor to UN mediator Folke Bernadotte, the American diplomat Ralph Bunche led the armistice negotiations on the island of Rhodes. Early in 1949 the armistice lines with Egypt, Syria, Lebanon, and Jordan were approved in their basic outlines. Following further discussions, agreements were signed in July (although rejected by Iraq), which more or less remained in effect until 1967. The Arab states had lacked a common strategy when entering the war, and they negotiated the armistice separately. Recognized international borders were only established much later, when Egypt made peace with Israel in 1979, followed in 1994 by Jordan. As of 2007, neither Syria nor Lebanon nor Iraq had taken this step, and Arab Palestine had not yet achieved independence.

Triumph and Catastrophe

In the first elections to the Israeli Knesset in 1949, victory went to the Labor Party (Mapai) under the leadership of David Ben-Gurion, with Chaim Weizmann elected president and Ben-Gurion himself prime minister. Following armed conflict between Irgun and the Hagana over a weapons shipment, which the Hagana claimed for itself as the official army of the State of Israel, Irgun surrendered and disbanded. Menachem Begin and a number of former Lehi fighters entered parliament (but not yet the government) as members of the Herut (Freedom) Party. Israel was able to build upon the institutions and structures of the Yishuv. In August 1949 the mortal remains of Theodor Herzl were transferred from Vienna to Jerusalem in a heavily symbolic act of state. Already in November 1948, the Israeli government had conducted a census, which set the number of Jews and Arabs at 782,000 and 69,000, respectively. By the end of 1949, the Jewish population had swelled from 600,000 to 1 million: in eighteen months, 350,000 Jews immigrated into the country.[36] The greater part did not come from Europe, but rather from the Near and Middle East. As a result of the first Arab-Israeli War, the foundation of Israel, and the ensuing flight and expulsion of Arab Palestinians, a "Jewish question" had now arisen in the Middle East where none had existed before, although it was of a very different character from the European one.

Palestinian defeat was total. The Israeli conquest of land was one factor that decisively influenced the further course of events; the refugee

---

[36] Morris (1987), pp. 188–96; Morris (2004), ch. 10, and Conclusion.

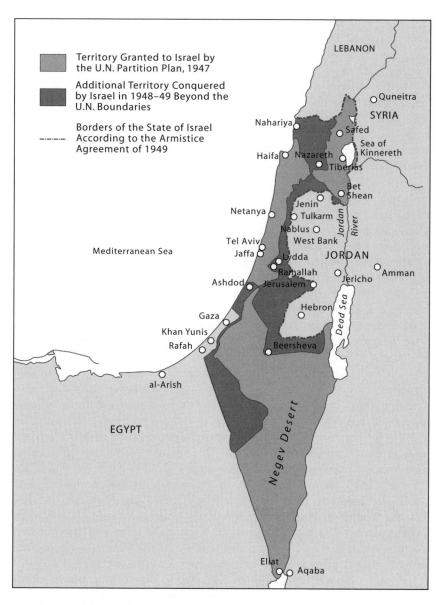

Map 8. The Armistice Lines of 1949

question was another. By the time the final armistice agreement was signed in July 1949, more than four hundred Arab villages had been abandoned, most of them destroyed and rendered uninhabitable— usually not through the war itself, but rather through deliberate action by the Israeli army and Jewish settlers. With the end of all restrictions on immigration, the number of Jewish immigrants to Israel soared, greatly increasing the pressure on the state and reducing its readiness to compromise. Arab villages, houses, fields, and businesses, which had been temporarily abandoned by their owners, were divided among the new Jewish immigrants. Not only did this create space, or *Lebensraum*, for them, it also served to eliminate any "fifth column" or prevent its appearance in the first place.[37] The policy was not uncontested. Many Israelis recognized that injustice was being done. The Socialist Mapam Party, for example, the coalition partner of Ben-Gurion's Mapai, spoke out against the "transfer" idea, against deportation, and in favor of the Arab right of return. But the opportunity resulting from the war to create an "Arab-free" Jewish territory was tempting—especially since a friendly attitude could hardly be expected from Arab returnees when they saw their property partly destroyed and partly plundered. The kibbutz movement was also opposed to a return of the refugees (despite their progressive attitudes, they were no champions of compromise with the Arabs). Others who were opposed included the authorities responsible for land and settlement, local Hagana commanders, and Jewish residents of isolated or formerly Arab-dominated areas such as Galilee.

Palestinians both inside and outside the occupied territories—occupied by Israel, Syria, Jordan, and Egypt—faced an uncertain future. Of the 1.4 million Arab residents living in Palestine at the end of the Mandate, around half (that is, between 700,000 and 760,000 people) either fled or were expelled between December 1947 and early 1949.[38] In the "West Bank," where hundreds of thousands of people had fled in 1947–49 from the areas conquered by Israel, King Abdallah installed his ally Raghib al-Nashashibi as military governor. Gaza was ruled by an Egyptian military administration. Even more uncertain was the fate of those who had fled beyond the borders of the Mandate region into neighboring Arab countries, or to Europe, America, or Australia.

We have spoken repeatedly of watersheds and turning points in the history of Palestine, deeply affecting its society, culture, and politics. The

---

[37] W. Khalidi (1992) covers events place by place, with maps and photographs. Morris (1987), ch. 5, and maps 2 and 3 (xii–xxii), lists the towns and villages from which Palestinians either fled or were expelled; Benvenisti (2000), esp. pp. 33–43, charts the campaign to rename settlements and sites after 1948 and thus erase the memories attached to them.

[38] Estimates in Morris (1987), pp. 297–98 (600,000 to 760,000); Morris (2001), p. 37 (700,000).

war of 1948–49 was such a watershed. For the Arab population, it was the catastrophe (al-nakba) plain and simple, the utter destruction of Arab Palestine as they had known it. For the Yishuv, it marked the realization of the bold dream of auto-emancipation and national self-determination, albeit not of security. For the surrounding Arab states and societies, it acted as a humiliating shock, highlighting the legitimacy crisis of the ruling elites (a crisis spurred not only by their failure in the first military conflict against a regional opponent). In those states that participated in the war (and other states as well), the defeat prompted radical political change: a series of military coups shook Syria, Egypt, and finally Iraq; in Jordan, King Abdallah fell victim to an assassin, though here unlike in Egypt no revolution occurred. The Arab-Israeli conflict over Palestine turned into one of the constituent elements of Middle Eastern politics. Even countries far beyond the Middle East, especially the United States and the Soviet Union, became entangled in it—whether willingly or not.

The myths and mystifications created by all parties, through which they hoped to make sense of events and to engender new forms of commitment and loyalty, would act for decades to shape collective notions of identity, justice, and injustice. In Israel critical historians began to question the official version of events at the close of the 1980s, spurred among other things by the 1982 Israeli invasion of Lebanon, and did so on the basis of the documents collected by the Jewish Yishuv and the Israeli state archives. They became known as the "new" or "revisionist" historians, though "revisionist" here was of course used in a completely different sense than in the political arena, where it referred to Jabotinsky's and Begin's notions of a Greater Israel. At the dawn of the twenty-first century, the Arab archives for the most crucial years remain sealed, and the political and intellectual climate in the Arab world is still unsuitable for a revisionist shattering of self-glorifying myths. In this respect, and not only in this respect, the asymmetry between the two sides persists.

BIBLIOGRAPHY

Aaronsohn, Ran (1990). "Cultural Landscape of Pre-Zionist Settlements." In *The Land That Became Israel*, edited by R. Kark, 147–163.

'Abd al-Ghani, 'Abd al-Rahman (1995). *Almaniya al-naziyya wa-filastin 1933–1945*. Beirut.

Abdel-Nour, Antoine (1982). *Introduction à l'histoire urbaine de la Syrie ottomane*. Beirut.

Abir, Mordechai (1975). "Local Leadership and Early Reforms in Palestine, 1800–1834." In *Studies on Palestine*, edited by M. Ma'oz, 284–310.

Abu-Husayn, A. R. (1985). *Provincial Leadership in Syria, 1575–1650*. Beirut.

Abu Jabir, Ra'uf Sa'd (2004). *al-Wujud al-masihi fi l-quds khilal al-qarnain al-tasi' 'ashar wa-l-'ishrin*. Beirut.

Abu-Manneh, Butrus (1986). "The Husaynis: The Rise of a Notable Family in 18th Century Palestine." In *Palestine in the Late Ottoman Period*, edited by D. Kushner, 93–108.

——— (1990). "Jerusalem in the Tanzimat Period: The New Ottoman Administration and the Notables." In *Die Welt des Islams*, 30: 1–44.

Adas, Michael (1981). "From Avoidance to Confrontation: Peasant Protest in Pre-colonial and Colonial Southeast Asia." In *Comparative Studies in Society and History*, 23: 217–247.

Aharoni, Yohanan, Michael Avi-Yonah, Anson F. Rainey, and Ze'ev Safrai (2002). *The Carta Bible Atlas*, fourth edition. Jerusalem.

Anderson, Benedict (1991). *Imagined Communities*, revised edition. London, New York.

Antonius, George (1969). *The Arab Awakening: The Story of the Arab National Movement*, reprint. Beirut.

Arbel, Ruth (ed.) (1996). *Blue and White in Color: Visual Images of Zionism, 1897–1947*. Tel Aviv.

al-'Arif, 'Arif (1944). *Bedouin Love, Law, and Legend, Dealing Exclusively with the Badu of Beersheba*. Jerusalem.

Arnon, Adar (1992). "The Quarters of Jerusalem in the Ottoman Period." In *Middle Eastern Studies*, 28,1: 1–65.

Arnon-Ohanna, Yuval (1981). "The Bands in the Palestinian Arab Revolt, 1936–1939: Structure and Organization." In *Asian and African Studies*, 15: 229–247.

al-'Asali, Bassam (1991a). *Thawrat al-buraq*. Beirut.

——— (1991b). *Thawrat al-shaikh 'Izz al-Din al-Qassam*. Beirut.

Asali, Kamil J. (ed.) (1997). *Jerusalem in History. 3000 B.C. to the Present Day*, revised edition. London, New York.

'Athamina, Khalil (2000). *Filastin fi khamsat qurun. Min al-fath al-islami hatta al-ghazw al-faranji (634–1099)*. Beirut.

Auld, Sylvia, and Robert Hillenbrand (eds.) (2000). *Ottoman Jerusalem. The Living City: 1517–1917.* 2 vols. Jerusalem.

Avci, Yasemin, and Vincent Lemire (2005). "De la modernité administrative à la modernisation urbaine: une réévaluation de la municipalité ottomane de Jérusalem (1867–1917)." In *Municipalités méditerranéennes. Les réformes urbaines ottomanes au miroir d'une histoire comparée (Moyen-Orient, Maghreb, Europe méridionale),* edited by N. Lafi, 73–138. Berlin.

Ayalon, Ami (2004). *Reading Palestine. Printing and Literacy, 1900–1948.* Austin.

Ayyad, Abdelaziz A. (1999). *Arab Nationalism and the Palestinians 1850–1939.* Jerusalem.

Bailey, Clinton (1980). "The Negev in the Nineteenth Century: Reconstructing History From Bedouin Oral Traditions." In *Asian and African Studies,* 14: 35–80.

——— (1990). "The Ottomans and the Bedouin Tribes of the Negev." In *Ottoman Palestine 1800–1914,* edited by G. Gilbar, 321–332.

Baldensperger, Philip J. (1893). "Religion of the Fellahin of Palestine." In *Palestine Exploration Fund. Quarterly Statement.* October 1893, 307–320.

Banse, Ewald (1934). *Das Buch vom Morgenlande,* third edition. Leipzig.

Ben-Arieh, Yehoshua (1984). *Jerusalem in the 19th Century: the Old City.* Jerusalem, New York.

——— (1979). *The Rediscovery of the Holy Land in the Nineteenth Century.* Jerusalem, Detroit.

Ben-Arieh, Yehoshua, and Moshe Davis (eds.) (1997). *Jerusalem in the Mind of the Western World, 1800–1948 (With Eyes toward Zion—V).* Westport, London.

Ben-David, Joseph (1990). "The Negev Bedouin: From Nomadism to Agriculture." In *The Land That Became Israel,* edited by R. Kark, 181–195.

Bentwich, Norman and Helen (1965). *Mandate Memoirs: 1918–1948.* London.

Benvenisti, Meron (2000). *Sacred Landscape. The Buried History of the Holy Land Since 1948.* Berkeley.

Berlin, Andrea M., and J. Andrew Overman (eds.) (2002). *The First Jewish Revolt: Archeology, History, and Ideology.* London, New York.

Bernstein, Deborah S. (2000). *Constructing Boundaries: Jewish and Arab Workers in Mandatory Palestine.* Albany, NY.

Bieberstein, Klaus, and Hanswulf Bloedhorn (1994). *Jerusalem. Grundzüge der Baugeschichte vom Chalkolithikum bis zur Frühzeit der osmanischen Herrschaft.* 3 vols. Wiesbaden.

Biger, Gideon (2004). *The Boundaries of Modern Palestine, 1840–1947.* London, New York.

——— (1990). "The Names and Boundaries of Eretz-Israel (Palestine) as Reflections of Stages in its History." In *The Land That Became Israel,* edited by R. Kark, 1–22.

Bimson, John J. (1991). "Merenptah's Israel and Recent Theories of Israelite Origins." In *Journal for the Study of the Old Testament,* 49: 3–29.

Birken, Andreas (1976). *Die Provinzen des Osmanischen Reiches.* Wiesbaden.

Black, Edwin (1984). *The Transfer Agreement: The Untold Story of the Secret Pact Between the Third Reich and Jewish Palestine.* New York, London.

Boehmer, Julius (1909). "Von Dan bis Berseba." In *Zeitschrift für die alttestamentliche Wissenschaft*, 29: 134–142.

Bowden, Tom (1977). *The Breakdown of Public Security: The Case of Ireland 1916–1921 and Palestine 1936–1939.* London, Beverly Hills.

Bowring, Sir John (1840). *Report on the Commercial Statistics of Syria.* London.

Braude, Benjamin, and Bernard Lewis (eds.) (1982). *Christians and Jews in the Ottoman Empire: The Functioning of a Plural Society.* 2 vols. New York.

Brenner, Michael (2002). *Geschichte des Zionismus.* Munich.

Brown, L. Carl (1984). *International Politics and the Middle East: Old Rules, Dangerous Games.* Princeton.

Budde, Hendrik, and Andreas Nachama (eds.) (1996). *Die Reise nach Jerusalem.* Berlin.

Burgoyne, Michael H. (1987). *Mamluk Jerusalem: An Architectural Study.* Buckhurst Hill.

Busailah, Reja-e (1981). "The Fall of Lydda, 1948: Impressions and Reminiscences." In *Arab Studies Quarterly*, 3: 123–151.

Busse, Heribert (1991). "Jerusalem in the Story of Muhammad's Night Journey and Ascension." In *Jerusalem Studies in Arabic and Islam*, 14: 1–40.

——— (1968). "The Sanctity of Jerusalem in Islam." In *Judaism*, 17: 441–468.

Campos, Michelle U. (2005). "Between 'Beloved Ottomania' and 'The Land of Israel': The Struggle over Ottomanism and Zionism Among Palestine's Sephardi Jews, 1908–13." In *International Journal of Middle East Studies*, 37: 461–483.

Canaan, Tewfik (1927). *Mohammedan Saints and Sanctuaries in Palestine.* Jerusalem.

Caplan, Neil (1983, 1986, 1997). *Futile Diplomacy.* 3 vols. London.

Carmel, Alex (2000). *Die Siedlungen der württembergischen Templer in Palästina 1868–1918*, third edition. Stuttgart.

Carmel, Alex, and Ejal Jakob Eisler (1999). *Der Kaiser reist ins Heilige Land. Die Palästinareise Wilhelms II. 1898.* Stuttgart.

Carmel, Alex, Peter Schäfer, and Yossi Ben-Artzi (eds.) (1990). *The Jewish Settlement in Palestine 634–1881.* Wiesbaden.

Cohen, Amnon (1989). *Economic Life in Ottoman Jerusalem.* Cambridge.

——— (2001). *The Guilds of Ottoman Jerusalem.* Leiden.

——— (1984). *Jewish Life under Islam: Jerusalem in the Sixteenth Century.* Cambridge.

——— (1973). *Palestine in the Eighteenth Century: Patterns of Government and Administration.* Jerusalem.

Cohen, Amnon, and Bernard Lewis (1978). *Population and Revenue in the Towns of Palestine in the Sixteenth Century.* Princeton.

Cohen, Michael J. (1978). *Palestine: Retreat from the Mandate: The Making of British Policy, 1936–45.* London.

Cohen, Shaye J. D. (1982). "Masada: Literary Tradition, Archaeological Remains, and the Credibility of Josephus." In *Journal of Jewish Studies*, 33, 1–2: 385–405.

Commins, David Dean (1990). *Islamic Reform: Politics and Social Change in Late Ottoman Syria*. New York, Oxford.

Courbage, Youssef, and Philippe Fargues (1992). *Chrétiens et Juifs dans l'Islam arabe et turc*. Paris.

Cuno, Kenneth M., and Michael J. Reimer (1997). "The Census Registers of Nineteenth-Century Egypt: A New Source for Social Historians." In *British Journal of Middle Eastern Studies*, 24: 193–216.

Dalman, Gustaf (1928–1941). *Arbeit und Sitte in Palästina*. 7 vols. Gütersloh.

—— (1925). *Hundert deutsche Fliegerbilder aus Palaestina*. Gütersloh.

Davis, John (1996). *The Landscape of Belief. Encountering the Holy Land in 19th Century American Art and Culture*. Princeton.

Davison, Roderic (1963). *Reform in the Ottoman Empire, 1856–1876*. Princeton.

Deringil, Selim (2002). "Jewish Immigration to the Ottoman Empire at the Time of the First Zionist Congresses: A Comment." In *The Last Ottoman Century and Beyond: The Jews in Turkey and the Balkans 1808–1945*, edited by M. Rozen. II: 141–149. Tel Aviv.

—— (1998). *The Well-Protected Domains: Ideology and the Legitimation of Power in the Ottoman Empire 1876–1909*. London, New York.

Divine, Donna Robinson (1994). *Politics and Society in Ottoman Palestine: The Arab Struggle for Survival and Power*. Boulder, London.

Dothan, Trude, and Moshe Dothan (1992). *People of the Sea: In Search for the Philistines*. New York.

Doumani, Beshara B. (1998). "Endowing Family: *Waqf*, Property Devolution, and Gender in Greater Syria, 1800 to 1860." In *Comparative Studies in Society and History*, 40: 3–41.

—— (1994). "The Political Economy of Population Counts in Ottoman Palestine: Nablus, circa 1850." In *International Journal of Middle East Studies*, 26: 1–17.

—— (1992). "Rediscovering Ottoman Palestine: Writing Palestinians into History." In *Journal of Palestine Studies*, 21: 5–28.

—— (1995). *Rediscovering Palestine: Merchants and Peasants in Jabal Nablus, 1700–1900*. Berkeley.

Douwes, Dick (2000). *The Ottomans in Syria: A History of Justice and Oppression*. London, New York.

Dumper, Michael (1994). *Islam and Israel: Muslim Religious Endowments and the Jewish State*. Washington, D.C.

Eckert, Willehad Paul, Nathan Peter Levinson, and Martin Stöhr (eds.) (1970). *Jüdisches Volk—gelobtes Land. Die biblischen Landverheißungen als Problem des jüdischen Selbstverständnisses und der christlichen Theologie*. Munich.

El-Eini, Roza I. M. (2006). *Mandated Landscape: British Imperial Rule in Palestine, 1929–1948*. London, New York.

Elad, Amikam (1995). *Medieval Jerusalem and Islamic Worship: Holy Places, Ceremonies, Pilgrimage*. Leiden.

—— (1996). "Pilgrims and Pilgrimage to Hebron (al-Khalil) During the Early

Muslim Period (638?–1099)." In *Pilgrims & Travelers*, edited by B. Le Beau and M. Mor, 21–62.

Elliot, Matthew (2004). "Dress codes in the Ottoman Empire: the case of the Franks." In *Ottoman Costumes*, edited by S. Faroqhi and C. Neumann, 103–123.

Elmendorf, Dwight L. (1912). *A Camera Crusade Through the Holy Land*. New York.

Elpeleg, Zvi (1993). *The Grand Mufti, Haj Amin al-Hussaini, Founder of the Palestinian National Movement*. London.

Enderwitz, Susanne (1996). "Die muslimische Eroberung Jerusalems." In *Die Reise nach Jerusalem*, edited by H. Budde and A. Nachama, 32–39.

—— (2002). *Unsere Situation schuf unsere Erinnerungen. Palästinensische Autobiographien zwischen 1967 und 2000*. Wiesbaden.

Eskenazi, Tamara C., and Kent H. Richards (eds.) (1994). *Second Temple Studies*. Sheffield.

Fahmy, Khaled (1998). "The Era of Muhammad 'Ali Pasha, 1805–1848." In *The Cambridge History of Egypt*, edited by M. W. Daly. II: 139–179. Cambridge.

Faroqhi, Suraiya (1990). *Herrscher über Mekka. Die Geschichte der Pilgerfahrt*. Munich, Zurich.

Faroqhi, Suraiya, Bruce McGowen, Donald Quataert, and Şevket Pamuk (1994). *An Economic and Social History of the Ottoman Empire. II: 1600–1914*. Cambridge.

Faroqhi, Suraiya, and Christoph K. Neumann (eds.) (2004). *Ottoman Costumes: From Textile to Identity*. Istanbul.

Farschid, Olaf, Manfred Kropp, and Stephan Dähne (eds.) (2006). *The First World War as Remembered in the Countries of the Eastern Mediterranean*. Beirut, Würzburg.

Findley, Carter V. (1980). *Bureaucratic Reform in the Ottoman Empire: The Sublime Porte, 1789–1922*. Princeton.

—— (1988). *Ottoman Civil Officialdom: A Social History*. Princeton.

Finkelstein, Israel (1988). *The Archaeology of the Israelite Settlement*. Jerusalem.

Finkelstein, Norman G. (1995). *Image and Reality of the Israel-Palestine Conflict*. London, New York.

Finn, James (1878). *Stirring Times*, edited by E. A. Finn. 2 vols. London.

Firestone, Ya'akov (1990). "The Land-Equalizing *musha'* Village: A Reassessment." In *Ottoman Palestine 1800–1914*, edited by G. Gilbar, 91–129.

Fischbach, Michael R. (2003). *Records of Dispossession: Palestinian Refugee Property and the Arab-Israeli Conflict*. New York.

Flapan, Simha (1987). *The Birth of Israel: Myths and Realities*. New York, Toronto.

Fleischmann, Ellen L. (2003). *The Nation and its "New" Women: The Palestinian Women's Movement 1920–1948*. Berkeley, Los Angeles.

Flores, Alexander (1980). *Nationalismus und Sozialismus im arabischen Osten. Kommunistische Partei und arabische Nationalbewegung in Palästina 1919–1948*. Münster.

Fohrer, Georg (1969). "Zion-Jerusalem im Alten Testament." In *Studien zur alttestamentlichen Theologie und Geschichte (1949–1966)*, edited by G. Fohrer, 195–241. Berlin.

Friedland, Roger, and Richard D. Hecht (1996). "The Pilgrimage to Nebi Musa and the Origins of Palestinian Nationalism." In *Pilgrims & Travelers to the Holy Land*, edited by B. Le Beau and M. Mor, 89–118.

Friling, Tuvia (2002). "Between Friendly and Hostile Neutrality: Turkey and the Jews during World War II." In *The Last Ottoman Century and Beyond: The Jews in Turkey and the Balkans 1808–1945*, edited by M. Rozen. II: 309–423. Tel Aviv.

Frischwasser-Ra'anan, H. F. (1976). *The Frontiers of a Nation: A re-examination of the forces which created the Palestine Mandate and determined its territorial shape*, reprint. Westport.

Fromkin, David (1989). *A Peace to End All Peace: Creating the Modern Middle East 1914–1922*. London.

Gafni, Isaiah (1981). "Reinterment in the Land of Israel: Notes on the Origin and Development of the Custom." In *The Jerusalem Cathedra* I: 96–104.

Galnoor, Itzhak (1995). *The Partition of Palestine: Decision Crossroads in the Zionist Movement*. Albany, NY.

Garfinkle, Adam M. (1991). "On the Origin, Meaning, Use and Abuse of a Phrase." In *Middle Eastern Studies*, 27: 539–550.

Gavish, Dov (1990). "Aerial Perspectives of Past Landscapes." In *The Land That Became Israel*, edited by R. Kark, 308–319.

Gelber, Joav (1997). *Jewish-Transjordanian Relations, 1921–48*. London, Portland.

Gelvin, James L. (1998). *Divided Loyalties: Nationalism and Mass Politics in Syria at the Close of Empire*. Berkeley.

Gensicke, Klaus (1988). *Der Mufti von Jerusalem, Amin el-Husseini, und die Nationalsozialisten*, Frankfurt.

Gerber, Haim (1985). *Ottoman Rule in Jerusalem, 1890–1914*. Berlin.

―――― (1998). "'Palestine' and Other Territorial Concepts in the 17th Century." In *International Journal of Middle East Studies*, 30: 563–572.

―――― (1979). "The Population of Syria and Palestine in the Nineteenth Century." In *Asian* and *African Studies*, 13: 58–80.

―――― (1987). *The Social Origins of the Modern Middle East*. Boulder.

Gershoni, Israel, and James Jankowski (eds.) (1997). *Rethinking Nationalism in the Arab Middle East*. New York.

Gidal, Nachum T. (1982). *Eternal Jerusalem, 1840–1917*. Munich, Lucerne.

Gil, Moshe (1997). *A History of Palestine, 634–1099*. Cambridge.

Gilbar, Gad (ed.) (1990). *Ottoman Palestine 1800–1914. Studies in Social and Economic History*. Leiden.

Gilbert, Martin (1994). *Jerusalem: Illustrated History Atlas*, third edition. Bnei Brak.

Gorni, Josef (1987). *Zionism and the Arabs, 1882–1948: A Study of Ideology*. Oxford.

Gottheil, Fred M. (1979). "The Population of Palestine, circa 1875." In *Middle Eastern Studies*, 15: 310–321.

Graham-Brown, Sarah (1980). *Palestinians and Their Society 1880–1946: A Photographic Essay*. London

—— (1982). "The Political Economy of the Jabal Nablus, 1920–48." In *Studies in the Economic and Social History of Palestine*, edited by R. Owen, 88–176.

Halper, Jeff (1991). *Between Redemption and Revival: The Jewish Yishuv of Jerusalem in the Nineteenth Century*. Boulder.

Hartmann, Martin (1883). "Die Ortschaftenliste des Liwa Jerusalem in dem türkischen Staatskalender für Syrien für das Jahr 1288 der Flucht (1871)." In *Zeitschrift des Deutschen Palästina-Vereins*, 6: 102–49.

Hasso, Frances S. (2000). "Modernity and Gender in Arab Accounts of the 1948 and 1967 Defeats." In *International Journal of Middle East Studies*, 32: 491–510.

Herzl, Theodor (1947). *The Jewish State*. New York.

—— (1936). *Der Judenstaat*, eleventh edition. Berlin.

Himadeh, Sa'id B. (ed.) (1938). *Economic Organization of Palestine*. Beirut.

Hobsbawm, Eric J. (1979). *Sozialrebellen. Archaische Sozialbewegungen im 19. und 20. Jahrhundert*. Giessen.

Hobsbawm, Eric, and Terence Ranger (eds.) (1983). *The Invention of Tradition*. Cambridge.

Hoexter, Miriam (1973). "The Role of the Qays and Yaman Factions in Local Political Divisions: Jabal Nablus Compared with the Judean Hills in the First Half of the Nineteenth Century." In *Asian and African Studies*, 9: 249–311.

Höpp, Gerhard (1999). "Der Gefangene im Dreieck. Zum Bild Amin al-Husseinis in Wissenschaft und Publizistik seit 1941. Ein bio-bibliographischer Abriß." In *Eine umstrittene Figur: Hadj Amin al-Husseini, Mufti von Jerusalem*, edited by R. Zimmer-Winkel, 5–23. Trier.

—— (ed.) (2001). *Mufti-Papiere. Briefe, Memoranden, Reden und Aufrufe Amin al-Husainis aus dem Exil, 1940–1945*. Berlin.

Höpp, Gerhard, Peter Wien, and René Wildangel (eds.) (2004). *Blind für die Geschichte? Arabische Begegnungen mit dem Nationalsozialismus*. Berlin.

Hopwood, Derek (1969). *The Russian Presence in Syria and Palestine, 1843–1914*. Oxford.

Hourani, Albert (1968). "Ottoman Reform and the Politics of Notables." In *Beginnings of Modernization in the Middle East*, edited by W. Polk and R. Chambers, 41–68. Chicago.

Howe, Kathleen Stewart (1997). *Revealing the Holy Land: The Photographic Exploration of Palestine*. Santa Barbara.

al-Husaini, Amin (1999). *Mudhakkirat al-hajj Muhammad Amin al-Husaini*, edited by 'Abd al-Karim al-'Umar. Damascus.

al-Hut, Bayan N. (1981). *al-Qiyadat wa-l-mu'assasat al-siyasiyya fi filastin, 1917–1948*. Beirut.

—— (ed.) (1979). *Watha'iq al-haraka al-wataniyya al-filastiniyya 1918–1939. Min awraq Akram Zu'aitir*. Beirut.

Hütteroth, Wolf-Dieter (1978). *Palästina und Transjordanien im 16. Jahrhundert. Wirtschaftsstruktur ländlicher Siedlungen nach osmanischen Steuerregistern*. Wiesbaden.

Hütteroth, Wolf-Dieter, and Kamal Abdulfattah (1977). *Historical Geography of Palestine, Transjordan and Southern Syria in the Late Sixteenth Century.* Erlangen.

Hyamson, A. M. (1939–41). *The British Consulate in Jerusalem in Relation to the Jews of Palestine 1838–1914.* London.

Inalcik, Halil (1977). "Centralization and Decentralization in the Ottoman Empire." In *Studies in Eighteenth-Century Islamic History,* edited by T. Naff and R. Owen, 27–52. Carbondale.

——— (1994). *An Economic and Social History of the Ottoman Empire. I: 1300–1600.* Cambridge.

Ingrams, Doreen (1972). *Palestine Papers 1917–1922. Seeds of Conflict.* London.

de Jong, Frederick (1983). "The Sufi Orders in Nineteenth and Twentieth Century Palestine: A Preliminary Survey concerning Their Identity, Organisational Characteristics and Continuity." In *Studia Islamica 58,* 149–181.

Joudah, Ahmad H. (1987). *Revolt in Palestine in the Eighteenth Century: The Era of Shaykh Zahir al-Umar.* Princeton.

Kaiser, Wolf (1992). *Palästina—Erez Israel. Deutschsprachige Reisebeschreibungen jüdischer Autoren von der Jahrhundertwende bis zum Zweiten Weltkrieg.* Hildesheim.

Kalkas, Barbara (1971). "The Revolt of 1936: A Chronicle of Events." In *The Transformation of Palestine,* edited by I. Abu-Lughod, 237–74. Evanston.

Kaplony, Andreas (2002). *The Haram of Jerusalem, 324–1099: Temple, Friday Mosque, Area of Spiritual Power.* Stuttgart.

Kark, Ruth (ed.) (1990). *The Land That Became Israel: Studies in Historical Geography.* New Haven.

——— (1990). "Transportation in Nineteenth-Century Palestine: Reintroduction of the Wheel." In *The Land That Became Israel,* edited by R. Kark, 57–76.

Karmi, Ghada, and Eugene Cotran (eds.) (1999). *The Palestinian Exodus 1948–1998.* Reading.

Karpat, Kemal H. (1974). "Ottoman Immigration Policies and Settlement in Palestine." In *Settler Regimes in Africa and the Arab World: The Illusion of Endurance,* edited by I. Abu-Lughod and B. Abu-Laban, 57–72. Wilmette, IL.

——— (1978). "Ottoman Population Records and the Census of 1881/82–1893." In *International Journal of Middle East Studies,* 9: 237–274.

Katz, Itamar, and Ruth Kark (2005). "The Greek Orthodox Patriarchate of Jerusalem and Its Congregation: Dissent over Real Estate." In *International Journal of Middle East Studies,* 37: 509–534.

Kayali, Hasan (1997). *Arabs and Young Turks: Ottomanism, Arabism, and Islamism in the Ottoman Empire, 1908–1918.* Los Angeles, London.

Kedourie, Elie (1978). *England and the Middle East,* second edition. Hassocks.

——— (1976). *In the Anglo-Arab Labyrinth: The McMahon-Husayn Correspondence and Its Interpretations 1914–1939.* Cambridge.

Khalaf, Issa (1991). *Politics in Palestine: Arab Factionalism and Social Disintegration, 1939–1948.* Albany, NY.

Khalidi, Rashid I. (1997). *Palestinian Identity: The Construction of Modern National Consciousness.* New York.

Khalidi, Rashid, et al. (eds.) (1991). *The Origins of Arab Nationalism*. New York.

Khalidi, Walid (1992). *All That Remains: The Palestinian Villages Occupied and Depopulated by Israel in 1948*. Washington.

—— (1984). *Before Their Diaspora: A Photographic History of the Palestinians 1876–1948*. Washington.

—— (1988). "Plan Dalet: Master Plan for the Conquest of Palestine." In *Journal of Palestine Studies*, 18: 4–70.

—— (1997). "Revisiting the UNGA Partition Resolution." In *Journal of Palestine Studies*, 27: 5–21.

Khoury, Philip S. (1983). *Urban Notables and Arab Nationalism: The Politics of Damascus 1860–1920*. Cambridge.

Klein, Samuel (1928). "Das tannaitische Grenzenverzeichnis Palästinas." In *Hebrew Union College Annual*, 5: 197–259.

Kobler, Franz (1956). *The Vision Was There: A History of the British Movement for the Restoration of the Jews to Palestine*. London.

Kolinsky, Martin (1993). *Law, Order and Riots in Mandatory Palestine, 1928–35*. London.

Konrad, Robert (1965). "Das himmlische und das irdische Jerusalem im mittelalterlichen Denken. Mystische Vorstellung und geschichtliche Wirkung." In *Speculum Historiale*, edited by C. Bauer, L. Boehm, and M. Müller, 523–540. Freiburg, Munich.

Krämer, Gudrun (2006). "Anti-Semitism in the Muslim World: A Critical Review." In *Die Welt des Islams*, 46,3: 243–276.

Kramer, Martin (1986). *Islam Assembled: The Advent of the Muslim Congresses*. New York.

Kreiser, Klaus (2005). "Turban and türban: 'Divider between belief and unbelief.' A political history of modern Turkish costume." In *European Review*, 13,3: 447–458.

Krüger, Jürgen (2000). *Die Grabeskirche zu Jerusalem. Geschichte—Gestalt—Bedeutung*. Regensburg.

Kühnel, Bianca (1987). *From the Earthly to the Heavenly Jerusalem: Representations of the Holy City in the Christian Art of the First Millenium*. Rome.

Kunt, Metin (1983). *The Sultan's Servants: The Transformation of Ottoman Provincial Government, 1550–1650*. New York.

Kupferschmidt, Uri M. (1986). "A Note on the Muslim Religious Hierarchy Towards the End of the Ottoman Period." In *Palestine in the Late Ottoman Period*, edited by D. Kushner, 123–129.

—— (1987). *The Supreme Muslim Council: Islam under the British Mandate for Palestine*. Leiden.

Kushner, David (1999). "The District of Jerusalem in the Eyes of Three Ottoman Governors at the End of the Hamidian Period." In *Middle Eastern Studies*, 35,2: 83–102.

—— (ed.) (1986), *Palestine in the Late Ottoman Period: Political, Social and Economic Transformation*. Jerusalem.

Lachman, Shai (1982). "Arab Rebellion and Terrorism in Palestine 1929–39: The Case of Sheikh Izz al-Din al-Qassam and His Movement." In *Zionism and Arabism in Palestine and Israel*, edited by E. Kedourie and S. Haim, 52–99. London.

Landau, Jacob M. (1979). *Abdul-Hamid's Palestine*. London.

Laurens, Henry (1999). *La Question de Palestine. I: 1799–1922. L'invention de la Terre sainte*. Paris.

Lazarus-Yafeh, Hava (1981). "The Sanctity of Jerusalem in Islam." In *Studies in the History of Religions*, 42: 58–71.

Le Beau, Bryan F., and Menachem Mor (eds.) (1996). *Pilgrims & Travelers to the Holy Land*. Omaha.

Lemche, Niels Peter (1991). *The Canaanites and Their Land: The Tradition of the Canaanites*. Sheffield.

——— (1994). "Is It Still Possible to Write a History of Ancient Israel?" In *Scandinavian Journal of the Old Testament*, 8: 165–190.

Lesch, Ann Mosely (1979). *Arab Politics in Palestine, 1917–1939: The Frustration of a Nationalist Movement*. Ithaca, NY.

LeVine, Mark (2005). *Overthrowing Geography: Jaffa, Tel Aviv, and the Struggle for Palestine, 1880–1948*. Berkeley.

Levy, Avigdor (ed.) (1994). *The Jews of the Ottoman Empire*. Princeton.

Lewis, Bernard (1980). "Palestine: On the History and Geography of a Name." In *The International History Review*, II: 1–12.

Lewis, Norman N. (1987). *Nomads and Settlers in Syria and Jordan, 1800–1980*. Cambridge.

Lindisfarne-Tapper, Nancy, and Bruce Ingham (1997). *Languages of Dress in the Middle East*. Richmond.

Lockman, Zachary (1996). *Comrades and Enemies: Arab and Jewish Workers in Palestine, 1906–1948*. Berkeley.

Luncz, A. M. (ed.) (1882). *Jerusalem. Jahrbuch zur Beförderung der wissenschaftlich genauen Kenntnis des jetzigen und des alten Palästinas*. Vienna.

Macalister, R. A. Stewart, and E.W.G. Masterman (1904–1906). "Occasional Papers on the Modern Inhabitants of Palestine." In *Palestine Exploration Fund: Quarterly Statement*, 1904: 150–160; 1905: 48–60, 343–356; 1906: 33–50.

Mandel, Neville (1976). *The Arabs and Zionism Before World War I*. Berkeley.

Manna', 'Adil (1998). *A'lam filastin fi awakhir al-'ahd al-'uthmani (1800–1918)*, third edition. Beirut.

——— (1992). "Continuity and Change in the Socio-Political Elite in Palestine During the late Ottoman Period." In *The Syrian Land*, edited by T. Philipp, 69–90.

——— (1999). *Tarikh filastin fi awakhir al-'ahd al-'uthmani: 1800–1918. qira'a jadida*. Beirut.

Ma'oz, Moshe (1968). *Ottoman Reform in Syria and Palestine 1840–1861*. Oxford.

——— (ed.) (1975). *Studies on Palestine During the Ottoman Period*. Jerusalem.

Marcus, Abraham (1989). *The Middle East on the Eve of Modernity: Aleppo in the Eighteenth Century*. New York.

Marsot, Afaf Lutfi al-Sayyid (1984). *Egypt in the Reign of Muhammad Ali*. Cambridge.

Masalha, Nur (1992). *Expulsion of the Palestinians: The Concept of "Transfer" in Zionist Political Thought 1882–1948*. Washington.

Mattar, Philip (1988). *The Mufti of Jerusalem: Al-Hajj Amin al-Husayni and the Palestinian National Movement*. New York.

Matthews, Charles D. (1936). "A Muslim Iconoclast (Ibn Taymiyyeh) on the 'Merits' of Jerusalem and Palestine." In *Journal of the American Oriental Society*, 56: 1–21.

Mayer, Thomas (1983). *Egypt and the Palestine Question, 1936–1945*. Berlin.

McCarthy, Justin (1990). *The Population of Palestine: Population Statistics of the Late Ottoman Period and the Mandate*. New York.

Mendes-Flohr, Paul, and Jehuda Reinharz (eds.) (1995). *The Jew in the Modern World: A Documentary History*, second edition. New York, Oxford.

Merkley, Paul C. (1998). *The Politics of Christian Zionism 1891–1948*. London, Portland.

Metzer, Jacob (1998). *The Divided Economy of Mandatory Palestine*. Cambridge.

Miller, Patrick D., Paul D. Hanson, and S. Dean McBride (eds.) (1987). *Ancient Israelite Religion: Essays in Honor of Frank Moore Cross*. Philadelphia.

Miller, Ylana N. (1985). *Government and Society in Rural Palestine 1920–1948*. Austin.

Mogannam, Matiel (1937). *The Arab Woman and the Palestine Problem*. London.

Monk, Daniel B. (2002). *An Aesthetic Occupation: The Immediacy of Architecture and the Palestine Conflict*. Durham, London.

Moors, Annelies (1995). *Women, Property, and Islam: Palestinian Experiences, 1920–1990*. Cambridge.

Morris, Benny (1987). *The Birth of the Palestinian Refugee Problem, 1947–1949*. Cambridge.

⸺ (2004). *The Birth of the Palestinian Refugee Problem Revisited*. Cambridge.

⸺ (2001). "Revisiting the Palestinian Exodus of 1948." In *The War for Palestine*, edited by E. Rogan and A. Shlaim, 37–59.

⸺ (2003). *The Road to Jerusalem: Glubb Pasha, Palestine and the Jews*. London, New York.

Mossek, M. (1978). *Palestine Immigration Policy under Sir Herbert Samuel: British, Zionist and Arab Attitudes*. London.

Munayyir, Isbir (1997). *al-Lidd fi ʿahday al-intidab wa-l-ihtilal*. Beirut.

Muslih, Muhammad Y. (1988). *The Origins of Palestinian Nationalism*. New York.

Nadan, Amos (2003). "Colonial Misunderstanding of an Efficient Peasant Institution: Land Settlement and *Mushaʿ* Tenure in Mandate Palestine, 1921–47." In *Journal of the Economic and Social History of the Orient*, 46: 320–354.

⸺ (2006). *The Palestinian Peasant Economy under the Mandate: A Story of Colonial Bungling*. Cambridge, London.

Nafi, Basheer (1998). *Arabism, Islamism and the Palestine Question 1908–1941: A Political History*. Reading.

⸺ (1997). "Shaykh ʿIzz al-Din al-Qassam: A Reformist and a Rebel Leader." In *Journal of Islamic Studies*, 8: 185–215.

al-Najjar, ʿAʾida (2005). *Sihafat filastin wa-l-haraka al-wataniyya fi nisf qarn, 1900–1948*. Beirut.

Naor, Mordecai (1998). *Eretz Israel. Das Zwanzigste Jahrhundert*. Cologne.

von Naredi-Rainer, Paul (1994). *Salomos Tempel und das Abendland. Monumentale Folgen historischer Irrtümer*. Cologne.

Nashashibi, Nasser Eddin (1990). *Jerusalem's Other Voice: Ragheb Nashashibi and Moderation in Palestinian Politics, 1920–1948*. Exeter.

Nebenzahl, Kenneth (1986). *Maps of the Holy Land*. New York.

Neuwirth, Angelika (1993). "Erste Qibla—Fernstes Masdschid? Jerusalem im Horizont des historischen Muhammad." In *Zion—Ort der Begegnung. Festschrift für L. Klein zur Vollendung des 65. Lebensjahres*, edited by F. Hahn et al., 227–270. Bodenheim.

——— (1996). "Jerusalem—Ein Ort auch islamischer Erinnerung." In *Die Reise nach Jerusalem*, edited by H. Budde and A. Nachama, 24–31.

Nicosia, Francis (1985). *The Third Reich and the Palestine Question*. Austin.

al-Nimr, Ihsan (1961–1975). *Tarikh Jabal Nablus wa-l-Balqaʾ*. 4 vols. Nablus.

Nir, Yeshayahu (1985). *The Bible and the Image: The History of Photography in the Holy Land, 1839–1899*. Philadelphia.

Norton, John (1997). "Faith and Fashion in Turkey." In *Languages of Dress*, edited by N. Lindisfarne-Tapper and B. Ingham, 147–177.

al-Nuʿaimi, Ahmad Nuri (1998). *al-Yahud fi l-dawla al-ʿuthmaniyya*, second edition. Jerusalem, Amman.

Osman, Colin (1999). *Jerusalem: Caught in Time*. Cairo.

al-Osta, Adel (1993). *Die Juden in der palästinensischen Literatur zwischen 1913 und 1987*. Berlin.

Owen, Roger (1981). *The Middle East in the World Economy, 1800–1914*. London, New York.

——— (ed.) (2000). *New Perspectives on Property and Land in the Middle East*. Cambridge.

——— (ed.) (1982). *Studies in the Economic and Social History of Palestine in the Nineteenth and Twentieth Centuries*. Carbondale, IL.

Pappe, Ilan (2004). *A History of Modern Palestine: One Land, Two Peoples*. Cambridge.

——— (ed.) (1999). *The Israel/Palestine Question: Rewriting Histories*. London, New York.

——— (1999). "Were They Expelled? The History, Historiography and Relevance of the Palestinian Refugee Problem." In *The Palestinian Exodus 1948–1998*, edited by G. Karmi and E. Cotran, 37–61.

Parfitt, Tudor (1987). *The Jews in Palestine 1800–1882*. Woodbridge, Wolfeboro.

Parry, Y. J., and Malcolm E. Yapp (eds.) (1975). *War, Technology, and Society in the Middle East*. London.

Parsons, Laila (2000). *The Druze between Palestine and Israel, 1947–49*. Houndmills, London.

The Peel Commission Report: Report of the Palestine Royal Commission presented by the Secretary of State for the Colonies to the United Kingdom Parliament by Command of His Britannic Majesty (July 1937). London.

Perlitt, Lothar (1983). "Motive und Schichten der Landtheologie im Deuteronomium." In *Das Land Israel in biblischer Zeit*, edited by G. Strecker, 46–58.

Petermann, Heinrich (1976). *Reisen im Orient 1852–1855*, reprint. Amsterdam.

Peters, F. E. (1986). *Jerusalem and Mecca: The Typology of the Holy City in the Near East*. New York.

Peters, Rudolph (1996). *Jihad in Classical and Modern Islam*. Princeton.

Philipp, Thomas (2001). *Acre: The Rise and Fall of a Palestinian City, 1730–1831*. New York.

—— (1998). "Highways and Sea Lanes in Southwest Syria in the 18th Century." In *The Syrian Land*, edited by T. Philipp and B. Schaebler, 3–18.

—— (ed.) (1992). *The Syrian Land in the Eighteenth and Nineteenth Century*. Stuttgart.

Philipp, Thomas, and Birgit Schaebler (eds.) (1998). *The Syrian Land: Processes of Integration and Fragmentation. Bilad Al-Sham from the 18th to the 20th Century*. Stuttgart.

Pierotti, Ermete (1864). *Customs and Traditions of Palestine Illustrating the Manners of the Ancient Hebrews*. Cambridge, London.

Porath, Yehoshua (1974). *The Emergence of the Palestinian Arab National Movement, 1918–1929*. London.

—— (1977). *The Palestinian Arab National Movement: From Riots to Rebellion*. London.

Provence, Michael (2005). *The Great Syrian Revolt and the Rise of Arab Nationalism*. Austin.

Al-Qattan, Najwa (2004). "*Safarbarlik*: Ottoman Syria and the Great War." In *From the Syrian Land to the States of Syria and Lebanon*, edited by T. Philipp and C. Schumann, 163–173. Beirut, Würzburg.

Quataert, Donald (1997). "Clothing Laws, State, and Society in the Ottoman Empire, 1720–1829." In *International Journal of Middle East Studies*, 29: 403–425.

Raby, Julian, and Jeremy Johns (eds.) (1992). *Bayt al-Maqdis. ʿAbd al-Malik's Jerusalem*. Part I, Oxford.

al-Radiʿi, Yusuf Rajab (1982). *Thawrat 1936 fi filastin: dirasa ʿaskariyya*. Beirut.

Rasmussen, Carl G. (2000). *Historisch-Geografischer Atlas zur Bibel*, second edition. Holzgerlingen.

Redford, Donald P. (1992). *Egypt, Canaan, and Israel in Ancient Times*. Princeton.

Reinkowski, Maurus (1995). *Filastin, Filistin und Eretz Israel. Die späte osmanische Herrschaft über Palästina in der arabischen, türkischen und israelischen Historiographie*. Berlin.

—— (1999). "Late Ottoman Rule over Palestine: Its Evaluation in Arab, Turkish and Israeli Histories, 1970–90." In *Middle Eastern Studies*, 35: 66–97.

Reiter, Yitzhak (1996). *Islamic Endowments in Jerusalem under British Mandate*. London, Portland.

Rogan, Eugene L., and Avi Shlaim (eds.) (2001). *The War for Palestine: Rewriting the History of 1948*. Cambridge.

Röhricht, Reinhold (1890). *Bibliotheca Geographica Palaestinae: Chronologisches Verzeichnis der auf die Geographie des Heiligen Landes bezüglichen Literatur von 333 bis 1878 und der Versuch einer Kartographie*, reprint. Berlin.

Rood, Judith Mendelsohn (2004). *Sacred Law in the Holy City: The Khedival Challenge to the Ottomans as seen from Jerusalem, 1829–1841*. Leiden.

Rosovsky, Nitza (ed.) (1996). *City of the Great King: Jerusalem from David to the Present*. Cambridge.

Rubin, Rehav (1999). *Image and Reality: Jerusalem in Maps and Views*. Jerusalem.

Safi, Khaled (2004). *The Egyptian Rule in Palestine 1831–1840: A Critical Reassessment*. Berlin.

Safrai, Shmuel (1983), "The Land of Israel in Tannaitic Halacha." In *Das Land Israel in biblischer Zeit*, edited by G. Strecker, 201–215.

Sakakini, Hala (1987). *Jerusalem and I: A Personal Record*. Jerusalem.

Salih, Muhsin Muhammad (1989). *al-Tayyar al-islami fi filastin wa-atharuhu fi harakat al-jihad, 1917–1948*, second edition. Kuwait.

Salmon, Yosef (2002). *Religion and Zionism: First Encounters*. Jerusalem.

Schaebler, Birgit (2000). "Practicing *Musha'*: Common Lands and the Common Good in Southern Syria under the Ottomans and the French." In *New Perspectives on Property and Land in the Middle East*, edited by R. Owen, 241–311.

Schatkowski Schilcher, Linda (1992). "The Famine of 1915–1918 in Greater Syria." In *Problems of the Modern Middle East in Historical Perspective: Essays in Honour of Albert Hourani*, edited by J. P. Spagnolo, 227–258. Oxford, Reading.

Scheben, Thomas (1991). *Verwaltungsreformen der frühen Tanzimatzeit. Gesetze, Maßnahmen, Auswirkungen*. Frankfurt.

Schleifer, S. Abdullah (1979). "The Life and Thought of 'Izz-id-Din al-Qassam." In *The Islamic Quarterly*, 23: 61–81.

Schlör, Joachim (1999). *Tel Aviv. Vom Traum zur Stadt*. Gerlingen.

Schmelz, Uziel O. (1990). "Population characteristics of Jerusalem and Hebron regions according to Ottoman census of 1905." In *Ottoman Palestine 1800–1914*, edited by G. Gilbar, 15–67.

——— (1975). "Some Demographic Peculiarities of the Jews of Jerusalem in the Nineteenth Century." In *Studies on Palestine*, edited by M. Ma'oz, 119–141.

Schölch, Alexander (1985). "The Demographic Development of Palestine, 1850–1882." In *International Journal of Middle East Studies*, 17: 485–505.

——— (1986). *Palästina im Umbruch*. Berlin.

Segev, Tom (2000). *One Palestine, Complete: Jews and Arabs under the British Mandate*. New York.

Seikaly, May (1998). *Haifa: Transformation of an Arab Society, 1918–1939*. London, New York.

Shabib, Samih (1988). *Hukumat 'umum filastin. Muqaddimat wa-nata'ij*. Nicosia.

Shafir, Gershon (1989). *Land, Labor and the Origins of the Israeli-Palestinian Conflict 1882–1914*. Cambridge.

Shama, Simon (1995). *Landscape and Memory*. New York.

Shamir, Ronen (2000). *The Colonies of Law: Colonialism, Zionism and Law in Early Mandate Palestine*. Cambridge.

Shapira, Anita (1992). *Land and Power. The Zionist Resort to Force, 1881–1948.* Stanford.

Shaw, Stanford J. (1975). "The Nineteenth-Century Ottoman Tax Reforms and Revenue System." In *International Journal of Middle East Studies,* 6: 421–459.

—— (1978). "The Ottoman Census System and Population, 1831–1914." In *International Journal of Middle East Studies,* 9: 325–338.

Sherman, A. J. (1997). *Mandate Days: British Lives in Palestine 1918–1948.* Baltimore, London.

Shilony, Zvi (1998). *Ideology and Settlement: The Jewish National Fund, 1897–1914.* Jerusalem.

Shimoni, Gideon (1995). *The Zionist Ideology.* Hanover, London.

Shlaim, Avi (2001). "Israel and the Arab Coalition in 1948." In *The War for Palestine,* edited by E. Rogan and A. Shlaim, 79–103.

—— (1990). *The Politics of Partition: King Abdullah, the Zionists and Palestine, 1921–1951.* Oxford.

Singer, Amy (1994). *Palestinian Peasants and Ottoman Officials: Rural administration around sixteenth-century Jerusalem.* Cambridge.

Sivan, Emmanuel (1995). *Mythes politiques arabes.* Paris.

Slyomovics, Susan (1998). *The Object of Memory: Arab and Jew Narrate the Palestinian Village.* Philadelphia.

Smith, Charles D. (1996). *Palestine and the Arab-Israeli Conflict,* third edition. New York.

Somel, Selçuk A. (2001). *The Modernization of Public Education in the Ottoman Empire 1839–1908. Islamization, Autocracy and Discipline.* Leiden.

Spyridon, S. N. (ed.) (1938). *Annals of Palestine, 1821–1841.* Jerusalem.

Stavrou, Theofanis G., and Peter R. Weisensel (1986). *Russian Travelers to the Christian East from the Twelfth to the Twentieth Century.* Columbus.

Stein, Kenneth W. (1984). *The Land Question in Palestine, 1917–1939.* Chapel Hill, London.

Stein, Leonard (1961). *The Balfour Declaration.* London.

Stemberger, Günter (1987). *Juden und Christen im Heiligen Land. Palästina unter Konstantin und Theodosius.* Munich.

Steppat, Fritz (1974). "Ein 'Contrat Social' in einer palästinischen Stadt 1854." In *Die Welt des Islams,* 15: 233–246.

Stillman, Y. K. (1979). *Palestinian Costume and Jewelry.* Santa Fe.

Storrs, Ronald (1945). *Orientations.* London.

Stoyanovsky, Jacob (1928). *The Mandate for Palestine.* London.

Strecker, Georg (ed.) (1983). *Das Land Israel in biblischer Zeit. Jerusalem-Symposium 1981 der Hebräischen Universität und der Georg-August-Universität.* Göttingen.

A Survey of Palestine 1946: Prepared in December 1945 and January 1946 for the Information of the Anglo-American Committee of Inquiry. 2 vols. Jerusalem.

Swedenburg, Ted (1995). *Memories of Revolt: The 1936–1939 Rebellion and the Palestinian National Past.* Minneapolis, London.

—— (1988). "The Role of the Palestinian Peasantry in the Great Revolt

(1936–1939)." In *Islam, Politics, and Social Movements*, edited by E. Burke and I. M. Lapidus, 169–203. Berkeley.

Tahbub, Fa'iq Hamadi (1982). *al-Haraka al-'ummaliyya wa-l-niqabiyya fi filastin 1920–1948*. Kuwait.

Talmon, Shemaryahu (1970). "Die Bedeutung Jerusalems in der Bibel." In *Jüdisches Volk—gelobtes Land*, edited by W. P. Eckert et al., 135–152.

Tamari, Salim (ed.) (1999). *Jerusalem 1948: The Arab Neighbourhoods and Their Fate in the War*. Jerusalem, Bethlehem.

Tauber, Eliezer (1993). *The Emergence of the Arab Movements*. London.

Tegart Papers 1938: Terrorism 1936–37. s.l.

Tergit, Gabriele (1996). *Im Schnellzug nach Haifa*, edited by J. Brüning. Berlin.

al-Tha'alibi, 'Abd al-'Aziz (1988). *Khalfiyyat al-mu'tamar al-islami bil-quds 1350h–1931m*. Beirut.

Thoma, Clemens (1970). "Das Land Israel in der rabbinischen Tradition." In *Jüdisches Volk—gelobtes Land*, edited by W. P. Eckert et al., 37–51.

Thompson, Elizabeth (2000). *Colonial Citizens: Republican Rights, Paternal Privilege, and Gender in French Syria and Lebanon*. New York.

Thomson, W. M. (1985). *The Land and the Book; or, Biblical Illustrations Drawn from the Manners and Customs, the Scenes and Scenery of the Holy Land*, reprint. London.

Tibawi, A. L. (1956). *Arab Education in Mandatory Palestine: A Study of Three Decades of British Administration*. London.

Tsimhoni, Daphne (1978). "The Arab Christians and the Palestinian Arab National Movement During the Formative Stage." In *The Palestinians and the Middle East Conflict*, edited by G. Ben-Dor, 73–98. Ramat Gan.

Tucker, Judith (1998). *In the House of the Law: Gender and Islamic Law in Ottoman Syria and Palestine*. Berkeley.

Tübinger Atlas des Vorderen Orients (TAVO)/Tübingen Atlas of the Near and Middle East (1977–1994). Wiesbaden.

Tütüncü, Mehmet (2006). *Turkish Jerusalem (1516–1917): Ottoman Inscriptions from Jerusalem and Other Palestinian Cities*. Haarlem.

van den Boogert, Maurits (2005). *The Capitulations and the Ottoman Legal System: Qadis, Courts and Beratlıs in the 18th Century*. Leiden.

Vashitz, Joseph (1983). "*Dhawat* and *'Isamiyyun*: Two Groups of Arab Community Leaders in Haifa during the British Mandate." In *Asian and African Studies*, 17: 95–120.

Verdery, Richard N. (1971). "Arab 'Disturbances' and the Commissions of Inquiry." In *The Transformation of Palestine*, edited by I. Abu-Lughod, 275–303. Evanston.

Vereté, Mayir (1992). *From Palmerston to Balfour: Collected Essays of Mayir Vereté*. London.

Vester, Bertha Stafford (1988). *Our Jerusalem: An American Family in the Holy City, 1881–1949*. Jerusalem.

Völger, Gisela, Karin Welck, and Katharina Hackstein (eds.) (1987). *Pracht und Geheimnis. Kleidung und Schmuck aus Palästina und Jordanien*. Cologne.

Wagner, Andreas (2002). *Die Juden Hebrons von der Lokalgesellschaft zur "Nationalen Heimstätte" (1904–1938)*. Berlin.

Wasserstein, Bernard (1978). *The British in Palestine: The Mandatory Government and the Arab-Jewish Conflict 1917–1929*. London.

Weinfeld, Moshe (1993). *The Promise of the Land: The Inheritance of the Land of Canaan by the Israelites*. Berkeley.

———— (1983). "Zion and Jerusalem as Religious and Political Capital: Ideology and Utopia." In *The Poet and the Historian: Essays in Literary and Historical Biblical Criticism*, edited by R. E. Friedman, 75–115. Chico, CA.

Weinstein, James M. (1981). "The Egyptian Empire in Palestine: A Reassessment." In *Bulletin of the American Schools of Oriental Research*, 241: 1–28.

Wharton, Annabel Jane (2006). *Selling Jerusalem: Relics, Replicas, Theme Parks*. Chicago, London.

Whitelam, Keith W. (1996). *The Invention of Ancient Israel: The Silencing of Palestinian History*. London, New York.

Whiting, John D. (1914). "Village Life in the Holy Land." In *The National Geographic Magazine*, 25: 249–314.

Wild, Stefan (2002). "Die arabische Rezeption der 'Protokolle der Weisen von Zion'." In *Islamstudien ohne Ende. Festschrift für Werner Ende zum 65. Geburtstag*, edited by R. Brunner et al., 517–528. Würzburg.

———— (1984). "Judentum, Christentum und Islam in der palästinensischen Poesie." In *Die Welt des Islams*, 23–24: 259–297.

———— (1985). "National Socialism in the Arab Near East between 1933 and 1939." In *Die Welt des Islams*, 25: 126–175.

Wildangel, René (2004). "'Der größte Feind der Menschheit.' Der Nationalsozialismus in der arabischen öffentlichen Meinung in Palästina während des Zweiten Weltkrieges." In *Blind für die Geschichte?* edited by G. Höpp, P. Wien, and R. Wildangel, 115–154.

Wilson, Mary C. (1987). *King Abdullah, Britain and the Making of Jordan*. Cambridge.

Wulf, Stefan (2005). *Jerusalem—Aleppo—Konstantinopel. Der Hamburger Tropenmediziner Peter Mühlens im Osmanischen Reich am Vorabend und zu Beginn des Ersten Weltkriegs*. Hamburg.

Yazbak, Mahmoud (1998). *Haifa in the Late Ottoman Period, 1864–1914: A Muslim Town in Transition*. Leiden.

Young, George (1905–1906). *Corps de droit ottoman*, 7 vols. Oxford.

Ze'evi, Dror (1996). *An Ottoman Century: The District of Jerusalem in the 1660s*. Albany, NY.

Zerubavel, Yael (1995). *Recovered Roots: Collective Memory and the Making of Israeli National Tradition*. Chicago, London.

Zürcher, Erik J. (1999). "The Ottoman Conscription System in Theory and Practice, 1844–1918." In *Arming the State: Military Conscription in the Middle East and Central Asia 1775–1925*, edited by E. Zürcher, 79–94. London, New York.

INDEX